... ...k
use of your time.
Enjoy!
B.S.
xx

England and the Papacy in the Early Middle Ages

England and the Papacy in the Early Middle Ages

Papal Privileges in European Perspective, c. 680–1073

BENJAMIN SAVILL

OXFORD
UNIVERSITY PRESS

OXFORD
UNIVERSITY PRESS

Great Clarendon Street, Oxford, OX2 6DP,
United Kingdom

Oxford University Press is a department of the University of Oxford.
It furthers the University's objective of excellence in research, scholarship,
and education by publishing worldwide. Oxford is a registered trade mark of
Oxford University Press in the UK and in certain other countries

Published in the United States of America by Oxford University Press
198 Madison Avenue, New York, NY 10016, United States of America

British Library Cataloguing in Publication Data
Data available

Library of Congress Control Number: 2023935783

ISBN 978–0–19–888705–8

DOI: 10.1093/oso/9780198887058.001.0001

Printed and bound in the UK by
TJ Books Limited

Acknowledgements

This is a complete reworking of my DPhil thesis, supervised by Sarah Foot and examined by Simon Keynes and Chris Wickham in 2017. The many debts I accumulated while preparing the original thesis are acknowledged therein, but I must thank again the Wolfson Foundation, Institute of Historical Research (IHR) and Royal Historical Society for funding my research, and the 'Jaffé 3'/'Papsturkunden des frühen und hohen Mittelalters' project, based at the Akademie der Wissenschaften zu Göttingen and Friedrich-Alexander-Universität Erlangen-Nürnberg, for inviting me to consult their unpublished materials and photographic collections in 2015–16. That thesis became this monograph during the Covid-19 lockdowns of 2020–21, with earlier groundwork put down at the British Library, Warburg Institute, IHR, Cambridge University Library, and University of East Anglia. It was brought to completion at Trinity College Dublin. Throughout this time I have been especially grateful for the support of David d'Avray, Caroline Goodson, Nicholas Vincent, Bryan Ward-Perkins, and Immo Warntjes. Individual chapters were read by Katy Cubitt, Tom Licence, Levi Roach, Alan Thacker, Francesca Tinti, and Judith Werner, and improved by their comments. Julia Crick lent invaluable palaeographic advice. Felicity Hill honoured the writing pact. The late Richard Sharpe gave much needed encouragement at a critical early stage. Works-in-progress were presented to the German Historical Institute Medieval Seminar, British Academy Anglo-Saxon Charters Symposium, IHR Earlier Middle Ages Seminar, Oxford Medieval Seminar, and the St Andrews Institute of Medieval Studies Seminar. Special thanks are due to OHM and OUP, their reader (later self-'revealed' as Janet Nelson), and above all Julia Smith as Advisory Editor. Any errors are my own.

Berlin, 2022

Contents

List of Figures

List of Maps

List of Abbreviations

AA inedita	*Acta pontificum Romanorum inedita*, ed. J. von Pflugk-Harttung, 3 vols. (Tübingen, 1880–8)
AAWI	*Regesta regum Anglo-Normannorum: the Acta of William I (1066–1087)*, ed. D. Bates (Oxford, 1998)
Abingdon	*Charters of Abingdon Abbey*, ed. S.E. Kelly, 2 vols. (Oxford, 2000–1)
AN	Paris, Archives nationales de France
ARTEM	*Chartes originales antérieures à 1121 conservées en France*, http://telma.irht.cnrs.fr/outils/originaux/index/
ASC	*The Anglo-Saxon Chronicle: a Collaborative Edition*, ed. D.N. Dumville and S. Keynes, 17 vols. (Cambridge, 1983–)
Barking	*Charters of Barking Abbey and Waltham Holy Cross*, ed. S.E. Kelly (Oxford, 2021)
Bath and Wells	*Charters of Bath and Wells*, ed. S.E. Kelly (Oxford, 2007)
BCS	*Cartularium Saxonicum: a Collection of Charters Relating to Anglo-Saxon History*, ed. W. de Gray Birch, 3 vols. (London, 1885–93)
BL	London, British Library
BnF	Paris, Bibliothèque nationale de France
Bobbio	*Codice diplomatico del Monastero di S. Colombano di Bobbio fino all'anno MCCVIII*, ed. C. Cipolla, 3 vols. (Rome, 1918)
Böhmer-Frech	K.A. Frech, *Regesta Imperii III. 5. Papstregesten 1024–1058*, 2 vols. (Cologne, Weimar and Vienna, 2006–11)
Böhmer-Zimmermann	H. Zimmermann, *Regesta Imperii II. 5. Papstregesten 911–1024*, 2nd edition (Vienna, Cologne, Weimar, 1998)
Chertsey	*Charters of Chertsey Abbey*, ed. S.E. Kelly (Oxford, 2015)
Christ Church	*Charters of Christ Church Canterbury*, ed. N.P. Brooks and S.E. Kelly, 2 vols. (Oxford, 2013)
Chron. Mos.	*Chronique ou livre du fondation du monastère de Mouzon*, ed. and trans. M. Bur (Paris, 1989)
Chron. Rames.	*Chronicon abbatiae Rameseiensis a saec. x. usque ad an. circiter 1200*, ed. W.D. Macray (London, 1886)
Chron. Winch.	*The Winchcombe and Coventry Chronicles: Hitherto Unnoticed Witnesses to the Work of John of Worcester*, ed. and trans. P.A. Hayward, 2 vols. (Tempe, 2010)

CS I	*Councils and Synods, With Other Documents Relating to the English Church I, A.D. 871–1204*, ed. D. Whitelock, M. Brett, and C.N.L. Brooke, 2 vols. (Oxford, 1981)
Davis	G.R.C. Davis, *Medieval Cartularies of Great Britain and Ireland*, rev. C. Breay, J. Harrison, and D.M. Smith (London, 2010)
De antiq.	William of Malmesbury, *De antiquitate Glastoniensis Ecclesie*, ed. J. Scott, in J. Scott, *The Early History of Glastonbury: an Edition, Translation and Study of William of Malemsbury's De antiquitate Glastonie Ecclesie* (Woodbridge, 1981), pp. 40–172
D&C	Dean and Chapter
ECEE	*The Early Charters of Eastern England*, ed. C.R. Hart (Leicester, 1966)
Glastonbury	*Charters of Glastonbury Abbey*, ed. S.E. Kelly (Oxford, 2012)
GP	William of Malmesbury, *Gesta pontificum Anglorum: the History of the English Bishops*, ed. and trans. M. Winterbottom with the assistance of R.M. Thomson, 2 vols. (Oxford, 2007)
GR	William of Malmesbury, *Gesta regum Anglorum: the History of the English Kings*, ed. and trans. R.A.B. Mynors, completed by R.M. Thomson and M. Winterbottom, 2 vols. (Oxford, 1998)
HA	Bede, *Historia abbatum*, in *Abbots of Wearmouth and Jarrow*, ed. and trans. C. Grocock and I.N. Wood (Oxford, 2013), pp. 21–75
HE	Bede, *Ecclesiastical History of the English People*, ed. and trans. B. Colgrave and R.A.B. Mynors (Oxford, 1969)
HN	Eadmer, *Historia novorum in Anglia*, ed. M. Rule (London, 1884)
HS	*Councils and Ecclesiastical Documents Relating to Great Britain and Ireland*, ed. A.W. Haddan and William Stubbs, 3 vols. (Oxford, 1869–78)
JE, JK, JL	P. Jaffé, *Regesta pontificum Romanorum ab condita ecclesia ad annum post Christum natum MCXCVIII*, 2nd edition, rev. W. Wattenbach, S. Loewenfeld, F. Kaltenbrunner, and P. Ewald, 2 vols. (Leipzig, 1885–8)
J³	P. Jaffé, *Regesta pontificum Romanorum ab condita ecclesia ad annum post Christum natum MCXCVIII*, 3rd edition, rev. K. Herbers, M. Schütz, J. Werner, et al., 4 vols. to date (Göttingen, 2016–) (Usually only cited when no entry in 2nd edition)

K	*Codex diplomaticus aevi Saxonici*, ed. J.M. Kemble, 6 vols. (London, 1839–48)
LD	*Liber diurnus Romanorum pontificum*, ed. Hans Foerster (Bern, 1958)
LP	*Le Liber pontificalis*, ed. L. Duchesne, 3 vols. (Paris, 1884–1957)
Malmesbury	*Charters of Malmesbury Abbey*, ed. S.E. Kelly (Oxford, 2005)
MGH Epp. I–VII	*Monumenta Germaniae Historica. Epistolae* I–VII, 7 vols. (Berlin, 1887–1928)
MGH Formulae	*Formulae Merowingici et Karolini aevi*, ed. K. Zeumer, *Monumenta Germaniae Historica. Leges V* (Hanover, 1886)
Northern Houses	*Charters of Northern Houses*, ed. D.A. Woodman (Oxford, 2012)
PAS	*Portable Antiquities Scheme*, https://finds.org.uk/database
Peterborough	*Charters of Peterborough Abbey*, ed. S.E. Kelly (Oxford, 2009)
PL	*Patrologiae cursus completus, series Latina*, ed. J.P. Migne, 221 vols. (Paris, 1841–64)
PRDP	*Pontificum Romanorum diplomata papyracea quae supersunt in tabulariis Hispaniae Italiae Germaniae*, ed. C. de Silva Tarouca and C. Erdmann (Rome, 1929)
PRO	London, The National Archives, Public Record Office
PUU	*Papsturkunden 896–1046*, ed. H. Zimmermann, 3 vols. (Vienna, 1984–9)
PUU England	*Papsturkunden in England*, ed. W. Holtzmann, 3 vols. (Berlin, 1930–52)
PUU Frankreich	*Papsturkunden in Frankreich*, ed. W. Wiederhold, 7 vols. (Berlin, 1906–13)
PUU Ile-de-France	*Papsturkunden in Frankreich, Neue Folge 7. Nördliche Ile-de-France und Vermandois*, ed. D. Lohrmann (Göttingen, 1976)
PUU Italien	*Papsturkunden in Italien. Reiseberichte zur Italia Pontificia*, ed. P. Kehr, 6 vols. (Vatican City, 1977)
PUU Saint-Denis	*Papsturkunden in Frankreich, Neue Folge 9. Diözese Paris II. Abtei Saint-Denis*, ed. R. Grosse (Göttingen, 1998)
PUU Spanien	*Papsturkunden in Spanien. Vorarbeiten zur Hispania Pontificia*, ed. P. Kehr, D. Berger, K. Herbers, and T. Schlauwitz, 3 vols. (Berlin, 1926–2020)
Reg.	Gregory the Great, *Registrum epistularum*, ed. D. Norberg, *Corpus Christianorum Series Latina 140–140A*, 2 vols. (Turnhout, 1982)

Rochester	*Charters of Rochester*, ed. A. Campbell (Oxford, 1973)
S	P.H. Sawyer, *Anglo-Saxon Charters: an Annotated List and Bibliography* (London, 1968); rev. S.E. Kelly, R. Rushforth et al. online at https://esawyer.lib.cam.ac.uk
St Albans	*Charters of St Albans*, ed. J. Crick (Oxford, 2007)
St Augustine's	*Charters of St Augustine's Abbey, Canterbury and Minster-in-Thanet*, ed. S.E. Kelly (Oxford, 1995)
St Paul's	*Charters of St Paul's, London*, ed. S.E. Kelly (Oxford, 2004)
Sherborne	*Charters of Sherborne*, ed. M.A. Donovan (Oxford, 1988)
VC	*Vita Ceolfridi*, in *Abbots of Wearmouth and Jarrow*, ed. and trans. C. Grocock and I.N. Wood (Oxford, 2013), pp. 77–121
VSW	Eddius Stephanus [Stephen of Ripon], *The Life of Bishop Wilfrid*, ed. and trans. B. Colgrave (Cambridge, 1927)
WBEASE	M. Lapidge, J. Blair, S.D. Keynes, and D. Scragg, eds., *The Wiley Blackwell Encyclopedia of Anglo-Saxon England*, 2nd edition (Oxford, 2014)
Winchester NM	*Charters of the New Minster, Winchester*, ed. S. Miller (Oxford, 2001)

Numbers in **bold** throughout the apparatus of this book refer to papal privileges in England catalogued in the Annotated Handlist (Chapter 3): the reader will find their full citation details there.

1

Introduction

As all fell silent after the reading, Berhtfrith, the king's top man, spoke to the archbishop: 'It would please those of us who need an interpretation to hear what the apostolic authority has to say.' The archbishop replied: 'Decisions of the apostolic see are expressed in a language which is tortuous and enigmatic – nevertheless, each document does reveal a single understanding of this matter at hand. I will untangle at least their sense in brief.'[1]

Our surviving evidence attests to the acquisition of a purported sixty-seven papal privileges relating to England in the early middle ages. Some are authentic, many forged, and only a few the subject of extended analysis: Berhtfrith would be alarmed to learn that there still remains much to unravel. The absence of a dedicated study has not gone unnoticed. Way back in 1839 John Mitchell Kemble, the godfather of modern Anglo-Saxon studies, promised a volume which failed to materialise before his untimely death. At the turn of the present century, two of the field's pre-eminent scholars reiterated the call for this 'urgent desideratum'.[2] Even had they not, the recurring appearance of these documents across almost all the *loca classica* of Anglo-Saxon historiography could not escape any student of the period. Papal privileges (documents issued in the names of the bishops of Rome, granting or confirming special rights to individuals or institutions) meet with repeat praise in the works of Bede and his contemporaries in the Northumbrian golden age. They stand out among the documentary records of the 'Mercian Supremacy'. Some of the most famous royal diplomas of the tenth and eleventh century cite them as precedents, while the suspicious discovery of long-lost privileges is characteristic of the archival creativity of post-Conquest England. They are tied to the names of such celebrated figures as Benedict Biscop and Aldhelm, Offa and Cynethryth of Mercia,

---

[1] *VSW*, 60, p. 130.
[2] Wormald, 'Æthelwold', p. 200, n. 89; Keynes, 'Foreword', p. xxi; *WBEASE*, p. 362.

England and the Papacy in the Early Middle Ages: Papal Privileges in European Perspective, c. 680–1073.
Benjamin Savill, Oxford University Press. © Benjamin Savill 2023. DOI: 10.1093/oso/9780198887058.003.0001

and Saints Wilfrid, Dunstan, Æthelwold, and Edward the Confessor. We find them in texts of diverse genres: history, chronicle, and hagiography; homily, gospel book, and liturgical collection; usually in Latin, but occasionally in Old English translation. They may have even made their way into our archaeological record. Yet still no study has brought all this material together and analysed it on its own terms. That's the task of this monograph.

The absence of such an examination can seem strange, since papal privileges represent a point of intersection between two of the major areas of research interest in Anglo-Saxon historiography: charter studies, and the relationship between the early English and Rome. The study of Anglo-Saxon charters has been revolutionised over the past half-century. Thanks to a number of influential secondary works, and the steady appearance of a series of high-calibre critical editions, a sophisticated engagement with these texts has now become a hallmark of scholarship on early medieval England.[3] Nevertheless, these studies have tended to focus predominantly on what one might call the native component of Anglo-Saxon documentary culture, with relatively little consideration about what happened when an additional, exotic genre of written instrument was imported into this same environment (and as we shall see, 'exotic' is the right word for these huge, metres-long scrolls of Mediterranean papyrus). This does not mean, of course, that Anglo-Saxon studies has shied away from exploring mainland European influences and connections in the history of pre-Conquest England. Since at least the time of the groundbreaking work of Wilhelm Levison, this has constituted a significant substratum of the field, and scholars—taking cues from Bede himself—have often placed England's relationship with Rome and its bishops at the forefront of these investigations.[4] In some cases that 'emotional connection' and 'close relationship' (or 'special relationship') with the papacy has been perceived as a 'characteristic phenomenon of the Anglo-Saxon period', perhaps exceptionally so, while one scholar has gone as far as to identify Rome as the Anglo-Saxon 'capital'.[5] Beyond, however, Levison's own major contributions, the documentary aspects of this relationship have, until quite recently,[6] not always been subjected to the same kind of attention or analytical rigour as one is used to seeing elsewhere. When discussion has taken place, it has often centred around either the earliest conversion-era letters known from Bede and Gregory the Great's

---

[3] WBEASE, pp. 97–9, 102–3, with bibliography.
[4] Levison, England; WBEASE, pp. 359–62, 409–10, with bibliography.
[5] Ortenberg, 'Anglo-Saxon Church', pp. 31–2, 58–62; Howe, 'Rome'.
[6] Here I refer especially to the important work of Susan Kelly, Joanna Story, and Francesca Tinti.

Register, or, at the other end of the spectrum, the post-Conquest 'Canterbury forgeries', principally of interest to Anglo-Normanists and twelfth-century specialists. Accordingly, the rich insights into early English religion, politics, and society made through advances in Anglo-Saxon charter studies over the past four or five decades have not extended as far as they might into the realm of Anglo-papal communications, despite the relative wealth of material available.

Most straightforwardly then, this book confronts this weak point in the scholarship by interrogating the full corpus of papal privileges in early medieval England with that same degree of scrutiny. Doing so is about more, however, than simply filling the gaps. It is a major contention of this study that papal privileges have a usefulness for historians which far surpasses what has hitherto been expected of them, at least by Anglo-Saxonists. Let's state this emphatically: papal privileges survive as a genre totally unique among our written sources for the early medieval west. Nowhere else, in this age of fragmented political and textual cultures, do we find another case of a single type of written document produced and authenticated at a single location, yet sought by, and transmitted to, individuals and institutions from diverse societies across Europe, often ones separated by different political configurations, and sometimes immense distances. It adds an exciting new dimension to the sorts of questions we can ask about early medieval England, if we reflect on the fact that privileges much like those we see at the Jarrow of Bede's day could also be found within the space of a few decades at the monasteries of Benevento, Farfa, and Fulda. Or: that one rare witness to Mercian inheritance strategies exists only as a generic template for scribes preserved in a single north-Italian manuscript, the earliest extant citation of which comes from a few decades later, on a still-surviving Egyptian papyrus addressed to post-Byzantine Ravenna. Or indeed: that a now-lost privilege sought in person at Rome by Archbishop Oswald of York would have had its immediate parallels in documents issued for his counterparts at Latin Europe's other frontiers, at Magdeburg, Salerno, and Catalan Vic. Reflective work on comparative methodology has stressed the need for historians to contrast only 'like with like', limiting comparisons to tightly controlled shared phenomena (e.g. bishops, castles, communes, coins) that might serve as *spie* ('peepholes') into the wider fabric of society.[7] As closely comparable, sometimes near-identical texts, produced under the 'control' of a single issuing body, yet

---

[7] Wickham, 'Problems', with reference to Ginzburg, 'Spie'.

found between diverse societies with otherwise few elements of extant source material in common, papal privileges have the potential to serve as just such *spie*. It is a potential so far largely untapped. This does not mean, of course, that we can just think of privileges as simple portals between, say, the Thames Valley and Val Trebbia, allowing us to juxtapose the two directly. As we shall see, the great differences between the existing conditions and frameworks of reference of such societies makes the application of privileges as completely straightforward comparators almost impossible. But the fact that texts much like those we are seeking to understand in England could be found elsewhere across the contemporary Latin west adds two crucial dimensions to this study. Firstly, we will not be able to speak with much authority about papal privileges in early medieval England unless we see how else they manifested themselves throughout Europe. Secondly, adopting such an approach will take this monograph beyond a basic study of a neglected genre of Anglo-Saxon evidence, and towards a far wider-ranging investigation, wherein we might pinpoint moments at which events in England correlated or contrasted with those in other societies, and ask why.

I. State of Research

Looking outside England therefore requires thinking beyond its historiographical boundaries. Here, however, the work of the historian of papal privileges in England becomes not challenged, but vastly enriched: the scale of output in this field is immense. For at least the early middle ages, the vast bulk of work on papal documents has been, and remains, Germanophone. Its roots and most significant advances lay in the same 'golden age' of German textual scholarship that saw the glory years of the *Monumenta Germaniae Historica*.[8] Taking off in the last decades of the nineteenth century and still enduring to this day, multi-volume projects by Germanophone scholars on papal documents (*Papsturkunden*) have dominated and defined the field as it now stands, in the form of registers (Jaffé, 1851; second edition 1885–8; third edition 2016–; the Göttingen Academy's *Pontificia* series, 1906–; the *Regesta Imperii*, 1968–), critical editions (the Göttingen *Papsturkunden* series, 1896–; the Austrian Academy's *Papsturkunden 896–1046*, 1984–9; the *Monumenta* itself from

---

[8] Wood, *Modern Origins*, pp. 156–61.

the 1890s), and diplomatic manuals. While these projects fed into a tradition of grand-type narrative historiography that reached its apogee in the mid-twentieth century,[9] they also appeared in dialogue with a number of important studies exploring largely diplomatic problems, such as the use of formulary books, the technology and aesthetics of the documents (script, layout, writing supports), and suppositions about papal chancery organisation.[10] Quite why the German historiographical tradition has invested so much into papal history is not self-evident, and one should at least be conscious of the political background that first set these gears in motion. Although the roots of a confessionalised scholarly preoccupation about the role of the papacy in sacred history date back to the publishing wars of the Reformation,[11] the institutionalisation of modern papal historiography—and with it, the elevation of *Papsturkunden* to a kind of canonical status in the study of European legal and constitutional history— must owe a good deal to a number of intersecting episodes in late nineteenth-century statecraft. If the professionalisation of the historical discipline and the maturity of the *Monumenta* and its related projects were fuelled by contemporary German nationalism and state-building, the kinds of subject matter and source material they prioritised also depended upon immediate developments in confessional high politics. The modern birth of early medieval studies in Germany cannot be viewed apart from the Taking of Rome and dissolution of the Papal States in 1870; the conclusion of the First Vatican Council and triumph of Ultramontanism that same year; the Catholic revival and Prussian-Vatican 'culture war' of the subsequent decade; followed by the opening of the Vatican Archives in 1882 and, in consequence, the foundation of the German Historical Institute at Rome six years later.[12] We therefore need to be wary of some of the statist and confessional baggage that this field inevitably brings. Less obviously, one also needs to be conscious that the preoccupation of that *fin de siècle* generation of researchers in the unravelling of the hidden mysteries of the papal chancery, and in the editing, ordering, and registration of papal documents as an end in itself, was in no small part a projection of the hyper-bureaucratic mentalities of their late nineteenth-century state.[13] Registers, editions, and diplomatic analyses can, anyway, only take us so

[9] Fuhrmann, 'Papstgeschichtsschreibung', pp. 157–61; Noble, 'Morbidity', pp. 506–11.
[10] See above all the work of Pflugk-Harttung, Sickel, Kehr, Santifaller, and Rabikauskas.
[11] Fuhrmann, 'Papstgeschichtsschreibung', pp. 143ff.
[12] Elze, 'Deutsche Historische Institut'; Clark and Kaiser, eds., *Culture Wars*.
[13] Mersiowsky, *Urkunde*, i, pp. 25, 29.

far. Without them, modern scholarship on papal history would be impossible. But defining the source material is only the beginning of analysis, and we must not fall into the trap of fine-tuning and fetishising the critical texts of *Papsturkunden* at the expense of further interpretation and the application of wider historical questions—something akin to what Mark Mersiowsky has called the *carta edita, causa finita* approach of certain strands of diplomatic scholarship.[14]

Important and wider-ranging interpretive work on earlier medieval *Papsturkunden* has nevertheless emerged in the latest generation of Germanophone scholarship, much of it a by-product of those more recent institutional efforts. Specialist studies by Hans-Henning Kortüm and Jochen Johrendt, together with a series of collected volumes published by the Göttingen Academy have demonstrated what scholars can achieve through a trans-regional approach to this unique corpus. These have applied questions about communication, memory, preservation, beneficiary influence, and regional identity across this continent-wide body of evidence, with a view in particular to the worlds of its recipients, rather than Rome.[15] This research has appeared alongside a smaller number of studies working within what has sometimes been called the 'new diplomatic', and has focused upon principally non-verbal aspects of papal privileges, analysing them as material artefacts and visual instruments of power.[16] Together, these projects have indicated how much is possible if we emancipate *Papsturkunden* from the confines of specialist textual analyses, thinking of them as more than just evidence for the administrative capacities of papal Rome. These studies have, however, entirely passed over England. There may be good reasons for this. Far fewer papal privileges (and no originals) survive from early medieval England, making it extremely difficult to integrate this material into the relatively big-data comparative analyses which these studies sometimes prefer. Indeed, the English evidence is comparably weakest from the later ninth to early twelfth centuries, the period with which this most recent wave of scholarship has largely concerned itself. Nevertheless: whatever sensible research considerations might lie behind this generational move away from

---

[14] Mersiowsky, 'Towards a Reappraisal', p. 19 ('charter edited, case closed').

[15] Kortüm, *Zur päpstlichen Urkundensprache*; Johrendt, *Papsttum*; Johrendt, 'Empängereinfluß'; Johrendt and Müller, eds., *Römisches Zentrum*; Johrendt and Müller, eds., *Rom und die Regionen*; Herbers and Fleisch, eds., *Erinnerung*; Herbers, Engel, and López Alsina, eds., *Das begrenzte Papsttum*; Herbers and Johrendt, eds., *Papsttum und das vielgestaltigte Italien*; Große, ed., *L'acte*; Herbers and Könighaus, eds., *Von Outremer*; Herbers and Müller, eds., *Lotharingien*.

[16] See below, Chapter 2.

the Anglo-papal evidence, its long-term effect has certainly been negative. It has cemented a trend within continental work on the early medieval papacy that treats England as a marginal outsider, and, within Anglo-Saxon studies, done little to remedy a reluctance to engage with non-Anglophone developments in papal historiography.

The single area in which scholarship on early medieval papal privileges has seriously expanded beyond the confines of German-language specialist literature, meanwhile, has been in dedicated studies of 'exemption' and 'protection'. This topic has seen important contributions over the past century from scholars across Europe and North America, covering material from both Anglo-Saxon England and continental Europe. The documents now labelled under these terms were undoubtedly important, and this book will turn to them on several occasions. Nevertheless, the predominance of this subject across much of the scholarship has probably had a distorting effect on wider perceptions of papal privileges in early medieval Europe. Firstly: grants of this kind made up only one part of the privileges issued by the popes, who from at least the later eighth century became increasingly preoccupied with guarantees for pre-existing church property. Focusing so much attention upon these quite particular kinds of privilege has therefore perpetuated a false impression that 'papal privileges' were essentially synonymous with grants of 'protection'/'exemption', an approach that significantly misrepresents the nature of most documents actually petitioned from Rome across these centuries. Secondly: these studies typically lean towards a pronounced teleological position, particularly one of a legalist-constitutionalist bent, something which continues to haunt many modern approaches to early papal history. 'Protection' and 'exemption' *would* emerge as highly important legal categories in the central middle ages, having a particular significance, for example, in the history of Cluniac monasticism. But in searching primarily for the 'growth' or 'origins' of these high-medieval phenomena across earlier centuries, many studies show only limited concern for early medieval developments in their own right, preferring instead to trace a line which culminates towards their author's period of core interest. Even Barbara Rosenwein's excellent *Negotiating Space* (1999) betrays this tendency, beginning with Urban II's privileging of Cluny in 1095, before tracing across 150 pages the developments leading *towards* that point, and then ending with an excursus on its implications for the United States Constitution.

Amidst all this, dedicated work on papal privileges in early medieval England has not flourished. Early twentieth-century contributions made by German scholars from the *Monumenta* school—the early medieval sections of Walther Holtzmann's *Papsturkunden in England* (1930–52), and Levison's *England and the Continent* (1946)—set an exceptionally high standard, and their work remains indispensable. What follows will very much be an exercise in standing on giants' shoulders. Yet these studies remain not just unsurpassed but also not substantially developed upon. The Göttingen Academy's planned *Anglia Pontificia* project currently sits on hiatus. More recent publications surveying the past and future of papal documentary scholarship seem almost to move England out of the picture altogether, celebrating the achievements made over the past century in studying papal documents at the 'core' of Europe (Italy, France, Germany), while looking forward to future progress in research on its 'peripheries' (Iberia, central and eastern Europe, Scandinavia).[17] It may not be too early to detect parallels here to the current political mood in Europe. This disinclination among papal specialists to engage with England has, anyway, not always been compensated by enthusiasm within Anglo-Saxonist scholarship. Hans Hubert Anton's ten-page study of 1975 on the authenticity of a number of Bede-era English privileges remains perhaps the most cited work.[18] The British Academy's *Anglo-Saxon Charters* series (1973–), while making invaluable contributions in this area, has remained inconsistent from volume to volume as to whether or not to include papal documents as part of the English documentary corpus: when they do appear, they have sometimes been relegated to appendices with more limited commentary. This is of course perfectly reasonable, given that papal documents did not fall within the original remit of the British Academy project, which already has the task of covering almost two thousand English charters, writs, and wills. But a result of this divided treatment is that, while Anglo-Saxon charter scholarship has exploded since the 1970s, and at the same time numerous volumes of both technical and interpretive work have appeared as a result of well-funded, institutionalised continental research on *Papsturkunden*, these two strands of scholarship have not only largely failed to interact, but have arguably become increasingly alienated from one another. Considering, as outlined above, the important potential of papal privileges as comparative tools, this parting of ways has implications beyond the relatively narrow world of diplomatic. It may have had a detrimental effect upon how both Anglophone and continental scholars have been prepared to situate Anglo-Saxon England within early medieval Europe more generally.

---

[17] Hiestand, ed., *Hundert Jahre*; Herbers, 'Im Dienste'.   [18] Anton, *Studien*, pp. 65–75.

II. This Book: Scope and Structure

This monograph therefore sets out to explore what we can learn from the surviving evidence for papal privileges in early medieval England. It fully engages with the advances made in both Anglo-Saxon studies and specialist papal historiography over the past century, while also using the rare, Channel-crossing potential privileges offer to investigate what insights they might generate about England within the wider European picture. It works on the basic premise that we should not treat papal documents in England separately from either the 'native' English texts among which they survive, nor the huge corpus of almost 800 papal privileges acquired elsewhere across the Latin west throughout this same period, of which they comprised only a small part (see Table 1.1).[19] It does so on the conviction that studying them in isolation creates a false divide that may have made little sense in light of contemporary practices; that such an approach allows

Table 1.1 Authentic papal privileges in western Europe, 590–1073: the state of the evidence

	Italy	Transalpine Europe	Iberia	England
Gregory I to Sergius I (590–701)	21 (*18 of which Gregory I*)	12–17 (*7 of which Gregory I*)	1 (*only Gregory I*)	6 (*1 of which Gregory I*) *+ 4 deperdita*
John VI to Hadrian I (701–795)	11	11–12	0	2 *+ 1 deperditum*
Leo III to John IX (795–900)	30	64	2	4 *+ 1 deperditum*
Benedict IV to Gregory V (900–999)	61	106	13	1–3 *+ 1 deperditum?*
Silvester II to Alexander II (999–1073)	210	175	23	7–8 *+ 4 deperdita*

[19] Table 1.1: figures for England are taken from Chapter 3; those for elsewhere are based on Santifaller, 'Verwendung', updated by current scholarship. The aim of this table is simply to make clear at a glance the scale and distribution of the *known* evidence.

us to generate new observations, connections, and comparisons so far overlooked; and that it also provides a much needed occasion to bring together bodies of scholarship traditionally divided between specialist fields. It addresses textual issues in the source material and establishes a preliminary groundwork for a workable corpus of authentically early medieval papal privileges in England, but treats this as a way towards asking wider and more interesting questions, rather than as an end in itself. Moreover, while a study of this size can only aim to do as much as to focus principally upon England, its explorations of what we might gain from taking a more regionalised, petitioner-focused approach to engagement with the papacy in this period will, I hope, be of value to those working on other parts of Europe as well. In a still-relevant intervention of 1995, Tom Noble complained of the 'morbidity' of much historical writing on the early medieval papacy within the wider field of early medieval studies. Whatever the transformations of the latter discipline since the mid-twentieth century, much work within the former has remained committed to tracing out a linear narrative, geared around the gradual realisation of a fixed papal 'idea' along a 'series of political-diplomatic encounters', ultimately looking forward to its supposed culmination under Innocent III (1198–1216) or Boniface VIII (1294–1303).[20] If it is now true that this kind of master-narrative no longer has many advocates, an alternative approach has yet to take its place. This book, focusing upon one region's engagement with papal documentary culture at particular moments across the early middle ages—and viewing those engagements primarily from the perspective of that regional society, rather than according to any developmental narrative of the papal centre— seeks to contribute to a new way of writing long-form early medieval papal history which might challenge at least some of the 'moribund' tendencies identified by Noble.

As for chronology, this book covers the period from c. 680 up to 1073: that is, from the point around which our evidence for authentic monastic privileges in the English kingdoms begins, up to the death of Alexander II (1061–73). Although Chapter 3 provides a review of all genuine and forged privileges from the Gregorian missions (597–604) onwards, the three authentic texts from these earliest decades pertain to the organisational efforts of the conversion, a topic which has already enjoyed extensive treatment. The study proper therefore commences with the pontificate of

---

[20] Noble, 'Morbidity'.

Agatho (678–81), when we first see English monastic leaders heading to Rome to acquire privileges in person. Ending at 1073 is a more arbitrary decision. But a study of this size covering more than four centuries would have only a limited usefulness, and the fact that acquisitions of privileges in England fall silent for a generation following the end of Alexander's pontificate, together with its rough proximity to the Norman Conquest, makes it an appropriate point at which to bring this early medieval investigation to a close. Altogether this period gives us sixty-seven purported privileges from the seventh to eleventh centuries, of which just under half can be considered authentic.

A necessary caveat: there is little chance that this figure accurately reflects the full number of acquisitions which actually took place. Historians of the early middle ages are now more attuned than ever to problems of archival losses and how they might have warped our understanding of the past.[21] Northumbria's early medieval records have come down to us in a state of especial devastation, and in parts of this book observations about 'England' refer more accurately to the Southumbrian polities. It is also the case, as we will see in Chapter 5, that the destruction and mutilation of documents could occur within a contemporary setting that was far from accidental. Nevertheless, there is still reason to believe that when it comes to papal privileges, the surviving record, for all its very real problems, has not distorted our picture of early medieval reality beyond all recognition.[22] Archival losses predominantly, if not exclusively, affect ephemera (e.g. letters of transitory import or deeds concerning perishables), lay or private charters (which in Anglo-Saxon England could be rendered in the vernacular, and thus especially vulnerable to later disposal), or memoranda and other notes of informal, minor interest. By contrast, early medieval papal privileges were extraordinary, maybe even quasi-sacral documents, whose very acquisition involved for the English an enormous investment of time and resources, and which were usually granted with perpetual validity. Meanwhile, although it is true that twelfth- and thirteenth-century processes of archival reorganisation would have led to the loss or at least corruption of

---

[21] Brown et al., eds., *Documentary Culture*; Whittow, 'Sources'.

[22] Cf. Koziol, *Politics*, pp. 307 ff. Note that the combination of relatively liberal UK metal-detector laws with the unusual phenomenon of papal documents having lead seals (*bullae*) means that we can, uniquely, also get a very loose picture of papal documentary culture in England independent of archival traditions. However crude the data, it is still noteworthy that of the 494 finds of loose medieval *bullae* currently listed on *PAS*, only two predate the twelfth century: see below, Chapter 3, p. 79.

many original papal documents (see discussion in Chapter 8), this will have also saved many of the texts from oblivion during the Reformation, when cartularies and other mixed-media codices had a much higher chance of survival than loose *papalia*.[23] Some destroyed or lost privileges (*deperdita*) have also left their trace in a number of narrative works, and even footprints in archives overseas. Moreover, the fact that the tenth century, the period for which our documentary survivals are *richest* in Anglo-Saxon England, is also when our evidence for papal privileges is *poorest* suggests that certain lacunae reflect more than just archival accidents. Overall, the reader must remain as cautious as ever of accepting an absence of evidence as evidence of absence. But our source base is sufficiently strong for us to think that, in what follows, arguments *about* silence are more than simply arguments *from* it.

Before we get started, it's important to be clear as to what we mean by papal privileges, as opposed to other *papalia*. We may define a papal privilege relatively widely in this book as any document issued, or purporting to have been issued, in the name of the bishop of Rome, granting or confirming some kind of special treatment to a particular named individual and/or institution, usually with perpetual validity. Across the continental corpus, these might concern rights over property or possessions, local economic arrangements, the use of liturgical vestments, rights of appeal to Rome, seating arrangements at councils, rights of authority over other persons or churches, or conversely the exclusion of the authority of other persons or churches. They were documents which, as with most other charters or diplomas, were perceived as having a limited applicability: what they granted pertained specifically to the named beneficiary, and was not meant as a general rule for the church at large. (In this respect they differ from what canonists would later call 'decretals': literally, privileges set out an instance of 'private law'—*priva lex*—rather than general law.)[24] While sometimes ambiguous and certainly not exclusive, the use of the term *priuilegium* for these papal documents is contemporary, and although

---

[23] Cheney, 'Some Features'. Readers who have used an English medieval cartulary will, however, have noticed the frequent erasure or cancellation of the word *papa* from many rubrics, probably the result of Henry VIII's proclamation of 9 June 1535, 'to cause all manner prayers, orisons, rubrics, canons in mass books, and all other books used in the churches, wherein the said Bishop of Rome is named or his presumptuous and proud pomp and authority preferred, utterly to be abolished, eradicated, and erased out, and his name and memory to be nevermore': *Tudor Royal Proclamations*, ed. Hughes and Larkin, i. 15 (my thanks to Jenna Gayle for this reference).

[24] Santifaller, 'Verwendung', pp. 22–33.

these texts were subject to wide variation, they nevertheless show certain consistent patterns in their structure, wording, content, and external appearance. This suggests that they would have been recognised at the time as a genre in their own right.

This definition is intentionally flexible. The later distinctions made by the lawyers of the twelfth century onwards, between 'solemn' and 'simple' privileges, are not useful for studying these earlier centuries.[25] Nevertheless this definition does not include all output attributed to the papal chancery, and one must be clear that this book is not concerned with papal texts in England *in toto*. Admonitory papal letters, replies on matters of church discipline or organisation, penitential letters, synodal decisions, or letters detailing Roman judicial proceedings are not included here. Admittedly, the dividing line between papal 'letters' and 'diplomas' such as privileges is not clear cut, especially since papal documents typically assumed an epistolary form ('X to Y, greetings...', '...Farewell'). In this book I follow the definition set out by Achim Thomas Hack between medieval letters and diplomas. Hack argues that, despite the limited contemporary vocabulary for the difference between these two categories, the typical 'dialogue-character' of a letter (as opposed to the one-way 'declaratory' style of a diploma), together with the usual assumption in a letter of a spatial and therefore temporal distance between sender and recipient (as opposed to the implication of a public grant made to an immediate, present recipient usually found in a diploma) does indicate a genuine distinction, one which contemporaries would have appreciated.[26] However, I depart from Hack in acknowledging that the functions and perceptions of such texts could change over time, or between different audiences. If a text that have might have initially fallen under the rubric of a letter (such as the admonitory message of one Pope John to an Ealdorman Ælfric, or Leo IX's remarks to Edward the Confessor concerning Exeter) came in due course to be preserved within an institution's archive as a written guarantee of its special status, then that letter could indeed *become* a diploma or 'privilege' in the eyes of some, whatever its originally intended genre or purpose. In some cases, therefore, the decisions taken in this book as to what qualifies as a 'privilege' are necessarily subjective. Yet that subjectivity may itself be historical, reflecting the probability that, to contemporaries, what did and what did not qualify as

---

[25] Frenz, *Papsturkunden*, pp. 19–21.   [26] Hack, *Codex*, i, pp. 32–6.

a papal *priuilegium* may not have always felt absolutely clear, and could well have become contested.

This book follows a bipartite structure. Part I lays the foundations, looking first at the immediate setting of papal privileges in early medieval Europe, exploring how they were petitioned, drawn-up, conveyed, and then introduced into their beneficiaries' regional societies (Chapter 2). It then turns to the known corpus of privileges for England, establishing as far as possible the shape and authenticity of the source base upon which a sustained analysis might rest, and in the process providing a working handlist for the reader (Chapter 3). Part II consists of four separate studies of papal privileges at work in four distinct periods of early medieval England. Chapter 4 investigates the significance of a handful of privileges acquired by English beneficiaries around the turn of the eighth century. It considers their implications for contemporary conceptions of monastic and episcopal space, while also setting these documents within (but also, outside of) a continental documentary culture beginning in fifth-century Provence. Chapter 5 takes the form of a more close-focus case study, investigating the ways in which royal men and women of the 'Mercian Supremacy' sought to use papal privileges to secure their own familial inheritance, and how these—initially, it seems, highly successful—efforts were later supressed, forgotten, and misremembered. Chapter 6 turns to the later tenth-century Cerdicing 'Kingdom of the English', and asks why we see such *little* evidence for papal privileges in this emerging polity, at just the same time as their use was proliferating across much of the post-Carolingian world. Chapter 7 then looks to the last decades of Anglo-Saxon England and the coming of the Norman Conquest, when a new generation of ecclesiastics sought to engage with the early leaders of the papal reform movement. To avoid as far as possible the imposition of a linear narrative, these four chapters each take the form of stand-alone studies, although the reader will see that there are ways in which Chapter 7 works like something of a sequel to that preceding. A book of this size can only go as far as to explore what we can know of these documents within their own immediate, early medieval setting, and needs to draw the line at investigating at any length their afterlife in the high middle ages. We cannot, however, ignore the fact that the changing attitudes and practices of that period had important implications for our own access to the earlier past: a brief 'coda' therefore addresses this issue (Chapter 8), before some final concluding remarks (Chapter 9).

PART I

UNDERSTANDING THE CORPUS

2

Getting to Grips with Papal Privileges in the Early Middle Ages

Printed critical editions of early medieval papal privileges deceive us. In their presentation of these documents as straightforward legal *acta*, arranged in sequential order under a modern typeface, they render them indistinguishable from the routine administrative output of a later medieval chancery, and reduced to simple, bureaucratic texts in a way that would have made little sense to contemporaries. Early papal privileges were not like that. In their original context, the arrival of these spectacular objects marked the culmination of a remarkable, months-long process. Before all else, papal privileges signalled an event. For much of the early middle ages, their acquisition demanded a return journey of perhaps over one thousand miles to the major cultic centre of the Latin west; personal supplication to the bishop of Rome for his special favour; and the publicising of his gift, embodied as a metres-long scroll of Egyptian papyrus, before an assembly of dignitaries in one's homeland. The most recent wave of scholarship on early medieval charters has stressed their importance as performative, symbolically charged objects.[1] Yet the degree to which the processes of acquisition and production peculiar to early papal privileges lent them a special quality within this wider genre has gone little explored. This chapter therefore seeks to introduce the reader to early medieval papal privileges, not by conjuring them out of thin air as self-evident diplomatic category, but by following step-by-step the route taken by their petitioner-pilgrims to the papal see and back. Its premise is that we cannot begin to study these documents within their beneficiaries' home societies until we first reconstruct how they came into existence, and in what material form. Given the paucity of our sources, it is necessarily wide-ranging, drawing on evidence found across Europe from the sixth to eleventh centuries. We need, of course, to be alert to the

---

[1] e.g. Rück, 'Urkunde'; Keller, 'Privilege'; Koziol, *Politics*; Mersiowsky, *Urkunde*.

England and the Papacy in the Early Middle Ages: Papal Privileges in European Perspective, c. 680–1073.
Benjamin Savill, Oxford University Press. © Benjamin Savill 2023. DOI: 10.1093/oso/9780198887058.003.0002

degree to which practices varied over this long period. And things would have varied according to place as well as time: where beneficiaries began and ended their journeys must have made significant differences to how these processes were undertaken and understood. As we shall see, the experiences of English petitioners fell within a European pattern, but were also subject to their own peculiarities—this matters, since it also suggests peculiarities in how the privileges were perceived and used.

I. The Petition

The most important point to establish is that papal privileges arose through petitions. That is to say, if we wish to understand how and why they came into being, we must look to initiatives taken within the beneficiaries' own societies, not papal Rome. This should not seem surprising. Scholars have long recognised that the papacy operated on a principle of 'rescript government' throughout the middle ages: reacting to problems brought to its door, rather than leading by pure initiative. This followed the conventions of Roman imperial government.[2] Practice naturally varied over the years, and especially from the mid-to-late eleventh century a number of popes began to operate *more often* (if still not most of the time) on their own initiative, with important consequences for high-medieval Christianity, as every textbook reader knows. For most of the period with which we are concerned, however, we find little evidence of popes making the first move. This was partly ideological. The early middle ages had a strong culture of petitioning, and the receipt of supplicants in the court of any ruler played a central role in royal self-representation, while at the same time determining a polity's patterns of government and documentary production.[3] Papal privileges usually opened with an *arenga*, an abstract statement in the issuer's voice on the rationale of a grant, and these often give us an insight into the importance of petitioning within papal political thought:

> Since...special care and attention is incumbent on the one who presides over this same apostolic see...it is entirely fitting that, if sometimes things which pertain to the honour and utility of the churches of God are sought

---

[2] Pitz, *Papstreskript*; for the continued importance of these dynamics into the later period, see now also Wiedemann, *Papal Overlordship*.

[3] Koziol, *Begging*; Mersiowsky, *Urkunde*, ii, pp. 546–604, 766–82.

from him, he should assent by making a kindly concession, and that those who, with the devotion of their own commendation, flow to the bosom of the mother – that is, to the home of the holy Roman church – ought to be received into its protection with a special kindness and affection.[4]

One problem: if receiving supplicants was so important to papal ideology, should we be wary of reading such 'propaganda' too literally? Perhaps, but the simple fact of the limited resources and administrative apparatus of the papacy throughout these centuries gives us reason for confidence. Without the initiative and expense undertaken by petitioners, it is difficult to see how the popes would have had the capacity to exert their influence very far beyond Rome at all.

A petition therefore meant a journey to Rome, and this takes us into the overlapping category of pilgrimage. Unlike their high-medieval counterparts, first-millennium popes could almost always be found in the Eternal City, where their role remained principally that of pastor of the *urbs* rather than *orbis*. There were a handful of momentary exceptions to this—for example, John VIII's West Frankish tour of 878–9, or the exiles of unpopular imperial candidates such as Gregory V (996–9)—while after 1046 things changed definitively with the coming of the semi-itinerant reform popes. In these instances the reception of many petitioners may have become easier, since Rome, well-placed as it had been as a Mediterranean imperial capital, was less accessible as a centre of European Christianity. As a general rule, however, petitioners travelled to Rome, probably in most cases making their way into the papal presence at either San Pietro or the basilica-palace complex of the Lateran. The identity of the place of petition with the 'threshold of the apostles', and of the route there with the foremost pilgrimage road in the Latin west, must have lent this process a sacral quality. Early medieval Rome was probably understood by outsiders more as a superlative cult site, with Peter's successor as its chief *impresario*, than as a centre of papal government per se. When (moving away from privileges for a moment) penitential pilgrims returned from Rome in the tenth and eleventh centuries with a papal certificate, this indicated that they had fulfilled their vow of visiting the city's shrines and found absolution through their power, not that they had been processed by any sort of penitentiary office in the later medieval sense.[5] Likewise with privileges, the ambiguous dual role of

---

[4] **64**; Fichtenau, *Arenga*, p. 106.   [5] See below, Appendix, pp. 284–5.

the petitioner-pilgrim invites us to consider whether the supplicant had primarily set out as a *peregrinus* ('out of a desire to see the apostolic shrines and atria', in the words of one seventh-century privilege),[6] with the acquisition of a privilege only arising as a secondary concern. Some early English examples would appear to indicate as much: Benedict Biscop acquired his privilege on his fourth trip to Rome, besides such 'spiritual wares' as books, relics, and a singing teacher; Aldhelm received his on a pilgrimage with his kinsman King Ceadwalla.[7] In practice, however, the distinction was not clear cut, and if anything privileges probably gained in stature through their blurry association with a pilgrimage and its rewards.

This aura of pilgrimage that would-be beneficiaries or their audiences might ascribe to a petition must have also much depended on the distances involved, and the degree to which any region was more or less routinely connected to Rome at any given time. Bernician or Aragonese petitioners probably saw things differently to their Beneventan counterparts. Whether that compensated for their difficulties of travel is less clear. Logistics must have been a major consideration, despite our sources rarely dwelling on the issue. Even travel within the Italian peninsula could be arduous: the ageing Bertulf of Bobbio collapsed in sickness on his return journey from acquiring his privilege in 628 (perhaps due to the midsummer heat—he was saved by an apparition of Saint Peter on his feast day, 29 June).[8] For some Anglo-Saxon petitioners, on their cross-Channel, transalpine adventure, perhaps as much as a couple of months' duration each way, the task could prove fatal.[9] At least two English metropolitans died en route to petition the pallium,[10] while the Mercian aristocrat Burgheard perished near Rheims, possibly while bringing back a privilege for the bishop of Dorchester-on-Thames, having succumbed to wounds sustained during an ambush in Lazio.[11] Our sources have such little to say about what impressions these journeys through diverse terrains, cultures, and climates must have made on their petitioners (especially those coming from rural, lowland Britain!),[12] that it is easy to forget that associations with these unique life experiences would have become embedded into the documents themselves. Political geography raised as many problems as the physical. There is much literature on the sorts of tolls and obstructions pilgrims or other travellers might have faced,[13]

[6] *MGH Formulae*, pp. 496–8 (JE 2105).   [7] *13, 20.
[8] Jonas, *Vita Columbani*, ii. 23, pp. 283–4.   [9] Matthews, *Road*.
[10] *HE*, iii. 29, pp. 318–19; B., *Vita s. Dunstani*, 26, pp. 80–1.
[11] See below Chapter 7, pp. 251–2.   [12] But see Aldhelm, *Opera*, p. 48.
[13] Matthews, *Road*, pp. 14–38.

and we know that Frankish travellers required episcopal letters in order to travel to Rome.[14] Authorities expressed more than once their anxieties about free-roaming pilgrims.[15] Distance typically meant, therefore, more political frontiers to cross, something which (when compared to many travelling from the more unified Carolingian or even post-Carolingian world) would have always remained a more serious matter of consideration for English petitioners. Such distances also demanded a huge input of time, resources, and knowledge. The farther one travelled, then presumably the greater the expense, and the need for contacts and intermediaries along the way. If this sounds like a simple point, it is nevertheless one too often ignored. The state-run *cursus publicus* ('post-service') that had sustained communications of this kind across the Roman Empire had vanished with it.[16] Throughout this period, the logistics of petition meant that those 'privileged' by the papacy *already* enjoyed the luxury of being among the richest and most influential institutions in their societies, perhaps all the more so as distance from Rome increased. One did not travel from Lindsey to the Lateran by faith alone.

The task of petition went in many instances to the leaders of these institutions. In the case of England, we can gather that such luminaries as Benedict Biscop, Aldhelm, Saints Wilfrid, Earconwald, and Dunstan, Giso of Wells, Ealdred of York, Ælfwine of Ramsey, Baldwin of Bury St Edmunds, and Thomas of Bayeux all obtained the privileges addressed to them in person.[17] Elsewhere the story was similar. If this looks inconvenient to us (as it may have done to many in the high and later middle ages), then it serves as a reminder that we are not dealing with a streamlined bureaucratic system, nor anything which aspired to such. Just as the great magnates of a realm sought diplomas from their sovereign in person, thus communicating their closeness to the ruler and the political centre,[18] so must have the opportunity to beseech the pope face-to-face, in the presence of Rome's saints, itself been a key incentive behind acquiring a privilege in the first place. These documents communicated proximity to the pope, even apostles, and ideally one must have wished to appear as closely associated as possible with their acquisition. Such high-status petitioners' encounters with the pope may

---

[14] *MGH Formulae*, pp. 104–5.

[15] Constable, 'Opposition'; Aronstam, 'Penitential Pilgrimages', pp. 67–9.

[16] Purcell, 'Postal Service'. Wood, 'Notes', p. 33, suggests that the *supplimentum publicum* which aided the petition in Jonas, *Vita Columbani*, ii. 23, p. 282, might indicate a remnant of this system in the Italian peninsula. This could, however, just be Jonas' term for a more ad hoc provision of resources from the Lombard king.

[17] *12–*13, 16–*17, 20, 41, *49, 57, 59, *62, 64–5.   [18] Keller, 'Privilege', p. 86.

have anyway concerned weightier matters, beyond the privilege alone. In many cases we can see that petitioners had arrived primarily in order to attend a council, during the course of which their acquisition of a privilege may have only been one of several concerns.[19] From the mid-tenth century, as the theatre for cross-continental, imperial politics came to take place more often in Italy, visits by high-status dignitaries assumed a more explicitly political aspect, as petitioners made their way into the papal (and sometimes imperial) presence in a quasi-ambassadorial context.[20] The opportunity to obtain a privilege might even have functioned as an incentive for those sent to act as representatives in royal or comital politicking. The rank of the petitioner may have depended on the gravity of the business at hand, although regional customs must have also played a part (in England, the most famous of these was the idea from the mid-tenth century that archbishops should acquire their pallia and accompanying privileges in person, something which the popes, bar some ninth-century gestures, do not seem to have required at all until the 1060s).[21] Nevertheless, institutions also sent envoys (*legati, missi, nuntii*) on their behalf as successful petitioners, although this is hardly reflected in the documents, which usually address the beneficiary as if present.[22]

Whatever their rank, petitioners needed to present written documentation. Any modern-day researcher visiting the Vatican will know the necessity of bearing the carefully worded recommendation of a local worthy, and we can see from the 650s similar expectations for intermediary-petitioners.[23] Yet even when the relevant prelate or patron came themselves, a written petition was probably required. Right through the early medieval centuries we have evidence that synods in Rome followed late antique legal procedure, whereby petitions were submitted as written texts and read aloud by an attending functionary.[24] Much has been made of a scene in Willibald's *Life of Boniface*, in which the saint submits a statement of faith to the pope in writing, as evidence of his difficulties with spoken Latin.[25] But this account may reflect this Anglo-Saxon hagiographer's attempt to make sense of Roman practices which were probably dictated by formal requirements, as

---

[19] e.g. *12, *13, 14, *49, ?†50, *51, 57–9.   [20] Below, Chapter 6, pp. 196–8.

[21] Schoenig, *Bonds*, pp. 37–8, 328–31.

[22] e.g. *23, ?†50, 58; this must have always been the case with authentic privileges addressed to English kings (29, 31–2, 36, 53–4).

[23] *MGH Formulae*, p. 497.

[24] Two examples of Anglo-Saxonist interest: VSW, 29–32, pp. 56–65; Boniface, *Epistolae*, 59, pp. 108–20. Cf. Feissel and Gascou, eds., *La pétition*; Rustow, *Lost Archive*, pp. 207–44.

[25] Willibald, *Vita Bonifatii*, 6, p. 28; Wright, *Sociophilological Study*, pp. 95–109.

much as it does communication issues. It is difficult to do more than generalise, since written petitions were ephemeral texts of little interest to archivists. We are, however, lucky enough to have a handful of surviving examples, few and far between: a letter of Faroald of Spoleto to John VII, for his foundation at Farfa (705); a letter of Abbo of Fleury, on behalf of a certain Hildegard (996/9); and another by Albert of Micy (1004/9). Farfa preserved the former for rare memorial purposes, as an effective foundation charter at the very beginning of its twelfth-century cartulary.[26] The latter two, however, both copied into the same eleventh-century French manuscript, may have had a more functional role as templates for future petitioners.[27] Whether petitioners were expected to bring further written proof to back up their claims probably varied, but there is evidence that they did so when their requests were more ambitious.[28] We can be more certain, however, that by the tenth century—as the 'confirmation politics' (*Bestätigungspolitik*) already prevalent in royal and imperial diplomatic began to influence continental attitudes to Rome, and as some institutions sought to have previous privileges confirmed and re-issued—one might be expected to present an older document (*Vorurkunde*) as proof and partial template.[29] Whether this was normally supposed to have been an original single-sheet rather than a copy is not clear. Considering, however, that originals were (as we shall see) unusually difficult to forge in a way that would have been convincing in Rome, and that we nevertheless have instances of authentic privileges citing what we now know to be forged documents, then it appears that the papal court must have sometimes permitted copies.[30] One could always make excuses, such as when the monks of Nienburg claimed that a fire had consumed all their originals.[31] There is little evidence that popes systematically registered the privileges issued in this period, and so such claims could not always be tested very rigorously, if at all.[32]

---

[26] *Regesto di Farfa*, ed. Giorgio and Balzani, ii. 1.

[27] *PL* 139. 421–2, 439–40 (BL, Add. 10,972, ff. 2r–v, 23r–v).

[28] Mostert, *Political Theology*, pp. 63, 66–76.

[29] Mersiowsky, *Urkunde*, ii, pp. 624–44, 749–66. Isolated evidence for this practice at Rome begins in the early-to-mid ninth century, but builds in momentum in the late ninth and tenth: Santifaller, 'Verwendung', pp. 92 ff.

[30] e.g. *Konzilien*, ed. Jasper, 25A (JL 4158), confirming the forgeries *PUU* †195 (JL 3736), †222 (JL 3768); †235 (JL 3783).

[31] *Codex diplomaticus Anhaltinus*, ed. Heinemann, i. 130 (JL 4334).

[32] See below, n. 53.

As for the act of petition, our sources reveal little. Beyond brief, stock formulae (*postulatis ut...*; *poposcitis ut...*; *petisti a nobis ut...*), papal diplomatic conventions did not allow for descriptions of supplicatory acts. We are therefore fortunate when we find rogue scribes diverging from the norm to reveal something of the process, as in a privilege of John XIII from the Ravennan Easter Synod of 967:

> When I, John...was residing in the city of Ravenna, together with my entourage (*cum meis*) and the most reverend bishops of Italy, there came into our presence the religious priests and deacons of the holy church of Bologna, and prostrating themselves to the ground before all the clergy gathered there, they kissed our feet and brought forward a letter of protection from Pope Leo V of holy memory, stating that they should pay no public dues. Whence, pricked by divine mercy, we gave our assent to their petition...[33]

This document does not necessarily reveal typical practice. It was issued outside Rome, at an abnormally large imperial assembly, and its formulation—if unique in the papal corpus—resembles royal-imperial *placita* (diplomas of legal judgements).[34] Nevertheless it remains as close as we can get to visualising early medieval papal petitioning. Its depiction of the petitioners' highly ritualised approach towards the pope and proskynesis before him; the public setting; and the bringing forth of a written document, would have at least sounded plausible to contemporaries.[35] Richer of Saint-Rémi, writing three decades later, depicted Archbishop Adalbero of Rheims petitioning the same pope after Christmas mass in Rome in 971, doing so in the presence of a number of other bishops who had participated in the service, who thereby provided a legitimating audience.[36] Unfortunately, we have reasons to doubt the precision of Richer's later account of the event, of which he must have heard at least second-hand (in reality the petitioner may not have been Adalbero but his archdeacon, and the occasion not Christmas 971 but Easter 972).[37] Nevertheless it seems improbable that the author

---

[33] *PUU* 175 (JL 3714).   [34] e.g. (from the same assembly): Otto I, *Diplomata*, 340.
[35] Koziol, *Begging*, pp. 59–76.   [36] Richer, *Historiae*, iii. 25–6, pp. 183–4.
[37] *Chron. Mos.*, ii. 6, p. 167 describes the acquisition of a different privilege and states that Adalbero had sent 'legates with letters' to undertake the petition *after* Christmas; the privileges themselves are both dated 23 Apr. 972: *PUU* 217–18 (JL 3762–3). Richer notes elsewhere that Adalbero's archdeacon 'G.' (Gerannus?) was in Rome at about that time: *Historiae*, iii. 43–5, pp. 191–3: presumably, he led the legation.

would have depicted a scene that sounded unbelievable, at least not to his immediate Rémois audience. In the long run, it was how *they* imagined the act of petition which mattered most for its continued validity.

II. Concession, Composition, and Conveyance

With the request made, how did the pope decide? Our sources survive in such a way that we almost never hear of rebuffs, but a handful of exceptions from the eleventh century shows that it remained a risk.[38] We can, nevertheless, hazard to guess that the bishops of Rome might have normally felt inclined to make a concession. Dispatching a happy recipient back to whatever far-flung region with a privilege in hand presented a comparatively rare opportunity for early medieval popes to make their presence felt abroad, while at the same time shoring up their image within Rome's competitive political community. Since the papacy had little real jurisdiction, this was not akin to a ruler granting away lands or prerogatives. In most cases, by confirming regional aspirations to rights and privileges, the popes lost nothing materially, and they had little obligation to check that their decrees were actually implemented—if problems arose, these would at worst just bounce back in the form of further petitions. The narrative technique of papal diplomatic, usually jumping straight from the *petitio* to the dispositive clause enacting the grant, gives the impression of an immediate response, but in reality petitions may have taken place across at least two stages: an off-stage hammering-out of the agreement, followed by a choreographed petition-and-concession in a more public setting.[39] While standard diplomatic depicts the pope alone as decision maker, he may well have sought counsel.[40] This could have taken place synodally, but perhaps in private, maybe in a way inaccessible to the petitioner. In a memorable scene from Stephen's *Life of Wilfrid*, the bishop and his followers stare on helplessly as the papal entourage discuss their case in Greek.[41] Those consulted might have intervened on the petitioner's behalf. Papal privileges did not as a rule include the 'intervention' clauses familiar to continental diplomatic,[42]

---

[38] e.g. **59**: Schoenig, 'Withholding', argues that denying pallium requests could be used as a 'tool of reform', but this could have applied to privileges generally.

[39] Cf. Althoff, 'Colloquium'.

[40] *Chron. Mos.*, ii. 6, p. 167, has a rare account of the pope 'seeking the judgement of his officials and fellow priests'.

[41] *VSW*, 53, pp. 112–13.   [42] Gilsdorf, *Favor.*

but decision-swaying intercessions by political or ecclesiastical heavyweights do occasionally appear in these documents,[43] and doubtlessly much went on unrecorded. After John XV had rebuffed Abbo of Fleury's first petition, the latter wrote to his confidant Leo, abbot of San Bonifacio in Rome, complaining about his desertion: 'in your absence, I confess, I was afflicted like a baby chicken, squawking away as the singular protection of its mother is snatched from it.'[44] Contacts, therefore, were unsurprisingly useful. Gifts, too, presumably played a critical role, although our documents stay quiet on the matter, being keen to portray only freely bestowed apostolic largesse. Our best evidence comes rather from occasions where acquisitions were criticised by others, and it proved advantageous to portray certain gift-exchanges in Rome as sale, and therefore in a sense simoniacal.[45] By the eleventh century this had become a sensitive topic, to say the least. Even then, however, we see ways by which the problem was side-stepped. In 1071, an English embassy on its way to petition Alexander II in Rome stopped at Lucca to donate relics to its church. In fact, Lucca's bishop at that time was Anselmo da Baggio—the alter ego of the pluralist Alexander—then renovating his Tuscan see.[46] The gifting necessary to win over Alexander in Rome could therefore take place some 200 miles north, in Anselmo's Lucca, a face-saving arrangement which must have suited both sides.

Once the pope and his familiars had agreed to the concession, the privilege could be drawn-up. Richer supposed that John XIII had, after giving verbal consent to Adalbero's privilege, 'thereupon ordered it to be put to writing, and then read in their presence'.[47] The contemporary *Chronicle of Mouzon* imagined the pope having a 'notary summoned to produce the privilege' once he had approved the grant.[48] We cannot know how far these outsiders' depictions of on-the-spot writing reflected actual practice. Nor is it clear whether this summoning might have happened after a formal, public petition, or rather the initial, behind-the-scenes stage proposed above. If the latter, the participants might have brought forth the ready-made privilege during a public petition-concession ceremony. The question of who these papal scribes were, and how and where they worked,

---

[43] Within the English corpus, **59** mentions Hildebrand. The imperial presence in Rome could provide a major swing factor: e.g. during the imperial reign of Otto I (962–73), 10 out of 34 privileges cited the emperor's intervention: *PUU* 152 (JL 3689), 153 (JL 3691) <159 (JL 3702), 177–8 (JL 3715–16), 184 (JL 3721), 186 (JL 3723), 192 (JL 3731), 197 (JL 3738), <199 (JL 3739).

[44] *PL* 139. 460.   [45] *VSW*, 34, pp. 70–1 (*12); *CS* I, i. 60–1.

[46] Savill, 'Prelude', pp. 798–9 (on the way to acquiring 64–5).

[47] Richer, *Historiae*, iii. 27, p. 185.   [48] *Chron. Mos.*, ii. 6, p. 167.

has preoccupied scholars of papal diplomatic more than any other. One can add little new here to their impressive body of work.[49] But it has not, characteristically, always 'seen the wood for the trees', and it will prove worthwhile to emphasise some points. First, we should dismiss any notion that this looked anything like the papal chancery of the high middle ages and beyond. We must work without teleologies. Nevertheless the term 'chancery' remains acceptable within an early medieval context, since for all its probable informality and fluidity, we can still detect something akin to a distinct body of scribes working within a sedentary, centralised milieu, and exhibiting a remarkable degree of continuity and consistency in their craft for over half a millennium. With its many churches and continuing lay notarial traditions, Rome must have had a large pool of scribes who could have gone into episcopal service. The *Liber pontificalis* indicates that by the sixth century a papal notariate had developed its own origin myths, imagining its genesis in the pontificates of Fabian (236–60) and Julius (337–52).[50] These scribes' continued use of a distinctive, Roman *curialis* script across our period presumably contributed to a sense of group identity. The same may have gone for the distinctive titles they adopted (*notarii* and *scriniarii*, headed variously by *primicerii* and *secunderii notariorum*, *bibliothecarii*, *protoscrinarii*, or *primiscrinarii*), although we should be cautious of imagining these as necessarily denoting precisely defined functions.[51] Their centre of operations was the *scrinium*, which probably doubled as both scriptorium and archive.[52] It is the single greatest tragedy of papal historiography that nothing of this early archive directly survives. We do not even have a sound understanding of what was kept there. Besides the exceptional case of Gregory I, we have no good evidence that early medieval popes systematically 'registered' outgoing documents, although we can see some bursts of activity in the later ninth and mid-eleventh centuries, doubtlessly in imitation of Gregory's legacy.[53] A few remote references place the *scrinium* at the

---

[49] Bresslau, *Handbuch*, remains essential. State-of-the-field: Johrendt, 'Papsturkunden'.

[50] *LP*, i. 21, 36, pp. 148, 205.

[51] Santifaller, *Saggio*; Unger, *Päpstliche Schriftlichkeit*, pp. 258–73.

[52] *LD* V 82; Unger, *Päpstliche Schriftlichkeit*, pp. 231–88.

[53] Evidence of systematic registration only begins under Innocent III (1198–1216). Besides Gregory I, *Reg.*, we have selective registers of John VIII and Gregory VII. The first two survive only through external copies, while the last two may well imitate the first. See generally Schieffer, 'Die päpstlichen Register'. A traditional view has held that *Reg.* followed late antique practices which continued into subsequent pontificates, making our three survivals the tip of the iceberg. The evidence for this is, however, quite thin on the ground, and Gregory I may have been exceptional within his own time. What survives of *Reg.* was copied in the eighth century. In the late ninth century, John the Deacon claimed this still existed as 14 papyral rolls in the *scrinium*

Lateran.[54] Considering both the practical and symbolic advantages of locating the production and retention of the papal written word at this palace centre, this sounds credible.

Chancery operations varied over time. It may not be too crude to say that one can perceive a decline in the quality of written output from the eighth century.[55] A hugely important shift came, however, in the 1040s, with the imperial imposition of the non-Roman reform party over the city's clergy. Hereafter we begin to see serious changes in papal diplomatic. One significant element of this was the effective emergence of two chanceries, in part the result of these outsider-popes spending much of their time outside the city. Despite overlaps, we can broadly identify one group working according to old Roman practices, still in a distinctive *curialis* script, when the pope was based in Rome; the other, probably non-Roman, travelled as part of the pope's entourage outside the city, producing documents in a northern European, 'diplomatic minuscule' hand.[56] The suddenness of this shift from the 1040s serves as reminder of just how consistent the previous half-millennium's diplomatic practices had been, and is revealing of the degree to which the Romans of the *scrinium* must have comprised a self-consciously distinct group.

Much of that consistency depended on the adoption by the *scriniarii* of a loose set of papal formulae (scribal templates) throughout the seventh to eleventh centuries, about one hundred of which survive in three north-Italian manuscripts. All three differ slightly in content, but they nevertheless bear witness to a shared, basic Roman formulary collection, now known as the *Liber diurnus*.[57] In the twentieth century, scholars raised doubts over this

---

(*PL* 75. 62, 223), but all citations in his *Life of Gregory* in fact derive from the eighth-century texts: Leyser, 'Memory', p. 192. There survive several further collections of letters of individual popes from the mid-to-late ninth century, but these are external compilations: Jasper, 'Beginning', pp. 108–31. We do find other references to an early medieval papal *regestum*, and even some appeals to using it as a resource, but this term may have just been a synonym for the *archivum/scrinium*: Unger, *Päpstliche Schriftlichkeit*, pp. 245–57. Rather than imagining a hidden pre-history of high-medieval-style 'registers', it may be preferable to conceive of the early medieval papal archive as a collection of *res gestae* in a looser sense: a repository of copies of miscellaneous items of noteworthy past business, maintained on an ad hoc basis with varying degrees of scrupulousness across the years—quite possibly with many older items deacquisitioned from time to time.

[54] Bresslau, *Handbuch*, i, pp. 152–3; Unger, *Päpstliche Schriftlichkeit*, pp. 249, 256–7.

[55] Pollard, 'Decline'; Hartmann, *Hadrian*, pp. 292–4.

[56] Kehr, 'Scrinium'; Rabikauskas, *Die römische Kuriale*, pp. 93–100.

[57] *LD* V (Vatican City, Archivio Segreto Vaticano, Misc. arm. xi, 19: Nonantola, s. viii/ix); C (Egmond-Binnen, Sint-Adelbertabdij, Bibliotheek Ms. G. ii: northern Italy, s. ix); A (Milan, Bibliotheca Ambrosiana, i. 2 sup.: Bobbio, s. ix/x).

text's status as a working papal formulary (a handbook for scribes composing papal documents) since, while elements of *Liber diurnus* formulae appear throughout the surviving corpus of the early medieval papacy, we find entire templates adopted only rarely.[58] The readiness with which this earlier generation of diplomatists despaired at the discovery that papal notaries did not slavishly follow the *Liber diurnus* says a lot about their own rigid conceptions of how an early medieval chancery 'ought' to have worked. One would do better to follow the lead of Alice Rio's work on the relationships between the Frankish formularies and charters of this period, recognising that scribes would have been savvy enough to have adapted the formulae they were using on a case-by-case basis.[59] As we shall see shortly, papal privileges were often composed in dialogue with their petitioners, and it is there that much of their interest lies. Moreover, the input of petitioners' initiatives and interests must have initially determined the very contents of the *Liber diurnus* in the seventh and eighth centuries, when its basic form took shape. Following the sequence of items in its earliest manuscript, the *Liber diurnus* comprises three layers: a core, thematically arranged collection of documents covering diverse themes, mostly from before *c.* 680 (nos. 1–63); a smaller, central section, perhaps from around 700 (nos. 64–81); and a second collection of items—often rubricated as *priuilegia* and frequently concerning the confirmation of property (nos. 82–99)—probably belonging to the pontificate of Hadrian I (772–95), who may have overseen the codification of the *Liber* in its existing form.[60] One can see from the retention of proper nouns in a couple of formulae that they are based on lost original documents, responding *de novo* to problems and petitions, copies of which were then kept for future use, probably because someone thought that such issues would arise again.[61] The *Liber diurnus* is therefore revealing in its own right about the matters dealt with in Rome across at least three stages of the seventh and eighth centuries, and what those attached to the *scrinium* then considered important. But it is also interesting to consider its own agency: petitioners from *c.* 680 onwards could find themselves receiving partly ready-prepared documents, the core components of which were originally drafted as bespoke responses to potentially very different requests,

---

[58] Santifaller, 'Verwendung'; Kortüm, *Zur päpstlichen Urkundensprache*, pp. 312–18, summarises the debate.

[59] Rio, *Legal Practice*, pp. 27–31.

[60] Sickel, 'Prolegomena'. Sansterre, 'La date', reviews subsequent historiography, adjusting dates for some formulae. *LD* numeration follows V; 11 further formulae are found in C and A.

[61] *LD* V 86, 93 (= **29**).

rooted within their own particular local circumstances. Formulae meant that some petitioners in Rome could, therefore, indirectly influence the reception and treatment of others—perhaps hundreds of miles, even centuries apart.

Collaboration between *scriniarii* and petitioners was, however, always necessary, and potentially extensive. The former always needed to know the names of the persons, institutions, or properties concerned, and the latter could provide them. That much is to be expected. Probably the most important advance over the last generation of early medieval papal diplomatic has, however, been the uncovering of the surprising degree to which petitioners sometimes influenced the wider composition of their privileges. Here the work of Hans-Henning Kortüm is fundamental. In a survey of the Latin of privileges addressed to petitioners from proto-Romance-speaking regions in the period 896–1046, Kortüm discovered that parts of documents would often diverge from standard chancery Latin and assume a more dialectic form particular to the beneficiary's own region (what we might call proto-Italian, proto-French, or proto-Catalan). The extent to which this affected a document might depend on what kind of privilege it was, and perhaps on the status of the petitioner. In many cases, however, it worked in dialogue with the *Liber diurnus*: the solemn, opening *arengae* and closing *sanctiones* of privileges drew upon parts of tried-and-tested set formulae, while the central section of the document was more directly shaped by the petitioner. As such, privileges often had a regionally determined 'core' (*Kern*), given legitimacy through a formalised, papal 'dressing-up' (*Einkleidung*).[62] Since local variations in grammar and orthography were reproduced textually, it appears that the *scriniarii* took written rather than oral cues from the petitioners: presumably, either letters of petition, pre-prepared drafts, or older documents presented to the pope for confirmation.[63] Kortüm's model of 'recipient influence' (*Empfängereinfluss*) has had extraordinary implications for our understanding of how the papacy worked in the early middle ages. It shows that regional, petitioner-driven demand not only determined who received a papal privilege and when, but in such a way that the documents were themselves sometimes partly authored by those same petitioners

---

[62] Kortüm, *Zur päpstlichen Urkundensprache*.

[63] One fascinating single-sheet allows us to see this process in action. Florence, Archivio capitolare, 1032 is a roughly contemporary copy of Benedict IX for Florence, 24 March 1038: *PUU* 609 (JL 4109). The copy has cancellations and interlinear annotations in a Roman hand, and this 'updated' text appears in the privilege of Leo IX for the same beneficiary, 15 July 1050: *PUU Italien*, i, pp. 440–1 (JL 4230). Clearly the single-sheet was passed to the *scrinium* who used it as a working draft: Kehr (ibid., pp. 435–44), identifies the annotating hand as that of the *bibliothecarius* Peter.

and beneficiaries, in line with regionally specific interests and ideas. Subsequent research has demonstrated that tenth- and eleventh-century petitioners might also choose which *Liber diurnus* formulae were incorporated into their privileges,[64] and even have some say over their graphic layout.[65]

We do not always need to deduce this diplomatically: some sources spell it out. Turning to what few petitions survive, we can see that this kind of influence was openly anticipated. Thus Albert of Micy in the first decade of the eleventh century:

> To the holy lord and venerable pope, John XVIII ... The place in which we live is called Micy ... a good woman, a *domna* named Regina, has granted much to the aforesaid place for her salvation ... and on account of this we urge your sanctity, that two charters which we have written in your name – one of which contains the property of the gifted benefice of this venerable woman, the other absolutely all the substance of our monastery – might be corroborated by your authority with the grant of your seal, and we will assiduously pray to God for you, both in life and death. For it is right, venerable father, that following the custom of your predecessors, you might confirm these monasteries with new papyri documents ...[66]

How far these practices of taking the liberty of arriving in Rome with 'charters written in the name' of the pope predated the tenth century is unfortunately not clear. The work of Kortüm and his successors is mostly limited to 896–1046, since it is only from this time that papal documents survive in relative abundance (with a suitable critical edition).[67] Outside the papal corpus, scholars recognise a general upswing in the beneficiary production of charters in much of Europe across this same period,[68] and so on one level Roman activities simply constituted one part of this wider phenomenon. Nevertheless, even if the long tenth century represents a high point, we do find occasional evidence of quite marked 'recipient influence' in elements of authentic papal privileges dating to as early as the pontificate of Gregory I.[69] We should, therefore, think of this practice as potentially affecting activity in the *scrinium* throughout the centuries under review in this study, albeit with variations of extent and frequency over time, and with

---

[64] Johrendt, 'Empfängereinfluß'.   [65] Werner, *Papsturkunden*.
[66] *PL* 139. 439–40.   [67] *PUU*.
[68] Guyotjeannin, Pycke, and Tock, *Diplomatique*, pp. 228–9.
[69] See below, Chapter 4, pp. 122-3.

the post-Carolingian period as a likely peak. At the extreme end of the spectrum, we even find a couple of early eleventh-century instances of *full* beneficiary creation of papal privileges (*Empfängerausfertigung*: that is, the beneficiaries drew up the entire final product themselves, only submitting it to the pope for his subscription and the attachment of a seal), although this appears to have occurred exceptionally rarely.[70] For most petitioners it was probably not desirable. As Albert of Micy explained, acquiring Roman papyri documents (*indiculorum bibli*) according to the custom (*mos*) of predecessors was a goal in itself. The 'dressing-up' mattered.

This brings us to the crucial issue of these privileges' spectacular material form (Figures 2.1–2.3). For the majority of recipients, in most of the period under review, they must have appeared truly unique—like no other written document. Three characteristics stand out. Firstly, they were comprised of sheets of glued-together papyrus: as far as we can tell, almost exclusively until the eleventh century, whereupon the material began to be phased out in favour of parchment, before effectively disappearing from 1049.[71] As typical as papyrus was in antiquity, its use had fallen into terminal decline across most of Latin Europe by *c.* 680, and by the later ninth and tenth centuries became so rarely encountered outside the documentary output of the *scrinium* that we see it described as a characteristically papal or Roman phenomenon.[72] What's especially remarkable is that the papal *scrinium* may have not only been the last major bastion of papyrus use in the Latin west, but perhaps globally. The Abbasid Caliphate had begun substantially adopting paper from the ninth century, a new tradition imitated by the Fatimid chancery in tenth-century Egypt, the centre of worldwide papyrus production. This ultimately meant the medium's death sentence.[73]

---

[70] Große, 'Frühe Papsturkunden'; Große, 'Die beiden ältesten Papsturkunden'.

[71] Parchment was first used regularly from 1005; papyrus last appears in 1057 (Victor II for Silva Candida, 8 May 1057: JL 4366—not surviving as an original, but described as papyrus in 1236: Gregory IX, *Les registres*, ii, col. 593): Werner, *Papsturkunden*, p. 512. The single pre-eleventh-century parchment privilege was produced at Ravenna, not Rome: above, n. 33 (Bologna, Archivio capitolare, Caps. 14 n. 1).

[72] *Chron. Mos.*, ii. 6; Goetting, 'Zur Kritik', p. 363. Decline: Santifaller, *Beiträge*, pp. 29–32, and now Internullo, 'Du papyrus' (stressing the much slower and more complex transition at port cities such as Ravenna, Naples, and Gaeta).

[73] Rustow, *Lost Archive*, pp. 113–37. From the ninth century there were also plantations in Iraq and Sicily; the latest date on an Arabic papyrus document is usually cited as 1087, but Grob considers this 'very doubtful': the last securely dated document may only be as late as 981: Sijpesteijn, 'Arabic Papyri', pp. 452–3; Grob, *Documentary Arabic*, p. 13. Ibn Hawqal (973/88), our single eyewitness for Sicilian papyrus cultivation, is explicit that most production was for ships' rope, with only a small portion prepared for local documentary use, and never for export: Ibn Hawqal, *Configuration*, pp. 121, 130. There is apparently no good evidence to support the 'modern myth' that any papal papyrus came from Sicily, nor that there existed pre-Islamic cultivation on the island: Internullo, 'Du papyrus', pp. 527–31.

Figure 2.1 The earliest surviving papyrus privilege: Paschal I for Ravenna, 819 (243 × 52 cm) (JE 2551): Ravenna, Archivio arcivescovile, Papiro n. 4, *in situ* in the present-day archiepiscopal archive (Arcidiocesi di Ravenna-Cervia, with permission).

Figure 2.2 Papyrus privileges of John XIII concerning Vic, 971 (JL 3746–7, 3750): Vic Arxiu Episcopal, 405–7, *in situ* in the present-day episcopal archive (Vic, Arxiu Episcopal, with permission).

The papacy's continued use of papyrus right through the early middle ages must have therefore been comparatively difficult and expensive to maintain, and was from that perspective clearly ideological. One finds clues that popes bought in bulk: one surviving privilege of 876 for Tournus retains an Arabic manufactory mark which may indicate its

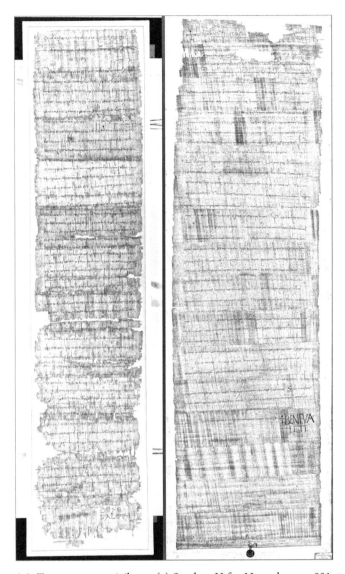

Figure 2.3 Two papyrus privileges: (a) Stephen V for Neeunheerse, 891
(145 × 32 cm: upper section missing) (JL 3468): Münster, Landesarchiv
NRW Abteilung Westfalen, B 605u/Stift Heerse/Urkunden Nr. 3 (Marburger
Lichtbildarchiv, with permission); (b) John XIII for Ató of Vic, 971
(237 × 66 cm; with *bulla*) (JL 3747): Vic, Arxiu Episcopal, 406
(Vic, Arxiu Episcopal, with permission).

production in Egypt in 838/41 (Figure 2.4).[74] A second characteristic was that these papyral privileges were astoundingly huge. Survivals begin from the eighth and ninth centuries, and show that they typically ran to around two and a half metres in length, and 300–700 millimetres in width.[75] One immense ninth-century privilege for Corbie—an unusual survival, but perhaps not an unusual production—shows that they could extend to almost seven metres.[76] Presumably they would have been read as scrolls, and normally kept rolled.[77]

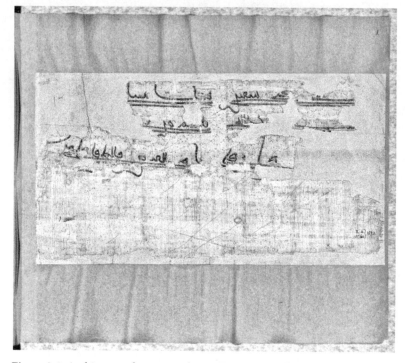

Figure 2.4 Arabic manufactory mark on a papyrus privilege: John VIII for Tournus, 876 (fragment 1 of 8) (55 cm wide; full privilege is 320 cm in length) (JL 3052): BnF, Lat. 8840 (Source: gallica.bnf.fr/BnF).

---

[74] John VIII for Tournus, 15 Oct. 876: see below, n. 86; Unger, *Regesta*, 196.

[75] According to the dimensions of the originals in *PRDP*.

[76] Benedict III for Corbie, 7 Oct. 855 (688 × 70 cm): see below, n. 86.

[77] Observable from the patterns of deterioration to the lengthwise edges of the extant papyri. The scroll was a characteristic medium for sovereign decrees elsewhere in the Mediterranean (Rustow, *Lost Archive*, pp. 381–401), but unusual in Latin Europe by this time: Giele, Peltzer, and Trede, 'Rollen', p. 686.

Lead *bullae* were attached by thread to the end of papyri.[78] Their purpose was as much functional as symbolic, keeping these huge documents tightly rolled up.[79] Thirdly, their layout often appears intentionally wasteful, taking up as much space as possible through widely separated lines of Roman *curialis* script (Figure 2.5). Although we see this script developing through approximately three stages across the early middle ages, the overall effect was one of consistency, conservatism, and increasingly uniqueness. A descendant of ancient Roman cursive, *curialis* made an obvious aesthetic appeal to antiquity that looked quite unlike anything else produced in most of Latin Europe by the ninth century, by which time it may have become increasingly difficult for outsiders even to read.[80]

Figure 2.5 *Curialis* script: from John VIII for Tournus, 876 (= Figure 2.4) (fragment 2 of 8) (Source: gallica.bnf.fr/BnF).

---

[78] Frenz, *Papsturkunden*, pp. 54–6.   [79] Fees, 'Bedeutung'.
[80] Rabikauskas, *Die römische Kuriale*.

The effect these classic-type papyral privileges had on their beneficiaries must have varied according to region and period. In an age in which charters could function as 'works of art',[81] however, we cannot doubt their almost unmatchable 'wow-effect' for many. Regardless of the content of these documents, this is what papal power *looked like*. Early medieval popes communicated their authority to pilgrims, envoys, and fellow Romans within their city's walls through artistic and architectural programmes.[82] Outside Rome, they made that same authority and presence felt through these unique material artefacts. Their distinct aesthetic communicated the distinct quality of papal power against that of other worldly or ecclesiastical authorities. Their huge size embodied the generosity of what they granted.[83] Scrolls usually appear in early medieval art as representations of Scripture: these privileges' conservative format thus evoked the authority of antiquity and the early church. It may have also aligned papal authority with that of the other 'great powers' of the Mediterranean. Little more than a fragment survives of Byzantine imperial documentary culture, but that which does suggests that papal privileges resembled (at least in the ninth century) contemporary Constantinopolitan diplomas. As such they could have expressed a kind of intertextual affinity, even parity, to the output of that chancery.[84] Metres-long decrees and privileges were also a prerogative of caliphal diplomatic:[85] at least some of the papacy's Mediterranean beneficiaries would have understood this resemblance. From our viewpoint as modern researchers, the papacy's use of huge papyral scrolls, *bullae*, and a unique, sometimes illegible script has further implications. At the time, these must have proved extremely difficult to forge as convincing pseudo-originals; later, they were unusually susceptible to physical degradation (only twenty-four, perhaps twenty-five, authentic papal papyri survive in their original form, in varying states of fragmentation),[86] presenting unique challenges for scribes seeking to transcribe them faithfully.

---

[81] Rück, 'Urkunde'.   [82] Goodson, *Rome*.   [83] Cf. Rustow, *Lost Archive*, p. 143.
[84] Cf. AN, K 17, n. 6; Brandi, 'Der byzantinische Kaiserbrief'.
[85] Rustow, *Lost Archive*, pp. 138–59.
[86] Hadrian I to Charlemagne, 788: AN, K 7 n. 9/2 (ARTEM 4502) (JE 2462); Paschal I for Ravenna, 11 July 819: Ravenna, Archivio arcivescovile, Papiro n. 4 (*PRDP* 1) (JE 2551); Leo IV for Ravenna, 31 Aug. 851: Vatican City, Biblioteca Apostolica Vaticana, Pap. vat. lat. 1 (*PRDP* 2) (JE 2606); Benedict III for Corbie, 7 Oct. 855: Amiens, Bibliothèque municipale, 526 n. 1 (ARTEM 4803) (JL 2663); Nicholas I for Saint-Denis, 28 Apr. 863: AN, K 13 n. 10/4 (ARTEM 3022) (JE 2718); John VIII for Tournus, 15 Oct. 876: BnF, Lat. 8840 (ARTEM 1786) (JL 3052); Stephen V for Neuenheerse (23 May or 22 June) 891: Münster, Landesarchiv Nordrhein-Westfalen Abteilung Westfalen, B 605u/Stift Heerse/Urkunden Nr. 3 (*PRDP* 3)

Under Leo IX (1049–54), the first truly effective pope of the eleventh-century reform movement, these traditions ended, and a new style of papal diplomatic emerged. Parchment ousted papyrus, thereby also scaling down the size of documents to dimensions more typical of other major western European diplomas (Figures 2.6–2.7). In the process, the *transversa carta* (length-greater-than-width) format of pre-reform papal privileges became less pronounced, and was sometimes joined by specimens in the *non transversa carta* (width-greater-than-length) style characteristic of Latin imperial diplomatic. *Curialis* meanwhile lost priority to 'diplomatic minuscule', an easily legible, caroline script widely used in the post-Carolingian world. While such changes downgraded these documents' aesthetic uniqueness, this was compensated by the novel introduction of two large graphic symbols of papal authority towards the end of privileges: on the right, the traditional papal farewell (*BENE VALETE*) became reimagined as an imposing monogram (again, resembling western imperial diplomatic practice) (Figures 2.8–2.9); on the left, a cross within a circle (the *rota*), bearing a written motif unique to each pope, functioned as a sign of papal subscription (Figure 2.10).[87] Not all of this diplomatic transition came as an absolutely clean break. Over the earlier eleventh century, the long-spurned medium of parchment had already crept into Roman use, probably as a consequence of global papyrus supplies terminally drying up. As a result the format of

(JL 3468); Formosus for Girona (891/2): Girona, Arxiu Capitular, Buttla del papa Formós (*PRDP* 4) (JL 3484); Formosus for Saint-Denis(?), 15 Oct. 893: AN, L 220 n. 3; K 15 n. 3/2 (ARTEM 4947) (JL 3497); Romanus for Girona, 15 Oct. 897: Girona, Arxiu Capitular, Buttla del papa Romà (*PRDP* 5) (JL 3516); John XIII for Vic, Jan. 971: Vic, Arxiu Episcopal, 405 (*PRDP* 6) (JL 3746); John XIII for Vic, Jan. 971: Vic, Arxiu Episcopal, 406 (*PRDP* 7) (JL 3747); John XIII to (Borrell of Barcelona, Jan. 971): Vic, Arxiu Episcopal, 407 (*PRDP* 8) (JL 3750); Benedict VII for Vic, 25 Feb. 978: Vic, Arxiu Episcopal, 445 (*PRDP* 9) (JL 3794); John XV for Dijon, 26 May 995: BnF, NAL 1609 (fragment 1: ARTEM 2587) and Dijon, Bibliothèque municipale, 909 (fragments 2–3) (JL 3858); Gregory V for Vic, May 998: Vic, Arxiu Episcopal, 624 (*PRDP* 10) (JL 3888); Silvester II for Le Puy, 23 Nov. 999: BnF, NAL 2507 (ARTEM 2593) (JL 3906); Silvester II for Urgell, May 1001: Urgell, Museu Diocesà, Butlla atorgada pel papa Silvestre II al bisbe Sala (*PRDP* 11) (JL 3918); Silvester II for Sant Cugat, Dec. 1002: Barcelona, Arxiu de la Corona d'Aragó, Butlla de Silvestre II (*PRDP* 12) (JL 3927); John XVIII for Isernia, Oct. 1004: Bergamo, Biblioteca civica, Papiro di Giovanni XVIII (*PRDP* 13) (JL 3942); John XVIII for Sant Cugat, Nov. 1007: Barcelona, Arxiu de la Corona d'Aragó, Butlla de Joan XVIII (*PRDP* 14) (JL 3956); Sergius IV for Saint-Martin du Canigou, Nov. 1011: Perpignan, Bibliothèque municipale, 72 (ARTEM 506) (JL 3976); Benedict VIII for Camprodon, 8 Jan. 1017: BnF, NAL 2580 (ARTEM 2605) (JL 4019); Leo IX for Le Puy, 20 May 1051: Le Puy, Bibliothèque municipale, 117 n. 1 (JL 4265). Radiciotti, 'Bolla', now argues that the 19-word fragment preserved as Rome, Biblioteca Angelica, ms. or. 62 (C.3.6), comes from a lost original of Sergius II for Sant'Ilario in Gallicata (846/7?) (J³ *5332). Another papyrus, Benedict VIII for Hildesheim, 1022 (JL 4036) was destroyed in 1943, but photographs remain: *PRDP* 15.

[87] Rück, 'Beiträge', pp. 30–5; Frenz, 'Graphische Symbole'; Frenz, *Papsturkunden*, pp. 19–23; Dahlhaus, 'Aufkommen'; cf. Garipzanov, *Graphic Signs*.

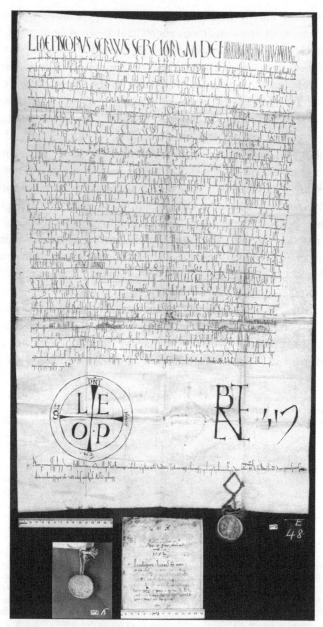

Figure 2.6 A 'reform-period' parchment privilege: Leo IX for Bamberg, 1052 (JL 4283): Munich, Bayerisches Hauptstaatsarchiv, Bamberg. Urk. 120 3 (Marburger Lichtbildarchiv, with permission).

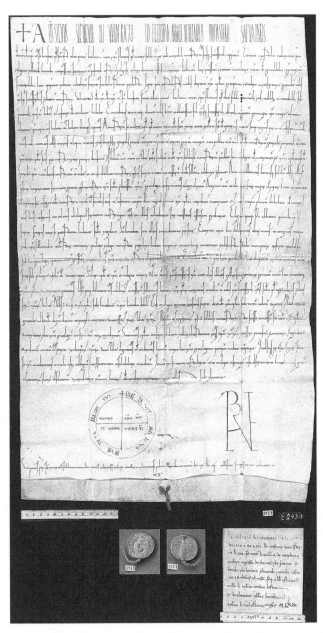

Figure 2.7 Another 'reform-period' parchment privilege: Alexander II for Fulda, 1064 (JL 4557): Marburg, Staatsarchiv, Stiftsarch. Fulda 1064 3 (Marburger Lichtbildarchiv, with permission).

Figure 2.8 Pre-'reform' *BENE VALETE* (detail, Figure 2.3b).

Figure 2.9 Monogrammatic *BENE VALETE* (with 'Komma') (detail, Figure 2.6).

Figure 2.10 *Rota* (detail, Figure 2.6).

privileges had already begun to look gradually more conventional.[88] On the other hand, as we have seen, traditionally trained *scriniarii* within the city continued after 1049 to use *curialis* when they could, and examples survive until as late as 1122.[89] The new reform style did not anyway emerge perfectly formed, but went through an experimental phase, before settling into its mature, high-medieval form under Paschal II (1099–1118). Nevertheless, the severity of the shift under Leo remains striking. On the one hand it was practical. He and his successors spent much time outside the city, and so the use of non-Roman personnel trained in non-Roman documentary conventions necessitated this change. Ideology, however, also played its part: a sudden, highly visible reworking of the materiality of papal documentary culture signalled the wider transformative programme of these new pontiffs. This was a reform aesthetic. It also meant that papal privileges increasingly resembled their German imperial counterparts.[90] If these documents now looked more modest than their epic early medieval forebears,

---

[88] Rück, 'Die hochmittelalterliche Papsturkunden', pp. 14–15.

[89] Rabikauskas, *Die römische Kuriale*, pp. 87–134; Werner, *Papsturkunden*, pp. 515–17.

[90] Rück, 'Die hochmittelalterliche Papsturkunden', p. 18.

they nevertheless stood on par with the sumptuous diplomas issued by the emperors of the west.

The aesthetic transformations of 1049 did not, however, disrupt a broad continuity in the internal, textual formulation of papal privileges throughout the whole period under review.[91] Returning, then, to our *scriniarii* at the Lateran, it may be helpful to outline what that basic diplomatic formulation was, since its technical terms will appear occasionally over the course of this book.[92] As an ideal-type—with countless case-to-case variations—a papal privilege proceeded as follows:

The **PROTOCOL** (πρωτόκολλον—literally, the 'first-glued' sheet of papyrus) sets the scene. Having usually solemnised the occasion with a sign of the cross (*inuocatio symbolica*), the text proper commences with the *intitulatio* of the pope's name and title (*X, episcopus, seruus seruorum Dei*) and then that of the addressee (*inscriptio*), also extending the address (in most circumstances, but not in pallium privileges) to their successors. The pope speaks in the first-person plural. This opening typically ends with a *formula perpetuitatis*, stating that the document holds good forever (*in perpetuum*).

The **CONTEXTUS** then forms the main body of the text, and follows a past-present-future narrative.[93] As we have seen, it opens with an *arenga*, a kind of rhetorical *exordium* that gives an abstract rationale for the grant, usually relating to the themes of papal authority, and the propriety of indulging petitioners. The *narratio*, in the past tense, then relates the background to the privilege. This unfortunately tends to be quite short, providing little contextual detail: that therefore makes it all the more worth paying attention on the rare occasions when this section does 'open up'. Usually, however, the *narratio* moves straight to a *formula petitionis*, acknowledging that a petition has been made. The *contextus* then cuts to the present tense for the *dispositio*. This is the core, *sine qua non* speech act of the privilege, where the grant is actually enacted—the pope states that he 'therefore grants/confirms...' what has been asked, and at this point the privilege comes into effect. Often this is followed by a *formula*

---

[91] Cf. Rustow, *Lost Archive*, p. 114, on 'continuity and innovation' in the switch from Abbasid to Fatimid diplomatic.

[92] Rabikauskas, *Diplomatica generalis*, pp. 22–32; Frenz, *Papsturkunden*, pp. 15–18, 21–3.

[93] Cf. Foot, 'Reading'.

pertinentiae, outlining what is included in the grant (for example, not just rights over a certain property, but also its slaves, tithes, etc.). This is usually then followed by the *clausulae*—more specific clauses on conditions of the privilege, written in the subjunctive rather than indicative, and therefore looking towards the future. These might include simple *clausulae praeceptiuae*, ordering the privilege to be observed by certain persons, and/or roughly equivalent *clausulae prohibitiuae*, stating that no harm should be done against it. These are then backed up by the sanctions (*sanctiones*) ensuring the document's future safeguarding. The *sanctio negatiua* systematically threatens anathema or excommunication upon the document's future transgressors (*poena spiritualis*); less often there is a *poena temporalis*, threatening a monetary sanction, but this is rare, especially when the beneficiary is far from Rome. By contrast, a *sanctio positiua* promises a blessing for the privilege's supporters. It is important to note that, since these penalties are presented in the subjunctive, they do not merely describe future sanctions, but actually embody them. 'If anyone…' (*Si quis…*) should one day transgress the privilege, this part of this ecclesiastical text would in theory become 'activated', and a malediction immediately enforced. The core part of the document ends here. In privileges written by Roman scribes from the pontificate of Hadrian I onwards, the *contextus* closes with the name of the *scriniarius/notarius* responsible, who also provides the month and indiction (the *Skriptumzeile*).[94]

The **ESCHATOCOL** (literally, the 'last-glued' papyrus) ends and authenticates the document, and is the work of other hands. The papal farewell (*BENE VALETE*) appears in pre-1049 privileges in a quasi-graphic format: written in a large, often ungainly majuscule, it is probably the pope's autograph.[95] Usually it is preceded by a cross (and sometimes followed by another), representing the pope's solemn subscription. As just seen, this splits from 1049 into two distinct graphic symbols: the cross becoming the *rota*, and the *BENE VALETE* a monogram.[96] Probably at least elements of the *rota* were autographic, but not the monogram. Below, the text ends with the dating clause (*datatio*), usually given in a third hand. The exact form of the date depends on the period concerned. The two most important points

---

[94] Not continued by the non-Roman, 'reform' scribes; it last appears in 1125: Frenz, *Papsturkunden*, p. 17.

[95] Frenz, 'Graphische Symbole', p. 403.

[96] Initially accompanied by a sign known as the *Komma*, whose purpose is unclear; used only intermittently, this disappears for good after 1092: Frenz, 'Graphische Symbole', pp. 400, 404–5.

to note are that from the earliest records to 771, then again 801–904 and 962–1039, the regnal year of the emperor (or, earlier, consul(s)) recognised in Rome is given; and, from the time of Hadrian I, the individual responsible for the *datatio* names himself. Below hangs the *bulla*.

At its roots this format is epistolary, following the strict letter-writing conventions of antiquity, which had become incorporated into late Roman legal practice.[97] Accordingly, its framework was not entirely unique, but shared across much of the post-Roman world. Most notably, royal and imperial diplomas in mainland Europe included many of the same internal features. The same was not, however, quite true of Anglo-Saxon diplomatic practice. We shall return to the implications of this distinction shortly. First, we need to get this privilege into our petitioner's hands.

We have few concrete details about how the conveyance of privileges worked, although our understanding of wider contemporary practice suggests that the act was probably public and ritualised, as with the formal petition.[98] The internal and external features of privileges indicate a multi-stage process, perhaps with the *eschatocol* not added until the moment of conveyance, and the *datatio* last of all.[99] The document may have been read aloud, either by the pope or a functionary.[100] The pope's personal handling of the privilege, and his autographic additions of the *BENE VALETE* and, later, elements of the *rota*, could have had a ritual quality, as a reference in the *Liber pontificalis* to John VIII confirming a document 'with his own holy fingers' suggests.[101] Whether that ritual also included, as sometimes observable elsewhere,[102] some sort of sanctifying contact between the document and an altar is uncertain. One finds exceptional, eighth-century

---

[97] Sharpe, 'Charters', p. 231.

[98] Keller, 'Privilege', pp. 86–9; Mersiowsky, *Urkunde*, ii, pp. 661–707.

[99] On a surviving single-sheet privilege of Leo IX for Fulda, 13 June 1049 (JL 4176), a mirror image of the monogram is imprinted to the left, suggesting that this was the last element added to the text, shortly before it was folded up (with the ink still wet): Marburg, Staatsarchiv, Stiftsarch. Fulda 1049 Jun. 13. Note that final authenticating elements are sometimes missing from surviving originals: e.g. Rabikauskas, 'Zur fehlenden und unvollständingen Skriptumzeile', pp. 107–16; for a study of where these absences may indicate that the recipient left Rome with the document before it was finally approved and conveyed, see Jarrett, 'Archbishop Ató'. In the case of the three incomplete Vic papyri studied by Jarrett (Vic, Arxiu Episcopal, 405–7: see above, n. 86), it is nevertheless noteworthy that while the *datatio* is missing, the *Bene Valete* (in Vic, Arxiu Episcopal, 405–6, but not 407, arguably a letter rather than a privilege) and *bulla* (in all three) are present, suggesting the order in which these final stages may have typically been processed.

[100] Richer, *Historiae*, iii. 27, p. 185.   [101] *LP*, ii. 105, p. 112.

[102] Fichtenau, *Urkundenwesen*, p. 63; Kelly, 'Anglo-Saxon Lay Society', p. 44.

references to important papal documents being placed over the tomb of Saint Peter.[103] It is tempting to imagine that this reflects wider practice, with these spectacular privileges thereby also becoming authentic Petrine contact relics, charged-up with the full power of the apostle himself. While this is possible, however, the evidence is lacking. One rare description of a privilege conveyance, from a tenth-century English pontifical, indicates something distinct: in 960 John XII had 'commanded' Dunstan to take his pallium from Peter's altar, but to receive his privilege 'from his own hands'.[104] That may not rule out the document spending time at the altar or tomb at an earlier stage, but it highlights what at least Dunstan and his circle deemed the climax of the ceremony: the moment at which pope and petitioner came together, passing the document from hand-to-hand. Artistic representations of such a ritual at Rome survive only from the twelfth century.[105] But a mosaic in Ravenna's Sant'Apollinare in Classe (668/85), depicts a scene which, however stylised, may give us a flavour of events in contemporary Rome. As an audience of lay and ecclesiastical dignitaries look on, an envoy of the archbishop of Ravenna approaches Emperor Constantine IV and meets him face-to-face. At the very centre of the mosaic's composition, the emperor proffers with his bare hands a large scroll emblazoned with the word PRIVILEGIA and passes it towards the envoy—whose own hands and arms, deferentially covered by the folds of his chasuble, are outstretched and waiting.[106]

III. Return and Recognition

For our petitioner-beneficiaries, this did not end the story. Indeed, for the audiences they needed to convince most, it had not yet begun. Geoffrey Koziol has made the most important recent contribution to our understanding of rulers' diplomas as tools of symbolic communication, casting them as 'performative acts' in the sense of Austinian 'speech act' theory. In this view, the ceremonial issuing of sovereign diplomas was not simply an exhibition of the pre-existing authority of the ruler, but the act through which that very

---

[103] *MGH Epp.* III, p. 563 (JE 2381); *LP*, i. 90, 97, pp. 389, 498. Unger, *Päpstliche Schriftlichkeit*, p. 248, n. 111, observes that evidence for this practice does not continue into the following century.

[104] BnF, Lat. 943, f. 7: see below, Chapter 6, pp. 190–94.

[105] Vatican City, Biblioteca Apostolica Vaticana, Vat. lat. 4939, ff. 142v, 145v, 147v, 151.

[106] 'Ravenna: S. Apollinare in Classe: Apse Mosaic: Constantine IV Pogonatus', *ARTSTOR*.

power was constructed and made 'live'. When a ruler's voice in a *dispositio* stated that 'we grant/confirm X...', this did not just describe a state of affairs, but actively brought it into being. Once archived, moreover, charters remained performative, recreating that same act whenever they were consulted: 'the charter of faith is not simply a record of a person's oath, it *is* his oath.'[107] Two key problems not directly addressed in this approach, however, and especially pertinent when thinking about papal privileges (especially in a more remote region such as England), are those of how (i) the meaning of the conveyance as a performative act might depend less on the virtuosity of the performer, than on its audience and their own frameworks of reference; and (ii) that audiences could vary widely, and therefore future readings of the performative act might vary accordingly, across both distance and time.[108] Papal privileges constitute an extreme (I think, *the* extreme) instance of a more general problem that beneficiaries would have encountered after diploma conveyances in super-scale polities such as the Carolingian, Ottonian, or Salian empires: that is, the audience before whom the initial conveyance took place may have had, in fact, little to do with the local political and social configurations in the region into which the document was being dispatched. No matter how well-received the initial ritual may have been, and no matter how much control the emperor or pope may have had over it, once a document arrived in its intended locality, that performative act would have to be realised again—before an audience with potentially very different expectations and codes of reference, and, usually, well beyond the control of the 'central' issuing authority.

Scholarly manuals on diplomatic show little interest in documents once they leave the chancery and place of issue.[109] Our sources do not often help: the privileges themselves can appear frozen in time at the moment of conveyance, while narrative accounts are rare. Nevertheless, we have important exceptions, several of which come from England. What evidence there is suggests that a privilege usually required recognition at an assembly and/or ecclesiastical council,[110] perhaps after a short period of remand in the beneficiary's archive.[111] Our best evidence is clustered. Stephen of Ripon (*c.* 713) describes Wilfrid's return to Northumbria in 680, whereupon he

---

[107] Koziol, *Politics*, pp. 40–62; Austin, *How.*
[108] 'Communicative distance': Koch, 'Urkunde', and Huschner, *Transalpine Kommunikation*, i, pp. 211–13.
[109] Mersiowsky, *Urkunde*, ii, p. 707.
[110] Assemblies and councils: Wickham, 'Consensus', with bibliography.
[111] Richer, *Historiae*, iii. 29, p. 185.

presented his sealed papal documents to the king, after which 'he summoned all the chief men who lived there as well as the servants of God to the synod's meeting-place' to hear (*ad audienda*) the texts and pass judgement. Bede (716/17) mirrors this with a story of his own Abbot Ceolfrith's privilege being 'openly shown to a synod, confirmed in writing... its authority attested both by the splendid King Aldfrith and by the bishops who were present, in the same way that the king and bishops publicly confirmed that other one of Benedict [Biscop]'s time in a synod'.[112] Almost three hundred years later, we find two separate accounts of Adalbero of Rheims convening a provincial council for the confirmation of his privileges of John XIII, where he ordered them to be read aloud, confirmed by an episcopal charter subscribed by the attendees, and then returned for safekeeping in the monastic archive.[113] Our most thorough account, however, comes from contemporary England, although it is not without problems. Byrhtferth's florid description in his largely imaginative *Life of Ecgwine* (after 1000, perhaps after 1016) of the return and confirmation of a papal privilege at the probably invented council of Alcester around the year 700 has little value for understanding the events of that time.[114] Yet as a recent analysis has shown, we may treat it cautiously as evidence for what the author might have known of meetings of the *witan* in his own day.[115] Byrhtferth's scene has parallels to what we see in the contemporary province of Rheims, with the key difference (as in Bede and Stephen) that the setting is a joint royal-episcopal assembly. It depicts the king ordering a privilege recently acquired for Evesham to be displayed and read aloud to those gathered; seeking, and receiving, the unanimous verbal consent of the assembly; and then ordering the archbishop of Canterbury to draw up a confirmatory *priuilegium*, to be ratified by the king and aristocracy. Finally—or so Byrhtferth imagines—the *priuilegium* (apparently the new confirmatory charter, but perhaps also the papal document) was brought to Evesham on a suitable feast day (All Saints, 1 November), and after mass placed 'in' the church's altar, while a prayer was read.

A few such confirmatory Anglo-Saxon charters survive. A short charter and list of subscriptions found beneath an eleventh-century copy of Sergius' privilege for Aldhelm may or may not reflect an authentic seventh-century

---

[112] *VSW*, 34, pp. 70–1 (*12); *HA*, 15, pp. 58–61 (*13, *23).
[113] *Chron. Mos.*, ii. 7, pp. 167–70; Richer, *Historiae*, iii. 30, p. 186.
[114] Byrhtferth, *Vita s. Ecgwini*, iii. 4–7, pp. 258–67 (cf. †24–5).
[115] Roach, *Kingship*, pp. 86, 167–8.

record, but even if it is a later forgery, it at least provides further evidence that such additional documentation was considered necessary by the later Anglo-Saxon period.[116] However, two further, more reliable, copies of seventh-century episcopal confirmation charters do exist,[117] while we see another two comparable charters, drawn-up at the *Clofesho* councils of 798 (probably) and 803 (certainly) which provide similar evidence from the time of the 'Mercian Supremacy'.[118] The latter survives as a single-sheet original.[119] What forms other charters might have taken is not clear, but it is possible that some confirmation documents may have been directly written onto the papyrus privilege. We at least know that others had this idea elsewhere: on an extant papyrus of Silvester II for Sant Cugat del Vallès (1002), a confirmatory comital charter has been inscribed directly into the space around the *eschatocol*, complete with multiple autograph subscriptions.[120] Given the massive size of papyral privileges, and the habit of *scriniarii* to leave a conspicuously large open area beneath their *eschatocol*, this rare survival may reveal a more commonplace occurrence. Nevertheless, confirmation by an assembly or synod was not guaranteed. The Council of Tribur of 895, presided over by the archbishops of Mainz, Cologne, and Trier, acknowledged the 'honour' due to the apostolic see, but ruled that those who brought back from Rome any 'false document' refuting their own authority would face incarceration.[121] Stephen reports that Wilfrid's papal documents were 'despised' and publicly rejected at a Northumbrian royal assembly;[122] there must be other cases where we simply do not hear of the privileges which failed to make it past this second stage. We can gather from Eadmer that Alexander II's privilege for Bury (1071) never even made it that far, having been confiscated immediately by Archbishop Lanfranc and not released until years later.[123] As time passed and political fortunes changed, some privileges were also brought back to light and reassessed at later councils. While Wilfrid's privilege for Ripon and Hexham finally found recognition at the Synod of Nidd (706),[124] others such as Hadrian's privilege for Lichfield (787/95) or Paschal's for the Coenwulfing family (817/18) were condemned at assemblies a generation after their first

---

[116] Rauer, 'Pope Sergius I's Privilege', p. 274.

[117] *ECEE*, pp. 122–3 (S 1246); *Chertsey*, 4 (S 1247).

[118] *Glastonbury*, 15b (S 152); *Christ Church*, 32 (S 1431a).

[119] BL, Cotton Augustus, ii. 61.   [120] Above, n. 86: full transcription in *PRDP* 12.

[121] *Capitularia*, ed. Boretius and Krause, ii. 252, pp. 230–1 (cap. 30); this less concerns forgeries than papal documents acquired under supposedly 'false' pretexts: see further Pitz, 'Erschleichung'.

[122] *VSW*, 34, pp. 70–1.   [123] *HN*, 3, p. 133.   [124] *VSW*, 60, pp. 128–33.

reception.[125] Condemnation might mean destruction, and this too could be ritualised: an account of a West Frankish assembly of 1008 depicts one especially controversial privilege almost thrown to the flames by its opponents.[126]

What determined these reactions? Without doubt, every case was different. Much depended on the contents of any one privilege, and pre-existing political and social relations within any given regional society. It seems unlikely that papal privileges typically functioned as game-changers to the existing on-the-ground situation, and successful 'privilegees' probably relied much on local standing and the acceptability of their claims prior to the petition. Our two contrasting earliest accounts are instructive. Wilfrid and Benedict Biscop acquired their privileges at the same time, from the same pope. These probably had similar contents. They returned to present their acquisitions before the same Northumbrian king, and so probably before assemblies composed of more or less the same dignitaries. But whereas Wilfrid, then the king's adversary, found his treated with contempt, Biscop's met with approval: incidentally, he also held the role of one of the same king's counsellors.[127] Yet beyond these more interpersonal factors, the success of privileges—both upon their initial reception, and then in their continuing implementation—must have also depended fundamentally upon the degree to which these documents could be reconciled with regional practices and experiences. This is vital to bear in mind when thinking about *early* medieval papal documentation, since in this period local practices might vary so much more widely, as might familiarity with the papacy, or understandings of what it was supposed to represent. Put briefly: papal privileges had to make sense, which was not guaranteed. On the one hand this depended on the compatibility of what was thought to have been granted with regional practices. As we shall see in Chapter 4, the kinds of monastic freedoms conveyed in seventh-century papal privileges bore much resemblance to political and religious configurations which already existed in parts of Francia and Italy, and so might have met with ready acceptance there; the same may not have applied to contemporary Britain. On another level, however, a privilege's chances of success also depended upon familiarity with certain documentary norms. Here the concept of diverse medieval 'documentary landscapes' (*Urkundenlandschaften*) is helpful.[128] Not all cultures of legal and documentary practice were the same, and these

[125] Below, Chapter 5, pp. 173, 181–2.   [126] André, *Vie de Gauzlin*, 18, pp. 50–3.
[127] Wood, 'Gifts', pp. 104–5; but see below, Chapter 4, p. 129.
[128] Härtel, *Notarielle und kirchliche Urkunden*, pp. 308–10.

distantly composed, exotic privileges must have been introduced into some more easily than others. Our giant papyri rolls undoubtedly had an awesome quality almost anywhere. But their internal diplomatic was not so different from those documents drawn up in the names of Merovingian, Lombard, Carolingian, or post-Carolingian sovereigns: they were in some ways complementary. As privileges took on a clearly post-Carolingian aesthetic from 1049, this must have only intensified. 'Recipient influence' meanwhile meant that papal documents might not just contain familiar ideas, but by the tenth and early eleventh centuries even express them, in some regions, in a proto-Romance that *sounded* familiar as well. None of this applied to England. The comparatively *sui generis* quality of Anglo-Saxon royal diplomatic—small public charters which resembled what only passed as private deeds elsewhere; were never issued solely in the king's name but with those of his counsellors; were effectively unvalidated (they lacked marks of notarial authentication, chancery corroboration, or seals); and usually alienated lands rather than rights—meant that among the English, papal charters looked far more alien. 'Documentary landscapes' could also change over time. The successful implementation of enough papal documents in any one region might further transform its documentary culture to become yet more amenable to these texts, once a society had become sufficiently familiar with (and confident in) them. We will see this in Chapters 6 and 7, set in tenth- and eleventh-century Europe. By then, papal privileges appear to have become effectively integrated into much of the shared post-Carolingian 'documentary landscape', but not that of the new Kingdom of the English.

All this underlines the crucial role of regional audiences in determining the fate of these privileges once they left Rome. Not only their success, but even their interpretation lay in this audience's hands. Understanding papal privileges in the early middle ages therefore requires us to embrace some of the basic lessons of reception theory: in Barthesian terms, to acknowledge a 'Death of the Author' (or in this case, pope) once these texts arrived in their destination societies. We cannot decipher any single meaning in them according to the original intentions of their authorship, but must accept that they were open to multiple readings and uses on the parts of their audiences, with whom their 'real' meaning lay. The theory-wary need not fear: all Barthes' essay does is alert us to the need for this change of perspective.[129] Better still for our purposes as historians is the more systematic work of

---

[129] Barthes, 'Death'.

Hans Robert Jauss.[130] For Jauss, the audience's perceptions are similarly of paramount importance, but their reading of a text is not open to their free will or whim. It depends rather upon their preceding experiences and points of comparison, what Jauss calls an audience's 'horizons of expectation' (*Erwartungshorizonte*). A text which does not fall into these horizons—which has a perceived 'aesthetic distance' to what is normally anticipated—will be read differently to one that does. The former may well be rejected, although in certain instances its shock-quality may also add to its perceived import.[131] One particular value of Jauss' approach is that it acknowledges that readings can change over time, as horizons shift: thus a 'new work', even if seen as having 'aesthetic distance' and making only a limited impact upon its first appearance, can potentially open up the way for similar 'works' to become accepted, even *expected*, in the future, as it causes an audience's horizons to widen.[132] Another—and here Jauss comes closer to Barthes—is that it reminds us that if we wish to understand the importance or meaning of a 'work' at any given time or place, then we need to get away from the point of production, and instead investigate 'how the contemporary *reader* could have viewed and understood the work' through 'the reconstruction of a horizon of expectations' at a located historical moment.[133]

In short, any work on early medieval papal privileges needs to focus at least as much on regional audiences as it does on Rome, since it was in the eyes of the former that their meaning became determined. That meaning could change according to place, and it could change according to time. Two privileges based on the same formulae, drawn-up by the same *scriniarius*, conveyed in Rome on the same occasion, but sent to two distinct ecclesiastical provinces, would not share an essential meaning. In their places of destination they would become something else, and that too would change over the centuries as they assumed archival form. If that makes comparative work more difficult, it also makes it more interesting—reminding us that across the varied landscape of early medieval Europe, a plurality of papacies existed at any one time.

IV. Conclusions

The importance of the world of the petitioner-beneficiaries has recurred throughout this chapter as its salient theme. The issuing of papal privileges

---

[130] Jauss, *Toward an Aesthetic.*   [131] Ibid., pp. 18–25.
[132] Ibid., pp. 20, 25, 32.   [133] Ibid., p. 28.

relied on petitioner initiative, and the success of a petition depended markedly upon a supplicant's own abilities, means, and circumstances. While the papal chancery could boast of its own comparatively sophisticated apparatus, even the composition of privileges often relied upon a significant degree of petitioner input. In the case of the practices outlined by Kortüm, this might even extend to something close to joint-authorship of the texts. When papal *scriniarii* contributed to these compositions via formulae from the *Liber diurnus* or elsewhere, these too ultimately looked back to bespoke responses to petitions made years earlier. The papacy presumably retained control over the ceremonies by which successful petitions were granted, and this would have done much to boost their own prestige in Rome. Once, however, the document passed into the petitioner's hands, its true fate— even *meaning*—depended upon what happened within that petitioner's society. There it needed to be publicly presented, confirmed, and kept in good standing by subsequent generations if it were to have any real validity or purpose. All of this lay beyond the pope's control, and was subject to variations across time and space. Many studies of the early medieval papacy have focused upon Rome, but this monograph will need to look in other directions. In what follows, the societies of petitioners and beneficiaries will be key. This is not to suggest that the Roman origins of these privileges did not loom large in the minds of those seeing, hearing, and using these privileges back in the regional world of the petitioners: one purpose of this chapter has been to map out some of the Roman background to the acquisitions which the following chapters will look at from a more regional perspective. But it has also highlighted three handy conceptual terms developed elsewhere in the scholarship, which we can use in what follows as analytical tools for thinking about those relationships and tensions between 'central' documentary production and 'peripheral' documentary culture: *Empfängereinfluss/*'recipient influence', *Urkundenlandschaften/*'documentary landscapes', and *Erwartungshorizonte/*'horizons of expectation'.

This book therefore focuses principally on England, although it does so comparatively, with an eye upon developments elsewhere. Some significant points of comparison have arisen in this chapter already. English petitioners usually had to travel further, for longer, and at presumably greater expense and risk than most of their continental counterparts. They came from kingdoms which were never politically integrated with Rome, nor the emperors who claimed rule over it and ensured that their names and regnal years appeared on papal documents. They faced serious geographical, political, cultural, and linguistic frontiers. The privileges they acquired resembled virtually nothing in Anglo-Saxon documentary culture—save, that is, other papal privileges, but since acquisitions probably took place comparatively rarely, familiarity with this genre may never have been great. This may not always have hindered their reception. On the contrary, their exotic quality, as strange scrolls brought across the sea by adventuring 'culture heroes' from the Latin world's foremost pilgrimage site[134]—as well-travelled artefacts, whose 'life histories' could be mapped in the Anglo-Saxon imaginary over the Alps, to the Mediterranean, perhaps as far as Egypt[135]—may well have sometimes enhanced their aura. But hindrance or otherwise, we have to acknowledge that a distance was always there: cultural, aesthetic, political, spatial. Papal privileges entered Anglo-Saxon archives as imports from a different world. It is to what survives of those archives that we must now turn.

[134] 'Culture heroes': Helms, *Craft*, with Blair, *Church*, pp. 77, 91–4.
[135] 'Life histories': Appadurai, 'Introduction', p. 41.

3

An Annotated Handlist of Papal Privileges in Early Medieval England

Now for the technical part. This chapter lays the foundations for Part II's discursive studies by providing for the first time a catalogue of all known papal privileges relating to England up to 1073. It includes privileges considered both authentic and forged (†), as well as reported lost privileges (*deperdita*) (*). It aims to do for papal privileges in early medieval England what Peter Sawyer's indispensable *Annotated List* of Anglo-Saxon charters did for the native documentary corpus: that is, to provide a usable conspectus of all the known material and its manuscript tradition, together with as much commentary on archives and authenticity as space allows.[1] Since we have almost seventy items to get through, that commentary is necessarily brief. As with Sawyer's *List*, this chapter cannot provide the full diplomatic analysis that only a future critical edition will permit, but it nevertheless presents a step towards that goal. Those who are not (yet) diehard fanatics of papal diplomatic or manuscript studies may wish to skip this section for now and head straight to Part II. Readers will, however, find this chapter a helpful resource to turn back to when looking for the details behind each individual privilege (numbered throughout this book in **bold**).

Before we begin, let's reiterate a point made in Chapter 1: this is a study of all documents which we might broadly class as *privileges*, and not every papal letter of every kind concerning early medieval England. Obviously, that has required some subjective judgement; for texts of ambiguous status, the reader is directed to the Appendix. Readers should note, moreover, that this chapter covers everything of which we have a trace—in Rumsfeldian terms, 'known knowns', and 'known unknowns'—but does not speculate on anything else we might have lost ('unknown unknowns').[2] What follows is what survives.

---

[1] Keynes, 'Provisional Checklist', was a precursor and model; *PUU England*'s archival surveys remain fundamental.

[2] Insley, 'Looking', p. 172. Speculated *deperdita* of pallium privileges are therefore not listed.

England and the Papacy in the Early Middle Ages: Papal Privileges in European Perspective, c. 680–1073.
Benjamin Savill, Oxford University Press. © Benjamin Savill 2023. DOI: 10.1093/oso/9780198887058.003.0003

A. Beginnings to the Mid-Eighth Century

1. 601, June 22
GREGORY I grants AUGUSTINE, BISHOP OF CANTERBURY the pal-
lium, and outlines privileges concerning future consecrations and the organ-
isation of the church

Incipit: Cum certum sit
Archive: Rome/Canterbury?/Wearmouth-Jarrow (preserved via Bede and
Gregory I's *Registrum*).
MSS: See MSS tradition for Bede (*HE*, pp. xxxix–lxxvi: earliest MS s. viii[1])
and Gregory (*Reg.*, pp. v–xii: *P* codices only, earliest MS s. viii).
Edited: *HE*, i. 29, pp. 104–7; *Reg.*, xi. 39, pp. 934–5.
Registered: JE 1826; J[3] 2956.

†2. 610, February 27
BONIFACE IV confirms to ÆTHELBERT, 'KING OF THE ENGLISH' the
privileges of the monastery of STS PETER AND PAUL, CANTERBURY

Incipit: Omnipotens Dei institutione
Archive: Canterbury, St Augustine's.
MSS: BL, Cotton Vespasian B. xx, ff. 279–80v (Davis 199.1) (s. xii[in]); BL,
Cotton Julius D. ii, f. 40 (Davis 192) (s. xiii[med]); BL, Cotton Claudius D. x, ff.
9v–10 (Davis 193) (s. xiii[2]).
Edited: BCS 11.
Registered: JE †1997; Conte, *Chiesa*, †10; J[3] †3184.

†3. 615
BONIFACE IV confirms to ÆTHELBERT, 'KING OF THE ENGLISH'
the privileges of the monastic community of CHRIST CHURCH,
CANTERBURY

Incipit: Dum Christianitatis uestrae
Archive: Canterbury, Christ Church.
MSS: See MSS tradition for Eadmer (*HN*, pp. ix–xv; earliest MS s. xii[1]) and
William of Malmesbury (*GP*, I, pp. xi–xxv: earliest MS *c.* 1125); BL, Cotton
Claudius A. iii, f. 7 (Davis 178) (s. xi/xii); BL, Cotton Cleopatra E. i, f. 40v
(Davis 162) (s. xii[in]); BL, Cotton Claudius E. v, f. 235v (s. xii[in]); Canterbury,
D&C, Register A, f. 1 (Davis 169) (s. xv[in]).

Edited: *HN*, 5, pp. 261–2; BCS 10; Boehmer, *Fälschungen*, pp. 145–6; *GP*, I, i. 30, pp. 62–3.
Registered: JE 1998; Conte, *Chiesa*, 11; J³ †3187.

†4. 624, February 7 (or 20)
HONORIUS I (sic) *confirms to the DOCTORS AND SCHOLARS of the UNIVERSITY OF CAMBRIDGE their privileges*

Incipit: Dilectissimi in Domino
Archive: Cambridge, University.
MSS: Cambridge, University Archives, Luard 115 (s. xiv^{ex}); Cambridge, University Archives, Luard 115*a* (s. xv^{in}); Cambridge, Gonville and Caius College, 249/277, f. 247 (s. xv); Oxford, Christ Church, 138 (s. xv^{3/4}), f. 1.
Edited: *Privileges of the University of Cambridge*, ed. Dyer, i, pp. 58–9.
Registered: J³ †3224.

5. (624, after April 24)
BONIFACE V grants JUSTUS, BISHOP OF CANTERBURY the pallium, and the privilege of consecrating bishops

Incipit: Quam deuote quamque
Archive: Rome?/Canterbury?/Wearmouth-Jarrow (preserved via Bede).
MSS: See MSS tradition for Bede (*HE*, pp. xxxix–lxxvi: earliest MS s. viii¹).
Edited: BCS 14; *HE*, ii. 8, pp. 158–61.
Registered: JE 2006; Conte, *Chiesa*, 30; J³ 3211.

†6. (624/5)
BONIFACE V grants JUSTUS, BISHOP OF CANTERBURY privileges concerning the metropolitan status of his see

Incipit: Susceptis uestrae dilectionis
Archive: Canterbury, Christ Church.
MSS: See MSS tradition for Eadmer (*HN*, pp. ix–xv; earliest MS s. xii¹) and William of Malmesbury (*GP*, I, pp. xi–xxv: earliest MS *c.* 1125); BL, Cotton Cleopatra E. i, f. 41 (Davis 162) (s. xii^{in}); BL, Cotton Claudius E. v, f. 235v (s. xii^{in}); BL, Cotton Faustina B. vi, f. 94v (Davis 178) (s. xii^{in}); Canterbury, D&C, Register A, f. 1 (Davis 169) (s. xv^{in}).

Edited: *HN*, 5, pp. 262–3; BCS 15; Boehmer, *Fälschungen*, pp. 147–8; *GP*, I, i. 31, pp. 62–5.
Registered: JE 2007; Conte, *Chiesa*, †31; J³ †3215.

7. 634, June 11

HONORIUS I grants HONORIUS, BISHOP OF CANTERBURY the pallium and outlines privileges concerning future consecrations (these privileges also applying to YORK).

Incipit: Inter plurima quae
Archive: Rome?/Canterbury?/Wearmouth-Jarrow (preserved via Bede); Echternach (with Willibrord's *Calendar*).
MSS: See MSS tradition for Bede (*HE*, pp. xxxix–lxxvi: earliest MS s. viii¹); BnF, Lat. 10837, ff. 33v–34 (s. viii^med).
Edited: BCS 19; *HE*, ii. 18, pp. 196–9.
Registered: JE 2020; Conte, *Chiesa*, 55; J³ 3243.

†8. (634/8)

HONORIUS I grants HONORIUS, BISHOP OF CANTERBURY privileges concerning the metropolitan status of this see

Incipit: Susceptis uestrae dilectionis
Archive: Canterbury, Christ Church.
MSS: See MSS tradition for Eadmer (*HN*, pp. ix–xv; earliest MS s. xii¹) and William of Malmesbury (*GP*, I, pp. xi–xxv: earliest MS *c*. 1125); BL, Cotton Cleopatra E. i, f. 41v (Davis 162) (s. xii^in); BL, Cotton Claudius E. v, f. 236 (s. xii^in); BL, Cotton Faustina B. vi, f. 94v (Davis 178) (s. xii^in); Canterbury, D&C, Register A, f. 1v (Davis 169) (s. xv^in).
Edited: *HN*, 5, pp. 263–5; BCS 20; Boehmer, *Fälschungen*, pp. 148–9; *GP*, I, i. 32, pp. 64–7.
Registered: JE 2021; Conte, *Chiesa*, †56; J³ †3246.

†*9. (664)

VITALIAN grants WULFHERE, KING OF KENT privileges for the monastery of MEDESHAMESTEDE

Incipit: n/a (*deperditum*/Old English paraphrase).
Archive: n/a (cited in Peterborough MS of *ASC*).

MSS: Oxford, Bodleian Library, Laud Misc. 636, ff. 16v (s. xii^{in}).
Edited: *ASC, s.a.* 656 E; Peterborough, 1B.
Registered: JE *2088; Conte, *Chiesa,* †183; J³ *†3426.

†10. (668/72)
*VITALIAN grants THEODORE, ARCHBISHOP OF CANTERBURY
privileges concerning the metropolitan status of this see*

Incipit: Inter plurima quae
Archive: Canterbury, Christ Church.
MSS: See MSS tradition for Eadmer (*HN*, pp. ix–xv; earliest MS s. xii¹) and
William of Malmesbury (*GP*, I, pp. xi–xxv: earliest MS *c.* 1125); BL, Cotton
Cleopatra E. i, f. 42 (Davis 162) (s. xii^{in}); BL, Cotton Claudius E. v, f. 236v
(s. xii^{in}); BL, Cotton Faustina B. vi, f. 97 (Davis 178) (s. xii^{in}); Canterbury,
D&C, Register A, f. 2 (Davis 169) (s. xv^{in}).
Edited: *HN*, 5, pp. 265–6; BCS 24; Boehmer, *Fälschungen,* pp. 149–50; *GP*,
I, i. 33, pp. 68–9.
Registered: JE 2095; Conte, *Chiesa,* †196; J³ †3440.

†11. (673/5), December 23
*ADEODATUS II grants HADRIAN, ABBOT OF STS PETER AND PAUL,
CANTERBURY privileges for his monastery*

Incipit: Euangelicis atque apostolicis
Archive: Canterbury, St Augustine's.
MSS: BL, Cotton Vespasian B. xx, ff. 280v–281 (Davis 199.1) (s. xii^{in}); BL,
Cotton Julius D. ii, f. 40v (Davis 192) (s. xiii^{med}); BL, Cotton Claudius D. x,
ff. 10r–v (Davis 193) (s. xiii²).
Edited: BCS 31.
Registered: JE 2104; Conte, *Chiesa,* †208; J³ ?3452.

*12. (679/80) [possibly 679, *c.* May 15]
*AGATHO grants WILFRID, BISHOP privileges for his monasteries of
ST PETER'S, RIPON and ST PAUL'S, HEXHAM*

Incipit: n/a (*deperditum*).
Archive: n/a (cited in Stephen's *Life of Wilfrid*).
MSS: See MSS tradition for Stephen: *VSW*, pp. xiii–xv: earliest MS s. xi).

Edited: *VSW*, 45, 47, 51, pp. 92–3, 96–7, 106–7.
Registered: JE *2112; Conte, *Chiesa*, †237; J³ *3484.

*13. (679, before late summer) [possibly *c.* May 15]
AGATHO grants BENEDICT BISCOP, ABBOT OF ST PETER'S, WEARMOUTH privileges for his monastery

Incipit: n/a (*deperditum*).
Archive: n/a (cited in texts composed at Wearmouth-Jarrow).
MSS: See MSS tradition for the historians of Wearmouth-Jarrow (*HA*, pp. xciv–cxiv; *HE*, pp. xxxix–lxxvi: earliest MS s. viii¹).
Edited: Bede, *Homelia*, pp. 16–17; *HA*, 6, 11, pp. 36–7, 48–9; *VC*, 16, p. 95; *HE*, iv. 18, pp. 388–9.
Registered: JE *2106; Conte, *Chiesa*, *221; J³ *3471.

14. (679?) May 15
AGATHO grants HADRIAN, ABBOT OF STS PETER AND PAUL, CANTERBURY privileges for his monastery

Incipit: Quoniam semper sunt
Archive: Canterbury, St Augustine's.
MSS: BL, Cotton Vespasian B. xx, ff. 281v–282 (Davis 199.1) (s. xii^in); BL, Cotton Julius D. ii, f. 40v (Davis 192) (s. xiii^med); BL, Cotton Claudius D. x, ff. 10v (Davis 193) (s. xiii²).
Edited: BCS 38.
Registered: Conte, *Chiesa*, †218; J³ ?3467.

†15. (680)
AGATHO grants ÆTHELRED, KING OF THE MERCIANS, ARCHBISHOP THEODORE OF CANTERBURY and SEAXWULF, BISHOP OF THE MIDDLE ANGLES AND MERCIANS privileges for the monastery of MEDESHAMSTEDE

Incipit: Dominus regnauit exultet
Archive: Peterborough.
MSS: Oxford, Bodleian Library, Laud Misc. 636, ff. 17v–18v (s. xii^in) [*Old English summary*]; London, Society of Antiquaries, 60, ff. 64–8 (Davis 754) (s. xii¹); Cambridge, University Library, Peterborough D&C I, ff. 88–9,

92–3 (Davis 757) (s. xiii^med); BL, Egerton 2733, ff. 99–106v (Davis 755) (s. xiii²).
Edited: BCS 48–9; *ASC, s.a.* 675 E; *Peterborough,* 2–2a.
Registered: JE †2111; Conte, *Chiesa,* †236; S 72; J³ †3486.

16. (678/81)
AGATHO grants EARCONWALD, BISHOP OF THE EAST SAXONS privileges for his monastery of ST PETER'S, CHERTSEY

Incipit: Quae ad securitatem
Archive: Chertsey.
MSS: BL, Cotton Vitellius A. xiii, ff. 25–6 (Davis 222) (s. xiii^med).
Edited: BCS 56; *Chertsey,* Appendix 1a.
Registered: JE †2115; Conte, *Chiesa,* †240; J³ †3488.

*17. (678/81)
AGATHO grants EARCONWALD, BISHOP OF THE EAST SAXONS privileges for his monastery of (ST MARY'S?), BARKING

Incipit: n/a (*deperditum*).
Archive: n/a (cited in a charter of Earconwald for Barking, 687/8(?) (S 1246)).
MSS: BL, Cotton Vespasian A. ix (s. xvi), f. 112; BL, Cotton Vespasian B. xv (s. xvi), f. 100.
Edited: BCS 87; *ECEE,* pp. 122–3; *Barking,* 2.
Registered: No (but cited in S 1246).

†18. (678/81)
AGATHO grants EARCONWALD, BISHOP OF THE EAST SAXONS privileges for his monastery of ST PAUL'S, LONDON

Incipit: Quae ad securitatem
Archive: London, St Paul's.
MSS: London, Metropolitan Archives, CLC/313/B/001/MS25504, ff. 6–7 (Davis 596) (s. xii¹); London, Metropolitan Archives, CLC/313/B/012/MS25501, ff. 61v–62 (Davis 597) (1241).
Edited: BCS 55.
Registered: JE †2114; Conte, *Chiesa,* †239; J³ †3487.

†*19. (678/81)
AGATHO grants HÆDDI, BISHOP OF THE WEST SAXONS permission to translate the body of Saint Birinus to WINCHESTER

Incipit: n/a (*deperditum*).
Archive: n/a (cited in a purported decree of Theodore, archbishop of Canterbury, supplied in Thomas Rudbourne's *Historia maior Wintoniensis*, ii. 3).
MSS: See MSS tradition for Thomas Rudbourne (Sharpe, *Handlist*, pp. 677–8; earliest MS s. xv^ex).
Edited: HS, iii, p. 126.
Registered: Conte, *Chiesa*, †222; J³ *?3475.

20. (687/701) [probably 689, *c.* April]
SERGIUS I grants ALDHELM, ABBOT OF STS PETER AND PAUL, MALMESBURY and ST JOHN THE BAPTIST'S, FROME privileges for his monasteries

Incipit: Ea quae religiosae/þa þincg þe
Archive: Malmesbury.
MSS: BL, Cotton Otho C. i/1, ff. 68–9 (s. xi^med) [*Old English*]; Cambridge, University Library, Kk 4. 6, ff. 269v–270 (s. xii^in) [*Latin: William of Malmesbury's Liber pontificalis 'C'*]; see MSS tradition for William of Malmesbury's *Gesta pontificum* (*GP*, I, pp. xi–xxv: earliest MS *c.* 1125) [*Latin*]; Oxford, Bodleian Library, Wood empt. 5, ff. 57–60 (Davis 641) (s. xiii^in) [*Latin*].
Edited: BCS 105–6; Aldhelm, *Opera*, pp. 512–14 [*Latin only*]; *GP*, I, v. 221, pp. 554–9 [*Latin only*]; Rauer, 'Pope Sergius' Privilege', pp. 270–6 [*Old English only*].
Registered: JE 2140; Conte, *Chiesa*, ?285; J³ 3595.

†21. 689, May 3
SERGIUS I confirms to the DOCTORS AND SCHOLARS of the UNIVERSITY OF CAMBRIDGE their privileges

Incipit: Quoniam fama bonae
Archive: Cambridge, University.
MSS: Cambridge, University Archives, Luard 115 (s. xiv^ex); Cambridge, University Archives, Luard 115a (s. xv^in); Dublin, Trinity College, 641,

f. 10 (s. xv[1]); Cambridge, Gonville and Caius College, 249/277, ff. 192v, 247 (s. xv); Oxford, Christ Church, 138, f. 1v (s. xv$^{3/4}$).
Edited: *Privileges of the University of Cambridge*, ed. Dyer, i, pp. 59–60.
Registered: J[3] †3559.

†22. (693)
SERGIUS I informs the BISHOPS OF 'ENGLAND' that he has received BERHTWALD, ARCHBISHOP OF CANTERBURY and confirms the privileges of his see

Incipit: Sicut nobis quibus
Archive: Canterbury, Christ Church.
MSS: See MSS tradition for Eadmer (*HN*, pp. ix–xv; earliest MS s. xii[1]) and William of Malmesbury (*GP*, I, pp. xi–xxv: earliest MS *c.* 1125); BL, Cotton Claudius, A. iii, f. 7v (Davis 178) (s. s.xii[in]); BL, Cotton Cleopatra E. i, f. 43 (Davis 162) (s. xii[in]); BL, Cotton Claudius E. v, f. 237 (s. xii[in]); BL, Cotton Faustina B. vi, f. 97 (Davis 178) (s. xii[in]); Canterbury, D&C, Register A, f. 2v (Davis 169) (s. xv[in]).
Edited: *HN*, 5, pp. 267–8; BCS 84; Boehmer, *Fälschungen*, pp. 152–3; *GP*, I, i. 35, pp. 70–5.
Registered: JE 2133; Conte, *Chiesa*, †281; J[3] †3569.

*23. (689/701)
SERGIUS I grants CEOLFRITH, ABBOT OF ST PAUL'S, JARROW privileges for his monastery

Incipit: n/a (*deperditum*).
Archive: n/a (cited in texts composed at Wearmouth-Jarrow).
MSS: See MSS tradition for the historians of Wearmouth-Jarrow (*HA*, pp. xciv–cxiv: earliest MS s. x[ex]).
Edited: *HA*, 15, pp. 58–9; *VC*, 20, pp. 98–9.
Registered: JE *2139; Conte, *Chiesa*, *294; J[3] *3596.

†24. 709
CONSTANTINE I directs BERHTWALD, 'PRIMATE OF THE CHURCHES OF BRITAIN' to hold a council and found a privileged monastery at the location of Bishop Ecgwine's vision of Saint Mary (EVESHAM)

Incipit: Venerabilem uirum Ecgwinum
Archive: Evesham; Canterbury, Christ Church.

MSS: Cambridge, University Library, Kk 4. 6, f. 272 (s. xii^{in}) [*William of Malmesbury's Liber pontificalis 'C'*]; BL, Cotton Cleopatra E. i, f. 34 (Davis 162) (s. xii^{in}); BL, Cotton Claudius E. v, f. 237 (s. xii^{in}); Evesham, Almonry Museum, 127 (*c.* 1200) [*single-sheet pseudo-original*]; BL, Cotton Vespasian B. xxiv, f. 76 (Davis 381) (s. xiii^{in}); Oxford, Bodleian Library, Rawlinson A 287, f. 162 (s. xiii^{in}) [*Thomas of Marlborough*]; BL, Harley 3763, f. 95 (Davis 382) (s. xiii); Canterbury, D&C, Register A, f. 10v (Davis 169) (s. xv^{in}).
Edited: BCS 126; Thomas of Marlborough, *History*, iii. 318–23, pp. 315–19.
Registered: JE †2147; J³ †3636.

†25. 713
CONSTANTINE I informs BERHTWALD, 'PRIMATE OF BRITAIN' that he has placed the monastery of Ecgwine (ST MARY'S, EVESHAM) under his authority, and granted it further privileges

Incipit: Diuina dispensatione ad
Archive: Evesham; Canterbury, Christ Church.
MSS: BL, Cotton Cleopatra E. i, f. 34v (Davis 162) (s. xii^{in}); ibid., ff. 64–5 (*c.* 1200) [*single-sheet pseudo-original*]; BL, Cotton Claudius E. v, f. 237v (s. xii^{in}); BL, Cotton Vespasian B. xxiv, f. 76v (Davis 381) (s. xiii^{in}); Oxford, Bodleian Library, Rawlinson A 287, ff. 162v–163 (s. xiii^{in}) [*Thomas of Marlborough*]; BL, Harley 3763, f. 95v (Davis 382) (s. xiii); Canterbury, D&C, Register A, f. 10v (Davis 169) (s. xv^{in}).
Edited: BCS 129; Thomas of Marlborough, *History*, iii. 324–8, pp. 318–21.
Registered: JE †2149; J³ †3667.

26. (708/15)
CONSTANTINE I grants HÆDDA, ABBOT OF ST PETER'S, BERMONDSEY AND WOKING privileges for his monastery

Incipit: Sicut religiosae uitae
Archive: Peterborough.
MSS: London, Society of Antiquaries, 60, ff. 55v–56v (Davis 754) (s. xii^1); Cambridge, University Library, Peterborough D&C I, f. 101 (Davis 757) (s. xiii^{med}).
Edited: BCS 133; *Peterborough*, Appendix 2.
Registered: JE 2148; J³ 3670.

†*27. (715/25)
GREGORY II grants INE, KING OF THE WEST SAXONS approval for his privileges for the monastery of ST MARY'S, GLASTONBURY

Incipit: n/a (*deperditum*).
Archive: n/a (cited in a forged charter of King Ine for Glastonbury, '725' (S 250)).
MSS: See MSS tradition for S 250 (*Glastonbury*, p. 262: earliest MS s. xii).
Edited: BCS 142; *De antiq.*, 42, pp. 100–1; *GR*, I, i. 36C, pp. 816–17; *Glastonbury*, 11.
Registered: No (but cited in S 250).

†28. (731/4)
GREGORY III confirms to the BISHOPS OF 'ENGLAND' the special privileges of the church of CANTERBURY

Incipit: Dei omnipotentis immensae
Archive: Canterbury, Christ Church.
MSS: See MSS tradition for Eadmer (*HN*, pp. ix–xv; earliest MS s. xii[1]) and William of Malmesbury (*GP*, I, pp. xi–xxv: earliest MS *c.* 1125); BL, Cotton Cleopatra E. i, f. 44 (Davis 162) (s. xii[in]); BL, Cotton Claudius E. v, f. 238 (s. xii[in]); BL, Cotton Faustina B. vi, f. 97 (Davis 178) (s. xii[in]); Canterbury, D&C, Register A, f. 3 (Davis 169) (s. xv[in]).
Edited: *HN*, 5, pp. 268–70; BCS 151; Boehmer, *Fälschungen*, pp. 153–4; *GP*, I, i. 36, pp. 74–7.
Registered: JE 2243; J[3] †3835.

(a) Conversion-Era Letters in Bede

Among the fifteen papal letters Bede includes in his *Ecclesiastical History* (731), three (1, 5, 7) concern the pallium and the metropolitan status of Canterbury, York, and initially London. Whether Bede knew the texts through copies made in the Roman archive, or from (copies of) the original papyri in England, remains a matter of debate.[3] We may class them as privileges. However, since they are well known, definitely genuine, and already the subject of an expert literature, they are not considered further in this study, which properly begins *c.* 680. Several points about their later reception nevertheless require special emphasis: that 7 had an early, probably independent, manuscript tradition in Frisia via a dossier connected to

---

[3] Story, 'Bede', pp. 786 ff., with bibliography.

the missionary Willibrord (d. 739);[4] that 1 would go on to feature in the manuscript tradition of Gregory I's *Register* (certainly copied from the Roman archive) only through the smaller eighth-century collection known as 'P' (54 letters; which also travelled with the 200-letter Cologne redaction, 'C'), and not the more influential collection compiled by Hadrian I (772–95) ('R': 684 letters);[5] that Gregory's *Register* anyway appears to have had a very limited readership in Anglo-Saxon England, if any at all;[6] and, lastly, that none of these privileges made it into the Old English translation of Bede's *History* of the later ninth or earlier tenth century.[7]

(b) Authentic Privileges for Monasteries, 678–715

Hans Hubert Anton's *tour de force* study of a privilege of Eugenius I (654–7) for Saint-Maurice d'Agaune also established the underlying authenticity of four privileges for English monasteries from the decades around the turn of the eighth century (**14, 16, 20, 26**).[8] All four share a similar core formulation, placing the beneficiary houses under the special authority of the Roman church. They survive in their Latin form in manuscripts of the twelfth century or later, and all with interpolations. Anton's judgements were based on the closeness of these privileges to *Liber diurnus* (*LD*) formulae 32 and 77; their similarity to other contemporary privileges from apparently unrelated continental archives; and the correspondences between these documents and those known from reliable, near-contemporary narrative reports (*12, *13, *23). Anton's analysis is convincing, although not perfect, since it gives insufficient consideration to the possibility of travelling forgers in later centuries. Nevertheless, there is further supporting evidence that Anton did not take into account (Anton was not an Anglo-Saxonist, and his study strictly diplomatic).

Agatho's privilege for Sts Peter and Paul (later St Augustine's), Canterbury (**14**) survives alongside a group of post-Conquest forgeries for the same house (including †2 and †11, discussed below). Compared to those texts, it is encouragingly simple, mostly following *LD* 32, with occasional readings from *LD* 77 and a further clause on abbatial elections found in

---

[4] Ibid., pp. 797 ff.   [5] Ewald, 'Studien'.
[6] Gretsch, *Ælfric*, pp. 46–9; Savill, 'Consul'.
[7] **1** and **7** are each mentioned as a *gewrit* (*Old English Version of Bede's Ecclesiastical History*, i. 16, ii. 15, pp. 90–1, 146–7); **5** is referred to only by its contents (ibid., ii. 7, pp. 118–19).
[8] Anton, *Studien*, pp. 49–92.

contemporary privileges in continental archives.[9] It is the least corrupted text of the group, but still presents problems. Its description of the monastery as 'founded by Æthelbert, first Christian king of the English' in the *inscriptio* looks bogus, and a brief nod to purported earlier privileges reads like an interpolation designed to support the more ambitious †2 and †11. Its dating clause is a mess. While sound in its diplomatic format, it gives the Ides (15) of May but with a range of incongruous imperial dates ranging 677–80, perhaps best explained by the illegibility of the flaking lower-end of the papyrus by the time of its copying. Since Agatho was not consecrated until 21 June 678, neither 15 May 677 nor 678 can work.[10] As we will see in Chapter 4, however, Benedict Biscop, a former abbot of Sts Peter and Paul and one-time companion of 14's addressee Hadrian, was in Rome in early-to-mid 679 as part of a Canterbury embassy (during which he also acquired *13),[11] and so a date of 15 May 679 is possible.

The other privileges in this group survive in poor condition. Chertsey's anachronistically lengthy 16 is severely corrupted and now undated, and invites extreme caution. Yet as Anton demonstrated, one can just about detect the wreckage of *LD* 32 beneath its surface.[12] What Anton may not have known is that another charter in the Chertsey archive in the name of Earconwald (16's addressee), now accepted as substantially genuine, outlines similar, apparently supporting arrangements for the monastery, doing so 'with the authority of blessed Peter, prince of the apostles', and is composed in such a way as to suggest the draftsman's familiarity with a contemporary papal privilege.[13] Together with our wider evidence for Earconwald's Channel-crossing aristocratic connections,[14] and a further indication in the Barking archive that he had personally travelled to Rome to meet Agatho,[15] this adds credibility to the argument for the privilege's underlying authenticity. Anton also recognised Malmesbury and Frome's 20 as having correspondences with *LD* 32, and judged it a more reliable text than 16. That there really was a seventh-century Latin original is now supported by Michael Lapidge's brilliant reconstruction of the career of 20's recipient

---

[9] Ibid., pp. 66–7; Santifaller, 'Verwendung', p. 88.   [10] Levison, *England*, pp. 189–90.
[11] Below, pp. 143–4.   [12] Anton, *Studien*, pp. 69–75, 91.
[13] *Chertsey*, 4 (S 1274), although I disagree with the argument (ibid., pp. 4, 120–1) that the privilege might have been drawn up as a guarantee before Earconwald's trip to Rome (as its problematic dating clause would suggest): the basic formulation of the document is so similar to that found in contemporary papal privileges, and so unlike known Anglo-Saxon diplomatic, that it looks highly likely that it took this papal document as its template. If this so, the extant indiction is a mistake or mistranscription. See also observations below on *17.
[14] Wormald, 'Earconwald'.   [15] Below, p. 70.

Aldhelm, which places him in Rome—and in the presence of Sergius—in April 689 as companion to King Ceadwalla.[16] This also gives us something close to a date for this privilege, now missing its *eschatocol*. Possibly unknown to Anton, the earliest copy is not in Latin, but in an Old English translation, added to a gospel book in a mid-eleventh century hand; on stylistic grounds, the translation may have taken place in the late tenth or early eleventh century.[17] This Old English copy is followed by a short confirmation charter in the names of Aldhelm (d. 710), King Ine of the West Saxons (688–726), and King Æthelred of the Mercians (674/5–706), also rendered in the vernacular but fragmented by fire damage.[18] The prospect that this translated a now-lost Latin charter (authentic or not) is now much improved following a recent editorial observation that William of Malmesbury left a long blank beneath his copy of **20** in his autograph *Gesta pontificum* (c. 1125).[19] In fact, a comparable seven-line gap also exists under this document (and no other) in Bodleian, Wood empt. 5, a later Malmesbury cartulary. The probability that **20** had always included the otherwise obscure monastery at Frome as its joint beneficiary is enhanced by William's remark that this house had long since 'relapsed into nothing, leaving only an insubstantial name behind'.[20] It would be odd to interpolate a non-existent institution as a co-beneficiary.

Anton further demonstrated the underlying authenticity of Bermondsey and Woking's **26** (also now undated) based on its correspondences to LD 32.[21] To this we may add that the unambitious, unusually conservative nature of this privilege—a modest document which makes no great claims for the two houses, and even outlines the limits of its abbots' prerogatives vis-à-vis the bishops—does not scream 'forgery', although it is surely corrupt in places. The absence of any other evidence for an early house at Bermondsey (let alone one tied to Woking) is potentially encouraging.[22] So is the survival of the text via the apparently uninterested archive

---

[16] Lapidge, 'Career', pp. 15–22.

[17] Rauer, 'Pope Sergius I's Privilege', which notes its 'parallels with [the] homiletic style' associated with Ælfric of Eynsham (c. 950–c. 1010).

[18] Ibid., p. 274.   [19] GP, II, p. 275.   [20] GP, I, v. 198, pp. 522–3.

[21] Anton, *Studien*, pp. 69–75, 91; Stenton, *Preparatory*, pp. 186–7, first recognised its value. Its dating-range can be slightly narrowed, since Constantine visited Constantinople Oct. 710–Oct. 711, taking his *scriniarius* Sergius with him: *LP*, i. 90, pp. 389–91.

[22] In the 1080s a Cluniac monastery was founded there: *Peterborough*, pp. 72–3. **26** makes none of the grand claims which one would expect of a forgery by the later Cluniac house (from whose archive it does not anyway survive).

of Peterborough. How and why it had entered that house's archive by the time of its twelfth-century copying is unknown.[23]

(c) Deperdita

Stephen of Ripon (*c.* 713), Bede (716/17, 731), and an anonymous author at Wearmouth-Jarrow (*c.* 717) report between them three lost privileges for their monasteries (*12, *13, *23). While tendentious, the basic reliability of these accounts is not in doubt. They indicate that Agatho's privileges for Wilfrid's Ripon and Hexham (*12) and Benedict Biscop's Wearmouth (*13) were acquired in early-to-mid 679 and 679/80 respectively, and it is argued in Chapter 4 that they were granted around the same time, plausibly alongside 14.[24] Scholars have sometimes dated the privilege of Sergius (687–701) for Abbot Ceolfrith's Jarrow (*23) to 701, since a delegation from that monastery is known to have visited Rome that year.[25] Ceolfrith could, however, have sent an earlier embassy to Sergius at any point following his accession in May 689 to the double abbacy of Wearmouth and Jarrow. These narratives are vague about the contents of these privileges, although I see no reason to doubt the scholarly consensus that they resembled our other surviving contemporary privileges for monasteries in England (14, 16, 20, 26) or mainland Europe (i.e. they were based on, or essentially replicated, *LD* 32 and/or 77).[26] We at least know that *23 closely resembled *13.[27] Although it has been argued that *13/*23 differed in content from *12 on the basis of their distinct representations in the above accounts,[28] this strikes me as simply the result of these narratives having different authors, with different agendas.[29]

---

[23] Bermondsey and Woking were once thought 'colonies' of *Medeshamstede*/Peterborough, but this is now contested: Keynes, *Councils*, pp. 37–48; Foot, *Monastic Life*, pp. 151–82; *Peterborough*, pp. 67–78.

[24] Below, pp. 143–4.   [25] *HA*, p. 59, n. 147.

[26] e.g. Wormald, 'Bede and Benedict Biscop', pp. 7–10, 28; Anton, *Studien*, pp. 62–5.

[27] *HA*, 15, p. 58.

[28] John, '"Secularium Prioratus"', pp. 221–3; Anton, *Studien*, pp. 90–2.

[29] On 4 occasions *VSW* (43, 47, 51, 52, pp. 88–9, 94–5, 104–5, 108–9) alludes to obscure rulings by Sergius and Benedict (II) (684–5) (J not listed). This has sometimes been read as evidence that *12 received further confirmations/reissues (Wormald, 'Bede and Benedict Biscop', p. 7; Cubitt, 'St Wilfrid', pp. 345–6), but *VSW* does not elaborate. These decrees probably concerned the reversal of Wilfrid's deposition at the Lateran Synod of 679, a separate matter.

To these *deperdita* we can tentatively add Barking's *17. At the end of his late seventh-century charter for the rights and properties of his foundation at Barking, Bishop Earconwald of the East Saxons (founder also of Chertsey, and addressee of 16) claims that 'permission (*licentia*) for this privilege was given and granted to me through the mouth (*per os*) of the most blessed Agatho, when I went to Rome ten years ago, in the year 677.'[30] This charter is not without problems. Surviving only in early modern copies, it has a potential context for forgery in the jurisdictional conflicts Barking faced with the post-Conquest bishops of London, something against which this charter broadly—although it must be said, not very explicitly—safeguards.[31] Its adoption of AD dating is exceptional, and anyway in its current form incorrect, since by 677 Agatho had not yet become pope. Nevertheless, there are reasons for confidence in its claims, and modern scholarly work has at times been positive (if never unanimously so) about the essential authenticity of this charter, which in its extant form includes various aspects which apparently derive from genuine seventh-century information, and is, on the whole, encouragingly unpretentious and contemporary in its language.[32] Only its dating elements have caused serious headaches, and even these are surmountable if we accept that such details may be interpolated, mistranscribed, or might even reflect contemporary error—unfamiliarity with the AD system could well explain its inaccurate usage. If the essentials of 16,

[30] *ECEE*, pp. 122–3 (S 1246), correcting the late copy of Cotton Vespasian B. xv ('18 annos') to agree with the indiction (the figure is illegible in Cotton Vespasian A. ix); but now cf. *Barking*, 2.

[31] Beaumont, 'Monastic Autonomy', which further suggests that S 1246 is a post-Conquest forgery, as its provisions against episcopal *dicio* suit the Barking–London tensions of this period. However, it is remarkable how brief this mention of *dicio* is: again, we might expect something more explicit and indeed ambitious from a high-medieval forgery drawn up with an agenda in mind.

[32] See comments listed by Sawyer (S 1246), with *ECEE*, pp. 125–7. To this must now be added the important discussion in *Barking*, pp. 23–5, 90–1, 142–9, which exercises more caution about the document, while still conceding that 'it is not beyond question that the charter is essentially authentic', and that there remains a plausible context for Earconwald's acquisition of dual privileges for Barking and Chertsey. Note, however, that the editor's caution is partly grounded in more pronounced doubts about the authenticity of 16 (revising the same scholar's previous position in *Chertsey*, and citing J³ †3488 to affirm that 'verbal links with a privilege of John XIX...in a continental archive suggest that it may have been produced in the mid-eleventh century or earlier.' Yet J³ only states that 16 is cited by Chertsey's own †48), together with the belief that 'it does seem remarkable that seventh-century religious women (however aristocratic) should have been accorded such a high level of autonomy and independence from episcopal supervision.' This does not seem so remarkable to me; indeed, two of the classic Gallic models of monasteries resisting local episcopal control (Arles, Poitiers) were foundations for women: see below, Chapter 4, p 119.

for Barking's sister house,[33] are after all authentic, then we already have a context for Earconwald (as noted, probably a figure of some stature, with kin in the highest mainland European aristocracy) reaching out to Agatho. My suggestion here is that the papal *licentia* which the charter cites was a written papal privilege for Barking, of the same kind we see elsewhere at this time: either very similar to Chertsey's **16**, or perhaps part of that same document in its original form (just as *12 and **20** covered two houses together). The remark that the grant came *per os* only indicates that Agatho also made the pronouncement orally, and/or that Earconwald petitioned him face-to-face. Perhaps the strongest evidence for the existence of *17, however, comes from the text itself of this seventh-century Barking charter. The structure and language of its initial *dispositio*—forbidding the exercise of episcopal 'jurisdiction', delineating the limits of the bishops' authority over the ordination of priests and consecration of nuns, before going on to outline the procedures of abbatial election after the abbess' death—is diplomatically strange within the Anglo-Saxon corpus, but just the sort of thing we see in papal privileges of the seventh and early eighth century from across the Latin west.[34] Its *intitulatio* even describes its issuer according to the quasi-papal formula *Ercanualdus episcopus...seruorum Dei seruus*. It is quite plausible that Earconwald's charter for Barking not only refers to a genuine, lost papal privilege which Agatho granted some ten years before, but that it took, directly or indirectly, that same text as a diplomatic template.[35]

(d) Forgeries and False Claims

Chief among the documents falsely attributed to this era are the famous Canterbury forgeries for the monks of Christ Church (†2), the primacy of its archbishop over York (†6, †8, †10, †22, †27), and the monastery of Sts Peter and Paul (†3, †11). Scholars have long recognised these as either spurious or substantially falsified in their extant form. Although there exist disagreements about dating, following Levison and Southern it is generally held that they belong to the early twelfth century, not long before their first known

---

[33] *HE*, iv. 5, pp. 354–7.

[34] *Regesto di Farfa*, ed. Giorgio and Balzani, ii. 2 (JE 2144); *MGH Epp.* II, pp. 468–9 (JE 1926). Comparable formulations appear in *Diplomata*, ed. Pardessus, ii. 302 (JE †2048), and *Bobbio*, i. 13 (JE 2053).

[35] I would extend this same logic to the relationship between Earconwald's charter for Chertsey (S 1274) and **16**: see above, n. 13.

manuscript appearances.[36] We will return to those contexts for forgery in Chapter 8, but for now we may put these *spuria* to one side.

Manuscripts of the early twelfth century onwards preserve other forged privileges which claim to date from this period. Peterborough's bombastic †15 is a long-recognised forgery, just one part of a wider 'dodgy dossier' of false claims for this house; the same goes for the alleged *†9, supposedly paraphrased in the twelfth-century Peterborough additions to the *Anglo-Saxon Chronicle*.[37] The unusual †18 for St Paul's, London has met with similar disregard.[38] It appears to adapt a version of 16 and/or the lost *17. Plausibly, when those privileges were brought forward by the mid-twelfth century *against* the claims of the bishop of London, they might have then come to the attention of his clergy at St Paul's, and formed the basis of this forgery. Two forgeries for Evesham (†24, †25) are noteworthy on two counts, since they survive as pseudo-originals of *c.* 1200, and are known through copies at the archiepiscopal archive of Canterbury as well as their beneficiary house. Presumably the Evesham privileges were of interest to Canterbury because of their description of Berhtwald as 'primate of Britain'.[39] The terminology used in the extant texts of the Evesham forgeries dates them to the early twelfth century,[40] but Byrhtferth's *Life of Ecgwine* (*c.* 1000, perhaps after 1016) reveals the existence of an earlier legend that Evesham had obtained papal privileges upon its foundation.[41] †24 and †25 thus look like later attempts to turn that myth into a 'reality'. None of the above forgeries is terribly convincing, but they all seem respectable when compared to the late medieval †4 and †21, which purport to confirm the prerogatives of the University of Cambridge some six centuries before

---

[36] Boehmer, *Fälschungen*; Levison, *England*, pp. 178–220; Southern, 'Canterbury'; Kelly, 'Some Forgeries'. The latter argues for at least †3 belonging to the eleventh century: see later discussion, p. 270, n. 11. Anton, *Studien*, p. 65, n. 62, hesitated to dismiss †11 as an outright forgery.

[37] *Peterborough*, pp. 159–74.

[38] Anton, *Studien*, p. 65, n. 62; it is cited in a forged diploma for the house, in the same early twelfth-century register in which the privilege first appears: *St Paul's*, 29 (S 1056).

[39] Sayers, '"Original"', pp. 371–80. The pseudo-original of †24 is now inserted into Cleopatra E. i; that of †25 was purchased from a private owner by Evesham council in 1964 (source: Ashleigh Jayes), but was apparently in the Arundel collection in 1812/30, when it was used for the revised *Monasticon*, ed. Dugdale, ii, pp. 14–15. Both single-sheets are by the same scribe, and datable to *c.* 1200. They are in an archaising script, which imitates some letter forms found in ninth- and eleventh-century Anglo-Saxon hands (Julia Crick, pers. comm.). For further detail see Savill, 'Donation'.

[40] Sayers, '"Original"', p. 376.

[41] Byrhtferth, *Vita s. Ecgwini*, iii. 3–8, pp. 256–7; see also above, p. 49.

its foundation.[42] Besides these texts, we know of two dubious claims to *deperdita*. A forged diploma in the name of King Ine, also a product of the early twelfth century, makes a passing reference to a privilege of Gregory II for Glastonbury (*†27).[43] We have no reason to take it seriously. The same goes for the much later claim of Thomas Rudbourne (d. after 1450), that Winchester had received permission from Pope Agatho to translate the body of Saint Birinus (*†19)—an unsupported and anachronistic assertion, with no contemporary parallels anywhere.

B. Late Eighth and Ninth Centuries

29. (772/95)
(HADRIAN I) confirms to (OFFA) AND CYNETHRYTH, (KING) AND QUEEN (OF THE MERCIANS) their rights and those of their 'genealogy' over their monasteries dedicated to St Peter

Incipit: Cum piae desiderium
Archive: n/a (fragment preserved only via *LD*).
MS: Vatican City, Archivio Segreto Vaticano, Misc. arm. xi, 19, ff. 96v–97v (s. viii^ex–ix^in).
Edited: *LD* V 93.
Registered: J³ 4612.

*30. (787/95)
HADRIAN I grants HYGEBERHT, ARCHBISHOP OF LICHFIELD privileges 'concerning his pallium and episcopal see'

Incipit: n/a (*deperditum*).
Archive: n/a (cited in a conciliar charter of *Clofesho*, 803, via Canterbury, Christ Church (S 1431a)).
MS: BL, Cotton Augustus ii. 61 (s. ix¹).
Edited: BCS 310; *Christ Church*, 32.
Registered: JE 2456; J³ *4519.

---

[42] The extant texts relate to fifteenth-century disputes, although their original composition could date back to the late thirteenth century: Hiatt, *Making*, pp. 70–101. Pseudo-Honorius' †4 claims that the University had already enjoyed a long tradition of papal privileges prior to the arrival of the Anglo-Saxons, and even insinuates that Honorius had studied there! †21 is cited in Nicholas Cantilupe's *Historiola fundationis uniuersitatis* (Sharpe, *Handlist*, p. 385).

[43] *Glastonbury*, pp. 266–72.

31. 798(?), March 8
LEO III *confirms to <CYNEHELM, 'KING'> his and his successors' rights over the monastery of ST MARY'S, GLASTONBURY, on the request of COENWULF, KING OF THE MERCIANS*

Incipit: Bone uoluntatis et
Archive: Glastonbury.
MS: Cambridge, Trinity College, R. 5. 33, ff. 10v–11 (s. xiii) [William of Malmesbury's *De antiquitate*].
Edited: BCS 284; *De antiq.*, 49–51, pp. 108–11; *Glastonbury*, 15a.
Registered: JE 2497; J³ 4646.

32. (796/816) [possibly 798, c. March 8]
LEO III *confirms to COENWULF, KING OF THE MERCIANS, his and his heirs' rights over their monasteries, <especially ST PETER'S, WINCHCOMBE>*

Incipit: Cum summe apostolice
Archive: Winchcombe.
MSS: BL, Cotton Tiberius E. iv, f. 13v (s. xii¹); Gloucester, Gloucestershire Archives, D678/1 M4/1, ff. 36–7 (Davis 1037) (s. xiii).
Edited: BCS 337; *Landboc*, ed. Royce, i, pp. 21–2; *PUU England*, iii. 1; *Chron. Winch.*, ii, *s.a.* 811.
Registered: Conte, *Regesto*, 31; J³ 4905.

*33. (796/816) [possibly 798, c. March 8]
LEO III *confirms to HRÆTHHUN, 'BISHOP AND ABBOT' OF ST MARY'S, ABINGDON privileges for his monastery*

Incipit: n/a (*deperditum*).
Archive: n/a (cited in a diploma of Æthelred II for Abingdon, 993 (S 876), and the *Historia* of Abingdon).
MSS: BL, Cotton Augustus ii. 38 (s. xᵉˣ) [*S 876 single-sheet diploma*]; BL, Cotton Claudius C. ix, f. 106v (1160s); BL, Cotton Claudius B. vi, f. 9 (s. xiiiᵐᵉᵈ).
Edited: *Abingdon*, 124; *Historia ecclesie Abbendonensis*, i. 9, B17, pp. 15–19, 254–7.
Registered: JE *2508; J³ *4741.

†*34. (796/816)
LEO III *confirms to (COENWULF, KING OF THE MERCIANS?) privileges for the priory at CULHAM, which is to revert to ST MARY'S, ABINGDON*

Incipit: n/a (*deperditum*).
Archive: n/a (cited in the *Historia* of Abingdon).
MSS: BL, Cotton Claudius B. vi, ff. 8–10 (s. xiii^med).
Edited: *Historia ecclesie Abbendonensis*, i. 9, B16, pp. 205–6.
Registered: JE *2505–6; J³ *4738–9.

35. 802, January 18(?)
LEO III confirms to ÆTHELHEARD, ARCHBISHOP OF CANTERBURY his metropolitan status

Incipit: Pontificali discretioni precipue
Archive: Canterbury, Christ Church.
MSS: See MSS tradition for Eadmer (*HN*, pp. ix–xv; earliest MS s. xii¹) and William of Malmesbury (*GP*, I, pp. xi–xxv: earliest MS *c.* 1125); BL, Cotton Cleopatra E. i, f. 44v (Davis 162) (s. xii^in); BL, Cotton Claudius E. v, f. 238 (s. xii^in); BL, Cotton Faustina B. vi, f. 97v (Davis 178) (s. xii^in); Canterbury, D&C, Register A, f. 3 (Davis 169) (s. xv^in).
Edited: *HN*, 5, pp. 270–1; BCS 305; Boehmer, *Fälschungen*, pp. 155–6; *GP*, I, i. 37, pp. 76–9.
Registered: JE 2510; J³ †4744.

36. (817, December 14/818, January 1)
PASCHAL I confirms to COENWULF, KING OF THE MERCIANS his and his heirs' rights over their monasteries

Incipit: Cum pie desiderium
Archive: Winchcombe.
MSS: BL, Cotton Tiberius E. iv, f. 15 (s. xii¹); Gloucester, Gloucestershire Archives, D678/1 M4/1, ff. 37–8 (Davis 1037) (s. xiii).
Edited: BCS 363; *Landboc*, ed. Royce, i, pp. 22–3; *PUU England*, iii. 2; *Chron. Winch.*, ii, *s.a.* 818.
Registered: J³ 5030.

†37. 857, May 11
BENEDICT III confirms to LOUIS, ABBOT OF SAINT-DENIS his monasteries' properties 'among the Anglo-Saxons . . . in the land of Britain'

Incipit: Questi estis filii
Archive: Saint-Denis.

MSS: AN, LL 1156, f. 80v (s. xiii); AN, LL 1158, p. 549, n. 1 (s. xiii^{ex}); AN, L 844, n. 3 (1460).
Edited: *PUU Saint-Denis*, 10.
Registered: JE 2666; Herbers, *Regesta*, 410; J³ 5647.

†38. (891/6)
FORMOSUS confirms to THE BISHOPS OF 'ENGLAND' the special privileges of the church of CANTERBURY

Incipit: Auditis nefandorum ritibus
Archive: Canterbury, Christ Church.
MSS: See MSS tradition for Eadmer (*HN*, pp. ix–xv; earliest MS s. xii¹) and William of Malmesbury (*GP*, I, pp. xi–xxv: earliest MS *c.* 1125); BL, Cotton Cleopatra E. i, f. 46 (Davis 162) (s. xii^{in}); BL, Cotton Claudius E. v, f. 241 (s. xii^{in}); BL, Cotton Faustina B. vi, f. 98v (Davis 178) (s. xii^{in}); Canterbury, D&C, Register A, f. 3 (Davis 169) (s. xv^{in}).
Edited: *HN*, 5, pp. 273–4; BCS 573; Boehmer, *Fälschungen*, pp. 157–9; *CS* I, i. 8; *GP*, I, i. 38, pp. 78–83.
Registered: JE 3506; J³ 7318.

(a) Authentic Privileges, 772–818

As long ago as 1687, Jean Mabillon recognised that the accidental retention of the proper name *Cynedrida* in a formula of the oldest of the three surviving copies of the *Liber diurnus* (*LD* V 93 = 29) left a clue that its lost exemplar had been addressed to an English beneficiary.[44] Two centuries later Theodor Sickel, in dating this section of *LD* to the pontificate of Hadrian I (772–95), could thereby also identify this *Cynedrida regina* as Cynethryth, queen of the Mercians (*c.* 770–96; d. in or after 798)—thus in turn revealing the remaining unnamed king of the text as her husband Offa (757–96).[45] Sickel's findings have since become relatively well-known through Wilhelm Levison's *England and the Continent*.[46] **29** is almost certainly a completely reliable text, if fragmentary: *LD* preserves only its *arenga* and *narratio*. It does not survive in England.

Levison further identified three more problematic texts from twelfth- and thirteenth-century English manuscripts as deriving from authentic papal

---

[44] Mabillon and Germain, *Museum*, I. ii, p. 37.   [45] Sickel, 'Prolegomena II', pp. 27–9.
[46] Levison, *England*, pp. 29–30.

documents of this period. Glastonbury's 31 is the most challenging of the group. Addressed by Leo III (795–816) to a mysterious 'King Cynehelm', this diplomatically unacceptable privilege is followed in William of Malmesbury's *On the Antiquity of the Church of Glastonbury* (c. 1130) by an Anglo-Saxon confirmation charter of '797' (for 798?).[47] Despite its obstacles, it has a number of unusual features that support its authenticity. Its problems of style can be explained in part by William's claim that he had rendered the text back into Latin from a now-lost Old English translation: indeed, the opening of the extant version has clear correspondences with *LD* 93, indicating that this text really does stand two removes of translation away from an authentic privilege of the time.[48] While the *eschatocol*, as so often in later copies, raises considerable difficulties in its current form and gives several possible dates (of which 8 March 798 seems the most acceptable),[49] its named authenticating officials, Eustachius and Paschal, do in fact appear in a number of authentic contemporary documents: Hadrian had even identified the latter as his nephew, and he is probably the same Paschal who would go on to lead the botched coup against Leo in April 799.[50] Its confirmatory charter (whose one-year-earlier dating probably reflects a scribal error somewhere along the line of transmission) includes an unusual but—in light what we know of 29—quite striking subscription by an 'Abbess Cynethryth' and her two kinswomen. Levison convincingly identified these as Offa's widow and two of their daughters.[51] The convergence of these oddities is encouraging. So is the fact that the privilege and its confirmation do no great favours for twelfth-century Glastonbury, asserting that the house should remain in familial possession, not something one would expect of a later monastic forger. 31 is without doubt a corrupted and twice-mistranslated text that needs treating with the upmost caution, but we can have reasonable confidence in its origins as an authentic privilege. We will return to its contents and further problems of interpretation in Chapter 5.

32 and 36, two privileges in the names of Leo and Paschal I (817–24), raise fewer obstacles. These appear in the twelfth-century *Winchcombe Chronicle* under the annals for 811 and 818, as well in Winchcombe's thirteenth-century cartulary (*Landboc*).[52] In the *Chronicle*, 32 immediately

---

[47] *Glastonbury*, 15b (S 152).   [48] Levison, *England*, p. 32.
[49] *Glastonbury*, pp. 299–301.   [50] Santifaller, *Saggio*, pp. 40–1; *LP*, ii. 98, pp. 4, 8.
[51] Levison, *England*, p. 251.
[52] Hayward argues that *Landboc* shared an exemplar with the *Chronicle*: *Chron. Winch.*, ii, pp. 253–8. Winchcombe archive: Levison, *England*, pp. 249–59.

precedes a forged foundation charter of Coenwulf, king of the Mercians (796–821) under the same annal.[53] In its extant form **32** is certainly defective and lacks a dating clause, but it follows elements of *LD* 86, 89, 90, 96, and 97, and looks essentially genuine. Holtzmann's edition provides a useful amended version, but there are problems even with his text: above all, its reading of Winchcombe as the privilege's chief beneficiary is an editorial intervention, unsupported by the manuscript witnesses.[54] This is not to rule out the possibility that Winchcombe was indeed the principal beneficiary, only that we cannot be sure that this was made explicit in the document drawn up in Rome. **32**'s position under the year 811 in the *Chronicle* has no grounds in the text of the privilege itself; Chapter 5 argues that it may have instead been acquired at the same time as **31**. Pope Paschal's **36** is fragmentary, with a more or less intact *protocol, arenga,* and *narratio* (based on *LD* 93), which then jumps immediately ahead to a mangled *datatio.* Holtzmann's edition incorporates Levison's expert reconstruction of the latter, which demonstrates that it was simply a best-attempt medieval transcription of what must have become a badly frayed and essentially illegible *eschatocol* at the end of the original papyrus.[55] Reconstructed, the clause dates to somewhere between 14 December 817 and 1 January 818. We will see in Chapter 5 that **36**'s deficit of a large section between its *narratio* and *datatio* probably results from an intentional obliteration of text, taking place about a decade after its original acquisition.

35, a privilege of Leo for Archbishop Æthelheard of Canterbury, restoring the metropolitan status of his see, is transmitted alongside the twelfth-century Canterbury primacy forgeries. Bar the surviving version's anachronistic claim that Canterbury should hold precedence over 'all the churches of the English', and its problematic-in-its-surviving-form *eschatocol* that renders its precise date doubtful,[56] its core text nevertheless appears essentially authentic,[57] and is supported by a number of contemporary sources.[58] Here it is worth adding that, in addition to the above texts, we now also have archaeological evidence for documents of

---

[53] BCS 338 (S 167).

[54] Holtzmann gives *Wincecumba* for *quamuis multa*: see Hayward's commentary, *Chron. Winch.,* ii, pp. 253–8.

[55] Levison, *England*, p. 256.   [56] Fichtenau, '"Politische" Datierung', pp. 497–8.

[57] Southern, 'Canterbury', p. 216.   [58] Noble, 'Rise'.

Figure 3.1 *Bulla* of Paschal I (817/24) (detached, now clipped at sides), discovered in Herefordshire, 2004: *PAS* HESH-ADE183 (Birmingham Museums Trust, CC BY-SA 4.0 licence).

these popes, in the form of loose *bullae* discovered by metal-detectorists in Kent (Leo III, 2014) and Herefordshire (Paschal I, 2004), that is, in regions approximate to two of the above beneficiaries (Figure 3.1).[59]

(b) Deperdita

A contemporary manuscript witness to a church council at *Clofesho*, 803, which essentially confirms **35**, also condemns *30, a privilege of Hadrian for the short-lived archbishopric of Lichfield (elevated 787).[60] Given the nature of this source—this act of condemnation explains why no other records survive—we must consider this an authentic *deperditum*. Much later, a charter of King Æthelred II for Abingdon (993) vaguely cites a privilege of Coenwulf and Leo (*33) for the 'freedom' of the house on behalf of Abbot Hræthhun. This claim would be taken up by the later *History* of the house (probably composed in the 1160s), which imagined Hræthhun, 'bishop and abbot', petitioning Leo for 'letters of his own authority, in which he urged the *princeps* of England to pay heed to the freedom of the church'.[61] These texts respectively frame this purported privilege within tenth- and twelfth-century debates about church 'freedom',[62] leaving the identity of Hræthhun something of a mystery.[63] However, I follow Susan Kelly and John Hudson in seeing *33 as probably an authentic echo of some kind of document acquired by Coenwulf or an associate from Leo around the time of **31** and **32**. It may have even been identical to the latter, which after all applied to multiple beneficiaries.[64]

(c) Forgeries and False Claims

A later recension of the Abingdon *History* adds a more elaborate spin to the story behind *33, wherein Coenwulf seeks, on behalf of his 'uterine sisters',

---

[59] *PAS*, KENT-01AD9F, HESH-ADE183: precise details of find locations are restricted. While it is tempting to link these *bullae* to our privileges, they could have been attached to papal letters of any kind. Such finds are rare. Of the 494 *bullae* in England and Wales listed on *PAS*, only these two predate the twelfth century. In addition, a *bulla* of Zacharias (741–52) is preserved as BL, Detached seal xxxviii. 5, while Norwich Castle Museum holds two finds attributed to Theodore I (642–9) and a 'John' (Naismith, 'Peter's Pence', p. 231). The latter is catalogued as John XI (931–5), but John XII (955–64) is also possible: Serafini, *Le monete*, i, p. lxxxvii.

[60] Cubitt, *Councils*, pp. 279–80.

[61] The later, thirteenth-century recension conceives of these more specifically as 'letters of his protection and privileges of apostolic authority': *Historia ecclesie Abbendonensis*, i. B17, pp. 254–7.

[62] Crick, '"Pristina"'; Roach, *Forgery*, pp. 113–52.

[63] Abingdon's early history: *Abingdon*, pp. cxciii–ccx; Hræthhun: Keynes, *Councils*, pp. 47–8.

[64] *Abingdon*, p. cciv; *Historia ecclesie Abbendonensis*, i, p. cxxv.

a privilege from Leo for the priory at Culham, due to revert to Abingdon after their deaths (†*34).[65] Abingdon sought papal confirmation of its rights over this priory in the mid-thirteenth century, and it is probably to around that time that we should date this bogus claim, which received no mention in the references to Leo of the 990s or 1160s.[66] It is nevertheless intriguing that this story should bring Coenwulf's female kin into the equation at all, since we shall see in Chapter 5 that they had in fact played an important role in his monastic politics and interactions with the papacy. Perhaps †*34 at least transmits a distant, distorted memory of the role of women in the Coenwulfing regime.

Across the sea, Saint-Denis preserved in thirteenth- and fifteenth-century copies †37, a privilege of Benedict III confirming the house's properties 'among the Anglo-Saxons' (*apud Anglos Saxones*). Its internal diplomatic deviates from contemporary papal chancery norms. Recent continental scholarship has, however, adopted an increasingly positive view,[67] pointing out a context (King Æthelwulf of the West Saxons visited Benedict III in 855–6, and on his return journey married Charles the Bald's daughter Judith in a ceremony conducted by Hincmar of Rheims, an alumnus of the school of Saint-Denis),[68] and some favourable internal features (there are, as usual, problems with the *eschatocol*'s dates, but this section is otherwise encouraging, with its named functionaries Theodore and Megistus found in authentic papal documents).[69] As for diplomatic irregularities, it's not impossible that a house of Saint-Denis' stature might have had a role in drafting its own papal documents in this period.[70] Overall, however, the argument is not compelling, and it is noteworthy that the privilege's advocates are continental specialists who have shown less interest in English contexts, or later motives for forgery. The charter of Æthelwulf which the privilege cites is, despite some minor positive features,[71] difficult to accept as genuine—just one of a series of highly dubious early 'English' diplomas claimed by Saint-Denis.[72] The transformations in cross-Channel politics and property holding from the eleventh century onwards would have given the

---

[65] Also cited in the spurious *Abingdon*, 9 (S 183). The sisters include one 'Keneswyth', possibly a confusion for Coenwulf's daughter Cwoenthryth.

[66] Oxford, Bodleian Library, Lyell 15, f. 19 (undated privilege of Gregory IX, 1227/41); *Abingdon*, p. 18; *Historia ecclesie Abbendonensis*, i., pp. lxviii.

[67] Atsma and Vezin, 'Le dossier'; *PUU Saint-Denis*, p. 91; Herbers, *Regesta*, 410.

[68] *LP*, ii. 106, p. 148; Atsma and Vezin, 'Le dossier', p. 231.

[69] Santifaller, *Saggio*, pp. 48–51; Atsma and Vezin, 'Le dossier', pp. 231–2.

[70] Cf. above, Chapter 2, pp. 30–32.   [71] Atsma and Vezin, 'Le dossier', pp. 231–2, 235.

[72] BCS 252, 259, 494, 1057 (S 133, 318, 686, 1186).

house a great incentive to assert the claims found here.[73] The Saint-Denis archive is anyway infamous for its forgeries, which sometimes reveal ingenious methods of deception, such as the gluing together of two sides of ancient papyri face-to-face, with a forgery then drawn-up on the dorse.[74] That *only* the *eschatocol* of †37 has genuine features may indicate comparable skulduggery. Saint-Denis was a centre of royal memory: it is plausible that later monks knew of Æthelwulf's 855–6 visit, and managed to find the exemplar of an authentic, contemporary papal dating clause to append to a forged text in order to lend it more clout. There remain too many problems with this privilege to allow us to take it especially seriously. Possibly, some kind of authentic papal communication once linked Æthelwulf, Benedict, and Saint-Denis.[75] But this is probably not it.

Lastly, Formosus' †38 is another text transmitted with the Canterbury forgeries. This presents an interesting case, since its underlying 'base' may well be an authentic *letter* of Formosus (891–6), admonishing the bishops of England for their alleged concessions to paganism amid the Viking invasions. Yet in its received and interpolated form, as a *privilege* confirming the prerogatives of Canterbury, it appears to be a falsification belonging to the early twelfth century, alongside the rest of the 'primacy' dossier.[76]

C. The Tenth Century

†39. (956?), April 22
JOHN (XII?) enjoins EADRED, KING, with 'all the bishops, duces, comites, *abbots and all the faithful of the English', to take into his care the monastery of STS PETER AND PAUL, CANTERBURY*

Incipit: Studio diuini cultus
Archive: Canterbury, St Augustine's.
MSS: BL, Cotton Vespasian B. xx, ff. 282–3 (Davis 199.1) (s. xii[in]); BL, Cotton Vitellius A. ii, ff. 10v–11 (Davis 191) (s. xii[ex]); BL, Cotton Julius D. ii,

---

[73] French monastic holdings in England post-1066: Burton, 'Monastic World', p. 121.

[74] Geary, *Phantoms*, pp. 107–13.

[75] Prof. Tinti (pers. comm.) draws to my attention the unusual reference to *Anglos Saxones* in this text, an identifier that may have originated on the continent: Tinti, *Europe*, pp. 3–4. This might further suggest some authentic underlying record, although again it would not be surprising if a house of Saint-Denis' stature had some other memorandum of the 855–6 visit.

[76] *CS* I, i. 8; Boehmer, *Fälschungen*, pp. 98–100, was less optimistic.

ff. 41v–42 (Davis 192) (s. xiii^med); BL, Cotton Claudius D. x, ff. 10v–11 (Davis 193) (s. xiii²); PRO, E 164/27, f. 46 (Davis 195) (s. xiv).
Edited: BCS 915; *PUU* †142.
Registered: JL †3678; Böhmer-Zimmermann †269; J³ †7752.

†40. (956?)
JOHN (XII?) confirms to EADRED, KING OF THE ENGLISH and ODA, ARCHBISHOP OF CANTERBURY the privileges of SS PETER AND PAUL, CANTERBURY

Incipit: Inter pręclaras sacrę
Archive: Canterbury, St Augustine's.
MSS: BL, Cotton Vespasian B. xx, ff. 283–4 (Davis 199.1) (s. xii^in); BL, Cotton Julius D. ii, f. 42 (Davis 192) (s. xiii^med); BL, Cotton Claudius D. x, f. 11 (Davis 193) (s. xiii²); PRO, E 164/27, ff. 46v–47 (Davis 195) (s. xiv).
Edited: BCS 916; *PUU* †143.
Registered: JL †3679; Böhmer-Zimmermann †270; J³ †7753.

41. 960, September 21
JOHN XII grants DUNSTAN, ARCHBISHOP OF CANTERBURY the pallium

Incipit: Si pastores ouium
Archive: Canterbury, Christ Church.
MSS: BnF, Lat. 943, ff. 7–8v (s. x^ex); see MSS tradition for Eadmer (*HN*, pp. ix–xv; earliest MS s. xii¹) and William of Malmesbury (*GP*, I, pp. xi–xxv: earliest MS *c.* 1125); BL, Cotton Cleopatra E. i, f. 46v (Davis 162) (s. xii^in); BL, Cotton Claudius E. v, f. 242 (s. xii^in); Canterbury, D&C, Register A, f. 11 (Davis 169) (s. xv^in).
Edited: *HN*, 5, pp. 274–6; BCS 1069; Boehmer, *Fälschungen*, pp. 159–61 (no. 10); *CS* I, i. 25 [*non-interpolated version*]; *PUU* 149 [*non-interpolated version*]; *GP*, I, i. 39, pp. 82–5.
Registered: JL 3687; Böhmer-Zimmermann 284; J³ 7767.

†42. (967?), January 24
JOHN (XIII?) confirms to EDGAR, KING OF THE ENGLISH the privileges of the monastery of ST PETER'S (WESTMINSTER)

Incipit: Quia literis tuę
Archive: Westminster.

MS: Oxford, Bodleian Library, Eng. hist. a. 2, no. iv (s. xiii^{med}) [*forged single-sheet diploma of Edgar of '969'* (S 774)].
Edited: BCS 1264; *Crawford Collection*, ed. Napier and Stevenson, 6; *PUU* †174.
Registered: JL 3712; Böhmer-Zimmermann †409; S 774; J³ †7908.

†43. (965/72)

JOHN (XIII?) gives notice that on the request of EDGAR, KING OF THE ENGLISH and DUNSTAN, ARCHBISHOP OF CANTERBURY he has granted privileges to the monastery of ST MARY'S, GLASTONBURY

Incipit: Noverit cunctorum notitia
Archive: Glastonbury.
MSS: BL, Royal 13 B. xix, f. 23v (s. xii^{ex}) [*William of Malmesbury's Gesta regum*]; Cambridge, Trinity College, R. 5. 33, f. 13 (s. xiii) [*William of Malmesbury's De antiquitate*]; Longleat, Marquess of Bath, 39, ff. 39, 61 (Davis 434) (s. xiv^{med}); Oxford, Bodleian Library, Wood empt. I, f. 68v (Davis 435) (s. xiv^{med}); Cambridge, Trinity College, R. 5. 16, pp. 75–6 (s. xiv^{ex}) [*John of Glastonbury*].
Edited: BCS 1070; *PUU* †211; *GR*, I, ii. 150B, pp. 826–8; *De antiq.*, 61, pp. 126–9; *Glastonbury*, Appendix 4b.
Registered: JL 3751; Böhmer-Zimmermann †482; J³ †7985.

?†44. (965/72?)

JOHN (XIII?) authorises EDGAR, KING OF THE ENGLISH, with 'all the bishops, duces, comites and abbots and all the faithful of the English', to expel the canons from the OLD MINSTER, WINCHESTER and confirms its privileges

Incipit: Quoniam semper sunt
Archive: Winchester, Old Minster.
MSS: Winchester, D&C, A/3/1, f. 5v (Davis 1044) (s. xiii^{ex}); Winchester, Hampshire Record Office, 21 M65/A1/1, ff. 166v–167 (c. 1300); Winchester, D&C, A/3/2, ff. 41v–42 (Davis 1044) (s. xiv^{med}); BL, Harley 1761, f. 77 (Davis 1048) (s. xiv).
Edited: BCS 1275; *CS* I, i. 29; *PUU* 212.
Registered: JL 3753; Böhmer-Zimmermann 483; J³ 7982.

*?†45. (970/72? 983/92?)

JOHN (XIII? XIV? XV?) grants OSWALD, as ABBOT OF ST BENEDICT'S, RAMSEY privileges for his monastery

Incipit: n/a (*deperditum*).
Archive: n/a (cited in Ramsey's *Liber benefactorum*).
MSS: Oxford, Bodleian Library, Rawlinson B. 333, ff. 6v, 13 (Davis 790) (s. xiii^{ex}); PRO, E 164/28, ff. 135v, 144 (Davis 788) (s. xiv^{in}).
Edited: *Chron. Rames.*, ii. 23, 59, pp. 48, 99.
Registered: Böhmer-Zimmermann 484; J³ *7983.

*†46. (971/2)
'FORMOSUS' (sic) (= JOHN XIII) grants OSWALD, ARCHBISHOP OF YORK the 'gift of the bishopric of WORCESTER'

Incipit: n/a (*deperditum*).
Archive: n/a (cited in a forged diploma of Edward the Confessor for York, '1065' (S 1037a)).
MS: York, Minster Library and Archives, L 2/1, pt. I, ff. 60v–61 (Davis 1087) (s. xiv^{med}).
Edited: *Northern Houses*, 11.
Registered: No (but cited in S 1037a).

47. (985/96?)
JOHN (XV?) threatens ÆLFRIC, EALDORMAN (OF HAMPSHIRE) with excommunication for his transgressions against the monastery of ST MARY'S, GLASTONBURY

Incipit: Relatione quorundam fidelium
Archive(s): Canterbury, Christ Church; Glastonbury(?).
MSS: BL, Cotton MS Tiberius A. xv, ff. 169v–70 (*c.* 1000); BL, Royal 13 D. ii, f. 38 (s. xii²) [*William of Malmesbury's Gesta regum*]; Cambridge, University Library, Ii. 2. 3, f. 45 (s. xii²) [ibid.]; BL, Royal D. v, f. 76v (s. xiii) [ibid.]; Cambridge, Trinity College, R. 5. 33, f. 13 (*c.* 1300) [*William of Malmesbury's De antiquitate, interpolation*].
Edited: *CS* I, i. 36; *PUU* <282; *GR*, I, ii. 151C, pp. 246–9; *De antiq.* pp. 203–4, n. 123; *Glastonbury*, Appendix 4a.
Registered: JL 3752; Böhmer-Zimmermann 623; J³ 8137.

(a) Authentic and Uncertain Privileges, 960–96

John XII's pallium privilege for Dunstan, archbishop of Canterbury (959–88) (41) is the only certainly authentic privilege from tenth-century

England. It survives as a near-contemporary copy in a liturgical codex either belonging to the prelate, or compiled shortly after his death.[77] This text closely follows *LD* 45, the standard pallium formula found across European archives.[78] Dunstan's tenth-century *Life* further attests to its acquisition.[79] An interpolated, twelfth-century version was far more widely transmitted as part of the Canterbury primacy forgeries: the survival of this earlier copy is therefore additionally illuminating in what it reveals of the workings of the later forgers and falsifiers.[80] Alongside 57, 41 is as close as we can get to an intact, contemporary witness to an authentic privilege from the Anglo-Saxon period.

Far more difficulties surround the undated ?†44 for the Old Minster, Winchester, preserved only in manuscripts of the thirteenth century onwards, although Matthew Parker transcribed a now-lost copy in the 1570s.[81] Written in the name of a 'Pope John' and addressed to King Edgar (957/9–75) and his subjects, it purports to approve a petition of Dunstan that the Old Minster, where Æthelwold (bishop of Winchester, 963–84) is installed, should have its canons expelled and replaced by monks, who will in future enjoy the right to elect their own abbot-bishops from amongst their own number. This request for papal approval does not appear in any contemporary witnesses. Moreover, ?†44's combination of named protagonists raises questions about its date which cast a shadow over its reliability. We know that the expulsion of canons took place on 20 February 964;[82] that Æthelwold was consecrated bishop on 29 November 963;[83] and that John XII (955–64) fled Rome on 2 November 963 before being deposed on 4 December and replaced by Leo VIII (963–5), against whom he briefly returned to contest the see from 26 February to April 964 (during which time he issued no further known privileges).[84] If we suppose, as did Dorothy Whitelock, that Edgar is unlikely to have 'acted before he obtained papal permission', then that leaves an almost impossibly narrow window for John XII to have received and granted the petition (unless one follows Whitelock in allowing for the possibility that the process had been initiated while Æthelwold was bishop-elect, although this pushes things quite far). An alternative, proposed by Francesca Tinti, is that the

---

[77] Below, Chapter 6, pp. 190–94.   [78] Santifaller, 'Verwendung', pp. 60, 63.
[79] B., *Vita s. Dunstani*, 28, pp. 84–5.   [80] Southern, 'Canterbury', pp. 205–6.
[81] Parker, *De antiquitate*, pp. 66–7.
[82] Wulfstan, *Life of St Æthelwold*, 17–18, pp. 30–3.
[83] *ASC, s.a.* 964 AEF; Wulfstan, *Life of St Æthelwold*, 16, pp. 28–31.
[84] John XII's last extant privilege dates 25 Apr. 963: *PUU* 157 (JL 3694); see further Böhmer-Zimmermann 318 ff.

petition left England soon after Æthelwold's election, but got delayed in Rome during the tumult of 963–4: it only later caught the attention of John XIII (965–72), by which time Edgar, Æthelwold, and Dunstan had already acted.[85] This scenario suggests a petition-by-letter, which then got stuck somewhere on the papacy's to-do list for well over a year. That sounds unusual for this period, when petitions tended to be conducted in-person by relatively high-profile delegations. A bureaucratic waiting-list in Rome is not otherwise attested at this time, and we must be wary of projecting backwards from high-medieval practices. One suspects that if Edgar's delegation had arrived within this late 963–4 period, they might have just lodged their petition with Leo VIII, the favoured imperial candidate: however, it is true that Leo only issued two known authentic privileges, both at the very beginning of his pontificate, and so some genuine disruption does seem to have occurred.[86] If the privilege is genuine, we mustn't anyway suppose that a *post factum* petition would have proved especially problematic. This was the tenth century, not the thirteenth, and *pace* Whitelock a petition lodged with John XIII in or after 965 for a privilege simply confirming events already long concluded seems quite possible, whatever the language of the document itself.

These issues with dating ?†44 constitute, however, only part of the problem. Considering the relatively loose standards of tenth-century papal diplomatic—and allowing for later losses, corruptions, and interpolations—this unpretentious text appears just about acceptable. It incorporates elements of *LD* 32 and 87. Yet a major stumbling-block is that its clause on episcopal-abbatial elections mirrors the *Regularis Concordia*, perhaps not issued until 966, and maybe not until as late as 973.[87] Traditionally, historians have followed one of two interpretations. Either the *Concordia* silently quotes this privilege of John XII/XIII[88] (improbable, given the absence of comparable papal pronouncements on the matter, or of references to the contemporary papacy anywhere in the *Concordia*); or, the privilege is simply a later forgery or falsification, copying this clause from this famous Æthelwoldian text.[89] Following Kortüm's findings on the prevalence of 'recipient-influence' in continental papal documents of the tenth century,[90] Tinti has more recently argued that the appearance of

[85] Tinti, 'England', pp. 175–6.   [86] *PUU* <159, <161 (JL 3701–2).
[87] *Regularis concordia*, p. 6; Liebermann, 'Aethelwolds'; Barrow, 'Chronology', pp. 212–13, 220–2.
[88] *CS* I, i. 29; Wright, 'Vercelli', p. 183.
[89] Liebermann, 'Aethelwolds'; Barrow, 'English Cathedral Communities', pp. 37–8.
[90] Above, Chapter 2, p. 30.

the *Concordia* clause in ?†44 could reflect that same phenomenon: the 'recipient-influence' of aspects of the original petition, perhaps composed by Æthelwold, becoming incorporated into the final document drawn up in Rome.[91] This is compelling, and makes good sense within a wider European context. But we should still proceed with caution. Kortüm's thesis permits us to be more open-minded, but it does not provide positive evidence for authenticity. Julia Barrow has shown that the privilege's *inscriptio*, an element of the document not necessarily affected by 'recipient-influence', is also irregular.[92] While this is not enough to discredit the document entirely,[93] Barrow points out elsewhere that there were very good reasons to forge this text in the twelfth century, when the Old Minster sought to protect its election privileges and monastic status from secular encroachment.[94] One might add further that, while references to prominent intercessors do feature in some contemporary papal documents, this privilege's name-checking of Edgar, Dunstan, and Æthelwold as a group looks suspicious—as if an attempt to conjure up all the benevolent ghosts of the tenth-century 'golden age' at once.[95] Overall, there is just about enough in this privilege's favour to think it potentially genuine. But taken together, the cumulation of issues raised by its late manuscript tradition, difficulties of dating, suspicious textual irregularities, and later motives for forgery add up to an alarming set of obstacles. Its authenticity does not lie beyond reasonable doubt. For now, let's suspend judgement on ?†44 as a text of uncertain status, and return to it in Chapter 6, when we can consider how far the wider context of tenth-century Anglo-papal interactions allowed for the possibility of its acquisition.

To this pair we may tentatively add 47, a short letter from another John to an Ælfric *dux*. I follow Stubbs', Keynes', and Kelly's identification of the latter as Ealdorman Ælfric of Hampshire (983–1016). Since the earliest manuscript probably dates to the time of Archbishop Ælfric of Canterbury (995–1005) and includes no other letters postdating *c.* 994, this probably identifies the pope as John XV (985–96).[96] Diplomatically, the letter is irregular, but then so are its contents—a threat against Ælfric for his

---

[91] Tinti, 'England', pp. 176–7: the *dispositio* may have been influenced by the English petition, whereas the *arenga* and *sanctio* follow LD 32 and 87.

[92] Barrow, 'English Cathedral Communities', p. 38.

[93] Cf. Unger, *Päpstliche Schriftlichkeit*, pp. 221–9, on the protocol formulae of *LD* falling out of use at the ninth-century *scrinium*.

[94] Barrow, *Clergy*, p. 97.

[95] See Robertson, 'Dunstan', on the twelfth-century reimagining of the protagonists of the English Benedictine movement.

[96] *Memorials*, ed. Stubbs, p. 396; Keynes, *Diplomas*, p. 177, n. 91; *Glastonbury*, pp. 567–70.

predations against Glastonbury. Because of its almost contemporary manu-script appearance, it must either be a bespoke, authentic missive acquired from the pope, or at worst a contemporary forgery. Even if the latter, we may nevertheless think of it as an authentic product of English understandings about Rome in the 980s–990s, and given the spirit of this age of 'recipient-influence', still a *de facto* papal document, just one entirely outsourced to the periphery. But is it a privilege? In the twelfth century, William of Malmesbury circulated via his *Gesta regum* an interpolated copy of the letter, which effectively made it a full-blown legal guarantee for Glastonbury's properties. The role of 47 in its original form is less certain. Nevertheless, one can find near-contemporary examples of continental monasteries archiving compar-able papal excommunication threats as if they were more conventional privileges. In Chapter 6 we can investigate this problem in detail.

(b) Deperditum?

Ramsey's *Liber benefactorum*, compiled in the mid-twelfth century but drawing upon earlier sources, twice claims that Oswald (bishop of Worcester, 961–92; archbishop of York, 971/2–92), the monastery's first abbot, had acquired through 'emissaries' *?†45, a privilege guaranteeing Ramsey's 'freedom', 'protection', and abbatial elections, in the name of another 'John'. It seems suspicious that the *Liber* does not provide a text for this document, since it functions elsewhere as a kind of cartulary-chronicle.[97] Nevertheless, such an acquisition was not impossible. We know Oswald travelled to Rome in 971/2 to receive the pallium from John XIII; that papal privileges safeguarding monastic 'freedom and protection', including abbatial elections, were acquired elsewhere in Europe at this time; that Ramsey had close links to Fleury, a house with strong commitments to its own 'papal-privileged' status; and that Byrhtferth of Ramsey (d. *c.* 1020), the author of Oswald's *Vita*, includes in a separate work an account of the bestowal of an eighth-century papal privilege—this depiction has nothing directly to do with either Oswald or Ramsey, but it may reflect in some way the author's own experiences. 'Suspicious but not impossible' feels like the best judgement at this stage. We can return to the wider context of this claim in Chapter 6.

---

[97] *ECEE*, p. 231.

(c) Forgeries and False Claims

It is not surprising, given the resonance of this period as a golden age of monastic refoundation, that numerous later forgeries were projected back to this time. Matters were probably helped by the ease of attributing undated documents to unspecified Popes John (the long tenth century had more than its share, running from John IX (898–900) to XIX (1024–32)). Besides the more uncertain cases above, scholarship has long recognised four further documents as spurious. They do not need close analysis here, but a few points of interest invite comment. †39–40 both belong to the early twelfth-century dossier of St Augustine's forgeries. Their *inscriptio* to King Eadred (946–55) is odd, since he overlapped with no known John. The only possibility is that the petitioners left before the king's death in November 955, arriving at Rome after John XII's assumption of the pontificate that December, but this again pushes things rather far. Levison considered both forgeries, with †39 based upon ?†44, which he thought genuine.[98] Whatever the authenticity of the latter, this possible link opens up interesting questions about inter-archive copying and forgery in the post-Conquest period. Westminster's †42 is cited in full in a 'gloriously spurious' pseudo-Edgarian diploma of '969' for that house, part of the mid-twelfth-century forgery project associated with Osbert de Clare.[99] It is extremely interesting that †42 claims to have been issued in Ravenna, since we know that John XIII co-presided over a synod there in Easter 967 where a number of other privileges were issued, a relatively rare occasion on which an early medieval pope was found outside Rome.[100] However, other elements of this forgery draw identifiably upon a model preserved in the archive of Saint-Denis, rather than anything known from England.[101] In that case it seems that if the forger did have a genuine, now-lost privilege from Ravenna before him, it was quite possibly not addressed to an English beneficiary.[102] The spectre of cross-Channel influences also haunts Glastonbury's †43, which again first appears in the twelfth century. Kelly's commentary on this document is essential.[103] One can add to it the observation that, while this privilege's 'notice' format

---

[98] Levison, *England*, pp. 195–8.

[99] *Crawford Collection*, ed. Napier and Stevenson, pp. 88–102; Chaplais, 'Original Charters', pp. 92–5; Keynes, 'King Æthelred's Charter', p. 58.

[100] See below, Chapter 6, p. 196, n. 44.

[101] Böhmer-Zimmermann, †409; its template is a forgery (s. xi) attributed to Nicholas I: *PUU Saint-Denis*, 13 (JE 2719).

[102] *Pace* Vollrath, *Synoden*, pp. 265–8.   [103] *Glastonbury*, pp. 510–14, 571–4.

('Let it be known to all the faithful...') looks highly unusual by the standards of contemporary papal diplomatic, it finds a parallel in a forgery of *c.* 1060 for Mont-Saint-Michel, also attributed to a Pope John. The lines of transmission are obscure, but is not impossible that this served as †43's model.[104]

One peculiar *deperditum* (*†46) was also later attributed to this period, although its proponents had a shaky grasp of tenth-century history. A forged diploma in the name of Edward the Confessor for York, preserved only in a fourteenth-century cartulary, possibly dates to the early-to-mid twelfth century.[105] It asserts that, when Archbishop Oswald of York went to Rome for his pallium, he also received from Pope Formosus a privilege granting York power over the see of Worcester. Supposedly, York later lost it in a fire. The statement betrays (and/or attempts to propagate) a warped understanding of the late Anglo-Saxon arrangement whereby archbishops of York sometimes also held the see of Worcester in plurality. The diploma also seems confused about papal history, replacing John XIII, who granted Oswald's pallium in 971/2, with Formosus, who had died some 75 years before. We can at least assume that Oswald had received a privilege for his pallium, and so we might (generously) consider *†46 at best a distant memory of that genuine acquisition.

D. From 1000 to 1073

†48. (1024/32?)
JOHN (XIX?) grants DANIEL, ABBOT OF ST PETER'S, CHERTSEY privileges for his monastery

Incipit: Ad sincerum Dei
Archive: Chertsey.
MS: BL, Cotton Vitellius A. xiii, ff. 27–8 (Davis 222) (s. xiii^med).
Edited: *PUU England*, i. 1; *PUU* †554; *Chertsey*, Appendix 1b.
Registered: Böhmer-Frech †25; J³ †8965.

*49. 1049 (*c.* October 1/6)
LEO IX grants ÆLFWINE, ABBOT OF ST BENEDICT'S, RAMSEY privileges for his monastery

---

[104] *PUU* †170 (JL 3757).   [105] *Northern Houses*, p. 170.

Incipit: n/a (*deperditum*).
Archive: n/a (cited in Ramsey's *Liber benefactorum*).
MSS: Oxford, Bodleian Library, Rawlinson B. 333, f. 22 (Davis 790) (s. xiii[ex]); PRO, E 164/28, f. 156 (Davis 788) (s. xiv[in]).
Edited: *Chron. Rames.*, iii. 115, p. 171.
Registered: JL *4178; Böhmer-Frech 624; J³ *9349.

?†50. (1049/50) [possibly 1049, *c.* October 1/6]
LEO IX orders EDWARD, KING OF THE ENGLISH to allow LEOFRIC, BISHOP to move his see from CREDITON to EXETER

Incipit: Si bene habes
Archive: Exeter.
MSS: Oxford, Bodleian Library, Bodley 579, f. 3v (s. xi[med]); Oxford, Bodleian Library, Bodley 718, f. 180v (s. xi²).
Edited: *CS* I, i. 70; *Leofric Missal*, ii, pp. 4–5.
Registered: JL 4208; Böhmer-Frech 512; J³ *9543.

*51. (1049, *c.* October 1/6?) or (1050, *c.* April 29/3 May?)
LEO IX grants (EADSIGE, ARCHBISHOP? and WULFRIC, ABBOT?) privileges for the ARCHBISHOPRIC OF CANTERBURY and the monastery of STS PETER AND PAUL, CANTERBURY

Incipit: n/a (*deperditum*).
Archive: n/a (cited in Goscelin, *Historia translationis sancti Augustini*).
MSS: BL, Cotton Vespasian B. xx, ff. 126v–127 (Davis 199.1) (s. xii[in]); see further MSS tradition for Goscelin (Sharpe, *Handlist*, p. 152).
Edited: Goscelin, *De translatione*, p. 433.
Registered: No.

†52. (1050, *c.* April 29/May 3)
LEO IX dispenses EDWARD, KING OF THE ENGLISH from his pilgrimage to Rome, orders him to found a monastery dedicated to ST PETER (WESTMINSTER), and grants it privileges

Incipit: Quoniam uoluntatem tuam
Archive: Westminster.
MSS: See MSS tradition for *Lives* of Edward the Confessor by Osbert de Clare (*La Vie de S. Édouard*, pp. 980–4: earliest MS s. xii/xiii) and Aelred of

Rievaulx (*Vita sancti Ædwardi*, pp. 13–63: earliest MS s. xii) [*short version*]; BL, Cotton Ch. vi. 2 (s. xii¹) [*single-sheet pseudo-original of* S 1043] [*short version*]; BL, Cotton Faustina A. iii, ff. 115–16v (s. xiii) (Davis 1011) [*long version*] (in S 1039); *inter multa alia, for full list see* S 1039, 1043.

Edited: *PUU England*, i. 2 [*long version*]; K 824 [*short version, within* S 1043]; Osbert de Clare, *La Vie de S. Édouard*, 7, p. 995 [*short version*]; Aelred of Rievaulx, *Vita sancti Ædwardi*, 11, pp. 115–16 [*short version*].

Registered: JL 4257; S 1039 [*long version*]; S 1043 [*short version*]; Böhmer-Frech †763; J³ †9473.

53. (1055/7)

VICTOR II informs EDWARD, KING OF THE ENGLISH and his **principes** *that he has confirmed the privileges of the monastery of ELY*

Incipit: Priuilegia apostolica et/Le privilege ki
Archive: Ely.
MSS: See MSS tradition for *Liber Eliensis* (ed. Blake, pp. xxiii–xxvii: earliest MS s. xii^ex) [*Latin*]; Cambridge, Trinity College, O. 2. 41, pp. 73–4 [*Anglo-Norman French*], pp. 102–4 [*Latin*] (Davis 364) (s. xii^med).
Edited: *PL* 143. 816 [*Latin*]; *Liber Eliensis*, ii. 93 [*Latin*]; *CS* I, i. 75 [*Latin*]; Short, 'Archives', p. 268 [*Anglo-Norman French*].
Registered: JL 4350; Böhmer-Frech 1199; J³ 10090.

54. (1055/7)

VICTOR II informs EDWARD, KING OF THE ENGLISH and his **principes** *that he has confirmed the privileges of the monastery of ST PETER'S, CHERTSEY*

Incipit: Priuilegia nostrum notum
Archive: Chertsey.
MS: PRO, C 52/4 (s. xiii^in).
Edited: *PUU England*, i. 4; *Cartae antiquae*, ed. Landon, 122; *CS* I, i. 74; *Chertsey*, Appendix 1c.
Registered: Böhmer-Frech 1201; J³ 10091.

†55. (1055/7)

VICTOR II confirms to the 'sons' of the monastery of ST PETER'S, CHERTSEY their privileges

Incipit: Iustis petentium desideriis
Archive: Chertsey.
MS: BL, Cotton Vitellius A. xiii, f. 28 (Davis 222) (s. xiii^{med}).
Edited: *PUU England*, i. 3; *Chertsey*, Appendix 1d.
Registered: Böhmer-Frech †1200; J³ 10117.

†56. (1055/7)
VICTOR II confirms a charter of GODGIFU, wife of Leofric, earl (of Mercia) for ST MARY'S, STOW

Incipit: Cum omni Christiane
Archive: Eynsham.
MS: Oxford, Christ Church, 341, f. 10v (Davis 399) (s. xii^{ex}).
Edited: *Eynsham Cartulary*, ed. Salter, i. 2; *PUU England*, iii. 3.
Registered: S 1233; Böhmer-Frech †1202; J³ †10113.

57. 1061, April 25
NICHOLAS II confirms to GISO, BISHOP OF WELLS his and his 'canonically promoted' successors' privileges

Incipit: Pontificii nostri est
Archive: Wells.
MS: Wells, D&C, C/F/3/2 (s. xi²) [*contemporary single-sheet copy/pseudo-original*].
Edited: *PUU England*, ii. 1; *CS* I, i. 77.
Registered: JL 4457; J³ 10418.

58. 1061, May 3
NICHOLAS II confirms to WULFWIG, BISHOP OF DORCHESTER-ON-THAMES his and his 'canonically promoted' successors' privileges

Incipit: Cum magna sollicitudine
Archive: Lincoln.
MSS: BL, Cotton Vespasian E. xvi, ff. 18–19 (Davis 581) (s. xiii^{in}); Lincoln, D&C, A/1/5, f. 169 (Davis 583) (s. xiii^{med}).
Edited: *PL* 143. 1356; *Registrum Antiquissimum*, ed. Foster and Major, i. 247; *CS* I, i. 78.
Registered: JL 4461; J³ 10425.

59. (1061, after April 22) [c. May 3?]
NICHOLAS II grants EALDRED, ARCHBISHOP OF YORK the pallium,
and outlines arrangements concerning the see of WORCESTER, which he
must renounce

Incipit: Quia diuinitatis occulta
Archive: York.
MSS: BL, Lansdowne 402, f. 29 (Davis 1085) (s. xiv^{in}); York, Minster Library
and Archives, L 2/1, pt. 1, f. 40v–41 (Davis 1087) (s. xiv^{med}).
Edited: Historians of the Church of York, ed. Raine, iii. 2; Tinti, 'Pallium',
pp. 21–3.
Registered: JL 4463; J³ 10486.

†60. (1059/61)
NICHOLAS II confirms to EDWARD, KING OF THE ENGLISH the privileges of his monastery dedicated to ST PETER (WESTMINSTER)

Incipit: Omnipotenti Deo referimus
Archive: Westminster.
MSS: See MSS tradition for Lives of Edward the Confessor by Osbert de
Clare (La Vie de S. Édouard, pp. 980–4: earliest MS s. xii/xiii) and Ælred of
Rievaulx (Vita sancti Ædwardi, pp. 13–63: earliest MS s. xii); London,
Westminster Abbey, W.A.M. xx (s. xii^{med}) [single-sheet pseudo-original of
S 1041]; BL, Cotton Faustina A. iii, ff. 33–4v (Davis 1011) (s. xiii); inter
multa alia: for full list see S 1041.
Edited: PL 143. 1358; K 825 [within S 1041]; Osbert de Clare, La Vie de
S. Édouard, 11, pp. 1001–2; Ælred of Rievaulx, Vita sancti Ædwardi, 17,
pp. 126–9.
Registered: JL 4462; S 1041; J³ 10484.

†61. '1043' (for 1063?)
ALEXANDER II confirms to EDWARD, KING OF THE ENGLISH the
privileges of the monastery of ST MARY'S, COVENTRY

Incipit: Scriptorum uestrorum eloquia
Archive: Coventry.
MSS: 15, all post-medieval: see MSS tradition for S 1000.
Edited: PL 146. 1299; K 916 [within S 1000].
Registered: JL 4543; S 1000; J³ 10677.

*62. (1061/5)
ALEXANDER II grants ÆLFWINE, ABBOT OF ST BENEDICT'S, RAMSEY privileges for his monastery

Incipit: n/a (*deperditum*).
Archive: n/a (cited in Ramsey's *Liber benefactorum*).
MSS: Oxford, Bodleian Library, Rawlinson B. 333, f. 23 (Davis 790) (s. xiii^{ex}); PRO, E 164/28, f. 157 (Davis 788) (s. xiv^{in}).
Edited: *Chron. Rames.*, iii. 118, p. 176.
Registered: J^3 *10781.

*63. (1061/70)
ALEXANDER II grants ÆTHELSIGE, ABBOT OF STS PETER AND PAUL, CANTERBURY privileges for his monastery

Incipit: n/a (*deperditum*).
Archive: n/a (cited in Goscelin, *Historia translationis sancti Augustini*).
MSS: BL, Cotton Vespasian B. xx, ff. 127v–128 (Davis 199.1) (s. xii^{in}); see further MSS tradition for Goscelin (Sharpe, *Handlist*, p. 152).
Edited: Goscelin, *De translatione*, p. 433.
Registered: No.

64. 1071, October 27
ALEXANDER II grants BALDWIN, ABBOT OF BURY ST EDMUNDS privileges for his monastery

Incipit: Quanquam sedes apostolica
Archives: Bury St Edmunds; Canterbury, Christ Church.
MSS: BL, Harley 76, ff. 139–40 (Davis 122) (s. xi^{ex}); BL, Cotton Cleopatra E. i, ff. 56–7 (Davis 162) (s. xii^{in}); BL, Cotton Otho A. xviii, f. 133 (s. xii^{in}); Oxford, Bodleian Library, Bodley 297, pp. 371–2 (1133/43); Cambridge, University Library, Mm. 4. 19, ff. 52–3 (Davis 118) (s. xiii^{in}); BL, Add. 14847, f. 3 (Davis 96) (s. xiii^{ex}); Canterbury, D&C, Register A, ff. 10v–11 (Davis 169) (s. xv^{in}); *inter al.: for full list see Savill, 'Prelude'.*
Edited: John of Worcester, *Chronicle*, ii. 646–8; Savill, 'Prelude', pp. 818–20.
Registered: JL 4692; J^3 11117.

65. (1071, *c*. October 27)
ALEXANDER II grants THOMAS, ARCHBISHOP OF YORK the pallium

Incipit: Si pastores ouium
Archive: York.
MSS: BL, Lansdowne 402, ff. 28v–29 (Davis 1085) (s. xiv^{in}); York, Minster Library and Archives, L 2/1, pt. 1, f. 41; pt. 2, f. 254v (Davis 1087) (s. xiv^{med}). Edited: *Historians of the Church of York*, ed. Raine, iii. 4; Cowdrey, 'Archbishop Thomas', pp. 32–4.
Registered: JL 4693; J^3 11118.

†66. (1070/73)
ALEXANDER II confirms to LANFRANC, ARCHBISHOP OF CANTERBURY the privileges of the monastic community of CHRIST CHURCH, CANTERBURY

Incipit: Accepimus a quibusdam
Archive: Canterbury, Christ Church; Durham
MSS: See MSS tradition for Eadmer (*HN*, pp. ix–xv; earliest MS s. xii^1), BL, Cotton Claudius E. v, f. 243v (s. xii^{in}); BL, Cotton Cleopatra E. i, f. 52 (Davis 162) (s. xii^{in}); Durham, Cathedral Library, B. iv. 18, f. 70 (s. xii^{in}); Cambridge, Peterhouse, 74, f. 118 (*c.* 1120/30); Cambridge, University Library, Kk 4. 6, f. 278 (s. xii^1) [*William of Malmesbury's Liber pontificalis* 'C']; BL, Harley 633, f. 59 (s. xii^{ex}) [*William of Malmesbury's Liber pontificalis* 'L']; Canterbury, D&C, Register A, f. 6v (Davis 169) (s. xv^{in}).
Edited: *PL* 146. 1415; *HN*, 1, pp. 19–21.
Registered: JL 4761; J^3 ?11126.

†67. (1070/73)
ALEXANDER II confirms to the monastic community of (the OLD MINSTER) WINCHESTER their privileges

Incipit: Legati nostri qui
Archive: Winchester, Old Minster (?).
MS: BL, Harley 633, f. 58v (s. xii^{ex}) [*William of Malmesbury's Liber pontificalis* 'L'].
Edited: *PL* 146. 1416.
Registered: JL 4763; J^3 ?11172.

(a) Authentic and Uncertain Privileges, 1049–71

Foremost among the genuine privileges for this period is Nicholas II's **57**, still preserved as a contemporary single-sheet manuscript at the cathedral of its recipient, Bishop Giso of Wells (Figure 3.2). Its internal text is surely an authentic product of the Roman Easter Synod of 1061: its diplomatic is impeccable; it closely matches the formulation of another, independently preserved episcopal privilege of two years before;[106] and Giso's attendance at the Synod is attested in other sources. It is necessary to stress, however, that this manuscript is *not*—as sometimes claimed—an original product of the papal chancery. As I have demonstrated elsewhere, its irregular script, incomplete *rota*, and absence of any trace of a *bulla* indicate that it is a contemporary facsimile. The hand is characteristic of Liège, Giso's place of origin. It is conceivably the handiwork of the bishop himself, or a member of his entourage.[107] Why such a copy was made is unclear. Perhaps Giso kept the original, with this facsimile going to Wells. In any case, its existence in this form somehow discouraged its later cartularisation: unlike other documents associated with Giso, this has no known further copies. It is interesting that the (surely deliberately) incomplete *rota* suggests that the facsimile was designed to replicate carefully the aesthetic of an original, while nevertheless making its non-original status evident. Historians should not, therefore, speak of any 'original' papal documents surviving from England before the twelfth century,[108] but this document is never-theless remarkable in its own right, as a unique example of Lotharingian, papal-imitative script at an Anglo-Saxon episcopal centre. 57 also provides an important methodological warning for the wider practice of Anglo-Saxon diplomatic, since there is a tendency in that field to assume that surviving single-sheets—which in the case of 'native' diplomas, lack any authenticating features—must be the 'originals'. As a papal document, 57 is our only pre-1066 single-sheet diploma where such marks of 'original' authentication can be tested—and indeed, it fails the test.

Four further privileges survive in later copies which we can confidently treat as authentic. Nicholas II's 58 for Wulfwig of Dorchester and 59 for Ealdred of York are products of the aftermath of the same 1061 Synod. 58 raises no problems. It is similar to 57, but with a different formulation drawing upon *LD* 89,[109] and with an impeccable dating clause acknowledg-ing recent changes in chancery personnel, confirmed elsewhere in the

---

[106] *PL* 143. 1311 (JL 4402).

[107] Savill, 'England and the Papacy', pp. 323–30. This missed a further crucial piece of evidence: the twelfth-century endorsement 'transcriptum priuilegii Nicholai papae'.

[108] *Pace* Keynes, 'Regenbald', p. 203, n. 105; Keynes, 'Giso', p. 255; *Bath and Wells*, p. 168; Baxter, 'Death', p. 279.

[109] Santifaller, 'Verwendung', p. 131.

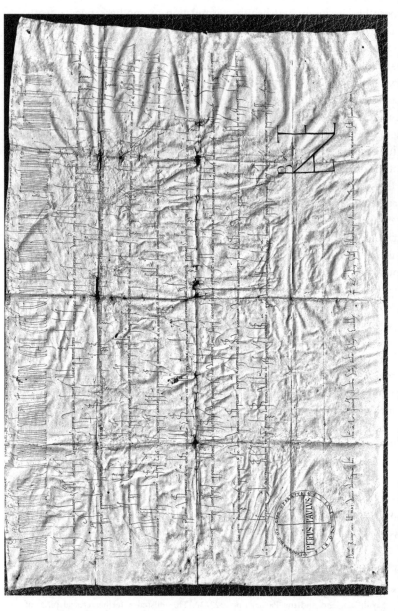

Figure 3.2 Nicholas II for Wells, 1061 (JL 4457), contemporary facsimile: Wells, D&C, CF/3/2 (Michael Blandford, by permission of the Chapter of Wells Cathedral).

continental corpus.[110] One probable corruption to the text is its remark about what Nicholas has learnt 'through the words of our legates' (*legatorum nostrorum*). In light of its context, 'our' looks like a copyist's error for 'your' (*uestrorum*), i.e. Wulfwig's *legati*.[111] **59** presents more difficulties. It is more irregularly formulated, lacks a dating clause, and appears only in much later manuscripts, but a study by Tinti has now quashed most doubts over its authenticity.[112] To this I will only add two further points. First, its limited long-term usefulness (it insists Ealdred must abandon his claims to Worcester, and extends this to his successors) does not look like the work of a forger. Second, its lost date may have been the same as, or very close to, that of **58** (3 May): we can pick up this point later in Chapter 7. **59** survives in the same fourteenth-century York cartularies as Alexander II's **65**, an entirely conventional pallium privilege for Ealdred's successor Thomas, based on *LD* 45 (the latest known text using this formula anywhere).[113] There are no grounds for not thinking it genuine. We can also gather from independent narrative sources that it must have been acquired at about the same time as Alexander's **64** for Abbot Baldwin of Bury St Edmunds, dated 27 October 1071.[114] I have demonstrated elsewhere its authenticity.[115] It is of particular interest that it is preserved in copies from the archives of both Bury and Christ Church, Canterbury. The latter tradition must result from an episode reported in Eadmer's *Historia novorum* (1109/16?), that Lanfranc, archbishop of Canterbury (1070–89), had confiscated the privilege shortly after its acquisition, returning it only shortly before his death.[116] One clause varies between manuscripts: a condition that the privilege's terms apply 'saving reverence to the apostolic see' in Bodley 297 appears in other copies as 'saving canonical reverence to the primate bishop', or is missing altogether. I argue elsewhere that the first clause probably represents the

---

[110] Bernard succeeds Humbert as *bibliothecarius* (Santifaller, *Saggio*, p. 177).

[111] No other sources indicate that Wulfwig attended the 1061 Synod, and there are no records of papal legates in England in the preceding years. By contrast, Nicholas states earlier in the privilege that Wulfwig's request has arrived via *legati* and *litterae*. Baxter has argued that the privilege was acquired with the help of representatives of the Leofwineson family, who had vested interests: Baxter, 'Death'; Baxter, *Earls*, pp. 182–8. Presumably these were the *legati*. Note that the term *legatus* applied generally to emissaries in this period and did not exclusively denote 'papal legates'—still an emerging concept—although this word could have confused a later copyist. It would be easy to mistranscribe the contraction 'urm' (*uestrorum*) as 'nrm' (*nostrorum*).

[112] Tinti, 'Pallium'; see also Licence, 'New Source'.

[113] Santifaller, 'Verwendung', pp. 60, 135.

[114] See above, Chapter 2, pp. 000.   [115] Savill, 'Prelude'.

[116] *HN*, 3, p. 133. Dating: Southern, *Saint Anselm*, pp. 298–309; but cf. Pohl, '(Un)Making'.

original formulation, whereas the second is an adjustment made to the text by Lanfranc during its confiscation (at which time the archbishop had begun asserting his 'primate' status, something never recognised by Alexander).[117]

Other items are less secure. Two now-undated privileges in the name of Victor II (1055–7) for Ely (53) and Chertsey (54) stand out by having close similarities to one another, but—perhaps disconcertingly—otherwise few affinities to any other privileges in the contemporary corpus. Their similarity could suggest they were issued at around the same time; it could also indicate that one was simply the copy of the other. Sympathetic commentators have suggested that their unusual acclamations (*Fiat? Fiat. Placet? Placet. Laudatis? Laudamus. Hoc sit stabile. Fiat, fiat, fiat*) point to a conciliar context,[118] but this is speculative. Nevertheless, there are some points in their favour. Excepting an almost certainly interpolated passage in 53 on Ely's rights of clerical exclusion and private justice,[119] it is encouraging that neither make especially ambitious claims, serving as fairly rote confirmations of unspecified monastic property rights. Papal diplomatic was, moreover, passing through a rare experimental phase at the time of Victor's accession, and since only nineteen privileges survive from his pontificate, we cannot pronounce too judiciously on 'norms'.[120] The diplomatic peculiarity of the two may even speak in their favour: it seems odd that later forgers might produce privileges which showed such *little* ambition in what they granted, but so *much* in their formulation. We have other, indirect evidence that Victorine documents reached England, so a context is possible.[121] Aspects of these privileges' archival history are also encouraging. Chertsey's 54 survives only via the Public Record Office's *Cartae antiquae* Rolls, copied in the early thirteenth century. In fact, Chertsey's mid-thirteenth-century cartulary omits the document, providing instead a patently spurious—and much more favourable—privilege in the same pope's name (†55). Perhaps Chertsey's archivists destroyed their texts of 54 once †55 was made, fearful that this more sober privilege undermined their preferred false document.[122] 53 is only securely attested from the mid-twelfth century, when it appears in the *Liber Eliensis* (c. 1170) and in a

[117] Savill, 'Prelude', pp. 804–11.   [118] *PUU England*, i, p. 221; Böhmer-Frech 1199.

[119] A dubious, recurring claim: *Liber Eliensis*, 'incipit', and ii. 54, 92, pp. 4, 135, 161–3 (the 'unquestionably spurious' S 1051); see Blake's note, p. 124, n. 4. 'Elements of private justice' existed in pre-Conquest England, but such liberties were very limited and diplomas claiming otherwise are 'largely or wholly bogus': Wormald, 'Lordship'.

[120] See above, Chapter 2, pp. 39–43.

[121] Later seals of Peterborough adopted the motif of Victor's *bullae*: Levison, *England*, p. 205.

[122] On the archive (and its 'terrible reputation'), see *Chertsey*, pp. 34–45.

slightly earlier Ely dossier of privileges in both Latin and Anglo-Norman French translations,[123] but its diplomatic may have been imitated as early as 1110/31 in an episcopal charter of Hervey of Ely for the church.[124] Overall, we should not invest too much into 53 and 54, and definitely consider the former interpolated. But there are just enough encouraging aspects to allow us to treat them cautiously for now as potentially genuine privileges.

Lastly, we should consider Leo IX's ?†50 concerning Leofric of Exeter as quasi-authentic. This short, undated text survives in two liturgical codices from the see, both in sections copied in the second half of the eleventh century. In the *Leofric Missal*, the earliest of the two, it is embedded within a narrative describing its acquisition, and an authentic diploma of Edward the Confessor (1042–66) for the same beneficiary appears to cite the text.[125] As we will see in Chapter 7, we know enough about other interconnections between Leo, Edward and Leofric's fellow Anglo-Lotharingians to suppose that such a document really was granted in 1049 or 1050 (possibly on the same occasion as *49). The only problem with ?†50 is that, while its essential formulation is unobjectionable, it is simply too succinct to pass as a full privilege of this type. What we now have probably represents an abbreviated or paraphrased memorandum of a lost original.

(b) Deperdita

Ramsey's twelfth-century *Liber benefactorum* (see *?†45) further claims that Abbot Ælfwine obtained *49 from Leo IX at the Council of Rheims (October 1049), confirming the monastery's *iura* (rights and/or properties). The vagueness of this statement is encouraging (again: one would expect more ambition from a false claim). We anyway know from both the *Anglo-Saxon Chronicle* and a Saint-Rémi source that Ælfwine attended Rheims,[126] and independent, continental archives show that several other privileges were granted at the event.[127] Changing circumstances in Ælfwine's East Anglia may have given him an increased incentive to seek support for his monastery.[128] The *Liber* also states that Ælfwine acquired *62 from

---

[123] Keynes, 'Ely', pp. 7–8; Short, 'Archives'.
[124] See Karn's notes to *English Episcopal Acta* XXXI, pp. cxxxvi, 8, although he considers 52 a probable forgery.
[125] *Leofric Missal*, ii. 1–6; *CS* I, i. 71 (S 1021).
[126] *ASC, s.a.* 1046 E, 1050 D; *Konzilien*, ed. Jasper, 27, p. 233.
[127] Santifaller, 'Verwendung', p. 122.   [128] Licence, *Edward*, p. 125.

Alexander II (1061–73) during a trip to Rome to pursue undisclosed business for Edward. A remark by the author suggests that he had intended to insert a copy of the document at around this point (*priuilegium quod inferius habetur*), but for whatever reason it does not materialise in either manuscript of the *Liber*. There is nothing out of the ordinary about these claims, which plausibly refer to genuine lost privileges.

Goscelin's *Translation of Saint Augustine* (1099/1109) reports two more unusual privileges, concerning conciliar seating prerogatives for the archbishops of Canterbury and the abbots of Sts Peter and Paul/St Augustine's (Leo IX: *51),[129] and the right of the latter to wear the mitre and sacerdotal sandals (Alexander II: *63). Continental archives reveal a number of comparable privileges granted to other institutions around this time (including for beneficiaries with 'apostolic' status, something to which the Canterbury churches also aspired at this point through their Augustinian cult).[130] Goscelin's claims thus look plausible. He may, however, have erred as to precisely how and when *51 was granted. His *Translation* reports that Abbot Wulfric acquired the privilege at the Council of Rheims (his attendance is corroborated by the same sources that indicate Ælfwine's), but states that Leo had been swayed on the matter sometime 'before' by Bishop Hermann of Ramsbury (d. 1078) at a 'huge meeting of bishops' at Rome. In fact, we know that Hermann was in Rome for the Easter Synod of 1050, where on 2 May he subscribed a privilege for the canonisation of Gerhard of Toul.[131] It was presumably also there, then, that *51 was both petitioned and acquired—that is, by Hermann on Canterbury's behalf. Since Goscelin had spent his youth under Hermann's tutelage,[132] he had probably heard the story from the man himself. Much later, he either confused the order of

---

[129] This could be the otherwise unidentified letter of Leo IX concerning Canterbury cited in Lanfranc, *Letters*, 4, p. 53.

[130] See below, Chapter 7, pp. 243–4. The monastery's transformation into an 'apostolic' cult site to Augustine is the theme of Goscelin's *Translation*; Echternach and Fulda (who had similar privileges) had 'apostolic' claims through Willibrord and Boniface. For this process at Canterbury as probably beginning in the 1030s/40s, see Hayward, 'Gregory', pp. 30–1, although he also suggests (ibid., p. 35) that Goscelin's later remarks about *51 and *63 were inventions, and should be seen in the same context as the St Augustine's forgeries (†2, †11, †39–40). Note, however, that Goscelin, perhaps writing as early as 1099, never cites those forgeries, whose content is anyway different in scope. Goscelin makes a single reference to the election of Wulfric taking place in line with 'the ancient custom of liberty and Roman privilege, first confirmed by apostolic authority' (*De translatione*, p. 432): if this assertion alludes to any document at all, then it is probably 14, which includes a simple clause on abbatial election.

[131] *Konzilien*, ed. Jasper, 30B, pp. 286–91.   [132] Barlow, 'Goscelin'.

events, or felt compelled by his new Canterbury patrons to emphasise Wulfric's agency, and thereby his closeness to Leo.

(c) Forgeries

An undated Chertsey privilege from 'John' to 'Abbot Daniel' (†48), preserved only in a mid-thirteenth-century cartulary and long considered a forgery,[133] has recently received more sympathetic treatment.[134] While allowances for Kortüm's thesis mean that one can no longer dismiss it with quite the same categorical certainty as before, it remains true that †48 has no positive features, and is too untrustworthy to use in a study of this kind. It is worth adding that this privilege's scholarly association with John XIX (1024–32) has no grounding in the evidence.[135] Chertsey's records have severe gaps, and Daniel, if he ever existed, could have held the abbacy almost anywhere between 693 and 964, or at various points after *c.* 1000,[136] thus opening up the range to as early as John VI (701–5) onwards. Considering what we have already seen of the frequency of this papal name and its later attraction as a generic designation on which to pin undated *spuria*, it seems likely that the later forger had no particular John in mind. The text probably belongs alongside the other Johannine forgeries discussed above (†39, †40, †42, †43; perhaps ?†44 and *?†45).

A great number of Anglo-Saxon diplomas purportedly belonging to the reign of Edward the Confessor are now deemed post-Conquest forgeries,[137] and the same goes for many of the papal privileges claiming to date from this time. †52 and †60 belong to the same Westminster forgery dossier as †42, whereupon they also entered Osbert de Clare's *Life of Edward* (1138), and then Aelred of Rievaulx's expanded *Life* of 1161. It is worth noting that these sources claim that †52 was acquired by Ealdred, Hermann, Ælfwine, and Wulfric—all genuine papal petitioners, as we have seen above—at a Roman synod, presumably alluding to the Easter Synod of 1050. Likewise, †60 is presented as having been petitioned from Nicholas II by Giso and Ealdred. We can at least say that the forgers had a reasonably solid grasp of the

---

[133] *PUU England*, i, p. 215; Santifaller, Rill, and Szaivert, 'Chronologisches Verzeichnis', pp. 40–1; Böhmer-Frech †25.
[134] *Chertsey*, pp. 24–5, 76 (nevertheless still rating it 'dubious').
[135] Holtzmann simply copied over the attribution from *Monasticon*, ed. Dugdale, i, p. 422.
[136] *Chertsey*, pp. 73–8.   [137] Clanchy, *From Memory*, pp. 318–19.

authentic Anglo-Roman interactions of the early papal reform period. Less impressive are Coventry's †56 and Stow's †61, part of a wider portfolio of forgeries concerning the foundations of Leofric of Mercia and his wife Godgifu.[138] †61 is unique: not a conventional privilege, but rather a charter in Godgifu's name, supposedly subscribed by Victor II. We do in fact know of rare instances of comparable papal confirmations appended to pre-existing diplomas in early eleventh-century France.[139] Yet no such practice is seen as late as the 1050s, and Godgifu's charter has anyway long failed all tests of Anglo-Saxon diplomatic. The older views that this curio is 'unquestionably spurious' and 'not very menacing' stand.[140] The same applies to †55, an unconvincing Victorine forgery from Chertsey, which we have already encountered as a possible thirteenth-century replacement for the restrained 54.

Two final, probable forgeries require separate treatment: those in the name of Alexander II for Christ Church, Canterbury (†66) and the Old Minster, Winchester (†67), apparently responses to Lanfranc's efforts to preserve the monastic order at both shortly after his appointment as archbishop.[141] If not outright suspicious, their formulation is nevertheless unconventional against the backdrop of Alexander's wider corpus; they receive no mention in contemporary sources, including Lanfranc's letter collection, which is strongly orientated towards Rome;[142] and they have a good context for forgery when they do first appear, during these communities' struggles to maintain their monastic identities in the twelfth century.[143] They probably belong to that period rather than Alexander's pontificate.[144] The two documents may nevertheless be among the earliest *spuria* considered in this chapter. Both appear in the manuscript tradition for William of Malmesbury's redaction of the *Liber pontificalis*, his earliest known work (1119 or shortly thereafter),[145] while †66 features in the first, almost

---

[138] Baxter, *Earls*, pp. 153–4, 183.   [139] See below, Chapter 6, pp. 000.

[140] Baxter, *Earls*, p. 183; *PUU England*, iii, p. 127.

[141] †67 does not mention Lanfranc but is apparently complementary to a forged or falsified letter of Alexander to the archbishop addressing the same issue: below, Appendix, p. 286. Note, however, that while that letter appears alongside †66 in both known copies of William of Malmesbury's *Liber pontificalis*, †67 does not feature in the earlier 'C' manuscript. Since 'C' also lacks a biographical notice for Alexander (typical for other popes, and immediately preceding †67 in 'L'), its omission probably results only from a copyist's oversight.

[142] Lanfranc, *Letters*.   [143] Barrow, *Clergy*, p. 97. Cf. †3 and ?†44.

[144] Clover, 'Alexander II's Letter'; Cowdrey, 'Lanfranc, the Papacy', pp. 489–95; Cowdrey, *Lanfranc*, pp. 150, 161.

[145] Thomson, *William*, pp. 119–38; but see above, n. 141.

certainly earlier section of Eadmer's *Historia novorum*, probably written around 1109/16.[146]

E. Summary

We have evidence for sixty-seven papal privileges concerning England which were purportedly acquired in the period up to 1073. It would appear that the texts of almost none have come down to us in wholly intact, authentic form, but we can identify **twenty-three as either substantially genuine, or as at least having a genuine basis.** Exactly zero survive as original products of the papal chancery—the closest we get to that are a handful of detached lead *bullae*, of uncertain origin. Nevertheless nine, arguably ten, texts are transmitted in pre-1100 manuscript copies, and six of these are contemporary (or very nearly contemporary) with their original beneficiaries (**29, 41, 47, ?†50, 58, 64**). The overwhelming majority of copies, however, exist in manuscripts of the twelfth century onwards. Besides these texts, reports of a further **eleven *deperdita* appear credible.** This leaves twenty-eight certain or probable forgeries, plus five unreliable reports. Most of these *spuria* can be securely dated to the twelfth century or later: interestingly, it is not clear that any Anglo-papal forgeries belong to the pre-1073 period.

Leaving aside the early, conversion-era privileges supplied by Bede, the evidence falls into five phases, which we can investigate in context in Part II: *c.* 680–*c.* 730 (Chapter 4); *c.* 770–*c.* 830 (Chapter 5); *c.* 960–*c.* 1000 (Chapter 6); 1049–73 (Chapter 7); and later copies, compilations, and forgeries (Chapter 8's 'Coda'). Now we know the corpus, let's see what we can make of it.

---

[146] Above, n. 116. Note that two copies of †66 appear in manuscripts associated with Symeon of Durham: in Peterhouse 74, it is the earliest of a number of privileges added to a copy (s. xi^ex) of the *Collectio Lanfranci* in Symeon's hand, *c.* 1120/30 (Thomson, *Descriptive Catalogue*, pp. 39–41), while Durham, Cathedral Library, B. iv. 18 is contemporary to his time as cantor: Gullick, 'Hand', pp. 18–23; Symeon, *Libellus*, pp. xlii–xliv. In his work on Durham's origins (1104/15), Symeon made the dubious claim that Gregory VII (1073–85) had issued a privilege upon its refoundation: ibid., iv. 2, pp. 226–9 (doubts: Foster, 'Custodians', p. 61). Symeon's (later?) interest in †66 probably derived from its relevance to contemporary aspirations at Durham. But it is remarkable that Symeon's Durham should have made multiple copies of †66 but not their own purported privilege of Gregory VII, further suggesting that the latter never existed as a text in Symeon's day. A later twelfth-century forgery of Gregory VII for Durham (*PUU England*, ii. 2: JL 5265) probably reflects a much later attempt to give this story documentary backing.

PART II

PAPAL PRIVILEGES IN ENGLAND: FOUR STUDIES

4

Papal Privileges in the 'Age of Bede'
(*c.* 680–*c.* 730)

Sometime after April 689, Aldhelm, abbot of Malmesbury, prince of the Gewisse, and 'the first English man of letters', set out from Rome with at least one less companion than he had brought with him, and a great many more texts. His kinsman Peter, known before his baptism on 10 April as King Ceadwalla of the Saxons, lay entombed beneath the portico of San Pietro in Vaticano. A copy of the epitaph freshly inscribed there, recording his death ten days after his entry into the faith, would have almost certainly made its way into Britain via Aldhelm's own baggage train, just one item amid what would become an important collection of inscriptions and itineraries, transcribed by the abbot from holy sites around the city.[1] Aldhelm's renown as a scholar derived in part from this visit to Rome,[2] and what we know of this famous compilation represents probably just the tip of the iceberg of the writings and other sacred paraphernalia he gathered during his stay. At least one artefact with which he must have returned, however, was not a copy, but a bespoke original, dedicated to no other holy place but his own: a sealed, papyral scroll addressed to him from Pope Sergius I, declaring that his monasteries at Malmesbury and Frome lay henceforth under the perpetual 'jurisdiction' of Saint Peter's church alone.[3]

One problem: what did this actually mean in practice? Standard accounts of the 'Age of Bede' usually include some remark on the monastic privileges of this type acquired not just by Aldhelm's foundations, but the Wearmouth of Benedict Biscop (679/80) and Jarrow of his successor Ceolfrith (689/701); Bishop Wilfrid's Ripon and Hexham (679/80); Sts Peter and Paul, Canterbury under Abbot Hadrian (*c.* 679/80); Bishop Earconwald's foundations at Chertsey, and probably Barking (678/81); and the more obscure houses of Bermondsey and Woking under Hædda

---

[1] *HE*, v. 7, pp. 468–73; Sharpe, 'King Ceadwalla's Roman Epitaph'; Lapidge, 'Career'; Thacker, 'Rome'.
[2] Aldhelm, *Opera*, p. 494; Story, 'Aldhelm'.   [3] **20**.

England and the Papacy in the Early Middle Ages: Papal Privileges in European Perspective, c. 680–1073.
Benjamin Savill, Oxford University Press. © Benjamin Savill 2023. DOI: 10.1093/oso/9780198887058.003.0004

(708/15).[4] The image of these figures returning from their long pilgrimage with these tokens of the pope's special favour fits in nicely with our wider ideas of this heroic age of the Anglo-Saxon church. Moreover, when we zoom out and see similar papal documents in Merovingian and Lombard archives—at the Columbanian houses of Bobbio (628, 643), Luxeuil (640/2), Rebais (641/2), possibly Remiremont (640/2), and an unidentified convent dedicated to Sts Mary, Columba, and Agatha (640/2);[5] the monasteries of Saint-Maurice d'Agaune (654/7), Saint-Martin at Tours (672/6), Farfa (705), and San Pietro fuori le Mura at Benevento (715/41);[6] together with a further group of elite beneficiaries in the opening decade of the Carolingian era at Fulda (751), Saint-Denis (757), and Brescia (762)[7]—all this chimes well with our sense of an early Anglo-Saxon church firmly rooted in wider continental activity (Map 4.1). Nevertheless, while it is easy to understand the appeal of these privileges as an evocative 'piece of Rome' to place alongside one's books and relics—perhaps in a church of Romanising design such as at Wilfrid's Ripon or Hexham—the actual implications of such distant institutions operating under Roman 'jurisdiction' are much harder to grasp. We know that Farfa, about 30 miles northeast of the Lateran and a recipient of one such privilege, lay quite beyond the orbit of papal control.[8] Indeed, the popes hardly held full sway over all the churches of Rome. What, then, might one have gained, or at least hoped to gain, from being under Roman 'jurisdiction' over one thousand miles away, in Northumbrian Tyneside or on the banks of the Thames?

This chapter addresses that conundrum by looking at these oft-cited but rarely studied texts within their immediate late seventh- and early

---

[4] *12, *13, 14, 16, *17, *23, 26.

[5] *Bobbio*, i. 10 (JE 2017); Tosi, 'I monachi', pp. 20–3 (JE 2053); *Cartulary of Montier-en-Der*, ed. Bouchard, 167 (JE †2045); *Diplomata*, ed. Pardessus, ii. 302–4 (JE †2046, †2048); *MGH Formulae*, pp. 498–500 (JE †2044). On these texts and ongoing debates over their authenticity: Ewig, 'Bermerkungen'; Anton, 'Liber'; Morelle, 'Liberté', with notes to J³ †3305, ?3311, ?3312, †3313, ?3319. The dedication to Columba (the virgin martyr) suggests that the unidentified convent may have been in the region of Sens, but the popularity of this saint makes this far from certain.

[6] Anton, *Studien*, pp. 12–23 (JE †2084); *MGH Formulae*, pp. 496–8 (JE 2105); *Regesto di Farfa*, ed. Giorgio and Balzani, ii. 2 (JE 2144); *MGH Epp.* II, pp. 468–9 (JE 1926).

[7] Boniface, *Epistolae*, 89a (JE 2293); *PUU Saint-Denis*, 2a (JE 2331); *Codex diplomaticus Langobardiae*, ed. Lambertenghi, 26 (JE 2350). While these texts have been rehabilitated by more recent scholarship, a further group of privileges, attributed to Martin I for Neustrian beneficiaries (JE †2073–7) are more unusual and still often dismissed as spurious. To avoid over-complicating matters they will be largely passed over in this chapter; but for a more positive assessment see now Wood, 'Between Rome', pp. 315–17.

[8] Costambeys, *Power*.

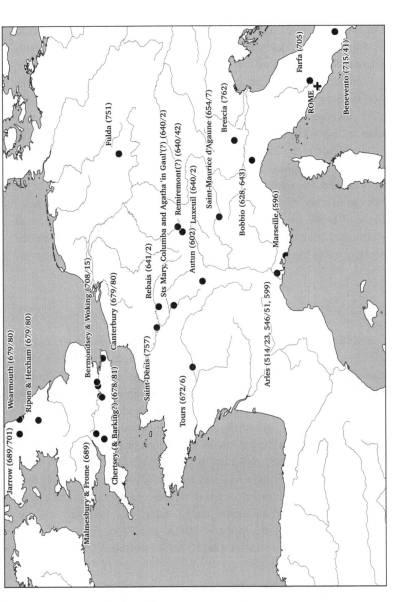

Map 4.1 Beneficiaries of papal privileges for monasteries, granting *iurisdicio* or comparable immunities, 514–762

eighth-century setting. First, it rejects the teleological notion that they functioned as early precursors to the legal privileges of monastic 'exemption' issued by high-medieval popes, arguing that we need if anything to begin by looking backwards rather than forwards, to the Gallo-Roman and Merovingian ecclesiastical culture from which the demand for these grants first arose. Next, it suggests that the dissimilarity between the Merovingian and Lombard religious and documentary landscapes and those of the still-crystallising Anglo-Saxon church means that we cannot just read our English privileges as simple transpositions of continental practice into an Insular setting: we must instead work comparatively to understand what was different about the English material and what it reveals. By doing so, we will see that our recipients may have adopted these documents in an attempt to work around a problem peculiar to lowland Britain around the turn of the eighth century: the effects of a sudden intensification of episcopal presence from the 670s–80s across an island full of newly founded monasteries, not all of which may have originally understood themselves as located 'within' the territory of a diocese, nor subject to any one bishop's personal authority.

I. The Continental Background

Let's first situate the contents of these privileges within their proper context. While this group of seventh- to mid-eighth-century documents vary in their details, they share between them enough core features that we may think of them as forming a distinct group. Generally speaking, their main dispositive clause declares that the monasteries to which they are addressed henceforth lie under the 'jurisdiction' (*iurisdicio, dicio*) or 'guardianship' (*tuitio*) of the Roman church alone, at the expense of the bishops or priests (*sacerdotes*) of any other. This is typically elaborated with a remark that, upon the abbot's death, the community should elect a successor amongst themselves, only then submitting him to a bishop for consecration; this arrangement might also be extended to the election of higher clergy within the monastery, for the purpose of performing masses, perhaps with the prohibition of external clergy entering the monastery also made explicit. This at least maps out an ideal type.[9]

---

[9] *LD* V 32: *sub iurisdictio, dicio*. In England: **14**: *sub iurisdicio, dicio* (incl. abbatial elections and uninvited entry ban); **16**: *sub tuicionem uidelicet ac regulam* (incl. abbatial elections, clerical elections, and uninvited entry ban); **20**: *sub iurisdictione ac tuitione* (incl. abbatial elections, clerical elections, and uninvited entry ban); **26**: *sub dicio* (incl. abbatial elections and clerical elections).

No one surviving privilege is exactly like the next, and some in their extant form come across as more nuanced or restrictive than others: notably, Pope Constantine's for Bermondsey and Woking gives the 'bishop of the place' (*episcopus loci*) more leeway, allowing him to still 'inquire into those things pertaining to the canons' while insisting that matters concerning property and its dispensation (*res, dispensatio*) remain the sole concern of the abbot and leading monks. But what is perhaps most notable about this group of texts as a whole (at least once we boil them down to their core, most reliably authentic components) is how much they *don't* say. Their clauses are few, and their grand claims about the imposition of papal 'jurisdiction' add nothing about the mechanisms of this arrangement, its enforcement, or what it means for the future relationship between the beneficiary monastery and the Roman see. By themselves, the texts reveal little.

Where the words of popes fail, however, the historians move in. In trying to fill in the gaps left by the brevity and imprecision of these privileges, over the past century scholars have tended to look to the future in order to ascertain what these documents 'really' meant. This literature is huge, and only a summary is needed here. One influential reading is that these documents represent the earliest examples of the high-medieval legal category of 'papal exemption', whereby select, privileged monasteries would be removed from regional ecclesiastical structures and placed directly under the authority of the pope. This arguably became a clever political tactic on the part of popes from the time of Gregory VII (1073–85) and Urban II (1088–99) onwards, providing a means by which they might have aggregated power away from the localities to the benefit of themselves in Rome. By projecting this much later legal category back into the golden age of seventh-century monasticism, an argument can therefore be made for that same, centralised (and centralising) papal policy as one with roots in a distant past: what we are seeing here, therefore, is essentially its more poorly documented, but more or less similar in principle, late antique/early medieval incarnation.[10] This of course simplifies an often complicated debate, and it is worth noting contrary positions. One alternative view is that, however generously we read the meagre set of clauses in these documents, they still fall well short of meeting the robust legal criteria needed for

---

[10] See above all Lemarignier, 'L'exemption' and Lemarignier, *Étude*; for full bibliography see Rennie, *Freedom*. On 'exemption' in later canon law: Fogliasso, 'Exemption', and Helmholz, *Spirit*, pp. 311–18. The term 'exemption' is used generally in the influential Anton, *Studien*, which may partly account for its continued vogue.

high-medieval 'exemption' privileges. Instead, some have recast them as very early instances of apostolic 'protection' privileges—another, slightly less impressive, if still prestigious, later legal category, whereby popes pledged to go out of their way to safeguard an institution against overbearing local powers.[11] Another school has rejected altogether reading the term *iurisdicio/dicio* as 'jurisdiction' in our modern (and both classical and later medieval) sense, noting that, within the sixth-to-twelfth-century papal documentary corpus at large, this word often denoted property rights. According to this interpretation, these privileges did not so much assert that Bobbio, Barking, and so forth were now under papal authority, but instead commended them into the Lateran's massive property portfolio.[12]

Whether one wishes to call these early manifestations of apostolic 'exemption', 'protection', or even 'commendation' (recent scholarship appears to have settled on a blur between the first two),[13] there remain serious problems with reading these documents according to these later classifications. It would be better if we dropped all three for good when studying this material. Firstly, it can almost go without saying that forcing our early medieval evidence into these categories is teleological. Whatever argument one might make for resemblances, even influences, between these seventh-century texts and their twelfth-century counterparts, approaching the former as merely a source for understanding the 'origins' of the latter is at best only useful for historians of high-medieval canon law or the later papacy, and doesn't tell us much about how contemporaries might have understood things. In taking such an approach, we run the risk of overlooking potentially revealing idiosyncrasies proper to this period, disregarding them on account of their perceived lack of importance for the twelfth-century-facing master-narrative. Second, hyper-legalist debates about the precise meaning of certain clauses, the implications of others being missing, or the correct definition of words such as *iurisdicio/dicio* are anachronistic: again, more appropriate to the world of high- and later medieval canon law than anything we see from these decades. That would be true if these texts survived intact; the fact that all of them have come down to us through imperfect (mistranscribed, interpolated) later copies makes laying too great a weight on any single clause or term all the more problematic. In any case,

[11] Appelt, 'Anfänge'; Schwarz, 'Jurisdicio'; and again for bibliography Rennie, *Freedom*. 'Protection' in later canon law: Dumas, 'Protection apostolique'.

[12] Rathsack, *Fuldaer Fälslschungen*, i, pp. 8–106.

[13] e.g. Rosenwein, *Negotiating*, pp. 106–9; Rennie, *Freedom*, pp. 69–87.

in a world without centralised canon-law norms and expectations, readers' interpretations of texts must have varied widely, perhaps more than in any other period. The above-cited argument that, in these years, *iurisdicio* was typically understood by papal scribes as indicating proprietorial control actually helps us very little, since the papal chancery in Rome was of course the one place where these privileges were *not* being implemented. *Iurisdicio* could have fluctuated in meaning everywhere—that may have even been part of its appeal. That connects to the final problem: that most studies of these privileges have taken a Rome-centred view, ruminating over what this sudden wave of concessions of *iurisdicio* meant for papal 'policy'. It is quite possible that at certain times popes were especially willing to make these grants, as we know probably also happened with papal gifts of relics.[14] But just as Roman 'relic policy' ultimately responded to desires, practices, and expectations generated further afield, so too were privileges granted in response to external petitions, and it is therefore to the worlds of those petitioners that we need to look. To assume a consistent and well-communicated policy emanating outwards from the Lateran is again ana-chronistic and forward-looking.

The unusually detailed *narratio* which opens Adeodatus II's privilege for Saint-Martin de Tours reveals, on the contrary, that as late as 672/6 some popes had little sense that, beyond Rome, select monasteries were enjoying the honour of operating without episcopal oversight. The idea might have even taken them aback:

When Aegiricus, the religious priest and abbot of the monastery of Saint Martin, where his venerable body lies, came (to Rome) out of a desire to see the apostolic shrines and atria, he presented himself before us, and brought forward a letter of commendation from our brother Chrodebert, bishop of the church of Tours, and he entreated with a humble voice whether, with apostolic authority, we might grant him a supporting (*subnixum*) privilege for the strengthening (*munitio*) of that venerable monastery... Yet we hesitated (*ambigimus*) on this point for a little while, since it is neither the custom nor tradition of our holy church to support the withdrawal (*secrenere*) of religious places from the provision of episcopal rule. But when we learned that his religiosity had brought forth a copy of the grant

---

[14] See Wood, 'Between Rome', p. 314, with Lin, 'Merovingian Kingdoms', pp. 242–3, for the possibility that promises of support in seventh-century Christological disputes may have helped sway the hands of individual popes.

made in writing by our aforesaid brother Chrodebert, bishop of Tours, for this monastic freedom, that is, this free licence of governance (*libera dispensandi licentia*), and we saw on this charter the subscriptions, added beneath, of other bishops from across Gaul giving their assent, we reckoned that there could be no way that the harmonious agreement of so many bishops might be contrary to reason and canonical rule. And therefore we have granted that what our brothers saw fit to confer...is to be confirmed once again.[15]

However stylised, Adeodatus' account of this petition brings to light three points of fundamental importance which the other, more straight-to-the-point papal *narrationes* of this period obscure: that monastic 'withdrawal' from regional episcopal oversight was strictly not considered either Roman practice or policy; that this was, rather, something emanating from Gaul, and not as a radical breakaway movement, but with the support, at least in select instances, of its church hierarchy; and that the papal privilege, once granted, did not function as a direct intervention, transforming local circumstances, but rather as an external support (*subnixum*) to a pre-existing situation, and moreover to a pre-existing set of documents, which had already ratified the arrangement.

Those pre-existing activities are not hard to find. That the act of granting 'immunities' conferring varying degrees of independence upon special, high-status monastic sites had played an important role in the royal and ecclesiastical politics of Merovingian Gaul (and, to a lesser degree, Lombard Italy) is well-established in the scholarly literature.[16] The crucial point here is that this movement appears to have been at first peculiar to southeast Gaul, disseminating from there outwards; and that there were at least inconsistent efforts to involve individual bishops of Rome as distant, third-party guarantors to these arrangements from as early as the sixth century. Their role, however, was as far as we can tell responsive: that is, simply adding a further layer of apostolic blessing to gears already set in motion by kings, queens, and bishops within the regions concerned.

---

[15] *MGH Formulae*, p. 497: the privilege opens with an apt *arenga*, reflecting on the responsibility of the bishops of Rome to preserve the traditions of the church fathers and their own predecessors, while at the same time respecting the decisions made by bishops of the wider church. The earliest extant text is missing some proper nouns, but can be reconstructed via its citation in an eighth-century episcopal charter (ibid., pp. 501–3) and later copies made at Tours (*Diplomata*, ed. Pardessus, ii. 374).

[16] See above all Rosenwein, *Negotiating*.

A quick chronological survey can establish the basic picture. Our earliest evidence of an attempt to limit the power of a bishop over a named monastery comes from a dispute settlement at Arles in favour of the monks at Lèrins (449/69), roughly contemporary with (and perhaps triggered by) the Council of Chalcedon's rulings (451) on the necessary subjection of monasteries to bishops.[17] Lèrins served as a finishing school for many Gallo-Roman prelates, and it is again from Arles, under the Lèrins-trained Bishop Caesarius, that we see the first recorded attempt to call upon papal aid in a local struggle to limit episcopal involvement in the monastic life, when Caesarius sought Pope Hormisdas' support (514/23) for his plans to keep his monastery for women out of the hands of his successors.[18] Caesarius had probably not turned to Rome because of any conviction about the see's special competence in such matters. His own extremely fragile position at Arles (the city tried to depose him on multiple occasions) was at that moment propped up by the Ostrogothic court ruling Italy and Provence, which had arranged to keep him in office through his extraordinary status as a 'papal vicar'.[19] Rome may have been one of the few places where he could have sought help at all. His decision, however, proved influential. Following the absorption of Arles into the Merovingian kingdoms, his *Rule for Virgins* travelled north to Queen Radegund's monastery at Poitiers (*c.* 560/70). Its significance there for an emerging style of Frankish royal monasticism which treated certain elite institutions as hands-off, independent sacred spaces is well-known.[20] What has tended to go overlooked, however, is that this *Rule* cited Hormisdas' support, and may have been transmitted with the text of his privilege, thus advertising the idea of the papacy as a distant guarantor for the integrity of the monastic life at this key moment in the development of Merovingian monasticism.[21] Back in Provence, Childebert I (d. 558) had meanwhile founded his own royal monastery in Arles, and his arrangements for the integrity of its property and free abbatial elections had been assured by Bishop Aurelian, who like his predecessor also requested a supporting guarantee from Pope Vigilius (546/51). That document no longer survives. Yet we do have the text of its renewal by Gregory I (599: probably mediated by Queen Brunhild, d. 613) whose responsiveness to a wave of such arrangements in the

---

[17] *Concilia*, ed. Munier, pp. 131–4; *Concilium*, ed. Schwartz, iii, pp. 437–8, 532–3.
[18] Caesarius, *Opera*, ii, pp. 125–7 (JK 864).   [19] Klingshirn, *Caesarius*.
[20] Gregory of Tours, *Libri*, ix. 40, 42, pp. 464–5, 470–4; Rosenwein, *Negotiating*, pp. 52–8; Rosenwein, 'Inaccessible Cloisters'.
[21] Caesarius, *Opera*, ii, p. 119; Munich, Bayerische Staatsbibliothek, Clm 28118, ff. 192–2v.

Provençal-Burgundian region is evident in his reply to a similar request for Saint-Cassien in Marseille, and for a series of comparable privileges for Autun, petitioned by Brunhild.[22] Significantly, Gregory's huge extant *Register* only shows him sending privileges of this type to this area.[23] That these impulses were regionally generated and did not in any case require papal involvement is observable at the Alpine fringes of the Burgundian polity, where the communities of the Juran Fathers and Saint-Maurice d'Agaune had long boasted quasi-independent status. The latter provided the model for the royal monastery of Saint-Marcel-lès-Chalon, whose exalted position as a holy space free of external interference was guaranteed by king and episcopate in 585. It likewise proved influential for an emerging model of Merovingian monasticism, in this instance entirely without reference to Rome.[24]

The seventh century saw these fits and starts erupt into what looks like a full-blown political culture of kings, aristocrats, and bishops removing high-status holy places from external oversight, together with the emergence of a systematic documentary culture to reinforce and advertise it. The royal (perhaps also Brunhildian) foundation at Luxeuil (593?), whose strict rules banning uninvited entry apparently extended even to kings, queens, and royal agents, had a huge influence over the subsequent generation of monastic foundations and renovations.[25] Following the unification of the Neustrian and Burgundian kingdoms in 626, a wave of diplomas bestowing royal and/or episcopal 'immunity' (explicit, self-imposed limitations at favoured monasteries) were acquired before the end of the century at Rebais, Saint-Denis, Sens, Sithiu, Corbie, Soissons, Montier-en-Der, Saint-Calais, Saint-Marie-des-Fossés, Saint-Marie de Blois, Saint-Germain-des-Prés,

---

[22] *Reg.*, vii. 12, ix. 217, xiii. 9–11 (JK *926, JE 1457, 1745, 1875–7).

[23] Attempts to mediate between conflicting Italian bishops and monasteries appear elsewhere among Gregory's letters, but in their contemporary setting they do not look like privileges per se: *Reg.*, i. 12, v. 47, 49, vi. 40, viii. 17 (JE 1079, 1362–3, 1486, 1504).

[24] *Fourth Book of the Chronicle of Fredegar*, 1, p. 4; *Concilia*, ed. de Clercq, pp. 234–6; Rosenwein, 'One Site'; Diem, 'Who'.

[25] For the importance of the local Burgundian context and monastic culture at this foundation given to Columbanus, see Wood, 'Prelude'; Wood, 'Jonas'; Wood, 'Irish'; Morelle, 'Liberté', p. 241. Entry ban: Jonas, *Vita Columbani*, i. 19–20, pp. 187–98, whose cartoonishly negative portrayal of Brunhild (written about 50 years later) doubtlessly resulted from her posthumous *damnatio memoriae*: O'Hara, *Jonas*; Wood, 'Jonas', p. 110. Note that Columbanus' own *Rule* ascribes no importance to the exclusion of the laity from monastic sites: O'Hara and Wood, 'Introduction', p. 14, n. 50, again suggesting there was little essentially 'Irish' or 'Columbanian' about the practices associated with Luxeuil and Bobbio; his writings do, however, show Caesarian influences: Stancliffe, 'Columbanus' Monasticism'; Wood, 'Columbanus'.

Saint-Martin de Tours and beyond,[26] with this influence also stretching into parts of Lombard Italy.[27] These diplomas often cited Lèrins, Saint-Maurice, Saint-Marcel, and Luxeuil as their models.[28] Why this peculiar movement— which would lose momentum in the eighth century, and become transformed into something rather different in the Carolingian age—emerged when it did and with what purposes has found various explanations: the sacral prestige accrued by rulers and bishops in banning even themselves from untouchable, 'taboo' holy sites;[29] the favours they might expect from the monks in return;[30] the need to relax economic burdens at large monasteries, in order to meet increasingly costly liturgical expenses;[31] the opportunity of limiting external influence as a way of breaking up rival networks of aristocratic power;[32] the ambiguities involved in many of these sites being non-urban and therefore more difficult to reconcile with conventional ecclesiastical structures.[33] As time passed, perhaps most important for those granting these 'immunities' was simply being seen to conform with accepted political and religious practice. If, in Adeodatus' words, it was 'neither the custom nor tradition' of the Roman church 'to support the withdrawal of religious places from the provision of episcopal rule', then just such a 'custom and tradition' had emerged in Gaul and parts of Italy by his time. As they sometimes spelled out in their diplomas, grantors of 'immunities' acted in order to advertise their role as legitimately following in their predecessors' footsteps. Although poor rates of survival mean that we can only occasionally observe the two acting in unison, it appears that royal diplomas granting monasteries worldly 'immunity' (freedoms from secular burdens, prohibitions of entry) were ideally supposed to work complementarily with those granted by bishops (bans on uninvited priestly visitations or usurpations of property, free abbatial elections).[34] One can see the importance of these two interlocking public diplomas to Merovingian political culture by the mid-seventh century (as well as their increasing standardisation) in the *Formulary of Marculf*, the

---

[26] Ewig, 'Beobachtungen'; Ewig, 'Privileg'; Rosenwein, *Negotiating*, pp. 66–96; Halfond, *Archaeology*, pp. 43–4; Morelle, 'Liberté'.

[27] See e.g. (685–754): *Codice diplomatico longobardo*, ed. Schiaparelli et al., i. 7, 13, 18, 30, 35, 50, 83, 96, 115; iv. 10, 12, 17, 18, 20, 23, 24.

[28] Prinz, *Frühes Mönchtum*, pp. 85–7.   [29] Rosenwein, *Negotiating*, pp. 19–23.

[30] Boureau, 'Privilege', p. 625; for *do ut des* gift economies: Davies and Fouracre, eds., *Languages*.

[31] Fouracre, 'Eternal Light'.   [32] Ewig, 'Privileg'; Fox, *Power*, pp. 68–9, 199–200, 217.

[33] See e.g. the query raised by the bishops in Jonas, *Vita Columbani*, ii. 23, p. 282.

[34] Rosenwein, *Negotiating*, p. 67.

widely circulated notarial handbook of the Frankish polity, which features the templates for these documents as its grandiose opening items.[35]

The critical point is that, by the time our corpus of papal privileges bestowing full Roman 'jurisdiction' begins from the second quarter of the seventh century, these documents appear essentially responsive to this new development; in many cases they clearly functioned as third-party, (in Adeodatus' words) 'supporting' decrees, bolstering those already enacted by regional lay and/or clerical elites. We have already seen this at Tours, and the same can be detected in the privileges for Luxeuil, Rebais, Saint-Maurice, and Sts Mary, Columba, and Agatha, which openly follow royal initiatives (and, quite plausibly, now-lost episcopal as well as royal diplomas).[36] These papal privileges add little to what we already see in *Marculf*-style 'immunities', save the quirk in their formulation which reimagines their independent status as somehow a manifestation of Roman *dicio/iurisdicio*.[37] Honorius' privilege for Bobbio (628), often referred to in the literature as 'the first papal exemption', appears at first glance a more original intervention. Yet Jonas of Susa's eyewitness account of its acquisition indicates that it too was petitioned with full royal (if not unanimous episcopal) support. It seems likely that it simply put into writing what was already practised at Bobbio, following the original arrangements of its mother-house at Luxeuil, thus taking us back again to the world of Brunhild (Jonas also reveals that the lead petitioner, Abbot Bertulf, was a Frank and Luxeuil graduate).[38] An argument has even been made for the beneficiary-composition of parts of Honorius' privilege by a member of the Bobbio petitioning party, maybe Jonas himself.[39] The same has been said of Gregory I's less ambitious, but still diplomatically unusual, privileges for Brunhild's Autun monasteries in his *Register*, once thought spurious but now deemed the work

---

[35] *MGH Formulae*, pp. 39–43. On *Marculf*: Rio, *Legal Practice*, pp. 81–101.

[36] In the case of Rebais just such an episcopal charter (636) does survive: *Diplomata*, ed. Pardessus, ii. 275.

[37] The privileges assert that they are following the initiative of Clovis II (639–57).

[38] Jonas, *Vita Columbani*, ii. 23, pp. 280–4; Morelle, 'Liberté'. Note that Pope Theodore's follow-up privilege of 643 states that it follows the petition of King Rothari (636–52). We arguably see something akin to the Merovingian pattern later elsewhere in Lombard Italy: royal and episcopal backing is indicated in the privilege for S. Salvatore, Brescia (762), while that for Farfa had the support of the duke of Spoleto (705). Costambeys, *Power*, pp. 2–4, suggests that Farfa may have been a conduit for Frankish 'immunity'-culture through its Provençal founder-abbot (and papal privilege recipient) Thomas of Maurienne.

[39] Rathsack, *Fuldaer Fälschungen*, ii, pp. 560–1. Jonas' role as Bobbio's archivist strengthens this hypothesis: Jonas, *Vita Columbani*, ii. 9, pp. 247–8; O'Hara, *Jonas*, pp. 103–4, 123.

of Merovingian chancery scribes.[40] A similar hypothesis would explain why the formulations of some of the papal privileges for Francia from the 640s–50s also look peculiar as Roman compositions—something long held against them in arguments about their authenticity—but fit more comfortably into what we know of Merovingian chancery practice. By *c.* 680, when the first version of the *Liber diurnus* came together, the basic templates of grants of papal *iurisdicio* had taken shape as formulae *LD* 32 and 77 (the latter possibly based on the Bobbio privilege of 628). They took their cue, however, from practices already underway well outside Rome; and their original texts may have even been partly drawn up by petitioners coming from that world.[41]

To sum up: the privileges granting papal 'jurisdiction' and its associated freedoms to monasteries in the Merovingian kingdoms and, later, parts of Lombard Italy, did not represent any novel intervention on the part of the Roman church into these institutions or surrounding polities, still less an attempt to pull them into the sphere of papal control, or its property portfolio. Instead, they responded to initiatives taken by local rulers and/ or bishops, and they concerned monasteries which were *already* beneficiaries of a regionalised culture of monastic 'immunity', which saw select, elite holy spaces withdrawn from conventional structures of authority, and bestowed with 'hands-off' freedoms from external interference. These papal privileges appear to have typically confirmed and supported these *pre-existing* arrangements, and moreover confirmed and supported the *pre-existing* diplomas enacting them. In some cases they used them as their textual models. These huge, spectacular papyri lent their prestigious apostolic blessing to those local arrangements, rhetorically framing this as a gift of papal 'jurisdiction' upon the beneficiaries concerned. We have no evidence of how that might have actually been enforced, but presumably the documents drew their continued validity from the regional guarantees to which they were now tied: as long as rulers and/or bishops continued to fulfil their own commitments to leaving certain monasteries alone, then by extension these houses' honorary status as operating under papal 'jurisdiction' remained in effect. Altogether, the evidence fits well into the categories we explored in Chapter 2 as important for the effective functioning of early medieval papal documents. These privileges would have met regional 'horizons of expectation' by corresponding to existing political and religious practice. They especially did so by resembling and re-confirming written

---

[40] *MGH Epp.* II, p. 378, n. 6; Anton, *Studien*, pp. 52–4; Markus, *Gregory*, p. 72, n. 26.
[41] Above, Chapter 2, pp. 28–31.

decrees already in effect within the local 'documentary landscape'. And this process was itself aided by the likelihood that the privileges mimicked, even in some cases reproduced, regional texts and legal formulae through 'recipient influence' on their composition.[42]

II. Exotic Imports? The View from England

The task now is to inquire as to whether this same idea of papal 'jurisdiction' as a prestigious confirmation of pre-existing practices of Frankish-style, selective 'immunity' of holy sites also applied in England, c. 680–c. 715. We can start by asking how far the reception of papal privileges in England might have been affected by the categories set out immediately above. Then we can turn to what evidence we have, if any, of their effective implementation in the narrative sources, and the significance attributed to them there.

Firstly, although we should exercise caution when arguing from silence, it must be said that there is no evidence at all that these privileges aligned with existing Anglo-Saxon 'horizons of expectation' about a recognised political culture of kings and bishops removing select holy sites from external interference. Whereas textual evidence for grants of monastic 'immunity' emerges in Gaul from the fifth century, and abounds in the seventh and earlier eighth, one finds no real equivalent in the early Anglo-Saxon church. A handful of texts bear only superficial resemblances. Two roughly contemporary decrees issued by King Wihtred of Kent (by law code, 695/6; and in more detail by charter, 699) and King Ine of the West Saxons (charter only, 704), announce freedom from public tribute for all the monasteries and churches under their rule, in exchange for obedience and spiritual support.[43] But the universal nature of these acts—promulgations of general law applying to *every* ecclesiastical institution—looks far removed from the selective privileging of a chosen few characteristic of continental 'immunity'. Moreover, these kingdom-wide decrees only concern royal tributes and burdens, and say nothing of entry bans or free elections. Much closer to Frankish episcopal diplomas of 'immunity' are Bishop Earconwald's charters for the monastic freedoms of his houses at Barking and Chertsey (678/93).[44] However, as

---

[42] Above, pp. 30, 51–4.

[43] *Christ Church*, 7 (= *St Augustine's*, 10) (S 20); *Gesetze*, ed. Liebermann, i, p. 12; *Malmesbury*, 10 (S 245); *Glastonbury*, 6 (S 246).

[44] BCS 87 (S 1246); *Chertsey*, 4 (S 1247).

outlined in Chapter 3, the best explanation for the markedly continental flavour of these documents is that they took Pope Agatho's privileges for Barking and Chertsey as their models. As such, these charters—notable for their otherwise unique formulation in the Anglo-Saxon corpus—do not provide evidence for any pre-existing culture of 'immunity' in early England, but rather the very opposite: in order to put his papal privileges into effect, Earconwald was compelled to reformulate them anew as these two local charters with local validity. What's more, since these quite unusual episcopal charters do not appear to have influenced subsequent documentary practice in England, one has reason to suspect that Earconwald's efforts may not have been particularly successful anyway. In sum, there is no evidence that the papal privileges acquired in England from *c.* 680 corresponded to already existing practices or expectations.

Next, as Earconwald's example has just demonstrated, we likewise find little evidence that papal privileges had any obvious compatibility with anything in the early Anglo-Saxon 'documentary landscape'. That we know of no English equivalents to diplomas of royal or episcopal 'immunity' with which these privileges might have been used alongside is already indicated above. The problem may, however, have run far deeper. The legal and documentary cultures of contemporary Gaul and Italy could trace back a direct line of continuity to those of the ancient world. Together with papal Rome, they benefited from a shared inheritance of diplomatic norms and practices. By contrast, Anglo-Saxon documentary culture appears to have only been in its infancy in the late seventh century, with no authentic charters datable to any earlier than the 670s.[45] This is not, of course, to conjure up a scene of baffled Anglo-Saxon illiterates scratching their heads over these privileges; besides all else, we know that occasional papal letters had made their way into England since the beginning of the century.[46] Nevertheless, in these formative decades it would be absurd to expect these highly formalised Roman documents to have been read in anything like the same way in Northumbria and Wessex as they might have been in, say, the contemporary Sabina or Provence. Essentially this is a point about intertextuality. Merovingian royal diplomas, episcopal charters, and papal privileges mirrored each other in form and function, and thereby reinforced each other's validity and meaning. Yet these decrees of

---

[45] When they were first used is disputed: Chaplais, 'Who'; Wormald, *Bede and the Conversion*, pp. 145–8; Kelly, 'Anglo-Saxon Lay Society', pp. 40–2; Snook, 'Who'.

[46] Above, Chapter 3, pp. 57–9, 66–7.

papal 'jurisdiction' may have stood out as far more exotic and extraordinary artefacts within the nascent Anglo-Saxon 'documentary landscape'.

That leads to the last point: that, in sharp contrast to some of their continental counterparts, one finds no indication that Anglo-Saxon petitioners had any substantial 'recipient influence' over this group of papal privileges. This is easier to hypothesise than prove, since the corrupt condition of the extant texts makes it difficult to speak securely about their original formulation. But with the possible, minor exception of the more subtle and nuanced privilege for Bermondsey and Woking, which dates somewhat later than the rest of the group, there is at least nothing to suggest that the acquired privileges went very far beyond the basic formulae ready at hand in the *Liber diurnus* by this date. Whereas many early petitioners coming to Rome from Gaul and Italy may have had their privileges tailor-made to suit their pre-existing local circumstances (in the process, as we saw with Adeodatus, even overriding some popes' own sense of propriety), from *c.* 680 their Anglo-Saxon counterparts probably picked up something far more 'ready-made', which they then had to implement back in their regional societies from scratch.

Overall, what little we know of the situation on-the-ground indicates that these privileges of papal 'jurisdiction' may have looked far more like exotic imports in England, *c.* 680, than they did in the European societies for which they had first been petitioned. There, they had corresponded much more organically to pre-existing conditions. As argued in Chapter 2, however, these privileges' exoticism and unfamiliarity in England did not necessarily preclude their effectiveness. Novelty and strangeness could have plausibly enhanced their 'wow-effect', rendering them more potent written instruments. Fortunately, we have some limited insight into the reception and use of these privileges, since those for Hexham, Ripon, and Wearmouth and Jarrow—while no longer extant themselves—appear several times in near-contemporary narrative accounts: Stephen's *Life of Wilfrid* (*c.* 713), Bede's *History of the Abbots* (716/17), and the anonymous *Life of Ceolfrith* (717). While in terms of their textual integrity these narrative sources prove far more reliable than our corrupted, much later cartulary copies of papal privileges, they bring with them their own methodological obstacles. They are tendentious, retrospective, selective, and allusive, although if we wish—as here—to learn about *perceptions of* and *reactions to* papal privileges, then we can nevertheless try to approach such impediments as objects of analysis in themselves. As we will see, all three narratives obscure more than they reveal about Anglo-Saxon practices of papal 'jurisdiction' or monastic 'immunity', and moreover suggest contemporary obstructions to these privileges' implementation. Nevertheless, the fact that the privileges receive repeat mention at all across the three narratives, however allusively, testifies to some continued recognition of their significance, at their beneficiary houses at least.

Let's start with Stephen, priest and perhaps cantor of Ripon. He composed his *Life* of Wilfrid, bishop of the Northumbrians (d. 710), only about three years after his subject's death, and more than three decades after Pope Agatho's grant of a papal privilege, jointly addressed to Ripon and its sister house of Hexham (679/80).[47] Stephen probably wrote from a position of anxiety and urgency, looking to secure the integrity of the Wilfridian communities and their landholdings after the passing of their long-controversial (twice deposed, and at least once excommunicated) bishop and abbot. Besides external difficulties, the Wilfridians may have also faced internal strife, following the possibly disputed succession of Acca as bishop-abbot of Hexham, and Tatberht as abbot of Ripon.[48] Stephen cites Agatho's privilege three times, asserting its continued validity, but reveals very little. He does not describe its original acquisition or the motives behind it, mentioning it only much later in his narrative of Wilfrid's career, as the bishop sought to recoup his confiscated properties. Nor does he reproduce the text, even though he is elsewhere keen to copy out papal documentation in full.[49] Stephen only tells us, vaguely, that the 'freedom' guaranteed by the privilege had been contravened when Ripon was converted into an episcopal see, against Wilfrid's wishes (temporarily, from *c.* 680); that the document concerned that house's abbot and 'community' (*familia*) together; and, several chapters later, that it covered both Hexham and Ripon in unison, as 'two monasteries...under one privilege' (*duo monasteria...sub uno priuilegio adscripta sunt*).[50] He says nothing about papal 'jurisdiction' in any way; nothing about free abbatial elections; and nothing about what Adeodatus had called 'the withdrawal of religious places from the provision of episcopal rule', nor their withdrawal from the interference of secular authorities or any named polities. It is evident that the documents faced obstruction, or were at least ignored, for most of Wilfrid's career.

---

[47] *12; VSW; Stancliffe, 'Dating'.   [48] Sowerby, 'Heirs'.
[49] VSW, 29–32 (*acta* of Lateran Synod of 679), 54 (letter of John VI, JE 2142), pp. 56–7, 116–21.
[50] VSW, 45, 47, 51, pp. 92–3, 96–7, 106–7.

But Stephen reveals little about what they were supposed to have achieved once recognised a few years before his hero's death.

These shortcomings in Stephen's presentation of this document probably resulted less from any defects within the privilege itself, than the likelihood that, by the time he wrote in *c.* 713, much of its content may have felt problematic. The claim made in standard papal 'jurisdiction' privileges, that no ecclesiastical authorities should hold power over a beneficiary monastery, might have looked awkward in light of Hexham's newly elevated status as an episcopal see in its own right from *c.* 680 (an arrangement with which—however much it had originally disturbed Wilfrid—Stephen's co-dedicatee Acca of Hexham must have been quite content; note that Stephen conspicuously passed over this detail when he complained that the very same thing had temporarily happened at Ripon). More importantly, a major function of Stephen's *Life* appears to have been its depiction of Wilfrid's personal appointment of Acca and Tatberht as his legitimate successors at Hexham and Ripon. In fact, a perceptive recent analysis has shown that this appointment possibly never took place.[51] Whatever the reality, Stephen's version of events contravened the terms a standard 'immunity' formula would have typically set out: that the community were to elect freely their head of house, *after* an incumbent's death. In light of this, the best way for us to understand Stephen's otherwise perplexing omission of the text of Agatho's privilege from his *Life* is to interpret this as a deliberate decision to suppress that document's uncomfortable finer details. Instead, Stephen selectively advertised the most important implications of the privilege from his own Riponian perspective, probably following the official narrative of his patrons Acca and Tatberht in *c.* 713. His three main assertions are that Agatho's pledge of 'freedom' meant above all that *Ripon* must not become an episcopal see; that the privilege outlived Wilfrid, applying to his *familia* at large; and, crucially, that Hexham and Ripon—a good 75 miles apart—were two monasteries joined together as one under its terms.

We learn more from the house histories of Wearmouth and Jarrow, composed about three to four years later. Bede's *History of the Abbots* and the anonymous *Life of Ceolfrith* provide some details about Benedict Biscop's privilege for Wearmouth, sought in person from Agatho (679/80), and Ceolfrith's for Jarrow, acquired from Sergius by his emissaries (689/701).[52] At face value, these privileges, as depicted in these narratives,

---

look more like an importation of Frankish-style 'immunity'. We are told that Agatho's privilege kept Wearmouth 'completely safe and free forever from every outside invasion' (*extricensa irruptione*),[53] while Sergius' made the community 'more secure from the invasion of unjust persons' (*ab improborum irruptione securiora*).[54] In contrast to Wilfrid's acquisitions, the two privileges apparently found royal and episcopal approval in Northumbria.[55] Moreover, we learn that the privileges also guaranteed, in conjunction with the Benedictine Rule, free abbatial elections from within the community. Those rulings were referred back to on two occasions: on the deathbed of Biscop, abbot of Wearmouth, in 689, after which Ceolfrith, already abbot of Jarrow, took control over both houses; and following Ceolfrith's retirement in 716, whereupon Hwætberht succeeded to this combined Wearmouth-Jarrow abbacy.[56] Both authors insist that Sergius' privilege replicated Agatho's for Wearmouth (*instar illius*).[57] Meanwhile, the anonymous biographer states quite forcefully that, once Ceolfrith had succeeded Biscop, Wearmouth and Jarrow became 'one monastery—positioned in two locations, but governed under one abbot, and protected under the same privilege' (*unum...monasterium, tametsi duobus in locis positum, uno semper abbati gubernatum, eodem priuilegii munimine tutatum*).[58] We must, however, take these writers' word for it, since (like Stephen) neither of the two in-house historians cared to copy out the texts of their otherwise much-vaunted privileges. Again, considering the enthusiasm they show elsewhere for quoting papal documents in full, this feels odd.[59]

Indeed, despite their seemingly more forthcoming approach, on closer inspection the strategy of these authors resembles Stephen's. They obscure the precise details of the Wearmouth and Jarrow privileges so as not to let them undermine the preferred version of events. Bede's claim that the king and his assembly gladly subscribed the privileges remains plausible, but the neatness of this image as an inversion of the scene in Stephen's *Life of Wilfrid*, where the bishop found his own papal documents 'despised' and rejected by the same group, arouses a hint of suspicion.[60] Regardless, neither of the Wearmouth-Jarrow authors speak of any pre-existing

---

[53] *HA*, 6, pp. 36–7.   [54] *VC*, 20, pp. 98–9.

[55] *HA*, 6, 15, pp. 36–7, 58–61; above, Chapter 2, pp. 47–9.

[56] *HA*, 11, 16, pp. 48–9, 62–3; *VC*, 16, pp. 94–5; cf. *Benedicti regula*, 64.

[57] *HA*, 15, pp. 58–9; *VC*, 20, pp. 98–9.   [58] *VC*, 16, pp. 94–5.

[59] *VC*, 39, pp. 119–21 (JE 2156); papal letters in Bede: above, Chapter 3, pp. 66–7; see also Goffart, *Narrators*, p. 278, n. 196.

[60] *VSW*, 34, pp. 70–1.

Merovingian-style culture of 'immunity' which these documents might have complemented. The remark about warding off the 'invasion' of 'unjust persons' suggests something quite different to continental 'immunity' and its noble sacrifices of royal and episcopal self-restraint. Most conspicuous is the speech put in the dying Biscop's mouth, when he urges the monks to follow Agatho's privilege and the Benedictine Rule by freely electing his successor as a community, and insists they shun anyone from his own kin. In fact, this runs entirely contrary to the events which followed, since Biscop anyway proceeded to appoint Ceolfrith of Jarrow as his successor at Wearmouth: in the process, not just overriding the Rule and the privilege, but choosing a kinsman after all.[61] As Ian Wood has shown, the anonymous biographer's assertion that Wearmouth and Jarrow were thenceforth united under one privilege as well as one abbot cannot give an accurate impression of Agatho's document (at that stage the only privilege acquired), since it predated Jarrow's foundation in 685.[62] At least as far into their narratives as their depiction of Biscop's death (689), the Wearmouth and Jarrow historians played loosely with the facts. Their reluctance to copy out their privileges is understandable.

To better understand the purpose of these two narratives and the significance their authors imputed to their houses' papal privileges, we need to turn to the election of Hwætberht as Ceolfrith's successor at both Wearmouth and Jarrow (Pentecost 716). Our two authors wrote in this election's immediate aftermath and had presumably participated in it. A recent study has convincingly identified Hwætberht as the leader of a scholarly 'reform party' at Wearmouth and Jarrow. Perhaps opposed to a faction more closely associated with Biscop's kin-group, the Baducings, this 'reform party' would have included Bede at the very least.[63] The composition of not one, but two distinct works documenting and legitimising the Pentecost election so shortly after it had taken place strongly suggests that it had not gone uncontested. Historians have long recognised that some of Ceolfrith's community may have feared the imposition of Baducing control following their abbot's departure. Presumably, this is what was meant by the 'invasion' of 'unjust persons'. But Baducing control over where? It is now generally accepted that Wearmouth and Jarrow originated as separate

---

[61] HA, 11, 16, pp. 46–51; VC, 16, pp. 94–7; Ceolfrith as a blood-relative: ibid., p. 95, n. 82.

[62] Wood, 'Foundation', pp. 84, 89–93; VC, p. 95, n. 80.

[63] O'Brien, 'Hwaetberht'. Tellingly, neither Bede nor the anonymous biographer provide Biscop's family name: for this we are reliant on VSW, 3, pp. 8–9.

institutions: the former Biscop's own, perhaps 'proprietary' monastery; the latter initially a royal foundation of King Ecgfrith (670–85). However, the point at which they formally united remains uncertain.[64] Normally this is thought to have happened upon Ceolfrith's dual succession in 689,[65] but contemporaries may have understood this as only a one-off arrangement. The real shift may have come two and a half decades later, upon his departure. The election of Hwætberht to both houses in 716 would in effect have snatched Wearmouth out of the Baducing inheritance by permanently aligning it to Jarrow on an institutional basis, rather than the ad hoc personal arrangement overseen by Ceolfrith (himself probably a Baducing). The grounds for this takeover may not have been strong, and any controversy justifiable. However, in the eyes of the Hwætberhtian party, there was a case for seeing the two houses as already combined by Sergius' privilege for Jarrow, and, at much more of a stretch, through the claim that even Agatho's earlier privilege had envisioned this arrangement. Bede hinted elsewhere that Hwætberht had taken personal responsibility for the acquisition of Sergius' privilege in Rome.[66] Perhaps this strategy was Hwætberht's own. The job of his two propagandists was therefore to obscure the fine-detail of the papal privileges while talking-up what his 'party' deemed their central purpose: the unshakeable union of Wearmouth and Jarrow, joined by a shared electoral regime which made no reference to the outside world.

All in all, it does not look as though we can ascribe quite the same meaning and function to these privileges of papal 'jurisdiction' in England as we can to their continental counterparts, nor the royal and episcopal 'immunities' the latter originally mimicked and supported, even if their texts may look very similar to us now. The same pre-existing conditions and expectations were not there. These were strange imports, which needed to be implemented from scratch. Meanwhile, what narrative sources we have indicate a combination of delayed implementation and selective interpretation, with an especial emphasis on the idea that these papal privileges offered the opportunity for a monastic *familia* divided between multiple locations to be kept together 'under one privilege'. The way forward, then, is not to assume simple commonalities between English and continental practice, but rather to approach the European-wide corpus comparatively, to see what was distinct about this cluster of Anglo-Saxon acquisitions.

---

[64] The key text is Wood, 'Foundation'.   [65] e.g. *VC*, p. 97, n. 96.
[66] *HA*, 18, pp. 66–7, linked to *23 by O'Brien, 'Hwaetberht', p. 318; possible connections between Hwætberht and Sergius: Thacker, 'Pope Sergius' Letter'.

What differences do we see, and what might they add to our understanding of the shape of the English church around the turn of the eighth century?

III. Episcopal Expansion, the 'Minster Boom', and Twinned Monasteries in England

Three things stand out as peculiar to privileges bestowing papal 'jurisdiction' upon monasteries in early Anglo-Saxon England.

What we might call 'twinning' is the first. We already saw above that St Peter's, Ripon shared its privilege with St Andrew's, Hexham, and that (at least according to its 716/17 commentators) the privilege for St Paul's, Jarrow secured its union with St Peter's, Wearmouth. Our Northumbrian narratives don't just hint at these arrangements: they underline them as central to the documents' purposes. Elsewhere a similar pattern emerges (Map 4.2). Aldhelm's privilege paired his more famous monastery of St Peter's, Malmesbury, with a now lesser-known foundation of St John the Baptist's, Frome. Hædda's privilege from Pope Constantine twinned his houses, both dedicated to Saint Peter, at Bermondsey and Woking. Earconwald's privilege for his men's monastery at St Peter's, Chertsey appears to have matched a lost privilege for his convent at St Mary's (?), Barking, run by his sister Æthelburh (or perhaps by this time her successor Hildelith). This pattern is striking in itself, but all the more so for its comparative uniqueness: elsewhere in the continental corpus, papal privileges do not reveal a twinning pattern.[67] This appears peculiarly English. But it also appears peculiarly *papal* when viewed *within* the English documentary corpus: native Anglo-Saxon charters do not 'twin' either. If we are looking for a specific purpose to these privileges, then here seems like the best place to start. One finds two early exceptions to this rule: Agatho's privileges for St Peter's, Wearmouth, and for St Peter and Paul's, Canterbury. Nevertheless, we have just seen that the Wearmouth privilege would at least become, within a generation, intentionally misremembered as having had a twinning effect. Moreover, as we will observe shortly, it may have actually been acquired at the same time, by the same petitioner, as the Canterbury privilege. We might therefore consider these two documents as early odd-ones-out, before the twinning pattern fully came into vogue.

---

[67] Gregory II or III's privilege for two monasteries outside Benevento (715/41) is the single instance.

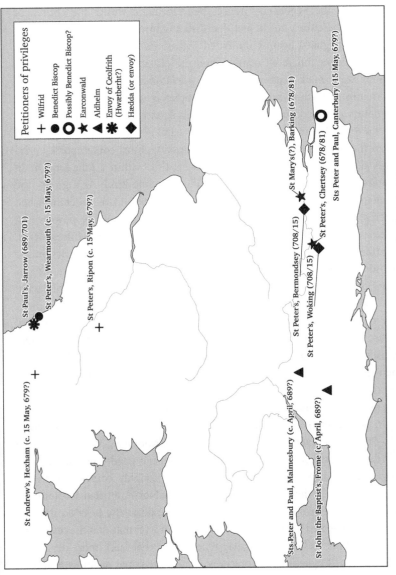

Map 4.2 Beneficiaries of papal privileges for monasteries in England, 678–715

Petitioners of privileges

+ Wilfrid
● Benedict Biscop
○ Possibly Benedict Biscop?
★ Earconwald
◀ Aldhelm
✱ Envoy of Ceolfrith (Hwætberht?)
◆ Haedda (or envoy)

St Andrew's, Hexham (c. 15 May, 679?)

St Paul's, Jarrow (689/701)
St Peter's, Wearmouth (c. 15 May, 679?)

St Peter's, Ripon (c. 15 May, 679?)

St Peter's, Bermondsey (708/15)
St Peter's, Woking (708/15)

St Mary's(?), Barking (678/81)

St Peter's, Chertsey (678/81)

Sts Peter and Paul, Canterbury (15 May, 679?)

Sts Peter and Paul, Malmesbury (c. April, 689?)

St John the Baptist's, Frome (c. April, 689?)

A second, more subtle characteristic is that in their extant form these English privileges make no reference to any specified secular or ecclesiastical authorities, nor to any kingdoms, regions, bishoprics, or territories. They declare that the beneficiary houses henceforth lie within the church of Rome's 'jurisdiction', but in fact that distant church is the only other place named; they guard against uninvited incursions by outsiders, but where those outsiders might be coming *from* is left unsaid. No local kings or bishops are named, neither as patrons, predators, nor otherwise. This lack of circumstantial information is not completely unique in the wider contemporary papal corpus, and it more or less squares with what we see in the *Liber diurnus* (although that is of course a set of generic templates, designed for further elaboration).[68] Yet generally speaking, most contemporary privileges do envision their beneficiaries as existing within a kingdom, or in relation to worldly or religious authorities of some kind. As a group, the Anglo-Saxon cluster is odd in its apparent rigidness to the unembellished *Liber diurnus* model, and its conspicuous silence about the powers and places surrounding its recipients—with the exception, that is, of Rome itself. Continental 'immunities' set out a process by which monasteries might 'withdraw' (*secrenere*) from regional power structures, but these Anglo-papal privileges did not acknowledge any such structures to begin with. This pattern also looks unusual when viewed against the English documentary corpus, since Anglo-Saxon royal diplomas publicised by their very nature kingly claims over named people and places. Privileges of papal 'jurisdiction' in England took a peculiar step in their failure to acknowledge their beneficiaries as having ever existed within an identifiable space or polity.

Thirdly, the time-frame of these documents is relatively narrow, and again particular to this region. With one exception all date within the period 678–701, maybe even as close as 679–89. The Bermondsey-Woking privilege postdates these a little (708/15), but even this can hardly belong to more than one political generation later; it anyway roughly coincides with the interest shown in these documents in the above Northumbrian accounts. As discussed, the Bermondsey-Woking privilege appears the (ever so slightly) more sophisticated composition of the group in its remark on the respective roles of abbots and bishops: it may reflect somewhat later, more developed reflections in England about precisely what these papal documents should

---

[68] Two exceptions are Bobbio's first privilege (628) and, much later, Fulda's (751): on the latter's lack of reference to external episcopal authorities, see Kéry, 'Klosterexemtion'.

and should not do. Nonetheless its basic formulation covers the same ground. This time-frame has no obvious correlation with what survives of the corpus of papal privileges elsewhere in Europe. It suggests that the acquisition of these documents corresponded to developments peculiar to lowland Britain, and that if we wish to understand their significance, then we need to turn to events taking place within the English church around those years.

My argument here is that the acquisition of this cluster of privileges represents the attempts of a select few Anglo-Saxon ecclesiastics to use these exotic Roman documents to negotiate their way around an immediate problem, peculiar to their own time and place. This was the clash between the 'boom' of monastic foundations beginning after *c.* 650, and the sudden amplification of episcopal presence and (probably) episcopal territoriality which followed the arrival of Theodore of Tarsus as archbishop of Canterbury (670–90). Most scholars now recognise that the 'minster boom'—the explosion of new foundations of rural monasteries by kings, queens, aristocrats, and clerics at this time—played perhaps *the* central role in determining the shape of English Christianity following the initial stages of conversion.[69] Early Anglo-Saxon bishops and bishoprics have, however, received far less attention. The last section of this chapter outlines a hypothesis that the 670s–80s saw a changing conception in the meaning of the bishop in much of lowland Britain. This involved a move away from a conversion-era model, where a small number of roaming bishops held a comparatively informal, interpersonal authority over the far-flung peoples and churches committed to them; and towards a comparatively more sharply defined phase, wherein a greater number of bishops in fixed sees (often, reappropriated monasteries) looked out over a flock conceived more along territorial than interpersonal lines, within an island-wide church divided by multiplied jurisdictional boundaries. When the 'minster boom' took off during the first, more fluid phase of the English episcopate, many monasteries, especially dispersed associations of houses, may not have automatically seen themselves as fixed within the territory of any one ecclesiastical polity. By the late seventh century, that might have come to look naïve. What I argue here is that the formulaic privileges bestowing papal 'jurisdiction', available from the Roman chancery of the 670s onwards, may have offered an opportunity for a select few monasteries to maintain

---

[69] Blair, *Church*, esp. pp. 73–108 (coining the term); see also Foot, *Monastic Life*.

their status quo and escape from that new, emerging territoriality. Hence these privileges' timing; hence their silence about any other regional authorities, places or spaces; and hence their insistence that monasteries distantly separated were in fact located together 'under one privilege' of Roman *iurisdicio* alone. This was not, therefore, about withdrawing from established structures, but rather an attempt to resist those which were newly emerging.

During the first decades of English Christianity, its few bishops appear to have often been associated with peoples rather than places or spaces: Bishop Agilbert of the West Saxons, Bishop Wilfrid of the Northumbrians, Bishop Felix of the East Angles, and so forth. This was not a rule, but a tendency is observable.[70] What these bishops actually got up to is barely documented, although we might suppose that they spent at least some of their time journeying around with the itinerant royal retinue, directing missionary work from there. 'Ethnic' bishoprics therefore corresponded to 'ethnic' polities, whose frontiers moved back and forth with the fortunes of war and succession, and anyway often overlapped/absorbed one another, as when the more powerful kings temporarily extended hegemony over multiple other peoples. This fluidity and ambiguity of jurisdiction could have become further complicated in these early years when bishops founded and consecrated churches and monasteries which later came under the sway of a different king or people, but with which they still maintained their earlier ties. Similarly, those whom bishops had locally baptised or ordained might later go on to operate in more distant regions, while still observing their older bonds of allegiance. 'Who knows how many bishops, priests and deacons he had ordained, and how many churches he had dedicated?' asked Stephen of Bishop Wilfrid's huge clerical *familia* and island-spanning 'realm of churches' (*regnum ecclesiarum*).[71] Wilfrid was exceptional, but we know

---

[70] The best contemporary witness is the *acta* of the Council of Hertford (672), reproduced in *HE*, iv. 5, pp. 348–55. Other references to early bishops over peoples: *HE*, iii. 22–3, pp. 282–3, 286–7 (East Saxons); *HE*, iii. 7, 25, 28, iv. 12; v. 18, v. 19, pp. 232–7, 298–9, 316–17, 368–9, 512–13, 522–3 (West Saxons/Gewisse); *HE*, iii. 20, pp. 276–7 (East Angles); *HE*, iii. 21, 24, iv. 3, 6, 12, pp. 280–1, 292–5, 336–7, 354–5, 368–9 (Mercians); *HE*, iv. 3, pp. 346–7 (*Lindisfari* and Middle Angles); *HE*, iii. 26, iv. 23, v. 19, 24, pp. 308–9, 406–7, 522–3, 562–3 (Northumbrians). References to early sees appear inconsistently, and in some cases suggest no fixed site (e.g. for the Mercians: *WBEASE*, p. 55). Note, however, that Canterbury and Rochester are normally named by see alone, the result of the unusually early division of the *Cantuarii* between two bishops; this was a model for what was later to apply more generally: *HE*, ii. 3, pp. 142–3. Roman sources always refer to English sees rather than peoples (i.e. London and York), in accordance with standard Mediterranean practice.

[71] *VSW*, 21, 66, pp. 42–5, 142–3.

of other prelates moving between kingdoms in this period, and his example was probably extreme rather than unique.

Comparison with parts of contemporary Gaul might help us to visualise this interpersonal model of episcopal power. Stimulating recent work on the continental medieval bishopric, led by Florian Mazel, has sketched out a process whereby the late antique conception of the episcopal diocese as a territorial entity disintegrated in the west in tandem with the break-up of the Roman state. As the Roman judicial and tax-collecting mechanisms which policed—and thereby performed and maintained—the administrative territory (*territorium*) surrounding the ancient city-state (*ciuitas*) collapsed in the fifth and sixth centuries, so too did the very possibility of this *territorium* as a homogeneous political space. Since Roman ecclesiastical structures mapped over political ones, this would have transformed in turn the concept of the 'diocese' (a term which fell into neglect for several centuries). What apparently emerged in its place was the episcopal *parrochia*: a predominantly interpersonal rather than territorial arrangement, whereby the bishop exerted influence beyond his city walls through an irregular network of relationships with the rural peoples or churches he and his successors had baptised, ordained, or consecrated.[72] Naturally, we cannot directly transpose this model onto the early English church, since the total implosion of Roman urban life and governmental structures in Britain well before the arrival of the missions from *c.* 600 ensured that there was no real *ciuitas*-rooted episcopacy to transition away from in the first place.[73] Mazel's hypothesis is, however, good to think with if we want to imagine how the early Anglo-Saxon episcopacy might have worked, even from day one: operating without clearly defined territorial dioceses, but instead through fluid *parrochiae* which were built up from associations and obligations between people, rather than imposed across objective space.

Things could, however, change. While fluidity and interpersonality probably remained the order of the day throughout this period, we have reason to suppose that English *parrochiae* nevertheless became comparatively more territorialised and spatially defined—as well as more intensively felt— following the arrival of the East Roman Archbishop Theodore. Critical here was Theodore's multiplication of bishops from *c.* 675/80 onwards. This took the number of recognised bishops on the island from the meagre

---

[72] Mazel, *L'évêque*; Mazel, ed., *L'espace*.
[73] Background: Blair, *Church*, pp. 10–34; Charles-Edwards, *Wales*, pp. 586–92.

six attending the Council of Hertford in 672,[74] up to a figure fluctuating over the following decades between sixteen and nineteen.[75] Shortly before his death in 735, Bede lamented that this had not still reached the target of twenty-four.[76] This threefold (threatened fourfold) increase had obvious consequences for the frequency and intensity of episcopal presence in the crudest terms, but it must have also affected how the *parrochia* became conceptualised. These new, smaller *parrochiae* were carved out from within the huge, 'peoples'-based bishoprics of the conversion period. In most cases they may no longer have correspond primarily to a named people or kingdom, but increasingly to a specified location which served as the fixed see of the new bishop. Thus, the single 'bishop of the Northumbrians' made way for the bishops of Hexham, York, Lindisfarne, and (temporarily) Ripon.[77] This meant multiple new boundaries, some of which surely sliced through older networks, allegiances, and *familiae*. But it also implied a more sharply territorial sense of what a *parrochia* involved, since episcopal frontiers no longer strictly corresponded to the fluctuating peoples under any one king's rule, but rather fell inside those polities, and therefore needed to correspond to a more concrete political geography. Monasteries (especially groups of monasteries) founded in more liminal spaces, or originally ambiguous in their political allegiances and orientation, may have felt increasingly pressured to see themselves as 'within' a single, more territorialised *parrochia*, run by a bishop in permanently closer proximity. Moreover, once it became clear in the wake of the 'minster boom' that the future of the almost totally rural Anglo-Saxon church lay with the monasteries, this new generation of bishops presumably became ever more preoccupied with exerting their influence over those same sites which their predecessors might have felt inclined to leave to their own devices. If ties between some monasteries and the local episcopate had not hitherto existed, that may have now begun to change, at the latter's initiative. To some degree

---

[74] *HE*, iv. 5, pp. 348–51.   [75] *WBEASE*, pp. 539–66.

[76] Bede, *Epistola*, 9, pp. 140–1.

[77] The plan was first proposed in canon 9 of Hertford 672, with further implications anticipated in canons 2, 3, 5, 6: *HE*, iv. 5, pp. 350–3. The East Angles' bishopric split between Dunwich and Elmham (?), *c.* 672/80; the Mercians' between Lichfield and temporarily Dorchester-on-Thames, *c.* 675 (later with a Middle Anglian see at Leicester), with further bishops added for the Hwicce (at Worcester?) and 'the people beyond the Severn' (at Hereford?), *c.* 680; the Northumbrians' between York, Hexham, Lindisfarne, temporarily Ripon, and Lincoln/Lindsey, 678/80, with further at Abercorn (temporarily, from *c.* 680), later Whithorn (before 731); the West Saxons' between Winchester and 'the west of the wood' (at Sherborne?), from *c.* 705: *HE*, iv. 5, 12, 23, 26, v. 18, 23, pp. 354–5, 370–1, 408–9, 428–9, 514–15, 558–61; *WBEASE*, pp. 539–66.

this would have involved appropriating monasteries as nodal points for the provision of pastoral care.[78] Yet it also meant tapping into their resources, as the monasteries increasingly became the chief hoards of the island's wealth (this could have felt all the more justified when, with episcopal numbers multiplying, many bishops may have deemed their share of the pie much diminished). In the absence of conventional urban centres, some high-status monasteries must have also held an attraction as sites to expropriate entirely, and convert into the necessary new sees for new bishops. This is precisely what happened within the space of a few years at Lichfield, Hexham, Ripon, Lindisfarne, Abercorn, and Selsey.

Our group of acquisitions of papal privileges bestowing papal 'jurisdiction' to pairs of monasteries, at the expense of acknowledging any other authority or territory, past or present, begins from the pontificate of Pope Agatho (678–81): that is, at just the moment this clash between the 'minster boom' and the transformation of the Anglo-Saxon episcopate could have arisen. It is difficult not to conjecture some link. If we now bear this context in mind and turn one-by-one to the English petitioners, we will see that a plausible reconstruction of their motives becomes possible after all.

Bishop Wilfrid may well have taken the first step. In 679–80 he had already made his way to Rome to press another, far more serious matter. There he was appealing against both his deposition as bishop of the Northumbrians in 678, and Theodore's carving-up of his super-*parrochia* and its reassignment to three, soon four other bishops.[79] The exact grounds for Wilfrid's deposition are obscure, but it had probably resulted from his resistance to the division of his *parrochia*, rather than being that division's cause (the fact that only three of the four new sees were initially filled suggests that one had originally been reserved for Wilfrid).[80] His appeal was addressed by the Lateran Synod of October 679. That concerned Wilfrid's episcopal career. But the future of his other role, as the founder and abbot of his two 'foremost monasteries' (*optima coenobia*) of Hexham and Ripon, together with their attached properties and communities, must have also preoccupied him. The most immediate problem was the seizure of both as sites of new episcopal sees, although that at Ripon only proved temporary. More concerning still would have been their future integrity as a

---

[78] Minsters and pastoral care: Blair, *Church*, pp. 68–72, 94, 160–6; Foot, 'By Water'; Foot, *Monastic Life*, pp. 283–336.

[79] *VSW*, 24–32, pp. 48–67; Cubitt, 'St Wilfrid', pp. 343–4.

[80] Roper, 'Wilfrid's Landholdings', pp. 74–5.

pair of institutions united under the authority of Wilfrid and his circle. Wilfrid had founded Hexham in 670/2 and refounded Ripon in 669/78, constructing both in corresponding Gallo-Roman architectural styles. The question of to whom they pertained would have hardly been asked, at least not while he still wielded his half-the-island-spanning super-jurisdiction as bishop of the Northumbrians.[81] Yet whether or not their founder's episcopal rank remained intact after his 679–80 appeal, the jurisdictional status of the two houses must have suddenly looked far more complicated against the transformation of the English episcopate at just this time. Whatever their shared history or aesthetic, the unity of two houses set 75 miles apart—split between the sub-kingdoms of Bernicia (Hexham) and Deira (Ripon), and divided by the *parrochia* boundaries of a new generation of bishops—cannot have now felt very secure to anyone. While pursuing his episcopal appeal in Rome, Wilfrid therefore had good reason to search for a separate solution to this abbatial matter as well. His unusually extensive familiarity with the Merovingian and Lombard polities may have meant that he already knew about Frankish-style 'immunities' and their papal confirmations.[82] Acquiring a formulaic document of the latter, straight from the *Liber diurnus*, presented an opportunity for him to negotiate his way cleverly out of this new predicament. By establishing Ripon and Hexham as 'two monasteries under one privilege', Wilfrid found a way by which they might be imagined as existing together within the helpfully distant—and helpfully vague—*iurisdicio* of the Roman church alone, with no other authority or territory acknowledged. Petitioning such a document might have involved an off-the-cuff gamble. But it would have offered at least one exit-plan for this pressing dilemma.

Stephen indicates that Wilfrid's acquisition did not receive immediate approval upon his return to Northumbria. Yet Theodore's insistence on annual, island-wide meetings of the English church provided a forum for its (at least informal) publicisation.[83] Those paying attention may have included Earconwald, bishop of the East Saxons (672/5–93). Before the arrival of Theodore and his own rise to episcopal status, Earconwald had participated in the 'minster boom' with his 'dual outstanding monasteries' (*duo praeclara monasteria*) at Chertsey and Barking (both *c.* 666?),

[81] *VSW*, 17, 22, pp. 34–7, 44–7; Cubitt, 'St Wilfrid', p. 343.
[82] By 679 Wilfrid had spent maybe over a decade of his career abroad: *VSW*, 3–7, 12–13, 24–5, pp. 8–15, 24–9, 50–7; Cubitt, 'St Wilfrid', pp. 342–4.
[83] *HE*, iv. 5, pp. 352–3.

founded about 30 miles apart, on the right and left banks of the Thames respectively.[84] The Thames Valley constituted a liminal space par excellence, with multiple, shifting political alliances and 'peoples' in all directions.[85] Its territorial ambiguities would have lent it a special appeal as a zone for monastic foundation. Although Barking lay on the margins of the kingdom of the East Saxons, since the death of their bishop Cedd in the plague of 664 their *parrochia* had received at best on-and-off canonical episcopal oversight.[86] It was almost certainly during that period that the house was strategically founded. Meanwhile, Chertsey's earliest charter proclaimed that the monastery had 'first been constructed under (*sub*)' Ecgberht, king of the distant people of Kent, but at the time of writing (672/5) recognised the (similarly distant, but in the other direction) kingship of the Mercians.[87] All this probably gave Earconwald's two Thameside monasteries significant room for manoeuvre, with closer links to one another than to any defined *parrochia*. Under Theodore, however, the situation at both houses changed. His deposition around 675 of Wynfrith, bishop of the Mercians, may have made way for the division of his sprawling ethno-bishopric into two smaller *parrochiae*, based between sees at Lichfield and Dorchester-on-Thames.[88] The latter would have brought episcopal presence far more tightly to bear upon downriver Chertsey. Meanwhile, Theodore consecrated Earconwald himself as bishop of the East Saxons at London, just eight miles along the riverbank from Barking. If Earconwald's elevation to the East Saxon see raised few problems for his relationship with that monastery, it presumably complicated his operations at Mercia-facing Chertsey, especially following Theodore's recent decrees against bishops 'invading' each other's wards.[89] The future integrity of his twin houses could not, moreover, be guaranteed following his death and replacement at London. Although we cannot be certain that Agatho's privileges for Earconwald's 'dual outstanding monasteries' of Barking-Chertsey postdated that for Wilfrid's 'foremost monasteries' of Ripon-Hexham, the similarity between the two arrangements is interesting. It is sorely tempting to see Earconwald's petition to Agatho for

---

[84] *HE*, iv. 6, pp. 354–7; Wormald, 'Earconwald'.

[85] Blair, 'Frithuwold's Kingdom'; Blair, 'Minsters'; Blair, *Church*, pp. 88–9.

[86] The bishopric was canonically vacant, 664–*c.* 675, save the uncertain episcopacy of Wine (*c.* 666?–before 672), who had been deposed as third bishop of the West Saxons, and thereafter held London simoniacally, having paid King Wulfhere of the Mercians for the *sedes*, apparently at that point in his gift: *HE*, iii. 7, pp. 234–5; *WBEASE*, p. 545.

[87] *Chertsey*, 1 (S 1165).   [88] *HE*, iv. 6, 23, pp. 354–5, 408–9; *WBEASE*, pp. 556–7.

[89] *HE*, iv. 5–6, pp. 350–1, 354–5; *WBEASE*, p. 545.

his blessing of exclusive Roman 'jurisdiction' over the two houses as an attempt to pursue a distinctly Wilfridian solution to his new predicament.

A generation later, Earconwald may have influenced his neighbours to try the same. Chertsey's seventh-century grounds bordered Hædda's monastery of Woking;[90] the latter's twin house of Bermondsey lay another 30 miles east along the south bank of the Thames, facing London. Together, their situation bears close comparison to that of Chertsey-Barking. Unlike the other abbots studied here, Hædda cuts an obscure figure. The original dates of his foundations are unknown, although he himself has been cautiously identified with Hædda, Mercian bishop of Lichfield (690–716/27).[91] The two houses were plausibly established along this liminal Thameside zone during the same mid-to-late seventh-century juncture as Earconwald's monasteries, when the see of London lay partly derelict, and the Chertsey-Woking area came under distant Mercian hegemony. Again, under Theodore that picture became more complicated; and it would complicate further still by the time of Hædda's petition to Pope Constantine (708/15), when Mercian power over the region south of the Thames had made way for that of the West Saxons, with the area incorporated into the *parrochia* of the bishop of Winchester.[92] Bermondsey and Woking therefore consisted of a pair of monasteries dedicated to St Peter at two disparate sites, possibly run by and belonging to a Mercian bishop based at distant Lichfield, and now split between the *parrochia* of West Saxon Winchester and the reach of a restored see of London. Seeking a document issued far beyond the Thames, conveniently pairing the two together under the shared jurisdiction of the Roman pontiff—and nowhere and no one else—might have had much to recommend it.

The Wilfridian 'two-monasteries-under-one-privilege' model probably also inspired Aldhelm. We should expect that he knew of Earconwald's and Wilfrid's acquisitions. Aldhelm wrote his famous treatise *On Virginity* (*c.* 675/86) for Barking, whose community included among its most prominent members his own sister, at just around the time it would have received Agatho's privilege. His extant correspondence meanwhile indicates his partisanship for the beleaguered Wilfridian *familia*.[93] We have good reason to believe that his journey to Rome with Ceadwalla in 689, with which this chapter began, had been orchestrated by no less than Wilfrid, then the dying

---

[90] *Chertsey*, pp. 53–8.   [91] Keynes, *Councils*, pp. 42–3; *Peterborough*, pp. 74–5.
[92] *Chertsey*, pp. 8–9.
[93] Aldhelm, *Opera*, pp. 228–9, 500–2; Lapidge, 'Career', pp. 17–21.

king's chief counsellor.[94] That trip also saw Aldhelm acquiring from Sergius his privilege for Malmesbury and Frome, two monasteries again about 30 miles apart. In this instance, no *parrochia* split was yet underway. Bishop Hæddi of the West Saxons would continue to oversee his mega-bishopric (in its latter years stretching out to incorporate also the South Saxons and the Isle of Wight) until his death in *c.* 705, when it at last split into two *parrochiae* under Daniel at Winchester and Aldhelm himself at Sherborne.[95] Still, given developments elsewhere in the 670s–80s, an abbot as learned as Aldhelm must have sensed early on which way the wind was blowing, and sought to take precautions. Indeed, it seems probable that Frome and Malmesbury had experienced only very loose episcopal oversight, if any at all, up to 689. Under Ceadwalla, the West Saxons had returned to pagan leadership through 685–8, and this following a decade of disunity under petty 'sub-kings' (*subreguli*)[96]—one suspects that Hæddi of Wessex's episcopate had lacked muscle. Malmesbury, set atop an Iron Age hillfort on the banks of the River Avon, lay along the Wessex–Mercian frontier zone.[97] If the later fragment of a purported treaty between Kings Ine of the West Saxons and Wulfhere of the Mercians (689/706?) bears any relation to a real historical event, then its statement that the rulers had agreed that neither of them might lay claim over this riverside monastery probably meant a formal recognition of the territorial ambiguities already benefiting the house since its foundation.[98] Malmesbury potentially stood in a no-man's-land, between and beyond direct West Saxon and Mercian rule. Sergius' privilege bestowing papal 'jurisdiction' and no other upon the house therefore allowed Aldhelm to enshrine his monastery's extra-territoriality in writing for perhaps the first time. Its Wilfridian 'twinning' technique did the same for Frome, while pre-empting any boundaries that might later be drawn between the two houses.

Agatho's privileges for Wearmouth and Sts Peter and Paul, Canterbury might seem like outliers against this pattern. A closer look, however, reveals that they too could have had their place in the above picture. Wilfrid and his retinue did not find themselves the only Englishmen in Rome when they appealed against his deposition in 679. We now know that the party

[94] Sharpe, 'King Ceadwalla and Bishop Wilfrid', pp. 216–17.
[95] *HE*, v. 18, pp. 514–15; *WBEASE*, pp. 548–9.
[96] *HE*, iv. 12, 16, v. 23, pp. 368–9, 382–5, 558–9; Sharpe, 'King Ceadwalla and Bishop Wilfrid', pp. 195–7, 208–9.
[97] Yorke, *Wessex*, pp. 61–2, 163; Blair, *Church*, p. 190.
[98] Rauer, 'Pope Sergius I's Privilege', p. 274.

representing Theodore's counter-appeal probably included Benedict Biscop, who would have acquired his Wearmouth privilege during this visit.[99] We can go further, and infer that Agatho had dismissed Biscop early, well in advance of the October Lateran Synod, since by September that year he had already brought Agatho's envoy John the Archcantor back to England, where he helped convene the Council of Hatfield.[100] That leaves only a small window, around late spring to early summer 679, when both Biscop and Wilfrid could have crossed paths in Rome.[101] Interestingly, the date of the extant Sts Peter and Paul, Canterbury privilege falls right within this time-frame, on 15 May. Biscop probably acquired that privilege as well: between 669 and 671 he had held Canterbury's abbacy in tandem with that of Wearmouth,[102] and he presumably maintained connections to the house. It would have been apt for Agatho to have issued all three privileges at about this same time. If so, that gives us something close to a date for the lost Northumbrian documents, but it also suggests an answer to the problem of why the pope granted the Wearmouth and Canterbury privileges at all. Wilfrid had perfectly good reasons to petition his privilege for Ripon and Hexham, and he may have been the prime mover in the trend outlined above. Viewed in isolation, the Wearmouth and Canterbury documents make less sense. However, if we suppose that Wilfrid and Biscop stood at loggerheads in Rome, and that the former had already secured his ambitious acquisition from Agatho, then the pope may have thought it wise to keep the peace, and grant two equivalent privileges for Biscop's principal houses of interest at Wearmouth and Canterbury. These would have balanced-out the gifts to Ripon and Hexham with consolation prizes for two minsters backed by Wilfrid's opponents. Placating Biscop would have been a shrewd move on Agatho's part, since he was in the process of sending Wearmouth's abbot home early before the appeal process had even begun, while at the same time expecting him to take care of his envoy John.

Wearmouth's privilege may not, therefore, have had any particular function ascribed to it during the monastery's earlier years. This helps explain Biscop's indifference to its provisions for free abbatial elections. Under the leadership of Ceolfrith and Hwætberht, however, the Wilfridian model

---

[99] Wood, 'Continental Journeys', pp. 208–10; Goldberg, 'King Ecgfrith' (I am grateful to Prof. Goldberg for sharing this unpublished paper).

[100] *HE*, iv. 17–18, pp. 384–91.

[101] Wilfrid had already spent the earlier part of 679 at the courts of Austrasia and Milan: *VSW*, 28, pp. 54–7; Cubitt, 'St Wilfrid', p. 344.

[102] *HA*, 3, pp. 26–9.

was embraced after all: the pairing of Wearmouth-Jarrow through the acquisition of Sergius' further privilege (and generous reinterpretation of Agatho's) resituated these houses under shared papal 'jurisdiction' in a manner already pioneered at Ripon-Hexham, Chertsey-Barking, and Malmesbury-Frome. We saw above that divided priorities, between Jarrow as a royal foundation and Wearmouth as a Baducing family monastery, may have encouraged this strategy. Did anxieties about changes in the Northumbrian episcopate from the 670s–80s also play a role? Unlike the other cases surveyed here, Wearmouth and Jarrow do not appear to have faced division through new or threatened *parrochia* boundaries. Nevertheless, looking out over the North Sea, at eight miles remove from one another between the mouths of the Tyne and Wear, these two houses may have had in their early days a greater air of spatial liminality about them than we now appreciate. Historians tend to speak reflexively of Wearmouth-Jarrow as part of the sub-kingdom of Bernicia at its hinterland. But more careful research has demonstrated that this is an assumption, one never spelled out in the sources (Bede certainly never refers to his location or himself as Bernician). Moreover, the siting of both monasteries on estates belonging to a royal line of the more southerly Deiran kingdom indicates territorial ambiguity.[103] When Biscop founded Wearmouth in 674 within this ambiguous Bernician-Deiran zone at the margins of the Northumbrian polity, in the age of the ethnic super-*parrochia*, he may have taken its autonomy for granted. By the turn of the century, that house and Jarrow lay surrounded by a constellation of new bishops at York, Lindisfarne, and Hexham, the latter just 30 miles upriver. Escaping into the imagined space of papal *iurisdicio* as a way of perpetuating that older autonomy, and disregarding local ideas about episcopal territory, would have had its attractions. Indeed, what evidence we have suggests that Wearmouth-Jarrow's most famous monk declined to recognise any of these Northumbrian *parrochiae* as touching upon his own back-yard. For all that modern historians have written about 'Bede's diocese' and his relationship with Bishop Acca of Hexham as 'his diocesan', Bede never expressed those ideas in his writings—nor, one suspects, much humoured them in his own mind.

*   *   *

One apparent glitch remains. If these privileges contributed to an effort at a select few monasteries to resist the rising tide of an amplified English

---

[103] Orton, Wood, and Lees, *Fragments*, pp. 108–15; Wood, 'Gifts', p. 97, n. 44.

episcopate, then how do we square that with the fact that some of their petitioners were bishops themselves (or in the case of Aldhelm, a bishop-in-waiting)? If Abbot Hædda of Bermondsey-Woking was also the Mercian bishop of the same name, then there is something jarring about his cameo appearance in Felix's *Life of Guthlac* (*c.* 720/49). There, we see him ferret out the nascent community of Crowland, deep in the marshy Fen borderlands of the Mercian and East Anglian kingdoms (an ambiguous space if ever one existed), so as to ordain Guthlac and consecrate his church, thus firmly 'entering' both 'onto the map' of his Lichfield *parrochia*.[104] Perhaps about the same time as Felix composed that *Life*, a dying Bede wrote to Bishop Ecgberht of York, aggressively outlining how he might requisition the more autonomous monasteries of Northumbria for episcopal use, and urging him to tear to shreds the charters in these houses' archives if it made their cowing easier.[105] So strong were Bede's words that one legal historian's classic study of these papal privileges doubted how far those of Wearmouth and Jarrow could have entailed any avoidance of bishops at all.[106]

Did Hædda and Bede change their minds? Or were they, with the former's episcopal colleagues, simply hypocrites? In fact, we need not see any contradictions. The exceptional nature of papal privileges of Roman *iurisdicio* did not have to undermine emerging patterns of regional episcopal authority: it could reinforce them. At the beginning of the 'minster boom', the question of whose monastery pertained to whose bishopric may have in many instances been left comfortably open. But the appearance on the scene of a select number of elite minsters, brandishing letters from the bishop of Rome to confirm that they only existed in papal 'jurisdiction', must have contributed to the erosion of much of that older ambiguity and room for manoeuvre at other, less fortunate houses. If figures such as Wilfrid, Earconwald, and Aldhelm had needed to travel over two thousand miles, twice 'traverse the sea's expanses' and 'cross by foot the clouded Alps'[107] to obtain the pope's personal support, embodied in a huge scroll of Egyptian bulrush, and all this simply to *maintain* their older autonomy ... well, then what hope for the little minsters and small-time abbots in their own *parrochiae*? By showing how far one had to go to circumvent the tightening

---

[104] Felix, *Life of St Guthlac*, 46–7, pp. 142–7. 'Entering onto the map': Scott, *Art*, pp. 120–1, borrowing a term from eighteenth-century Qing bureaucracy.
[105] Bede, *Epistola*, 7–17, pp. 134–61.   [106] Schwarz, 'Jurisdicio', pp. 65–70.
[107] Aldhelm, *Opera*, p. 15.

episcopal regimes of post-670s England, papal privileges confirmed rather than undermined them.[108] The exceptions proved the rule.

IV. Conclusions

To summarise. If we wish to get a sense of what contemporaries thought about papal privileges bestowing Roman 'jurisdiction' upon monasteries in seventh- and early eighth-century England, then it is to the world of those immediate beneficiaries that we need primarily to look. Just because these documents resembled, and (probably only indirectly) influenced the much later privileges of papal 'exemption' characteristic of late eleventh- to thirteenth-century ecclesiastical politics does not mean that we can project either the legal thinking or centralised, Rome-driven policies of that era back onto this age. Nor is it necessarily the case that these privileges had the same function or significance in England as they did in contemporary Francia or Italy. Their origins lay in the context of a primarily Merovingian culture, where the gifting of self-restraining royal and episcopal 'immunities' to super high-status holy sites played a key role in political and religious practice. Petitioners from that world might go to Rome to seek additional, papal guarantees to back up and add a further layer of prestige to those pre-existing arrangements, and at least some popes acquiesced—framing this as a largely rhetorical extension of papal 'jurisdiction' over said sites—albeit not without expressing doubts about the validity of the whole business. Those papal 'jurisdiction' privileges therefore grew out of, and fed back into and reinforced, an already existing set of norms, expectations, and documentary practices; and since those do not appear to have existed in England, then we cannot expect the same kinds of privileges to have worked there in quite the same way. What this stream of continental petitioners did do by the later 670s, however, was to leave their mark in the documentary formulae of the papal chancery, so that visitors to Rome from quite different worlds might come away with superficially similar privileges, and then attempt to apply them as solutions to their own, distinct problems. This appears to have been what happened in England, 679–715. There, a

---

[108] Cf. d'Avray, *Medieval Religious Rationalities*, pp. 23–6, 150–63, on systems of 'formal rationality' (here, the standard, generally applied *parrochia* system) versus one-off instances of 'substantive rationality' (the papal privileges for specific beneficiaries, which paid no attention to it). In the case studied here, however, the two systems are not at odds: rather the latter more sharply delineates (and so strengthens and affirms) the former.

small group of elite ecclesiastics may have sought to use these formulaic documents' vague pledge of a distant papal 'jurisdiction' which acknowledged no other authorities or territories as a way of both (1) tying together separated pairs of monasteries under their charge, whose future unity could not be taken for granted; and (2) preserving those houses' original semi-autonomy, newly threatened by the sudden expansion and redefinition of the Anglo-Saxon episcopate from the 670s.

Did they have much impact in the long run? There's reason to be pessimistic. Stephen and Bede both indicated that, even within their own lifetimes, their houses' privileges had faced delayed implementation. After 708/15 no comparable 'jurisdiction' privileges appear again in the record for Anglo-Saxon England, while with the passing of Bede, even these acquisitions seem to have faded into obscurity, until a minor revival of interest in the late tenth and eleventh centuries. Yet to evaluate them according to these forward-looking criteria is to get sucked into the centuries-spanning papal master-narrative. In their immediate setting, these privileges were extraordinary: the fruits of a multi-generational effort by a group of astonishingly well-travelled 'culture heroes', reappropriating for their own ends a set of exotic texts preserved in a Mediterranean chancery, and importing them back into a distant, barely Christianised island in an attempt to maintain their local power and prestige.[109] They emphasise in particular much of what must have made a city as massive and complex as Rome so exciting to the early Anglo-Saxons—not just its magnetic pull as a symbol of authority, but its potentiality as a huge resource of myriad texts, materials, and ideas, which could be reapplied to regional problems, far removed from their original setting or purpose. For us, these privileges also have a value quite outside the constraints of papal historiography, since they highlight an aspect of the first century of Anglo-Saxon Christianity that has arguably gone overlooked: that its 'minster boom' first flourished at a time when episcopal presence was unusually thin on the ground, a state of affairs which must have raised tensions as the number of bishops suddenly accelerated after Theodore's arrival. Whether our cluster of privileges actually did much to affect those developments in the long run is a different matter, but one irrelevant to their significance for immediate contemporaries. Besides, Anglo-Saxon England was rapidly transforming. As we will see in the next chapter, by the time a new wave of papal privileges began to appear on the island from the 770s/790s, things would look very different indeed.

---

[109] 'Culture heroes': above, Chapter 2, pp. 54–5.

5

Papal Privileges and the 'Mercian Supremacy' (*c.* 770–*c.* 830)

Sometimes, God prefers to communicate in English. The Winchcombe redactor of the *Life and Miracles of Saint Kenelm* (*c.* 1070) told how once, when Pope Leo III (795–816) had begun to say mass at San Pietro,

> ...a dove whiter than snow appeared from above in the sight of everyone, and it carried in its gentle beak a snow-white parchment inscribed with golden letters in English, which it put down upon the altar of Saint Peter...The holy and apostolic father looks trembling at the crisp white sheet written all over with unfamiliar words and letters, and implores the throng of diverse nations flocking together to Saint Peter, to indicate whether anyone among them might understand anything of the text of this letter. There were, among the assembly of so many lands, a good number of English, even Mercians...By them the holy letter is read out, and its interpretation is as follows: 'In Clent Cow-Valley, Kenelm king's-son lies under a thorn bush, deprived of his head.'[1]

Leo at once sent legates bearing his documents into England, investing Wulfred, archbishop of Canterbury (805–32) with 'apostolic authority', so that he might lead a search party to retrieve the young boy's corpse from its revealed location, and convey it back to the nearby monastery of Winchcombe. There lay already the body of his father Coenwulf, king of the Mercians, in the church of Saint Mary which 'he himself founded and dedicated in kingly fashion'. As the cortège approached the minster, Kenelm's sister Cwoenthryth, who had seized control of the realm following the death of her male kin, looked out from its church dedicated to Saint Peter, and 'consumed with anger, indignation and bitterness', began to chant Psalm 109 (108). 'By some kind of witchcraft', she did so backwards.

[1] *Vita et miraculi sancti Kenelmi*, 10–11, pp. 64–7.

England and the Papacy in the Early Middle Ages: Papal Privileges in European Perspective, c. 680–1073.
Benjamin Savill, Oxford University Press. © Benjamin Savill 2023. DOI: 10.1093/oso/9780198887058.003.0005

Proof came soon enough of her complicity in her brother's murder, as her eyeballs dropped from their sockets and rolled across the psalter page. She soon died. Her body was tossed in a ditch.[2]

So much for the edifying narratives of a golden age—Bede's day had long passed. In this chapter, we leave behind the heroic era he nostalgically depicted in his last years, and turn instead to the new political landscape which had already begun to take shape by the time of his death: the 'Mercian Supremacy' of the eighth and early ninth centuries. Under Æthelbald (716–57), Offa (757–96; briefly followed by his son Ecgfrith, 796), and Coenwulf (796–821), the Mercian kingdom of the Midlands dominated southern Britain for almost a century. While contemporary with the early Carolingians, theirs was not a great era of dynasty-building or integrative structural reform. Each of these three kings came from distinct kinship groups. After seizing power, each had to establish his huge personal dominion from the ground up, exercising from Mercia a mixture of direct rule and varying degrees of overlordship over the peoples south of the River Humber. Following Coenwulf's death that pattern could not be sustained, and the 'Supremacy' rapidly fell apart in the 820s–30s. Besides sheer force, these kings maintained their hegemony in no small part through the absorption and reappropriation of the vast networks of monastic property, infrastructure, and labour-resources built up during the previous century's 'minster boom'.[3] Our record of papal documentation duly reflects that shift in the relationship between these increasingly mighty kings and subordinate monasteries: in these decades, the autonomy-confirming papal privileges of the kind discussed in Chapter 4 disappear altogether. Instead, by the end of the eighth century, we see a new wave of very different, tailor-made privileges arriving in England—this time, not ostensibly at the request of the abbots or monasteries concerned, but of the kings who sought to control them. In this chapter, we will explore the role played by this unique group of privileges in the controversial exercise of Mercian hegemony, discovering what these documents can tell us about the peculiar nature of Mercian power; the role of women and family-held monastic property within it; and the ways in which it was remembered—or rather, obscured and misremembered— after the fallout of the 820s–30s collapse.

---

[2] Ibid., 11–16, pp. 66–73.
[3] See generally Keynes, 'England, 700–900', pp. 21–38, now with Blair, *Building*, pp. 179–231; 'Supremacy': Stenton, *Anglo-Saxon England*, pp. 206 ff.; 'boom': above, p. 135.

This chapter harbours, however, a central paradox: the *c.* 780–*c.* 820 apex of Mercian overlordship saw papal privileges employed more effectively than at any other point in early medieval English history, while leaving to posterity some of the weakest and most distorted evidence for their application. The following investigation therefore necessitates a change of scale. Zooming-in to undertake some micro-historical detective work, it reconstructs the petitioning and use of papal privileges through three generations of Mercian rulers by examining documentary caesurae and scribal slips, and deciphering clues from warped later accounts. And as unprepossessing as it looks at first sight, Winchcombe's eleventh-century legend of 'Kenelm king's-son' and his murderous witch-sister Cwoenthryth provides this detective story's unlikely point of departure.

* * *

The Winchcombe *Life* admittedly has little worth as a conventional record of ninth-century events. Its chronology does not work; contemporary records report no such royal fratricide; no 'Queen Cwoenthryth' is known to have ruled; nor do we find a 'Saint Kenelm' venerated until the later tenth century. The story, identifiable through its fairy-tale motifs as a variation on what would eventually become the Brothers Grimm's 'Juniper Tree', bears all the hallmarks of an oral narrative, only later set to writing in its surviving hagiographic form.[4] Historians have long recognised, however, that at least elements of the *Life* echo something more than fiction. Places and protagonists appear elsewhere. Winchcombe, now believed on archaeological grounds to have housed a ninth-century royal mausoleum,[5] retained in its twelfth-century chronicle copies of a purported royal diploma of Coenwulf (a forgery, but perhaps based on a genuine tradition) and, far more significantly, two imperfect but essentially authentic privileges granted to the king by Leo III and his successor-but-one Paschal I (817–24).[6] This evidence that documents of 'apostolic authority' of some description linked Rome, the king, and Winchcombe has recently been enhanced by the discovery of lead *bullae* bearing these same popes' names in Kent and the Mercian heartlands.[7] Other archives leave further hints, at least some independent of the *Life*. William of Malmesbury's *On the Antiquity of Glastonbury* (*c.* 1130) preserves a further papal privilege and confirmatory royal diploma

---

[4] Grimm, *Kinder- und Hausmärchen*, 47, pp. 229–38; Blair, 'Saint', pp. 481–2.
[5] Bassett, 'Probable Mercian Mausoleum'.   [6] BCS 338 (S 167); 32, 36.
[7] Above, Chapter 3, p. 79.

linking Glastonbury to Leo, Coenwulf, and a certain Cynehelm/Kenelm, while at Abingdon a tradition going at least as far back as the 990s commemorated the joint patronage of Coenwulf and Leo.[8] Most intriguing of all, however, is a charter of 826/7 surviving via two contemporary, single-sheet duplicate-originals from Christ Church, Canterbury. It records a bitter and protracted property dispute between Archbishop Wulfred and Coenwulf, and subsequently the latter's heir—no less than an Abbess Cwoenthryth, whom the charter links to Winchcombe.[9]

This charter of 826/7 holds remarkable value in its own right as a detailed narrative, however one-sided, of a major clash between the king and archbishop of which no other record now survives. The greater part of the document appears to derive from a joint royal-ecclesiastical assembly at the unidentified site of *Clofesho* in 825. This relates how, at an unspecified point, Coenwulf and Wulfred had fallen into dispute over who might control the Kentish monasteries of Reculver and Minster-in-Thanet. Tensions flared to such a degree that the king, in his 'enmity, violence and avarice', somehow brought it about 'through his order and insinuation overseas at the apostolic see' that Wulfred was deprived of these monasteries and their properties, and (most striking to us, since it is never mentioned elsewhere) that 'the whole people of the English were deprived of his primordial authority and ministry of holy baptism for altogether six years.' At an undefined time 'after this', Coenwulf summoned Wulfred to an assembly at London, and declared that he would lose all properties and find himself banished from the realm, so that 'neither the words of the lord pope nor *cæsar*' might help him; that is, unless he met the terms of the 'reconciliation' by handing over three hundred hides at Eynsham and paying £120. Wulfred eventually agreed: he was restored 'to all the power and obedience that pertained to his episcopal see...just as his predecessors had held in former times', and Coenwulf promised to keep him 'safe and secure as regards (*contra*) the lord pope from all accusations and discord'.

'None of this agreement was implemented', however, and for three years Minster-in-Thanet rendered neither dues nor 'obedience' to the archiepiscopal see, 'and in many other places its *parrochia* was dishonoured'. Only in the reign of Beornwulf (823–5: a new king, of a new dynasty, in the years

---

[8]   31; *Glastonbury*, 15b (S 152); *33.

[9]   BL, Cotton Augustus ii. 78; BL, Stowe Ch. 15: *Christ Church*, 59 (S 1436). Brooks' and Kelly's brilliant commentary in ibid., pp. 598–604 is indispensable for making sense of this complex (and poorly written) text, although I have not followed this on all points.

historians now recognise as the tipping-point of Mercian collapse), did Wulfred invite Coenwulf's daughter and 'heir', Abbess Cwoenthryth, to the aforesaid *Clofesho* council of 825, to demand redress for the wrongs done against him. Beornwulf, however, mindful of the 'friendship' of Coenwulf's heirs, agreed to Cwoenthryth's plea that he might act as her 'intercessor and patron', and mediated a renewed 'reconciliation' through her gift of four properties totalling one hundred hides. Yet within a year— and at this stage the narrative appears to switch to a lengthy addendum to the original *Clofesho* text—it transpired that Cwoenthryth had failed to hand over all these estates, and still owed £47 to Wulfred. This prompted a third and final meeting at *Oslafeshau* in the province of the Hwicce (the same midland region as Winchcombe and 'Clent Cow-Valley'), seemingly without royal oversight. There, Wulfred humiliated Cwoenthryth, and forced her to confess her 'foolishness'; since the *Clofesho* agreement had now been for- feited by the abbesses' actions, he now declared himself 'free from all the old *causae* which they had previously reconciled'. In a final attempt to receive the triumphant archbishop's 'friendship', Cwoenthryth promised to make amends on all losses, and gifted two further properties. It was then proposed that 'the heirs of Coenwulf and all his inheritance (*hereditas*) were freed' of further accusations. Wulfred agreed, on the 'condition' that the records of the concerned estates were erased from certain 'old privileges' by Cwoenthryth's party at Winchcombe, who had to promise never to bring these forward as evidence again.[10] A new record of events was drawn-up, of which our two surviving manuscripts presumably represent original exem- plars. Remarkably for a woman in the corpus of Anglo-Saxon charters, Cwoenthryth's subscription appears first. She then vanishes from history until her pantomime turn as the witch and fratricide of the eleventh-century Winchcombe *Life*.

This unique account touches upon developments of truly enormous magnitude which remain unexplained. We know from elsewhere that Wulfred worked as a vigorous 'reformer', and as a zealous maintainer, at times even forger, of Canterbury's documentary records; he may well have cut a contentious figure.[11] Yet this charter's suggestion that Coenwulf had suspended him from office, annulling his 'primordial authority and ministry

---

[10] '...ut omnis hereditas Coenpulfi heredesque illius firmaliter liberati. Tuncque episcopus hoc idem consensit. hanc condicione ut illorum prædictorum agellorum nomina de antiquis priuilegiis quæ sunt æt Þincelcumbe eradati fuerint. iterumque inposterum non sunt prolati.'

[11] Brooks, *Early History*, pp. 132–42; Cubitt, *Councils*, pp. 191–213; Cubitt, 'Finding'.

of baptism' for as long as six years, reveals a period of turmoil which receives no other mention elsewhere, although it is corroborated by a break in surviving Canterbury documents between 815 and 821/2,[12] and a phase in which Canterbury moneyers ceased to mint in the archbishop's name.[13] The charter hardly explains why or how this momentous suspension came about. It is evident that monastic property played a part, and, we are told, that Coenwulf has brought 'insinuations' to Rome, causing him to threaten Wulfred with the authority of pope or even *cæsar* (Emperor Louis the Pious?). Scholars have long acknowledged the gravity of the situation to which these crabbed sentences fleetingly refer: a 'major clash of Church and State';[14] a 'quarrel [which] comes into general history' and 'must have affected every aspect of English public life'.[15] But how exactly any of this happened still requires an explanation. The same mystery surrounds the remarkable tenacity of Cwoenthryth in retaining control over the properties of her family, from its fall from power following the overthrow of Coenwulf's brother Ceolwulf in 823, right up to Wulfred's triumph in 826/7. The dispute's links to the mangled papal privileges in the Winchcombe archive have not gone unnoticed, but remain yet to be fully explored.[16] Likewise, the fact that the dispute's protagonists would arise again in Winchcombe's oral lore some two and half centuries later—this time, with Cwoenthryth not as the guardian of the house's interests but as its stereotyped tyrant, and with Wulfred not threatened by the pope, but acting on his behalf to defeat the evil abbess—has only been treated as at best an interesting curio or coincidence.

The rest of this chapter seeks to demonstrate how we may after all make sense of this dispute if we bring together these individually defective sources from disparate archives, and ask *why* they present such difficulties. As already remarked above, there is good reason to think that papal privileges played an unusually effective role in the royal politics of this period, something that looks paradoxical, since the surviving evidence for papal interactions of these decades is so riddled with distortions and lacunae. The argument that will be presented here is that those later gaps and misrepresentations in the record can in this instance be taken as evidence *for* that contemporary potency. Moreover, part of that potency appears to relate to

---

[12] *Christ Church*, 51 (18 Mar. 815: S 178); 53 (821: S 1619) (only surviving as a later memorandum and perhaps unreliable); 52 (17 Sept. 822: S 186).

[13] Cubitt, *Councils*, p. 199.   [14] Ibid., p. 598; Brooks, *Early History*, p. 182.

[15] Stenton, *Anglo-Saxon England*, pp. 229–30.

[16] Brooks, *Early History*, pp. 185–6; Story, *Carolingian Connections*, pp. 208–9.

the signs that, within these years, the papal privileges acquired by the Mercian hegemons were unusually tailored towards local circumstances, with few exact parallels elsewhere. Most studies of English interactions with the papacy during the 'Mercian Supremacy' have, understandably, focused upon connections with the Carolingian world, 'international' high politics, and the Anglo-Saxons' adoption of certain Carolingian practices. Instead, this chapter investigates the ways in which Mercian kings, queens, and their daughters made novel uses of the resource of papal authority which were unique to their political environment, and asks how much we might learn from this—not about the themes of 'Church and State' per se, but of problems of royal property, kinship, and inheritance that may have in fact had little resonance in the Carolingian world. These developments came to their explosive culmination in the Coenwulf–Wulfred–Cwoenthryth dispute, as tendentiously recorded in the Canterbury charter, and still dimly remembered at Winchcombe centuries later. The first foundations, however, were laid by King Offa and Queen Cynethryth several decades before. Let's start with them first. Impressively, the unique piece of manuscript evidence for their innovations takes us one thousand miles southeast of Mercia, to the Italian monastery of Nonantola.

I. Property and Genealogy: Offa, Cynethryth, and Hadrian

We saw in Chapter 3 that we can identify a fragmentary document, now only preserved in northern Italian manuscripts of the *Liber diurnus*, as the opening *arenga* and *narratio* of a privilege addressed to Offa, king of the Mercians, and his wife Cynethryth (queen from *c.* 770), dating to the pontificate of Pope Hadrian I (772–95).[17] That the recipients are only identifiable thanks to the accidental retention of Cynethryth's name in what should have been an all-purpose formula by one manuscript's scribe, working at Nonantola in the late eighth or early ninth century, is astounding in itself: we have here a near-contemporary witness to Mercian political history, known only through Italian archives, and hanging by the thread of a single scribal error (Figure 5.1). While the text has attracted attention before, the implications of its absence from the English archival record have

---

[17] **29** = *LD* V 93.

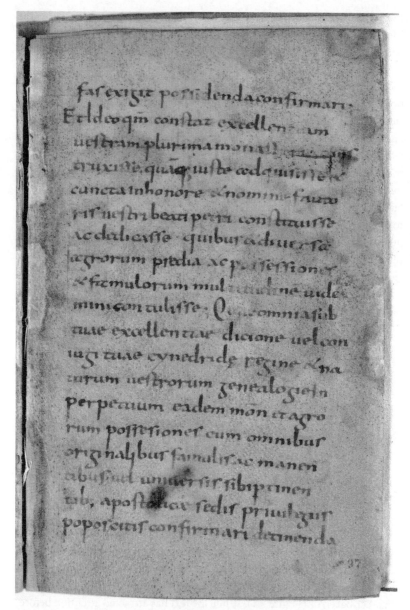

Figure 5.1 'Cynedridę regine' in *Liber diurnus* V 93: Vatican City, Archivio Segreto Vaticano, Misc. arm. xi, 19, f. 97 (© 2022 Archivio Apostolico Vaticano; by permission of Archivio Apostolico Vaticano, all rights reserved).

occasioned less comment. What remains of the text suggests a major confirmatory monastic privilege by Hadrian, which looks unlike anything we find in previous centuries. Following an apparently original *arenga* on the importance of granting privileges for the confirmation of 'those things which are done legally', Hadrian notes that his recipients' 'excellency' has overseen the construction and 'just acquisition' of many monasteries, dedicated 'in the honour and name of your patron, the blessed Peter', to which pertain many lands, estates, possessions, and slaves. The pope then commits to granting what they have 'requested': that by 'privileges of the apostolic see', these same monasteries, and all that pertains to them, will be confirmed as being held under the 'authority' (*dicio*) of Offa, Cynethryth, and those born of their *genealogia*. At this point the privilege begins to move into its dispositive clause, and states that it is about to name the places concerned— but here the text as we have it suddenly ends: anything further would be circumstantial detail, inappropriate for a formulary.

For historians this sudden end to the fragment is enormously frustrating. Educated guesses have been made about the identities of these 'many monasteries', with Bedford, Bath, Bredon, Chertsey, and Woking among the chief candidates.[18] The following discussion will press the case for Cookham, Glastonbury, and Winchcombe in particular. All, however, are possible, even probable, and the full list conceivably came to some length, since a great proportion of Anglo-Saxon minsters had their primary church dedicated to Peter.[19] Offa and Cynethryth's decision to adopt the saint as their personal 'patron', and seek approval from his successor in Rome for their 'acquisitions' opened up the route to the confirmation of a potentially huge portfolio of monastic lands and renders. The evidence fits in well with what we know of Offa's more imperial phase of rule from *c.* 770 onwards, as he asserted more direct control over the Southumbrian kingdoms beyond the Mercian heartlands, taking hold as he went of numerous minsters, by then the principal foci of wealth and political power across Britain.[20] Control of monasteries also meant access to prayers, masses, and enormous religious capital, an aspect of Offa's rule we need to take just as seriously. The king did not have an Asser or Einhard to sing his praises (or no evidence of one survives), and historians have often been quick to stress the more cynical

---

[18] Levison, *England*, p. 31; Sims-Williams, *Religion*, p. 161; Cubitt, *Councils*, p. 226; *Peterborough*, p. 200; *Chertsey*, pp. 11–12.

[19] Levison, *England*, pp. 33–6, 259–65; but see also Gittos, *Liturgy*, pp. 75–116.

[20] Brooks, *Early History*, pp. 184–5; Sims-Williams, *Religion*, pp. 154–68; Blair, *Church*, pp. 121–3; Wood, *Proprietary Church*, pp. 241–3.

aspects of his accumulation and control over churches where they emphasise the devotional concerns of his Carolingian or later West Saxon counterparts. Frankish kings had long drawn intense spiritual authority from their association with the monastery of Saint-Denis, and their cultivation of 'Lord Dionysius' as 'our personal patron' (*peculiaris patronus noster*).[21] Offa's move to adopt no less than the prince of the apostles as his patron, and to do so by associating himself with the cult activity not of a single holy place, but a multitude—named and confirmed by a privilege issued near that saint's own Roman tomb—reveals a Southumbrian twist on the same ideas.[22] Besides: the dual spiritual and economic benefits of controlling monasteries were complementary rather than contradictory.[23] By acquiring and constructing shrines to Peter as he exerted his hegemony across southern Britain, Offa at once unlocked access to huge material resources, the power of the divine, and the island's core nodes of local networks and European connectivity. All were crucial to the construction of the 'Mercian Supremacy'. Hadrian's privilege represents both a contemporary witness to that moment, and an attempt to articulate it, advertise it, and render it more secure.

It also meant a sharp break with the papal privileges for monasteries we saw in Chapter 4. The differences between this document and those of the *c*. 680–*c*. 715 period, as well as its distinct relationship to the other papal privileges found elsewhere in Europe around this time, can reveal much about the workings of Mercian power in these decades, and are vital for understanding the background of the royal-episcopal property disputes of the 790s–830s, to which we will turn shortly. Three things about this text stand out as especially important.

Firstly, the privilege concerns the large-scale confirmation of property (that is, of both properties belonging to churches, and through their over-lordship, effectively churches *as* property) and of specifically familial rather than 'royal' or 'public' property per se. It is important to stress that the most obvious distinction between this privilege and those discussed in Chapter 4—the move away from papal limitations on external interests in monasteries (by newly placing them under Roman *dicio*), to one confirming their properties, under the control of a ruler (acknowledging

---

[21] *Urkunden der Merowinger*, ed. Kölzer, 22, is the earliest example (584/628), but the designation became standard.

[22] Leo III later remembered Offa as Peter's 'standard bearer and retainer': *MGH Epp.* IV, p. 188 (JE 2494).

[23] Innes, *State*, p. 17; Costambeys, *Power*, pp. 48–50.

their subjugation under the petitioner's royal *dicio*)—reflects a broader development throughout the continental corpus of papal, royal, and episcopal diplomas around this time. In Francia and the lands under its control, evidence for the time-honoured tradition of complementary grants of episcopal and royal 'immunity' for selected, high-status monasteries evaporates in the second half of the eighth century, becoming superseded by more vigorous assertions of kingly 'protection' or 'defence' over such sites. This flipped matters on their head. Elite religious houses now enjoyed the honour of being taken into the king's personal care and drawn closer into worldly power structures, rather than theoretically excluded from them. Under this transition, the word 'immunity' became equated with and absorbed into the idea of royal 'protection'/'defence'; equivalent episcopal grants meanwhile became a dead letter, and disappeared entirely. This process has generated reams of scholarly discussion.[24] Of chief interest here is the support it lends to the argument made in the previous chapter, that early, continental grants of papal privileges placing monasteries under Roman 'jurisdiction' served principally as a third-party, reactive confirmation to existing regional traditions of royal and episcopal immunity. For, once that tradition ended under the Carolingians in the later eighth century, so too, abruptly, did the record for equivalent papal privileges.[25] Instead, if the contents of the surviving manuscripts of the *Liber diurnus* have been reliably dated, we can observe a

---

[24] Rosenwein, *Negotiating*, pp. 99–134; Wood, *Proprietary Church*, pp. 230–5, 251–9, with bibliography.

[25] The latest known privileges of the *LD* V 32/77 'jurisdiction' type from this period are those for the high-profile cases of Fulda (752), Saint-Denis (757), and Brescia (762): see above, Chapter 4, p. 112, n. 7; it seems that even in these final instances, direct royal 'defence' was already emerging as the norm: although our earliest copy of Fulda's privilege comes from within *c.* 50 years of its issue (Munich, Bayerische Staatsbibliothek, Clm 8112, f. 54), Eigil's account of the archiepiscopal-monastic conflict that erupted during this time makes little mention of the papacy in its original recension (*c.* 794), and chiefly understands the position of the monastery as guaranteed only by King Pippin's grant of his exclusive 'defence': Eigil, *Vita Sturmi*, 17–20, pp. 151–6. Elsewhere surviving papal privileges for monasteries and bishops of the early Carolingian period concern themselves only with responding to requests of straightforward guarantees of lordship and property: thus, Paul I to Pippin for Soracte (761/2): *MGH Epp.* III, pp. 526–7 (JE 2349); Hadrian for Ravenna, 782: *Annales camaldulensis*, ed. Mittarelli and Costadoni, i, app. 3, cols. 10–12 (JE 2437); Hadrian for Saint-Denis (774/84): *PUU Saint-Denis*, 7 (JE 2443—a hybrid privilege: states that churches in the Valtellina do not lie in any episcopal *ius*, but only so the region can be claimed by Fulrad of Saint-Denis); Paschal I for Ravenna, 819: *PRDP* 1 (JE 2551). At Farfa, John VII's 705 privilege (above, Chapter 4, pp. 112, n. 6) become effectively overridden after the Frankish conquest by a number of royal and imperial diplomas (*Urkunden*, ed. Dopsch et al., 98–9; *Urkunden Ludwigs*, ed. Kölzer, 71, 177; *Regesto di Farfa*, ed. Giorgio and Balzani, ii. 272, 282). Thereafter papal privileges for Farfa concern instead only guarantees of judicial restitution (Hadrian, 772: ibid., ii. 90) (JE 2395), or property (Stephen IV, 817, and Paschal, 817: ibid., ii. 224–5) (JE 2544, 2546).

shift in papal diplomatic practice in the last decades of the eighth century, towards a situation in which the confirmation of the properties of monasteries and churches had suddenly become the major business of the papal chancery.[26] This probably had a lot to do with immediately local circumstances. The Frankish conquest of the Lombard kingdom of 773–4 must have unleashed a shockwave of property disputes across central and northern Italy.[27] It makes good sense that this move to issuing guarantees to proprietorial title appears to characterise the record of the papacy's diplomatic activity from around this same time. When Offa's envoys arrived in Rome in the 770s/790s, they may have therefore found themselves in an environment with a very different documentary culture to that encountered by Wilfrid or Aldhelm a century before. Grants of Roman 'jurisdiction' to abbots of distant, bishop-excluding monasteries (as in Chapter 4) had perhaps entirely ceased, while the confirmation of churches' estates, slaves, and other possessions was suddenly becoming papal Big Business.

If this proprietorial function of Offa's privilege seems obvious, it remains necessary to emphasise that the text does *not* strictly speaking purport to confirm 'royal' property. This is not a point of minor nuance, but critical to understanding the long-term function of the document. The privilege's forward-looking guarantee that the acquired monasteries and their estates should remain under the authority of not only the addressees but 'those born of your *genealogia*' reminds us of Offa's famous efforts to have his son Ecgfrith (d. 796) anointed as his royal successor, a scheme probably involving a degree of papal backing.[28] This text appears at first sight an extension of that project: an appeal for a sacral, Rome-sanctioned guarantee for the material basis of Ecgfrith's royal inheritance as well as his kingly office. In fact, almost the opposite may be true. The term *genealogia* appears rarely in contemporary diplomatic, and its adoption here is noteworthy.[29] By specifying that these monasteries, with their lands and possessions, lay under not only Offa and Cynethryth's *dicio* but that of their blood relations, the privilege outlines a way in which these might remain in familial possession even if this family were to lose royal title, and kingship were to pass to another line. We know little about Anglo-Saxon land law at this time, but passing royal property to a royal heir was probably a relatively

---

[26] Above, Chapter 2, pp. 28–9.   [27] Costambeys, *Power*, pp. 273 ff.
[28] Story, *Carolingian Connections*, pp. 178–80.
[29] Two other appearances: *Urkunden*, ed. Dopsch et al., 51, 89; Hadrian also uses it in a letter to Charlemagne (May/Sept. 781): *MGH Epp.* III, pp. 598–9 (JE 2441).

straightforward affair. Retaining those claims when the royal title moved to a different kin-group presumably presented more serious difficulties. This privilege may represent one attempt to set up a safety-net in case of such events. It is perhaps less an expression of kingly self-confidence than a reminder that Offa may have had profound doubts about his ability to secure the royal title for his descendants.

This leads to the second point: that Queen Cynethryth holds a far more significant role in this privilege than simply providing a handy clue to the modern researcher. She may be central to its purpose. Cynethryth held a uniquely prominent role in the Mercian kingdom. She was one of the first royal consorts to rule as 'queen', and attested Offa's charters. Her image even appeared on coins minted in her name, a prerogative unique among Anglo-Saxon women, and almost unmatched anywhere in the early medieval world.[30] Her appearance in Hadrian's privilege fits into that pattern, but its implications may go further. The loss of the text's *inscriptio* means we cannot tell whether the document was addressed only to Offa (the usual assumption), or to the king and queen together. Yet some of the surviving text's language may hold a clue. Whatever his might in southern England, from the perspective of Rome's Franco-Byzantine political stage Offa may have looked like something of a provincial sub-king, and we cannot be sure whether papal protocol would have systematically referred to him as *uos* rather than *tu*. In a privilege such as this, which has the character of a confirmation of private, familial property, the former may have been even less likely. The *genealogia* clause may be revealing. Hadrian's *tutoiement* in referring to the monasteries concerned as 'all under the authority of your [*sing.*] excellency and your [*sing.*] wife Queen Cynethryth and those born of your [*pl.*] genealogy' (*omnia sub tuae excellentiae dicione uel coniugi tuae cynedridae regine et natorum uestrorum genealogie*) could suggest that his earlier remarks on 'your excellency' (*excellentiam uestram*) and Peter, 'your patron' (*fautoris uestri*) may have been plural rather than deferential, and that the privilege was therefore aimed and addressed at both the king and queen. Even if this is not the case, the switch within the same clause from singular *tu* when speaking of the pair's respective *dicio*, to plural *uestrorum* when speaking of their *genealogia* has important implications: it may indicate that only those born of *both* Offa and Cynethryth's union could become heirs to this monastic portfolio, and/or those of their family on *both* sides.

---

[30] Stafford, 'Political Women', pp. 36–42; Kelly, 'Cynethryth'; Naismith, *Medieval European Coinage*, p. 138, figs. 1171–2.

Moreover, its phrasing indicates that Cynethryth laid claim to significant monastic properties distinct from those of her husband, which were becoming combined under the new arrangement.

There is context to this. Several studies have demonstrated the increased importance tied to maternal bloodlines and matrilineal descent in western Europe around the turn of the ninth century, affecting both laws of inheritance and trends in 'genealogical thinking'. This also manifested itself in the contemporary development of the cult of Mary as Queen Mother, especially its emphasis on Christ's Marian bloodline.[31] Pauline Stafford has moreover hinted that Cynethryth's unusual prominence in Offa's kingdom could have resulted from the latter's efforts to marry-in to a position of greater security. Whereas Offa, who seized power after the murder of King Æthelbald, may have come from a kin-group with only limited 'king-worthiness', Cynethryth possibly claimed direct descent from the celebrated King Penda (d. 655). If so, her own *genealogia* could well have bolstered Offa and his children's otherwise shaky legitimacy.[32] Whatever its fragmentary nature, Hadrian's privilege appears to support Stafford's proposition through its emphasis on the *genealogia* of both the king and queen, and we may add it to the increasing evidence of the later eighth century as a time of heightened articulation in thinking about matrilineality. So too may it further develop Stafford's suggestion that Offa had married into kingly legitimacy, by reminding us that this probably also meant marrying into substantial (monastic) property.

The third point, which we can only make by stepping back from these minutiae to a position of synchronic and diachronic comparison, is that this sort of privilege appears unique to England within the years of the 'Mercian Supremacy'. Nowhere else in Europe do we find evidence that papal privileges of this type were petitioned, granted, or forged. Considering that the core formulation of the privilege had entered the *Liber diurnus*, and was

---

[31] Wood, 'Genealogy'; Leyser, 'From Maternal Kin'; McDougall, *Royal Bastards*, pp. 66–93. Note also that our earliest text of the 'Anglian Royal Genealogies' comes from a Mercian MS datable to 805/14 (BL, Cotton Vespasian B. vi/1, ff. 104–9), which may derive from a lost original from the time around Offa's death: Dumville, 'Anglian Collection'. We also have evidence that the *Gospel of Pseudo-Matthew*, the eighth-century Carolingian text detailing Mary's bloodline, was known in England, perhaps Mercia, around this time: its Old English translation may be Mercian, while the original influenced the *Old English Martyrology*, tentatively located to ninth-century Mercia, although much remains uncertain: Clayton, *Apocryphal Gospels*, pp. 136–41; Clayton, *Cult*, pp. 23, 214–17; *Old English Martyrology*, pp. 1–11, 176–9, 290.

[32] Stafford, 'Political Women', p. 36. 'King-worthy' lines: Charles-Edwards, 'Anglo-Saxon Kinship'.

therefore signposted for future use, this is especially surprising. As we saw in Chapter 4, such formulary collections could provide a route by which responses to developments particular to one region might be repurposed as responses to circumstances arising elsewhere at a later date. Assuredly, we do see formula 93's *arenga* on the importance of providing apostolic confirmations, as well as elements of its *narratio* reused in other privileges over the next three centuries, and so we cannot quite say it was added to the *Liber diurnus* in vain.[33] But the unique, core idea of the formula, on the accumulation and construction of monasteries and monastic properties, and their confirmation under the *dicio* of two rulers and their *genealogia*, does not reappear in any form whatsoever outside Mercian contexts within these same decades. Again, one needs to be cautious about making arguments from silence, but considering the tight concentration of this evidence against the expansive backdrop of the early medieval papal corpus, it does appear as though the original privilege that became *Liber diurnus* 93 was a response to developments peculiar to Mercian kingship and its relationship to monasteries at a particular point in time. It had a special usefulness at a turn-of-the-century moment in Southumbrian politics, which did not arise again, nor have immediate parallels elsewhere. Once more, it is important to note not the similarities but differences between the Carolingians and Mercians here. These were not, as in the Frankish super-state, claims to lordship over 'public', 'royal' monasteries, but those held and controlled by a particular family; and that family was not—as in the singular Frankish tradition—synonymous with the concept of kingship and the *regnum* itself, but just one of many aristocratic, 'king-worthy' lines. In short, we might see this privilege as a response to a problem within royal monastic lordship that was harder to conceive of under the single-bloodline, 'public'-minded Carolingian system.[34]

Whereas, then, the monastic privileges in Chapter 4 derived heavily from pre-existing formulae found in Rome, Hadrian's privilege for Offa and Cynethryth looks like an original composition, tailor-made to address Southumbrian developments. What first prompted the king and queen to attempt such a strategy? We know that some of the religious houses swallowed up into Offa's power base during his conquests had, back in the days

---

[33] John XII for Subiaco, 10 May 958, *PUU* 148 (JL 3648) substantially follows *LD* V 93 but is addressed to the abbot of a single monastery and guarantees abbatial rather than familial succession. *Arenga* only: Paschal I for Ravenna (the oldest extant original privilege): above, n. 25; Leo IX for Toul, 12 May 1050: ARTEM 222 (JL 4224).

[34] But cf. later parallels at the very beginning of the Ottonian regime: Otto I, *Diplomata*, 1.

of the 'minster boom', acquired papal privileges notionally safeguarding their independence. We might like to imagine the abbots of Chertsey or Woking hurriedly unfurling their already-crumbling papyrus scrolls before Offa and his henchmen as they took the monasteries into their possession, and arguing in vain that the foundations lay under the authority of the Roman church alone.[35] Perhaps confrontations of such a kind, however futile, at least put ideas into the heads of the king and his counsellors about possible alternative forms of authority through which their gains might be made more secure, or by which meddling bishops and regional elites might be kept at arm's length. Either way, we should think it a testament to the self-confidence and innovative nature of Offa and Cynethryth's reign that the petition they sent to Hadrian required the drafting of a papal privilege of an entirely new kind—one indebted neither to older papal diplomatic traditions, nor contemporary developments in the Carolingian world. Most striking of all, the events shortly following Offa's death suggest that it really *worked*.

II. Consolidation, 798: Coenwulf, Cynethryth, and Leo

In December 796 Ecgfrith died just six months into his reign, abruptly ending forever his father's dynastic ambitions. Kent, where Cynethryth had minted her coins, was already in rebellion. The Mercian kingship passed to Coenwulf, scion of a wholly different (and indeed probably rival) *genealogia*, who upon asserting his own overlordship over Kent in 798 and installing his brother Cuthred as their king,[36] at once began to press the newly elected Leo III to dismantle Offa's pet project of a second Southumbrian archbishopric at Lichfield. The pope, effectively out of office for most of 799–800 following an attempted coup, granted the petition in 802, to Canterbury's great jubilation.[37] It would seem as though Offa's forty-year legacy were being briskly taken apart. But amid all this, the future of his kindred's property may have presented a quite different matter. A crucial meeting in 798 of the Southumbrian council of *Clofesho*, held under Coenwulf's auspices, did not result in great seizures of estates or the *damnatio memoriae* of the Offing line, but rather the public confirmation

---

[35] Offa's influence over the two houses is indicated by his charters in favour of Woking (757/96): *Peterborough*, 6 (S 144); and Chertsey, 787: *Chertsey*, 5 (S 127). Both ignore **16** and **26**.
[36] Keynes, 'Control', pp. 112–18.   [37] See below, pp. 171–4.

of the rights of the dead king's heirs to (at least some) of their familial monastic holdings. In a much-studied Canterbury charter issued at that assembly, Archbishop Æthelheard (792–805) conceded control over the important minsters of Cookham and *Pectanege* to no less than Cynethryth herself, now styled 'abbess', in recognition of which he received a scattering of Kentish estates.[38] *Pectanege* remains unidentified, but the charter tells us that Cookham, a strategically significant Thameside minster reminiscent of those at neighbouring Chertsey or Woking,[39] had fallen into Offa's hands during his reign, and that despite Canterbury's historical claims to the house and the retention of its charters, he had seized it and passed it to his heirs. The events of 796–8 would have put Cynethryth in a considerably vulnerable position by the time of *Clofesho*,[40] and so her emergence from this dispute with what looks like the upper hand is remarkable. Coenwulf's presiding at the settlement must have had some role in swaying events, whatever their direction, and there were presumably numerous, now-irrecoverable developments that pushed things in the widow's favour. Given the circumstances, however, it is extremely tempting to link Cynethryth's retention of Offa's familial minsters with the above-discussed privilege of Pope Hadrian—a critical detail wholly overlooked by Æthelheard or his scribe. In fact, an independent text from Somerset strongly indicates that the role of papal privileges, together with Coenwulf's approval of them, lay at the very heart of such a settlement, and that the Canterbury charter reports only one of a conceivably far wider group of settlements made for the Offa–Cynethryth portfolio that year.

Chapter 3 introduced a strange Glastonbury composite document, re-translated back from Old English into Latin by William of Malmesbury, *c.* 1130: a privilege of Leo III of March 798, accompanied by a confirmation charter of Coenwulf, in turn attested by Cynethryth and her daughters.[41] The extant text is a wreck. Garbled by two stages of translation and probably multi-generational mistranscriptions and interpolations, we can only read around its outlines. The basics are as follows. Leo's privilege, following a *Liber diurnus* 93-type *arenga* (probably the single most reliable part of the document's papal component), confirms the rights of an otherwise unattested 'King' Cynehelm over the monastery of Glastonbury and its

---

[38] *Christ Church*, 27 (S 1258): see Brooks, *Early History*, pp. 103–4; Wood, *Proprietary Church*, pp. 242–4; Blair, *Church*, pp. 130–1. *Clofesho*: Cubitt, *Councils*; Keynes, *Councils*.
[39] Blair, 'Minsters', pp. 8–9, 23.　　[40] *Christ Church*, p. 431.
[41] 31; *Glastonbury*, 15b (S 152).

properties, supposedly first conveyed to him by Ecgfrith, and now confirmed by Coenwulf. In the addendum, dated (wrongly, if it really did follow the papal privilege) to 797, the new king states that he has acquired Leo's privilege on Cynehelm's behalf, and confirms again the 'freedom' granted by Ecgfrith, announcing that this was written 'in the second year of my reign' (Dec. 797–Dec. 798) at the 'venerable place which is called Glastonbury'. There it was subscribed by the two southern archbishops ('York' is incorrectly, but from a later copyist's perspective, understandably given in place of soon-to-be-suppressed Lichfield), with nine bishops, thirteen abbots, and six *principes*, all of whom follow Abbess Cynethryth and her 'dearest kin'. Even this bare-bones summation of the text has its stumbling-blocks, although there are ways around them. The charter's list of subscribers suggests a full provincial council of the Southumbrian church, something which in this period never took place anywhere near the Wessex heartland,[42] and so 'Glastonbury' as a location looks like a later error. Perhaps the lost original read *Clofesho*? Meanwhile, Leo's addressee 'King' Cynehelm is otherwise unknown and surely erroneous, even if tantalisingly reminiscent of the high-medieval legend of Coenwulf's son 'Saint Kenelm', whom we met at the beginning of this chapter. A *dux* of that name does, however, appear in the king's retinue in an authentic charter of 811: he may well have been the original aristocratic beneficiary to this 'Glastonbury' settlement, and plausibly if not necessarily of Coenwulfing blood.[43]

Perhaps the best clue to the original character of the 'Glastonbury' settlement comes, however, from the subscription of Abbess Cynethryth and her daughters, which is sufficiently unusual to merit closer reading. Effectively a short charter in its own right, it has Cynethryth declaring that she has not only 'subscribed to' but 'granted' the Glastonbury arrangement, with the condition that 'if it should happen later that a person of another lineage (*alterius progeniei homo*) should take up the possession and power (*possessio et potestas*) of the venerable place of Glastonbury, Cynehelm and his successors (*successores*) should firmly and faithfully remain there,

---

[42] Cubitt, *Councils*, pp. 27–39, 263–88.

[43] *Rochester*, 17 (S 165). Probably the best explanation for the attribution of *rex* to Cynehelm in the Glastonbury text is an enthusiastic copyist's conflation of the beneficiary with the legendary 'Kenelm king's-son' after the cult of the latter had taken off in the intervening centuries: Thacker, 'Kings', pp. 8–12. This does not rule out the possibility of some link between the *dux* and future saint: among the other subscribers to Coenwulf's grant in S 165 were Æthelburh *regina*, Cwoenthryth *filia regis*, and Cyneberht and Coenwald, both *propinqui regis*. If Stafford, 'Political Women', p. 41, is right that this looks like a 'meeting of royal heirs', then Cynehelm's presence suggests royal kinship.

without disruption, in their perpetual peace and liberty'. This passage is awkward enough to suggest that it is not obviously an interpolation or falsification, and the word *progenies*, while unusual in early medieval diplomatic, is very close to the similarly rare *genealogia*, and quite possibly the outcome of that word in the course of the text's Latin-to-English-to-Latin translation history. Considering that it appears here relating to a concession made by Cynethryth with her family members, it is difficult not to see this clause as in some way a reference to Pope Hadrian's privilege. The obscure phrasing has nevertheless raised difficulties of interpretation. Cynethryth's 'condition' (*ratio*) appears to contradict itself: how could Glastonbury still remain with Cynehelm and his successors if its 'possession and power' had passed to a 'person of another lineage'?[44] The problem here may be the assumption that this *possessio et potestas* was ever Cynehelm's—that is, presuming that, when Cynethryth speaks of this passing one day to an *alterius progeniei homo*, the *homo*-in-power at the time of writing must have been Cynehelm, with his *successores* necessarily members of his own *progenies*. Instead, the passage makes perfect sense if we understand that the 'possession and power' (or however this was phrased in the eighth-century original) still remained after this settlement with Cynethryth and her kin— as confirmed in Hadrian's original privilege—and that the situation imagined in her 'condition' is that there existed at least the possibility that in the course of time this might pass to a *progenies/genealogia* other than her own (here it is worth recalling that *homo* means 'person', not 'man'). What Cynehelm secured from this whole process may have only been an indefinite lease,[45] or a sort of (lay) abbacy, and/or right to appoint abbots. Susan Wood has shown that abbatial *successio* could in this period denote abbots elected by whatever means, and did not have to imply familial inheritance.[46]

With this in mind, the best reading of this composite text may be as follows. At some point in his short reign, Offa's anointed heir King Ecgfrith had granted to one Cynehelm the monastery at Glastonbury and its estates. This was part of the wide network of minsters 'justly acquired' by the members of his *genealogia*, and guaranteed to them perpetually through Hadrian's privilege for his mother and father. As such the grant may not have been one of full alienation, or was perhaps made on ambiguous terms.

---

[44] Cubitt, *Councils*, p. 276; *Glastonbury*, pp. 303–4.
[45] That leases of monasteries were not infrequent is indicated by the 816 Council of Chelsea: HS, iii, p. 582.
[46] Wood, *Proprietary Church*, pp. 127–39.

Following the sudden death of Ecgfrith and apparent collapse of the Offing legacy, control over the house (as perhaps many others) became hotly disputed. Amid the likely disorder following the king's death, Cynehelm may have claimed full right, while Cynethryth and her daughters, as the beneficiaries of Hadrian's privilege, continued to assert theirs. At this point Coenwulf, the new king, could have intervened, arbitrating a settlement to the advantage of both parties. With his envoys dispatched to acquire from Leo III in March 798 a new, *Liber diurnus* 93-type privilege somehow concerning the minster (perhaps addressed to himself, Cynehelm, or even Cynethryth's family, renewing the terms of Hadrian's privilege—the state of the extant text does not allow us to say), the settlement was formalised at a major Southumbrian council later that year. Cynehelm and those he appointed as *successores* could have retained use of Glastonbury and its estates, while Cynethryth and her *genealogia* ultimately retained their full 'power and possession' (= *dicio*?), giving Cynehelm the reassurance that even were this to pass elsewhere, his own rights to the house would not be jeopardised.

Even if only the outlines of this deliberately loose reconstruction ring true to the events of the 790s, its core element—Coenwulf's conciliar intervention to protect the claims of Cynethryth to her familial monastic property— closely mirrors the events described in the more reliable and better known Canterbury charter concerning Cookham. It also shows very clearly (in a way the evasively penned Cookham charter does not) that papal privileges played an important role in such settlements. It is here that we probably see the guarantees pledged in Hadrian's privilege for Offa and Cynethryth's *genealogia* actually made good by a later king and his assembly. In fact, despite their great differences in their current form, the Canterbury and Glastonbury charters probably originated as two records of the same event. The large-scale assembly indicated by the subscriptions to the Cynehelm settlement, together with its dating discrepancies, suggests that it was not, as the surviving text claims, the result of a transaction at Glastonbury in 797, but at a full-scale provincial church council, conceivably at the most frequently chosen site of *Clofesho*, in Coenwulf's second year of 798. Those assemblies usually took place in June–November,[47] which would have given enough time for an embassy to Leo III in March that year to have returned with supporting documentation. A *Clofesho* meeting of 798 is, of course, the

---

[47] Cubitt, *Councils*, pp. 25–6.

context reliably asserted by our charter for the Cookham agreement. What we are probably seeing in both charters, therefore, are two fragments of the documentation generated by a major meeting in the summer or autumn of 798 of the prelates and magnates of all the kingdoms under the 'Mercian Supremacy', following its consolidation under the new regime of Coenwulf. Here, presumably amongst other matters, it was publicly decided as to what would become of the huge, trans-regional monastic holdings of Offa and Cynethryth's kindred, now that they had ceased to hold the royal title. The resolutions over Cookham, *Pectanage*, and Glastonbury may have only been the tip of the iceberg. With some concessions here and there, the case of Cynethryth and her *genealogia* seems to have won out. The guarantees first made in Pope Hadrian's privilege may have played the trump card.

But why would Coenwulf have overseen, perhaps even forced through, such pro-Offing settlements? Was there not much to gain from seizing, repurposing, and redistributing such sites? And was Coenwulf not elsewhere wiping the slate clean of Offa's legacy: arrogating royal titles to his own family, and, at Lichfield, already preparing for the scrap-heap the dead king's reforms to the structure of the English episcopate? Doubtlessly, there were situational considerations that we cannot now recover. Nor should it entirely surprise us if Coenwulf's position by mid-798 had become geared towards a degree of public peace-making: taking up the role of the king as defender of widows and orphans had its obvious virtues.[48] With regard to safeguarding the legacy of Offa and Cynethryth's Petrine minsters, however, two factors in particular appear to have come into play. First, *quid pro quo*: in recognition for protecting some or most of these monasteries, Coenwulf may have felt entitled to lay claim to a certain select few for himself and his heirs. Second, there was the issue of setting a precedent of royal recognition of such papal privileges, in the event that Coenwulf and his family might also hope to benefit from comparable guarantees in the longer term. Coenwulf may have perceived the benefits of Offa and Cynethryth's scheme, but it needed his well-publicised recognition and support in 798 if a similar claim by his own heirs in the future were ever to be accepted. In fact, we may have evidence that both such strategies were already underway in that same year. Here we return to the monastery of Winchcombe.

The earliest section of the *Winchcombe Chronicle* (1122/*c*. 1150) includes under the year 811 a now-undated privilege of Leo III for Coenwulf, confirming

---

[48] Cf. Halfond, 'Caring'.

his monasteries and estates, immediately adjoined to a purported foundation charter for Winchcombe in Coenwulf's name, dated to November that year.[49] However corrupted in its current form, Leo's document appears authentic in its essentials, and while not based upon *Liber diurnus* 93, broadly follows it sense-for-sense if not word-for-word, granting the same sort of privileges to Coenwulf as Hadrian had to Offa and Cynethryth: Leo confirms to Coenwulf and his heirs 'all the monasteries and diverse places' he has procured, held through kin, or justly acquired, and sanctions against their future interference, including by future kings. Whether this extant text's clause on Coenwulf's burial, prayers for his sins, or freedoms from secular service reflects Leo's original privilege is obscure. Similarly uncertain are the 'monasteries and diverse places' the text concerns, although Winchcombe was probably chief among them.[50] In any case, the document appears to have made the crucial distinction between the monasteries secured for Coenwulf and his 'heirs' (*hereditas, heredes*), and the machinations of future generations and kings (*posteri successoresque reges*). That is, it does *not* assume that the two were one and the same, nor does it equate 'royal monasteries' with 'familial' ones. Just as he had overseen the safeguarding of Hadrian's privilege for Offa and Cynethryth in 798, Coenwulf appears here to have acquired a wide-ranging papal guarantee that, were his own family to lose the royal title, they would not lose their network of monastic properties.

In fact, we may even be looking at an arrangement made that same year, perhaps at this same *Clofesho* assembly. Coenwulf's accompanying 'foundation charter' is certainly bogus, and its date of 811 may only derive from the lost *acta* of an 811 synod at Chelsea.[51] We need turn only one folio back in the *Chronicle*'s manuscript to find our clue. While the better part of the *Winchcombe Chronicle* is based on the work of John of Worcester, some entries for the years around the turn of the ninth century are unique, and leave little doubt that this was a house closely associated with the memory of Coenwulf and his family, a 'man magnificent and happy in his holy offspring...who constructed this monastery called Winchcombe', as the entry for his succession under 795 (*sic*) reads, paying little attention to Offa and Ecgfrith.[52] However, a later, twelfth- or thirteenth-century hand has added in the margins for 787 that it was in fact Offa who had first

[49]   32; BCS 338 (S 167); BL, Cotton Tiberius E. iv, ff. 13v–14.
[50]   Abingdon was probably also covered: *33.   [51]   Cubitt, *Councils*, p. 284.
[52]   BL, Cotton Tiberius E. iv, f. 13; *Chron. Winch.*, i, pp. 99–146.

founded Winchcombe, installing women religious, before adding at 798 that Coenwulf built (another?) monastery there in that year, when it was dedicated by thirteen bishops.[53] The sources for this information are not known.[54] But it is difficult to see what high-medieval Winchcombe stood to gain from these claims. The argument of the *Chronicle*'s recent editor, that the documents preserved under 811 serve as more reliable witnesses,[55] can hardly be true for dating the house's foundation, since Coenwulf's foundation charter is almost completely forged, while Pope Leo's privilege has lost its dating clause, and speaks only of acquisitions, not foundations. The annotator's dating of 798 for Coenwulf's addition of a further church at Winchcombe is suggestive, particularly in light of its apparent independence from the other documents from that year discussed above. Given the circumstances, it seems a most plausible original date for the Leo privilege now copied under the entry for 811.[56] If so, then we are probably looking at the *Clofesho* assembly of 798, following an embassy to Rome in March that year, as not only the occasion on which the new king gave his guarantee for most of the papal-secured monasteries claimed by the fallen Offing dynasty, but where he also promulgated his own privilege, newly acquired from Leo, which safeguarded under Peter's authority the properties of his own *heredes* against the predations of *posteri successoresque reges*. The two acts went hand-in-hand. Coenwulf's legitimation of Offa and Cynethryth's papal privilege meant the legitimation of his own. And at the centre of the settlement stood Winchcombe: first founded by Offa in 787; covered by Hadrian's original guarantee (its principal dedication was to Peter); then handed over to the new king in 798 in due recognition of his arbitration, becoming apparently the heart of the new Coenwulfing dynasty's own monastic network.

*   *   *

One last detail from this same year needs quickly revisiting: the matter of the Canterbury and Lichfield archbishoprics. A twelfth-century tradition held that, after Coenwulf had crushed the Kentish uprising in 798, he blinded and

---

[53] Reconstructed by Hayward: *Chron. Winch.*, i, pp. 246, 249, ii, pp. 450, 452.

[54] The same passages appeared a generation earlier in the *Quedam Chronica de Anglia*: *Chron. Winch.*, i, pp. 248–9.

[55] *Chron. Winch.*, i, p. 248.

[56] 798 is also the date given for Winchcombe's foundation in a narrative passage in the monastery's thirteenth-century cartulary: Gloucester, Gloucestershire Archives, D678/1 M4/1, f. 33; *Landboc*, ed. Royce, i, p. 17. The date of 811 given for **30** by Royce in the margins of his edition (ibid., p. 21) is his own intervention.

mutilated its leader, Eadberht Præn, and imprisoned him at Winchcombe.[57] If this is true, it would have proved a fitting gesture within what we can now discern of Coenwulf's wider programme that year of consolidating his regime change, and asserting his right to Winchcombe as his new dynastic centre. Eadberht's removal also meant that the pro-Mercian Archbishop Æthelheard could return to Canterbury.[58] It is understandable, then, that 798 is the year usually attributed to Coenwulf's sole surviving letter to Leo III, a petition for the suppression of Offa's Lichfield archbishopric (first approved by Hadrian in 787/95), which accompanied a now-lost letter of Æthelheard on the same theme.[59] Katy Cubitt has argued that Coenwulf's remark in his letter, stating that this petition was drawn up 'with all the bishops of our province', indicates a synodal context.[60] It is conceivable that this too originated at our *Clofesho* council of summer–autumn 798. The letter also refers to a mishandled earlier petition on the same matter, conveyed to Leo by one Abbot Wada: perhaps he was part of the conjectured first Coenwulfing embassy to Rome that March, acquiring the above-discussed monastic privileges. It is now generally accepted that Coenwulf had sought through his second embassy not just the dissolution of Offa's Lichfield project, but the relocation of the southern archbishopric to Mercian-controlled London. This would have realised the original plan of Gregory I, probably best known to the king and his counsellors through Bede's *Ecclesiastical History*.[61] Leo, in his non-committal letter of reply (798/9?), at least made clear that he had understood Coenwulf to have meant as much.[62] It is necessary to emphasise, however, that while Coenwulf's letter speaks of the Gregorian plan, he only does so only in order to introduce his account of how the archbishopric ultimately became established in Canterbury, Augustine's burial place, since 'it seemed right to all the wise men of our nation that the metropolitan dignity should be established in that city, where rest the bodily relics of him who implanted the true faith in these regions.' This is his last word on the matter. Modern scholarship may have put too much weight on Leo's reply. It is possible that the pope had misread the situation; that those bearing the letter to Rome had communicated otherwise;[63] or—as seems most likely—that Leo's remarks referred back to the earlier embassy of Wada, who had dealt with the matter,

[57] *ASC*, s.a. 796 F; *GR*, I, i. 95, pp. 138–9; Brooks, *Early History*, pp. 124–5.

[58] Brooks, *Early History*, p. 125; *Christ Church*, pp. 197–8.   [59] *GR*, I, i. 88, pp. 125–9.

[60] Cubitt, *Councils*, pp. 277–8.

[61] Brooks, *Early History*, pp. 123–5; Noble, 'Rise', pp. 297–9; *HE*, i. 29, pp. 104–7 (1).

[62] *MGH Epp.* IV, pp. 187–9 (JE 2494).   [63] Brooks, *Early History*, pp. 123–4.

Coenwulf regretted, 'unwisely'. By mid-798, with Kent subdued and Eadberht in chains, it looks as though the king had already firmly set his sights on acquiring a papal privilege that would restore Canterbury to its full archiepiscopal dignity.

To what advantage? I argue here that one of Coenwulf's primary objectives with seeing this through would have been the legitimacy it would have given to his own papal privileges protecting his family's monasteries. In a world with effectively no mechanisms of enforcement coming from the papacy itself for its rulings, a consensus about the inviolability of papal privileges needed to be continually established 'on the ground' within any given society if there were any chance of these documents having any effect. Offa's innovative Hadrianic privileges—the one for his family monasteries, and the other for the elevation of Lichfield[64]—may not have initially enjoyed much recognition. Coenwulf would probably not have faced much opposition if he had simply torn them up. As we have seen, however, the king needed to recognise Hadrian's privilege for the properties of Offa and Cynethryth's *genealogia* if he were also to secure recognition for his own. Moreover, if Hadrian's proprietorial privilege had to be respected, the same would therefore need to apply for this pope's document raising Lichfield. Coenwulf therefore found himself compelled to do things 'by the book', refer the case to Rome, and acquire a new privilege from Pope Leo, if this atmosphere of legitimacy so beneficial to him were to be constructed and maintained. In fact, the agonisingly slow process of the affair (three embassies; hundreds of *mancuses* in gifts; synodal meetings of the entire Southumbrian church; and no final resolution until the promulgation of Leo's restoration-privilege for Canterbury at the *Clofesho* council of 803)[65] surely helped Coenwulf's case. It publicised the idea that papal rulings needed to be regarded as matters of superlative importance, and that simply ignoring them was not a serious option.

This may have felt new. What looks like the relative ineffectiveness of the privileges discussed in Chapter 4 implies that such a consensus about the inviolability of papal rulings was *not* the norm in seventh- and earlier

---

[64] *30 was condemned at *Clofesho* 803: *Christ Church*, 32 (S 1431a).

[65] Leo's restoration privilege (35) required another embassy led by Æthelheard in 801–2. In his letter to Coenwulf accompanying the privilege (*GR*, I, i. 89, pp. 130–3: JE 2511) Leo remarks that he had received 120 *mancuses* in gift from the king, probably in addition to the 120 Coenwulf had pledged to send with the bearers of his 798 letter (*GR*, I, i. 88, pp. 128–9). The privilege did not receive full synodal promulgation until 12 Oct. 803: above, n. 64. See further Brooks, *Early History*, pp. 125–7.

eighth-century England. After all, even Gregory's letters had gone ignored when it came to the continued pre-eminence of Canterbury after Augustine's death. Coenwulf and his counsellors therefore made an extremely shrewd move in securing from Leo a privilege granting Canterbury its full archiepiscopal status south of the Humber, since doing so gave, for the first time ever, an honour that had formerly been based only on tradition a fully documented legal grounding. From 802/3 Canterbury owed its position to a contemporary papal privilege alone. If it wished—let's say, by also asserting lordship over certain monasteries—to challenge the legitimacy of Coenwulf's familial papal privileges, it could not do so without jeopardising its own legal security. As it happened, just such a situation arose.

III. Confrontation: Wulfred, Cwoenthryth, and Paschal

The Coenwulfings' hold over their network of proprietorial family monasteries was not without its opponents in the Southumbrian church hierarchy. Across the following two decades, enormous tensions grew between the king and Canterbury over the control of certain high-profile minsters, principally in Kent. Matters exploded with the suspension of Æthelheard's successor Wulfred between c. 816/17 and c. 821/2, and what looks like the freezing of all activity at his archepiscopal see. This momentous event has conspicuously left almost no trace in the record. It is solely and obscurely addressed in the Canterbury charter for the Wulfred–Cwoenthryth 'reconciliation' of 826/7 (with which this chapter began) as principally concerning the monasteries of Reculver and Minster-in-Thanet, with Wulfred's defrocking brought about through the instigation of Coenwulf, who had sent dispatches of some kind to Rome, and whose threats against the archbishop obscurely invoked the pope and even emperor.[66] The details of the build-up to this event, and its background in decades-old tensions between opposing lay and episcopal claims to monastic lordship, have been expertly covered by Nicholas Brooks, Susan Wood, and John Blair.[67] It is worth stressing that the nature of the dispute by the early ninth century seems to have been less a case of bishops seeking to 'free' churches out of 'worldly' control and into some sort of abstract vacuum of autonomy, than the exertions of these

---

[66] Above, pp. 152–3.
[67] Brooks, *Early History*, pp. 175–206; Wood, *Proprietary Church*, pp. 152–60, 239–44; Blair, *Church*, pp. 79–134.

prelates towards claiming their own, alternative proprietorial lordship over such sites. Essentially the matter was fought over which 'family' controlled any one church: the kin-group of a king or lay aristocrat, or the corporate *familia* gathered around a bishop. Under Archbishop Wulfred (803–32), whom we know from other sources to have been especially prominent in enriching the Canterbury Christ Church *familia*, these claims to episcopal lordship intensified, finding their most forceful expression at the Council of Chelsea of 816. As Cubitt has shown, Chelsea's *acta* took a cavalier approach to late antique canon law. These misrepresented the rulings of Chalcedon (451) on episcopal oversight of monasteries within their *parrochia* and the inviolability of monastic property as if they extended to full episcopal lordship, and with that the 'fuzzy' implication of proprietorial control.[68] Coenwulf and his leading nobles attended that council; the archbishopric of Canterbury was suspended shortly thereafter. Only during the troubled reign of the king's brother Ceolwulf (821–3) did Wulfred return to Canterbury; and only after Ceolwulf's overthrow and the Coenwulfings' fall from power—and soon after, the collapse of Mercian hegemony altogether[69]—did the archbishop at last, if only gradually, take hold over the disputed monasteries and clear his name. Even then, Coenwulf's daughter managed to defy Wulfred for a surprisingly long time. This much we have seen uniquely recorded at the beginning of this chapter in the Canterbury charter of 826/7.

What triggered Wulfred's dethronement? And why was the archbishop still finding himself outmanoeuvred by the king's daughter for six years after his death? Earlier studies have raised the possibility that Coenwulf's papal privileges for his monasteries—that of Leo III (798?), supported by another of Paschal (817/18)—played a role in this crisis.[70] In fact, we need to treat them as absolutely central to it. They provide the key to making sense of Wulfred's deposition, and allow us to understand Cwoenthryth's years-long resistance to the resurgent archbishop. An important clue lies in the evidence that this dispute endured long after Coenwulf's death and his family's loss of the royal title. This points directly towards the situation envisioned and insured against in Leo III's privilege: one in which Coenwulf's *heredes* and *hereditas* (two terms from the papal document which reappear to describe the party led by Cwoenthryth in the 826/7 charter) continued to

---

[68] HS iii, pp. 579–85; Cubitt, *Councils*, pp. 191–204. 'Fuzzy' boundaries between lordship and ownership: Nelson, 'Church Properties', pp. 369–72.

[69] Keynes, 'England, 700–900', pp. 35–8.   [70] Above, n. 16.

claim lordship over the king's monasteries against the predations of future generations. As first outlined in Hadrian's precedent-setting privilege for Offa and Cynethryth, this was not about protecting public, 'royal monasteries', but those held within a kinship group, once that family no longer held royal title. The 826/7 charter reveals that Wulfred's final victory over Cwoenthryth took place at an assembly in the vicinity of Winchcombe. This strongly suggests a connection. The position of Abbess Cwoenthryth (formerly the king's daughter) after the fall of her dynasty in 823–7 looks a lot like that of Abbess Cynethryth (formerly queen) in 796–8. Her ability to retain for years some hold over her familial minsters probably rested on just the same documentary means as Cynethryth had done, with Leo and Paschal in the place of Hadrian. The former queen's case may well have been recalled as a precedent. What differed this time was, following the disintegration of Mercian power in the mid-820s, the absence of a strong king to act as final guarantor for those privileges in 826/7, that is, as Coenwulf had done in 798. Wulfred finally got his way, but only as the whole edifice of the 'Mercian Supremacy' suddenly collapsed around him. By contrast, Coenwulf seems to have enjoyed exceptional success in pursuing his cause, plausibly using the archbishop's claims upon the monasteries covered by his papal privileges as the grounds for defrocking him shortly after 816.

His ability to do so need not have required invoking anything beyond the privileges themselves. Again: the papacy had virtually no enforcement mechanisms of its own, and the implementation of its documents was solely a matter for the societies of their addressees. This applied to the punishment of transgressions as much as the positive fulfilment of privileges, the former being outlined in the negative *sanctiones* of contemporary papal documents. These typically imposed excommunication or anathematisation upon opponents of the texts. All that was needed was a sufficiently wide consensus that papal privileges were rulings of the highest significance, even inviolable, something which the tortuous turn-of-the-century negotiations over the positions of Canterbury and Lichfield may have temporarily achieved. Some modern readings of the 826/7 charter's references to the king's 'insinuations' (*inmissio*) in Rome, and to the 'lord pope' and *caesar*, have suggested that the procedure leading to Wulfred's suspension had taken on international dimensions, in which Pope Paschal (817–24) became 'deeply involved', and which had even drawn in Louis the Pious (814–41).[71]

---

[71] Stenton, *Anglo-Saxon England*, pp. 229–30; *Christ Church*, pp. 598–601.

Inmissio need only indicate, however, a negative gloss on the kinds of embassies Coenwulf must have dispatched to acquire his monastic privileges, and need not imply any high-level intrigue at the Aachen or Lateran palaces. Coenwulf's reported offer to keep Wulfred 'secure against the lord pope' if he fell into line, and warning that 'neither the words of the lord pope nor *caesar*' would aid him if he did not, could meanwhile simply indicate that the king and his assembly had threatened to enforce the papal privilege's sanctions upon him for interfering with his monasteries. The reference to *caesar* is intelligible when we recall that contemporary papal documents dramatically ended with their authentication in the name of the emperor, 'crowned by God'.[72] That the single legal guarantee of Canterbury's own position as metropolitan see now depended upon a comparable papal privilege of 802, ending with just such a clause, would have made the gravity and legitimacy of this invocation difficult to argue against.

With good reason, then, Canterbury under Wulfred's leadership began to act evasively about the nature of papal authority. Much has been made of the *Anglo-Saxon Chronicle*'s remark on the archbishop's visit to Leo for his 'blessing' in 815–16, timed as it was just before the Council of Chelsea and his subsequent suspension.[73] He appears, however, to have returned empty-handed. It says a lot that, despite Canterbury's interest in the use of written proofs across these years,[74] Wulfred and his successors never contended that they had ever received any papal rulings backing their claims to the Kentish minsters (nor any others). One can detect a change of mood at the archbishopric in the first decade of the century. Synodal injunctions about the need to respect papal privileges had featured among the canons of the 'Legatine Councils' of 786, and again at the *Clofesho* meeting of 803 held under Æthelheard.[75] The latter was the same meeting at which Leo's privilege for Canterbury's pre-eminence was promulgated, and the archbishop took the opportunity to claim that the pope had also 'mandated' to him that (all?) monasteries should be permitted to elect their own abbots, 'and not presume to choose lay and secular lords over the *hereditas* of the Lord'. There is no evidence that this referred to an official papal decree formulated around 800/2 for general promulgation in the Latin west.[76] A generic pledge

---

[72] Above, Chapter 2, p. 45.

[73] *ASC, s.a.* 813 ACDE, 815 F; Brooks, *Early History*, p. 186; Cubitt, *Councils*, p. 191; Story, *Carolingian Connections*, pp. 207–8.

[74] HS iii, p. 583. Unusual density of documentation from these decades: *Christ Church*, pp. 42–3.

[75] *MGH Epp.* IV, p. 22; *Christ Church*, 33 (S 1431b).   [76] *Pace Christ Church*, pp. 461–2.

that 'justice' be done for the monasteries as well as 'dioceses' in Canterbury's jurisdiction appears in Leo's second letter to Coenwulf:[77] Æthelheard's conciliar announcement may have just reflected an attempt to formalise that gesture. Whatever the case, upon Wulfred's succession evidence of pro-papal sentiment at Canterbury ceases, and one gets the impression that the perceived strength of Coenwulf's claim to holding his disputed monasteries through papal authority had made Rome a difficult subject for the arch-bishop. We can see this in the forged documents drawn up at Canterbury in those same years. Wulfred's scriptorium almost certainly fabricated two documents attributed to King Wihtred of Kent (purportedly 699/716) and Æthelbald, king of the Mercians ('742'), together with a false decree of the Council of Hatfield of '680' (sic, for 679). These sought to project back into the distant past the causes dearest to early ninth-century Canterbury—in the case of forged charters, the safety of the 'free' monasteries from lay or royal lordship; in 'Pseudo-Hatfield', the see's full and unchallenged archiepiscopal status in Southumbria.[78] What has gone undervalued, however, is the fact that these forgeries do not merely imagine a past wherein Canterbury's contemporary interests were defended, but moreover they do so largely *without* deference to Rome. They advance much the same claims as Æthelheard had in 803 in the name of Leo III, yet they locate them in a pre-Leonine, pre-Hadrianic age, without recourse to papal authority, only the supremacy of Insular royal and conciliar decisions. It is in fact remark-able, in light of recent events—not least his visit to Rome only months before—that Wulfred made no invocation of papal authority at his Chelsea Synod of 816, his last great set-piece and claim to the Kentish minsters before his suspension.[79] This was, given the circumstances, an *anti*-papal council. Leo's privilege might have given Coenwulf such a winning hand in the dispute that Wulfred found himself compelled to seek out entirely alternative sources of authority. That path drove him to forgery.

The smoking gun for the central role of papal privileges in the murky events of 816/17–826/7 comes, however, from the extant text of Coenwulf's second privilege for his familial monasteries and estates, acquired from Pope Paschal (14 Dec. 817/1 Jan. 818). Nicholas Brooks noted the significance of this document's dating: only shortly after the Council of Chelsea, and at just

---

[77] *GR*, I, i. 89, pp. 130–3 (JE 2511).

[78] *Christ Church*, 8, 12 (S 22, 90); Brooks, *Early History*, pp. 191–7; Cubitt, 'Finding'.

[79] Cubitt, *Councils*, p. 192, remarks that Wulfred put special weight in his Chelsea legislation upon 'the authority of the canons of the Roman church'. But these were only 'Roman' in that they belonged to the late antique conciliar tradition (i.e. Nicaea and Chalcedon).

the point the archbishop disappears from the record. Nevertheless the text, also preserved in the twelfth-century *Winchcombe Chronicle* (*sub anno* 818), has proven difficult to interpret due to its fragmentary state.[80] As shown in Part I, the bulk of what survives closely mirrors what we know of Pope Hadrian's privilege for Offa and Cynethryth (and thus *Liber diurnus* 93), its only real differences being its single addressee and reference to *heredes* instead of 'those born of your *genealogia*'. Its dating clause, while horribly mangled in its extant form, has an authentic basis. The more serious problem of the Paschal text is that it follows the *Liber diurnus* formula far *too* well, as demonstrated in a side-by-side comparison of the closing lines of both:

Liber diurnus V 93	*Paschal I for Coenwulf*
...in perpetuum eadem monasteria et agrorum possesiones cum omnibus originalibus famulis ac manentibus. uel uniuersis sibi pertinentibus apostolicae sedis priuilegiis poposcitis confirmari detinenda sicuti inferius adscripta eadem loca atque agrorum predia continere monstratur scilic& [*Text ends*]	...in perpetuum eadem monasteria et agrorum possessiones cum omnibus originalibus famulis ac manentibus uel uniuersis sibi pertinentibus apostolicę sedis priuilegio poposcitis confirmari detinenda sicuti inferius asscripta eadem loca atque agrorum predia continere monstratur. [D]a[t(um)...] Kal[enda]s Ianua[r]i[a]s p[e]r [m]an[um] Theodo[ri] [n]um[encul]atoris [s(an)c(t)ae] s[edis a]po[stolicae, imp(erante) d(omi)n(o) n(ostro) H]ludouuic[o] piiss(imo) [p(er) p(etuo)] august[o] a Deo coronat[o] magn[o] imper[ato]re anno [q]u[a]r[t]o [et p(ost) c(onsulatus) eius anno quarto] s [ed] et [H]lothari[o] novo imperatore eius filio anno primo indictione XI. [*Text ends*]

[80] 36; BL, Cotton Tiberius E. iv, f. 15; Brooks, *Early History*, p. 186.

Translation of final section of LD V 93: '...you have asked to be confirmed to be held forever, with privileges of the apostolic see, those same monasteries, and possessions of lands, with all their native slaves and tenants, and everything that pertains to them: that is, those same ascribed places and estates of land shown to be included below, namely [Text ends]'.

Translation of final extant section of Paschal I for Coenwulf: '...you have asked to be confirmed to be held forever, with a privilege of the apostolic see, those same monasteries, and possessions of lands, with all their native slaves and tenants, and everything that pertains to them: that is, those same ascribed places and estates of land shown to be included below Given on the [...] Kalends of January through the hand of Theodore, *numenculator* of the holy apostolic see, in the fourth year of the imperial reign of our lord Louis the most pious, forever augustus, the great emperor crowned by God, and in the fourth year after his consulship, but also in the first year of the reign of his son Lothar, the new emperor, in the eleventh indiction' [Text ends].'

We can see that both abruptly cut short just as they introduce the crucial dispositive clause listing the monasteries and properties confirmed. This is perfectly understandable in the *Liber diurnus* manuscript, since it presents the document as a reusable formula. Yet for the same rupture to appear at precisely the same spot in the later Winchcombe copies of Paschal's privilege for Coenwulf hardly seems intelligible. Rather, it is almost infuriating: we find ourselves just about to discover which specific minsters and estates Coenwulf sought to protect immediately after the 816 council, indeed just as his conflict with the archbishop blew up—and then the section breaks off mid-sentence. Instead, the document immediately jumps ahead to its final section, the *datatio*. Pierre Chaplais argued that the bizarre coincidence between this Italian formulary and twelfth-century English text could only point to the latter being a forgery, copied, he claimed, from an (otherwise unattested) *Liber diurnus* manuscript in England.[81] As Brooks rightly pointed out, this accusation of forgery plainly lacks a motive. Why would Winchcombe use a formula to forge a text that granted or confirmed absolutely nothing?[82] However, Brooks' alternative hypothesis—that the original papyrus had simply worn away over the centuries, causing the copyist's exemplar to cut off at this point—does not suffice either. The poor quality of the dating clause indicates that the very bottom of the original papyrus sheet was in a sorry state by the time the privilege was copied, but this cannot explain why the preceding sections of the document are entirely missing. We have continental examples of degraded papyrus originals, and none follow such a peculiar pattern of textual loss.[83] For the papyrus to have fallen apart as cleanly as Brooks suggested—ending *immediately* before the concerned properties are introduced, and resuming suddenly for the dating clause—would be an incredible turns of events if it really did result from accidental degradation within the archive. This caesura looks man-made.

In fact, if we study this fragmentary Winchcombe text alongside the settlement charter of 826/7 preserved only at Canterbury, we find that the deficiencies of Paschal's privilege as it survives may, paradoxically, reveal a great deal about its function and effectiveness, and perhaps even resolve the matter of how and why Wulfred vanishes from our records at just this time. Towards the end of its description of the final stages of the dispute with Coenwulf and Cwoenthryth over the Kentish minsters of Reculver and Minster-in-Thanet, the Canterbury charter has the archbishop declare that

---

[81] Chaplais, 'Some Anglo-Saxon Diplomas,' pp. 355–6.
[82] Brooks, *Early History*, pp. 185–6.   [83] For the full corpus see above, Chapter 2, n. 000.

he has at last been freed from all *causae*, and is willing to reconcile with the humiliated and defeated abbess,

> on this condition: that the names of the aforesaid lands are erased from the old privileges at Winchcombe, and not brought forth again.[84]

Could we link these demands for erasures with the missing section of Paschal's privilege? Thanks to the relatively systematic diplomatic employed by papal scribes, outlined in Chapter 2, we can reconstruct with some confidence what the original document would have looked like, progressing from the opening *protocol*; to *arenga, narratio*, then *dispositio* (including the list of pertaining properties); then the *sanctiones*; before the closing *eschatocol* (*BENE VALETE* and dating clause). Our surviving text of the privilege retains the first three in their entirety; excepting the *BENE VALETE* (easily left untranscribed, since on the original papyrus it would have stood out as distinct from the main text in its oversized, quasi-graphic form), it also preserves the *eschatocol*. What it precisely lacks, therefore, is (i) the *dispositio*, which would have in this case consisted of the list of the names of the monastic properties and pertaining estates protected by the document; and (ii) the *sanctio*, with which transgressors would be punished, typically by declaring them anathematised and barred from the company of the faithful. These are abruptly missing from the surviving version of the privilege, whereas the rest remains close to intact.

Using these telling silences, let's now attempt at last a reconstruction of events. Following the Council of Chelsea of 816, tensions between Coenwulf and Wulfred over the disputed lordship of the Kentish monasteries had reached their peak. Coenwulf thereupon proceeded to double-down on his (impressive, but admittedly somewhat imprecise) privilege of Leo III for his family's properties by dispatching to Rome envoys to meet the newly elected Paschal. There, at the very end of 817, they acquired for the king a further privilege closely resembling that which Hadrian had granted to Offa and Cynethryth. This not only confirmed Coenwulf and his heirs' lordship over their monasteries and estates, but listed them by name. Based on the contentions of the later charter of 826/7, we can surmise that Reculver, Minster-in-Thanet, and their vast holdings were chief among them the places enumerated. With this second privilege now brought before the bishops and *principes* of Southumbria—that is, by a king as powerful as

---

[84] Above, n. 10.

Coenwulf, and in a society with as sufficiently secure a consensus about the potency and inviolability of papal rulings as early ninth-century England may have become—Wulfred's continued refusal to back down from his own assertions of lordship over these sites would have now looked indefensible. His forged charters, depicting a bygone world in which the archbishopric of Canterbury and the 'freedom' of his minsters were guaranteed by powers other than the pope, were not enough to save him. Paschal's privilege would have ordered automatic condemnation and anathematisation of any who defied its terms. Coenwulf seems to have had enough support on the ground by now to put this into effect. Wulfred may have thus found himself publicly anathematised: we know that his church now ceased to issue charters; ceased to organise synods; and ceased to mint coins—in the words of the later account, 'the whole people of the English were deprived of his primordial authority and ministry of holy baptism for altogether six years.'

As the 820s progressed, Wulfred slowly began to claw back his position, thanks to the death of Coenwulf, the deposition of his brother, and collapse of Mercian hegemony under a succession of weakened kings. Even as late as 826/7, however, Cwoenthryth appears to have held on to Leo and Paschal's privileges at her familial minster (and now her father's mausoleum?) at Winchcombe. She invoked them effectively enough to still exercise power over distant Minster-in-Thanet, long after Wulfred thought he had the issue settled. Only at the 826/7 council of *Oslafeshau* did Wulfred finally close the matter, publicly humiliating the abbess. No documentation survives from the archbishop's wilderness years, and we should not be surprised if he had them destroyed. Yet by ordering Cwoenthryth to make erasures to her archive at Winchcombe, Wulfred, in his moment of triumph, inadvertently left us in the Canterbury charter a clue to the central document which instigated his downfall. Centuries later, when a high-medieval scribe of Winchcombe copied down what remained of the papyral scroll he unfurled before him, two parts *precisely* were completely missing: its list of monas-teries and their estates, and a promise to condemn to anathema whoever laid claim to them. In what that copyist could not find, we can pinpoint precisely how, when, why, and in whose name Archbishop Wulfred fell from power.

IV. Conclusions

When we met Cwoenthryth at the beginning of this chapter, it was in the guise she assumed in the oral memory of eleventh-century Winchcombe: as a usurper and murderess, striving through witchcraft to fight off Archbishop Wulfred, who had hurried to the monastery's rescue on the orders of Pope Leo. Her cause of death, reading Psalm 109 (108) backwards, represents a classic example of the fairy-tale 'spell turned back on itself' trope. Psalm 109 was a cursing psalm, employed in contemporary rituals of excommunication and anathema;[85] by aiming it towards Wulfred, but speaking the words in reverse, she only cursed herself. In light of what we can now reconstruct of ninth-century events, there is a wonderful irony here. In reality, it may well have been Wulfred who found himself anathematised in the 810s–20s, on the explicit pretext of a contemporary papal sanction; we might like to imagine Psalm 109 being read over his own lowered head by an assembly of bishops, as Cwoenthryth and her father watched on.[86] At the very least, we know that the historical abbess had long persisted as the defender of Winchcombe's interests, and Wulfred its predator. Considering the remarkable role reversals that had taken place in the house's collective memory by the later eleventh century, it feels apt that the anathema which Cwoenthryth's high-medieval incarnation directed at the archbishop only ended up bouncing back upon her.

The warped ironies of Winchcombe's later traditions present us with something more, however, than a curious endnote. They are a testament to the degree to which these peculiar developments of the 770s–820s—wherein three generations of Mercian royal-aristocratic families successfully harnessed papal authority to protect their own monastic inheritance against the episcopate—had become successfully obliterated from historical memory. As the adopted central cult site of Coenwulfing power, and the family's archive and mausoleum, Winchcombe had meant to serve as a 'place of memory' of the highest order. While the legends that had accrued there around Coenwulf, Cwoenthryth, and the mysterious 'Kenelm king's-son' by the time of the Norman Conquest show that remnants of this survived, they had become little more than empty names to which new, *topos*-laden stories were attached. Memories of the Coenwulfings appear to have lost most of their textual basis. Following the densely packed set of entries and documentary insertions concerning Coenwulf and the early history of Winchcombe that appear in its twelfth-century *Chronicle* under

---

[85] e.g. Cambridge, Corpus Christi College, 146, f. 329 (from Winchcombe's diocese of Worcester, 1096/1112); Jaser, *Ecclesia*, pp. 178–82.

[86] Psalm 109 is used in this way in an episcopal deposition ritual in Gregory of Tours, *Libri*, v. 18, p. 223.

the years 798–818, we find nothing more about either the family or the house itself after a confused entry on Coenwulf's death (misdated to 819). The Winchcombe record only resumes with entries for the house's 'Benedictine Reform'-era abbots, beginning with Germanus (966), and these anyway belong to the hand of a still later, thirteenth-century scribe.[87] The early ninth to later tenth century had become a zone of oblivion for the house. These sudden lacunae could have owed something to the disruptions of the 'Viking Age'; the house's refoundation in the 960s as an all-male, Benedictine monastery;[88] and perhaps also a reported fire in 1090.[89] Yet the later *Chronicle*'s concentration of evidence from the years leading right up to Cwoenthryth's abbacy, parts of which reproduced authentic documentary sources, suggests that through all these years some genuine kernel of texts remained, even if they cut short in the 820s. Wulfred's demand that Winchcombe's archives be pruned of their evidence of the Coenwulfing inheritance, and the selective deletions observable in Paschal's privilege, serve as important reminders that archival losses need not always have come as a result of the vicissitudes of time, nor later, epoch-shaking moments such as the Viking wars or subsequent waves of reform. Sometimes, the destruction of evidence could depend upon on-the-spot decisions made in the wake of sudden shifts of power, with obliterative effects on a house's identity. With Abbess Cwoenthryth reduced to merely a name in the eleventh-century Winchcombe tradition, confused oral traditions of her power became linked to the community's retention of two fragmentary, barely comprehensible papal letters, spawning a legend in which she had not been Winchcombe's defender, but its tyrant, who was finally defeated through the dispatch of papal edicts. As the foregoing has shown, a reconstruction of her historical role is only possible if we explore contemporary charters independently preserved at the other side of the country, at Canterbury.

My core argument here is that the intentional destruction and suppression of papal privileges, and even of evidence for their use, indicates their fundamental potency in England at the turn of the ninth century. We have seen through these years instances where the successful invocation of papal

---

[87] BL, Cotton Tiberius E. iv, ff. 15, 17v; the 819 entry leads into a short account of the Kenelm-Cwoenthryth legend, ultimately derived from *Vita et miraculi sancti Kenelmi* (via John of Worcester, *Chronicle*, *s.a.* [819]). There is one further piece of evidence concerning pre-Benedictine Winchcombe, preserved elsewhere, via Worcester's archive: a charter (897) concerning land held on a three-lifetime lease from the *hereditas* of Coenwulf, although the precise arrangement is obscure, as is the identity of the 'Cynethryth' mentioned in the charter: BCS 575 (S 1442).

[88] Foot, *Veiled Women*, ii, pp. 239–41.   [89] John of Worcester, *Chronicle*, *s.a.* (1090).

documents in disputes went glaringly unmentioned (Canterbury's 'loser's narrative' of the Cookham settlement, 798); where other privileges were publicly denounced (Hadrian's privilege for Lichfield at *Clofesho* 803, which appropriately no longer survives); and where documentary erasures were demanded in public, a destructive act still leaving its mark in later copies (*Oslafeshau*/Winchcombe, 826/7). The fact we have to go as far as Nonantola to find a manuscript of Hadrian's privilege for Offa and Cynethryth's Southumbrian monasteries may in fact stand as the best evidence for its potency that we have: its English copies were in time destroyed. It is a great paradox (but not a contradiction) of the period studied in this chapter, that it has at one and the same time given us perhaps our best evidence for the successful implementation of papal privileges in England, and some of the worst evidence for their longer-term survival. These complement each other.

It was also a phase that would stand out as an anomaly in the papal master-narrative as it had already begun to develop by the central middle ages. Studies of social memory and oral tradition have shown how all-purpose 'fairy-tale' components can enter and restructure oral narratives when some of their original elements become (say, with time) decontextualised and no longer carry the same meaning.[90] The story of the Cwoenthryth–Rome–Wulfred triangle as it was first told at Winchcombe may have no longer made much sense to the monastery's eleventh-century, all-male Benedictine community. How, they might have asked, could a woman have rightfully inherited by blood full lordship over their house? And how could the great Pope Leo III have taken her side, against that of the reforming archbishop? The dispute's eventual reshaping beyond all recognition into a variant on 'The Juniper Tree' might, ironically, have produced a version of events more comprehensible to a community with high-medieval ideas of the relationship between the papacy and monasticism than one based on early ninth-century realities.

The papal privileges for the monasteries of the 'Mercian Supremacy' were, then, unique to their time. They were also unique to their region: granted in Rome, but petitioned and drafted as tailor-made solutions to problems specific to that time and place. Accordingly, this has been the least explicitly comparative chapter in this book, since no evidence survives in the Carolingian world of equivalent acquisitions from Rome. Could this itself be explained? The myriad differences between the workings of the empire of

---

[90] Fentress and Wickham, *Social Memory*, pp. 68–80, 88–97.

Charlemagne and Louis the Pious and that of their Mercian contemporaries (let alone the nature of their relationship to Rome) render impossible any single, straightforward answer. One issue that surely made a difference, however, was that of the distinction between royal monasteries and familial monasteries that these Anglo-papal documents presuppose. The Mercian disputes were not, as once thought, between the monoliths of 'Church and State', but conflicts over the suddenly ballooning wealth of 'churches' in the plural, fought out between multiple aristocratic families for whom the office of king came and went, and by the episcopal *familiae* who closely identified with none of them. The Carolingian achievement of establishing one family as 'natural lords', thereby co-identifying the concepts of a single *genealogia* with a single *imperium*,[91] and so too (at least in theory) a single *ecclesia*, opened up a vast gulf between political practice either side of the Channel. Only in the tenth century would something similar become established in England. But by then, as we will see in the following chapter, continental affairs had already begun to develop along a new, still different path.

[91] Airlie, '*Semper fideles?*', and now Airlie, *Making*.

6

Papal Privileges and the English Benedictine Movement (*c.* 960–*c.* 1000)

After Cwoenthryth—silence. With the collapse of Mercian hegemony, papal privileges disappear from the English record until the later tenth century. By then, we are once again looking at a transformed landscape, typically characterised by the unification of a single kingdom of the English under the West Saxon Cerdicing dynasty, and the 'Benedictine Reform' of its church under King Edgar (957/9–75) and the prelates Æthelwold (bishop of Winchester, 963–84), Dunstan (bishop of London and Worcester, 957/9, archbishop of Canterbury, 959–88), and Oswald (bishop of Worcester, 961–92, archbishop of York, 971–92).[1] Whatever the leading Mercian families had done to set a template for effective papal documentary interventions in English politics, such precedents were swept away by the rising West Saxon regime. As early as the 830s we see the ascendant King Ecgberht (802–39) and his son Æthelwulf (839–58) asserting a new kind of direct royal lordship over the 'episcopal' churches and monasteries of their newly conquered lands, reminiscent of the kind of public patronage exercised by the Carolingians, and free of any reference to external authorities, least of all the bishops of Rome.[2] Even when we begin to detect papal privileges in England again from the 960s, the evidence looks slight indeed. This by itself is remarkable, since the West Saxon royal court intensively cultivated its relationship with Rome throughout this period. Æthelwulf travelled in state to the papal court, and as a child his son Alfred (871–99) may have gone twice. In the years that followed, English emissaries began conveying to the Roman see the 'national' tribute of Peter's Pence, a unique monetary gift that would become enshrined in royal law by the later tenth century, and which must have involved huge sums of English coinage flowing into Rome

---

[1] Molyneaux, *Formation*. For the term 'reform' see Barrow, 'Ideas', but cf. Leyser, 'Church Reform'.

[2] *Christ Church*, 69 (S 1438); Blair, *Church*, pp. 124, 132–2; Wood, *Proprietary Church*, pp. 241–2.

England and the Papacy in the Early Middle Ages: Papal Privileges in European Perspective, c. 680–1073.
Benjamin Savill, Oxford University Press. © Benjamin Savill 2023. DOI: 10.1093/oso/9780198887058.003.0006

every year.[3] At the turn of the millennium, we find a papal emissary assisting at Rouen in a peace treaty between English and Norman delegates,[4] and around the same time we begin to see evidence of English bishops dispatching individual penitents to Rome to seek absolution at the apostolic see.[5] Yet throughout this period, hard evidence for Anglo-Saxon churches acquiring papal guarantees of their rights or properties appears negligible-to-non-existent.

Documentary absences of this kind look stranger still when we step back to observe developments elsewhere in Europe around this time. The later Carolingian period saw an acutely heightened articulation of the concept of papal authority and the right of ecclesiastics to petition for its intervention, reaching its apogee between the pontificates of Leo IV (847–55) and John VIII (872–82).[6] Besides such highlights as the crafting of the Pseudo-Isidorian forgeries (a canon law collection largely consisting of forged late antique papal decrees, probably concocted near Rheims, perhaps as late as *c.* 850),[7] and the appeal for Nicholas I (858–67) to wade into the divorce case of Lothar II (855–69),[8] the number of individual papal privileges acquired across the Carolingian empire rose exponentially in these decades. This new momentum survived the break-up of the Carolingian world and continued into the tenth century.[9] Historians once dismissed the institution of the papacy between the waning of the Carolingians and the coming of the mid-eleventh-century 'papal reform' as an inert and degenerate 'pornocracy', the epitome of all that was wrong with this supposed age of iron.[10] It is true that the individual bishops of Rome struggled, if they tried at all, to exercise much power beyond the city on their own initiative in these years. They also found themselves subject to local political upheavals and bouts of institutional amnesia.[11] Yet if we take a model of the papacy that looks not to the workings of the Roman institution itself, but to how political and religious communities on the outside perceived it, a case could be made for the 'long tenth century' as one in which papal authority remained highly

---

[3] Story, *Carolingian Connections*, pp. 225–8, 234–40; Naismith and Tinti, 'Origins'.
[4] *PUU* †307 (JL 3840).
[5] Aronstam, 'Penitential Pilgrimages': see below, Appendix, pp. 284–5.
[6] Scholz, *Politik*, pp. 172–239; Herbers, *Geschichte*, pp. 80–95.
[7] See *inter alia* Fuhrmann, 'Pseudo-Isidorian Forgeries'; Knibbs, 'Ebo'.
[8] d'Avray, *Dissolving*, pp. 11–43.
[9] As a rough guide, Santifaller, 'Verwendung', lists 88 surviving texts of apparently authentic papal privileges, 847–900, and 69 for 900–55. By contrast, for 752–847 only 25 authentic privileges are listed.
[10] Squatriti, 'Pornocracy'.   [11] Amnesia: Roberts, *Flodoard*, p. 165.

articulated and sought after throughout the post-Carolingian world. Collections of papal laws and letters such as Pseudo-Isidore continued to be copied and used;[12] appeals for papal emissaries to be sent up from Rome to participate in transalpine disputes (however fruitlessly) would still be made;[13] and petitions and acquisitions of new papal documents across East and West Francia, Italy and Catalonia rocketed to a new high, numbering over 450 in total across the period 896–1046 (over 500 if we include contemporary forgeries).[14] That this same era saw the high point in the 'recipient influence' of continental papal privileges, as identified by Kortüm, only reinforces this point about the continued, even increased vitality of the concept of Roman authority in the post-Carolingian world, as do the number of forgeries dating from this time. From the 960s, moreover, these regional initiatives to seek privileges in Rome became intertwined with the enormous energy invested in the city as a political focal point by the hegemonic East Frankish regime. After the imperial coronation of 962, Otto I (936–73), Otto II (961–83), and Otto III (983–1002) spent between them almost seventeen years ruling in Italy;[15] as a general rule, all papal privileges were authenticated in their name. The lines between seeking papal documentary support and participating in the Ottonian political community would have become blurred.

Against this backdrop, the evidence for papal privileges in England during this period looks all the more meagre. Altogether we have only one bona fide privilege: a document for Dunstan's use of the archiepiscopal pallium from John XII. It is joined by a doubtful privilege of John XIII(?) for the Old Minster, Winchester; a (not wholly convincing) twelfth-century claim of a lost privilege granted by another Pope John to Oswald, for his foundation at Ramsey; and an authentic-but-unusual undated letter of John XV, threatening Ælfric, ealdorman of Hampshire, with excommunication for his predations upon Glastonbury—not impossibly, a hint of some sort of concept of 'papal protection' at the monastery.[16] Recent scholarship has brought these long-neglected texts back into the spotlight, rightly asserting that Anglo-Saxonists need to pay more attention to interactions between Rome and England during the 'Benedictine Reform' period.[17] What remains to be done, however, is to frame them within their much more sizeable

---

[12] Kéry, *Canonical Collections*, pp. 87–202; Fuhrmann, *Einfluß*, ii, pp. 408–585; Roberts, *Flodoard*, p. 68; Roberts, 'Bishops'.

[13] Rennie, *Foundations*, pp. 167–9.   [14] Johrendt, *Papsttum*, pp. 16–19. Edition: *PUU*.

[15] Müller-Mertens, 'Ottonians', p. 260.   [16] 41, ?†44, ?†*45, 47.

[17] Tinti, 'England'.

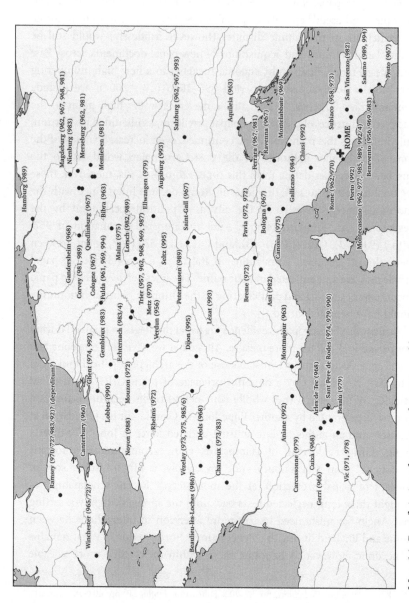

Map 6.1 Beneficiaries of extant authentic/possibly authentic papal privileges, 955–96

continental context. The period between the pontificates of John XII (955–64) and John XV (985–96) provides a suitable sample for comparison: 96 authentic privileges from East Francia (40), Italy (30), West Francia (17), and Catalonia (9),[18] of which 29 beneficiaries are archbishoprics/bishoprics, 62 monasteries, alongside five outliers (Map 6.1).[19] Jochen Johrendt has analysed this tenth-century corpus on its own terms, although without integrating the scraps of Anglo-Saxon material.[20] That's the goal of this chapter, which intends to be candid about just how little survives. It asks why we see so few papal privileges in England during this key juncture in its state formation, that is, at a time when acquisitions of privileges increased exponentially elsewhere, and when the West Saxon court's political interactions with Rome may have reached an all-time peak.

I. The Pallium Privilege: Dunstan and His Continental Counterparts

> Here begins the letter of privilege which Archbishop Dunstan, having received the blessing of Pope John, took from his hands upon his command. But the pallium he did not take from his hands but, upon his command, from the altar of Saint Peter the apostle.

Thus the opening rubric of the Dunstan Pontifical, the liturgical handbook compiled for (and perhaps by) the archbishop within his lifetime.[21] A copy of John XII's privilege of 960 follows over the next four sides (Figure 6.1). It outlines Dunstan's personal right to use the pallium, the limited days on which he might do so, and concludes with a rumination on proper episcopal conduct.[22] The pallium was a distinctive white stole worn by the bishop of Rome. From the sixth century it was granted as a papal gift to bishops of exceptional importance, and by the later Carolingian period to most western archbishops (itself part of the seventh-to-ninth-century process whereby

---

[18] These divisions are crude, but follow Kortüm, *Zur päpstlichen Urkundensprache*, and Johrendt, *Papsttum*. Lotharingia is treated here as East Frankish, and Flanders as part of the West Frankish zone.

[19] Outliers: *PUU* 175, 205, 240, 284, <290 (JL 3714, 3742, 3787, 3824, 4069).

[20] Johrendt, *Papsttum*.

[21] BnF, Lat. 943, f. 7; Rosenthal, 'Pontifical'; Rasmussen, *Les pontificaux*, pp. 258–317.

[22] 41: BnF, Lat. 943, ff. 7–8v.

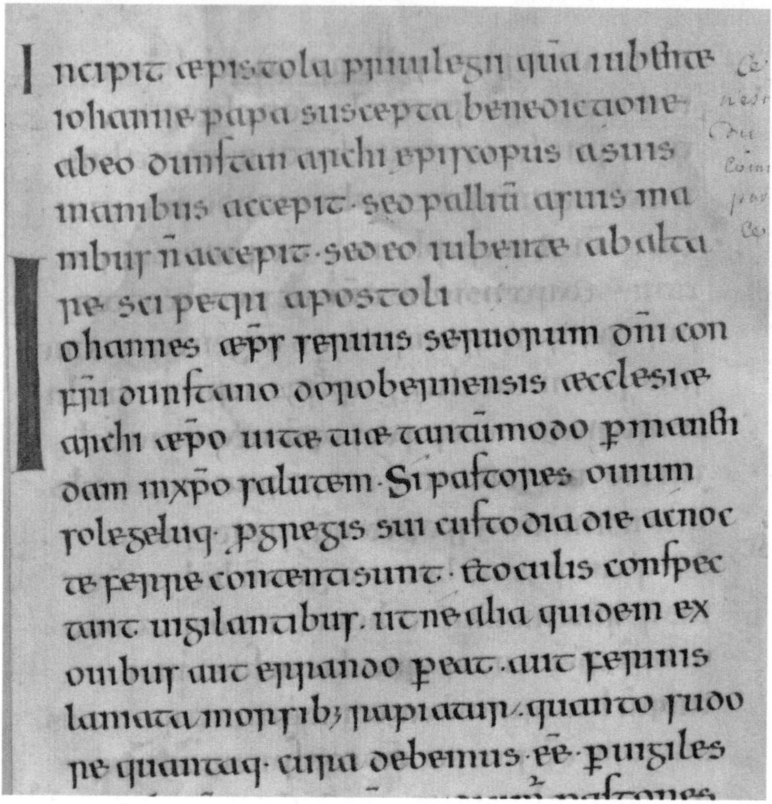

Figure 6.1 John XII's privilege for Dunstan, 960 (JL 3687), copy in the Dunstan Pontifical: BnF, Lat. 943, f. 7 (detail) (Source: gallica.bnf.fr/BnF).

this office arose to supersede that of the provincial 'metropolitan'). Its history has enjoyed exhaustive attention in recent scholarship.[23] Here, we need only discuss Dunstan's privilege and its context. The metropolitans/ archbishops of Canterbury had received the pallium since 601,[24] and their York counterparts, after a false start, from 735. What changed in Dunstan's lifetime was that from perhaps as early as 927 the archbishops of Canterbury had begun to head to Rome to receive the garment in person, a custom imitated at York from c. 959 or 971/2.[25] This seems to have come as an English initiative, and was not practised habitually elsewhere. The major

[23] Tinti, 'Archiepiscopal Pallium'; Schoenig, *Bonds*. [24] 1.
[25] Tinti, 'Archiepiscopal Pallium', pp. 311–19; Bullough, 'St Oswald', pp. 7–8.

change, however, probably revolved less around the dispatch of an embassy, than the presence of the archbishop himself within it. Historians sometimes portray early medieval popes simply dispatching pallia to distant archiepiscopal sees, but there remains some uncertainty as to how this might have worked in practice. Most probably—as with any other papal privilege—envoys bearing gifts would have travelled to Rome to announce the election of a new archbishop, and once there petitioned a fresh garment and the accompanying privilege for its use. The *Liber diurnus* shows that routine texts for the latter existed since at least the seventh century.[26] However, regional archives only began to preserve these intermittently from the turn of the ninth century, and the one that opens Dunstan's pontifical is the first surviving example from England, and the last until the 1060s.[27]

Its content is singularly unexceptional. However splendid its presentation in Dunstan's book, the document lacks the features that make many of its continental counterparts interesting, perhaps instructively. Scholarly interest has hitherto focused less on the text than its unique rubric. Francesca Tinti has suggested that its description of a two-stage conveyance—privilege from the pope's hands, pallium from Peter's altar—may reflect the rubricator's wish to distance Dunstan from any tainted association with John XII, whom the Ottonians deposed in 963, and whose reputation soon fell to ruins.[28] Just how far Anglo-Saxon circles were moved by these events is, however, unknown. It is anyway difficult to see why, if the rubricator was so concerned by the implications of John's unworthiness in this ritual (itself a theological matter),[29] he had bothered even to mention that Dunstan had received his blessing, acted on his commands, or received the document 'from his hands'.

The rubric may make more sense if read within its context as the opening of a 'pontifical'. These books, collections of liturgical materials pertaining to the office of bishop, first appeared in the tenth century and have received renewed attention in recent years. Besides exploring the importance of pontificals as markers of episcopal self-identity, these studies have revealed the creative variety found within this nascent genre, with diverse liturgical texts compiled for encyclopaedic purposes, as well as practical use.[30] Dunstan's is the only pontifical from across Europe to include a pallium privilege. In this manuscript its preservation may point foremost to liturgical

---

[26] *LD* V 45–8.   [27] Santifaller, 'Verwendung', pp. 60–1.
[28] Tinti, 'England', pp. 172–3.   [29] Leyser, 'Episcopal Office'.
[30] Rasmussen, *Les pontificaux*; Hamilton, 'Early Pontificals'; Parkes, *Making*.

interest: the document is, after all, about the right to wear a liturgical garment, and the specific feasts it outlines as suitable occasions for its use might be easily cross-referenced with the *ordines* for those days further on in the manuscript. The visual format of the text moreover aligns with that found in the main body of this liturgical codex, where short, direct rubrics of ritual 'stage directions' are given in red ink, followed by lengthy spoken-word parts (prayers, blessings, etc.) in black.[31] Seen within this context, the insertion of the privilege at the opening of the pontifical hardly indicates any kind of conventional archiving of a legal document, but is itself an *ordo*: the inelegant rubric gives the physical directions for John's blessing and two-stage ritual of conveyance (document from hands, garment from altar), and then the black text of the privilege recreates the speech of John himself addressing Dunstan in the first person. It was not, of course, an *ordo* ever to be performed again in England. But by capturing here in a liturgical 'script' both the words and movements of the precise ritual moment in San Pietro when he became a fully palliated archbishop, Dunstan and his circle were able to reconjure this performance whenever they opened his pontifical, and verbally recreate the act anew for the many who could not follow him there.

Those same Anglo-Saxon audiences would presumably not have noticed the rigid conservatism of the privilege. Its text follows *Liber diurnus* 45 almost word-for-word, and approves the formulaic minimum of pallium-days: Christmas, Epiphany, Easter Sunday, Ascension, Pentecost, the Assumption, the feast days of the apostles, 'your anniversary' (*in natalicio tui*), and the consecrations of bishops and churches (the otherwise-standard day of the feast of John the Baptist is excluded, although it is not clear if this reflects scribal oversight, or further minimalism).[32] Impressive enough. But if the pontifical's readers had our omniscient historians' view of the contemporary corpus of pallium privileges, they may have felt short-changed. Elsewhere around this same time, prelates across the Ottonian polity successfully began to petition for upgrades to their standard package of pallium-days, with concessions for its further use on the feast days of local patron saints granted to the archbishops of Magdeburg (Maurice), Benevento (Bartholomew), and Salzburg (Rupert). The latter, together with Trier and Hamburg, also received permission for added pallium-days for the feasts of Laurence and (again)

---

[32] *LD* V 45 does not include the formula for 'pallium-days', but it can be deduced from contemporary privileges elsewhere. *In natalicio tui* probably refers to the anniversary of the recipient's ordination: Niermeyer, *Mediae latinitis lexicon*, *s.v.* 'natalicius'.

Maurice, two saints especially cultivated by the Ottonian dynasty. Hamburg's privilege even added the stipulation that it was within the archbishop's rights to wear the garment either side of the Elbe.[33] These details add to our evidence for Ottonian cult and liturgy, but they also point towards competitive gestures of differentiation and one-upmanship within the highest ranks of the Latin archiepiscopate.[34] They are matched by the further clauses added to archiepiscopal privileges, outlining special areas of honour and jurisdiction, e.g. over peoples beyond the frontier (the 'Slavs' at Magdeburg, the 'Danes' at Hamburg); over the rights of consecrating particular sees (Salerno); or of 'primacy' in 'Gaul and Germany' (Mainz).[35] All this fits into our picture of what we know elsewhere of the tensions over ambiguous and overlapping claims to precedence, jurisdiction, and hierarchy within the Ottonian church, whether between the ancient churches of Mainz, Trier, and Cologne; with the neighbouring West Frankish see of Rheims; or in relations with the new archbishoprics controversially carved out at Magdeburg, Benevento, and Salerno.[36] The continued interest throughout the tenth century in the Pseudo-Isidorian forgeries, much of which revolved around invented ideas of super-archiepiscopal 'primacies',[37] formed part of this same environment. As strange as it looks to us, seeking from Rome a pallium and its accompanying letter of personalised privileges seems to have worked as an important part of the armoury of tools with which these prelates might push their claims to pre-eminence among the tangled hierarchies of the tenth century. (In the 950s Rheims went as far as to advertise a forged privilege for the late Archbishop Hincmar (845–82), granting him the right to wear the pallium *every* day: an extreme example, but nevertheless instructive.)[38] The unadorned simplicity of Dunstan's privilege, and the wider negligence in England even to archive documents of this kind, helpfully reminds us of how little the later Anglo-Saxon church resembled the world of hierarchical entanglements and ambiguities characteristic of much of post-Carolingian Europe. Canterbury and York seem to have had little challenge to their episcopal pre-eminence either side of the Humber: what would have been the use of asking the pope to grant them extra little honours here and there?

---

[33] *PUU* 152–3, 190, 197, <301 (JL 3689, 3691, 3728, 3738, 3835).

[34] Zotz, 'Pallium'; Johrendt, *Papsttum*, pp. 72–5.

[35] *PUU* 190, 237, 299, <301, 320 (JL 3728, 3784, 3833, 3835, 3852).

[36] Boshof, 'Köln'; Beumann, *Theutonum*; Zimmermann, 'Ottonische Studien', pp. 1–25; Roberts, *Flodoard*, pp. 66–74; Huschner, 'Benevent'.

[37] Fuhrmann, 'Pseudo-Isidorian Forgeries', p. 143.

[38] Flodoard, *Historia*, iii. 10, p. 206 (JE 2608); Roberts, *Flodoard*, pp. 125–7.

The Anglo-Saxon archbishops therefore probably concerned themselves less with the nuanced legal advantages that their pallium acquisitions would bring them in England, than the event itself of their journey to Rome. As his pontifical's rubric emphasises, what really mattered was that Dunstan was *there*. Why did these archbishop-led embassies begin in the tenth century? A prevailing argument is that the archbishops must have sought a dispensation from the pope for the canonical transgression of translating sees, since these journeys commenced at just the same time as these archbishops began to be appointed from among the already-existing English episcopate.[39] Certainly, the taboo of episcopal translation had generated controversy at Rome at the end of the ninth century, and would remain very much on the agenda in the mid-eleventh, as we will see in the next chapter.[40] But this had little bearing in Anglo-Saxon England, which during the tenth century bucked all continental anxieties by developing an unusual predilection for episcopal translation, in which an effective *cursus honorum* of 'stepping-stone sees' led up to Canterbury and York.[41] The idea that the tenth-century popes had either the means or the will to clamp down on this feels anachronistic. Rather than the translations themselves, a more important context behind these journeys to Rome was probably the political situation that caused them in the first place: the meteoric rise of the West Saxon Cerdicing dynasty. Translations began to Canterbury, and later York, at about the same time as their Southumbrian and Northumbrian provinces became fully integrated into their fledgling Kingdom of the English, and these appointments lay in the West Saxon king's hand.[42] Those same rulers excelled in building up their political connections abroad, and their ties to the Ottonian polity are well-documented.[43] Around the same time Italy became a core arena of political activity for the Ottonian regime. Its political set-pieces in Rome and Ravenna brought together prelates, ambassadors, princes, and reformers from throughout post-Carolingian Europe; emperors and popes presided together over councils.[44] One can imagine that the new, imperial-minded 'kings of the English' would have also wished to assert their place upon this 'international' stage at Rome, even while taking a cautious

---

[39] Brooks, 'Canterbury', pp. 228–9; Tinti, 'Archiepiscopal Pallium', p. 313.

[40] Below, pp. 000.   [41] Cubitt, 'Bishops', p. 121.

[42] *Christ Church*, p. 205; Molyneaux, *Formation*, pp. 66–7, 177–9.

[43] Leyser, 'Ottonians'; Foot, *Æthelstan*, pp. 44–52; Bihrer, *Begegnungen*.

[44] Major papal-imperial 'set-pieces' for granting privileges: e.g. Otto I's imperial coronation: Böhmer-Zimmermann 293–305 (*PUU* 152–4, JL 3689–91); the Ravennan Synod of Easter 967: Böhmer-Zimmermann 411–23 (*PUU* 175–80, JL 3713–18); and the Otto-Theophanu wedding of Easter 972: Böhmer-Zimmermann 492–502 (*PUU* 216–20, JL 3761–5).

distance from its politics. The privileging of archbishops played a key part in these Ottonian-papal gatherings: among the numerous grants of pallium privileges in the period under review, no less than five were granted in person to the archbishops of newly raised sees with all the ceremony of the Ottonian court's backing: Magdeburg (in three stages: 962, 967, and 968), Capua (966), Benevento (969), Vic (971), and Salerno (983).[45] The case of Vic, on the Catalan-Andalusi frontier, is especially noteworthy. That Count Borrell of Barcelona joined the petitioning-party and presented his archiepiscopal candidateAtó to the emperor attests to the nature of these later tenth-century pallium expeditions as highly politicised occasions.[46] Later tenth-century Italy was a place where Christendom's highest priests were invested before European-wide audiences, and the Anglo-Saxons may well have consciously participated in this stagecraft. Oswald's journey to Rome probably coincided with the spectacular Otto II-Theophanu wedding and coronation of Easter 972, during which John XIII granted a number of papal privileges for beneficiaries across Europe.[47] The archbishop of York may have been among them. At the end of the century, the pallium expedition of Ælfric of Canterbury (995–1005) probably led him only as far as the imperial city of Pavia, where Gregory V (996–9) and his circle had taken exile. Ælfric may have arrived in time for the Council of Pavia of February 997, where among the items on the agenda were the schism at the archbishopric of Rheims; the threatened excommunication of King Robert the Pious (989–1031) by his West Frankish episcopate; and the renewal of the privileges of the high-status sites of Fulda and Otto III's palatine church at Aachen.[48] If so, one doubts this timing was merely fortuitous.

Overall, what little evidence we have for pallium privileges in England may indicate a distinction between 'foreign' and 'domestic' policy. By heading to Italy for these honours, the Anglo-Saxon prelacy—and, by extension, the new Kingdom of the English—made itself visible on the European stage, ostentatiously participating in a distinctly post-Carolingian political community: a

---

[45] *PUU* 154, 177, 190, 197, 476–7 (JL 3690, 3715, 3728, 3738, 3747). Capua's and Salerno's privileges are lost, but see Böhmer-Zimmermann 393, 618.

[46] Richer, *Historiae*, iii. 43–4, pp. 191–3.

[47] Byrhtferth, *Vita s. Oswaldi*, iv. 5, pp. 102–5; Nelson, 'Second English *Ordo*', pp. 373–4.

[48] *ASC*, *s.a.* 997 F (s. xi/xii) reports that Ælfric went to Rome for his pallium, but the destination must be a later assumption since Gregory was not in the city that year. We know the pope met with the archbishop since Abbo of Fleury's letter collection preserves a note from Gregory asking after Ælfric's well-being on his return home: *PUU* 344 (JL 3879). On the February council, its privileges (*PUU* 339–40; JL 3874–5) and Ælfric's possible attendance, see Böhmer-Zimmermann 786–9, 791.

'Europe of Bishops',[49] with the continent-spanning, palliated archbishops at its head. However, whereas those archbishops from within the imperial church and its orbit sought these pallium privileges in order to negotiate their contested authority back in their own political ecosystem—utilising these insignia in their 'strategies of distinction'[50]—we find no evidence that these documents played a comparable role in England. There, the petitioned privileges seem to have taken a simplistic form, and did not attract much attention from contemporary archivists. Our single survival does not belie this, since the Dunstan Pontifical's presentation of the text appears chiefly liturgical, focusing more on the role of Dunstan himself than the institutional rights of Canterbury. By the turn of the millennium the codex had anyway left the archiepiscopal see for Sherborne.[51] The pallium had an unusually long history among the Anglo-Saxons, and was certainly revered. Yet we see little sign that the novel phenomenon of English archbishops heading to Rome to petition it had a serious role to play in the internal politics of the tenth-century formation of the kingdom. Nor did it contribute to the restructuring of its church, which had begun to develop an enthusiasm for episcopal translation and plurality that looked quite out of step with the tensions flaring up elsewhere in the Latin west. What mattered most was the role of these pilgrim-archbishops as stately ambassadors of the West Saxon *imperium* to the wider European and Mediterranean world. They were there to be seen.

II. Privileges for Tenth-Century Monasteries: Winchester and Ramsey in (and out of) Context

The connection between the English kingdom's two ancient archbishoprics and Rome was one thing: what about its growing number of newly founded or refounded Benedictine monasteries? The rise of the great abbeys of the 'Benedictine Reform' has long dominated accounts of tenth-century Anglo-Saxon Christianity, just as the wave of continental foundations associated with contemporary European 'reform monasticism' has preoccupied scholars working on the wider European church.[52] But while the role of papal support has taken a central position in studies of the latter, the possibility of some level of Roman institutional backing for the English

---

[49] Reuter, 'Europe'.   [50] Bourdieu, *Distinction*, p. 59.
[51] Rosenthal, 'Pontifical', p. 162.
[52] 'Reform monasticism': for an overview and critique see Wollasch, 'Monasticism'.

Benedictine foundations has only been seriously entertained relatively recently.[53] The problem stems from a lack of evidence. It is nevertheless intriguing that the *cause célèbre* of the English movement—the royally sanctioned expulsion of the clerics of the Old Minster, Winchester by Bishop Æthelwold, and the refoundation of the site as a Benedictine monastic cathedral—also finds support from the single potentially genuine papal privilege for an English monastery surviving from between the 810s and 1050s. As we saw in Part I, however, the extant text of this now-undated document of John XIII (authorising the expulsion of the canons, and arranging for the free election of future abbot-bishops from among its monastic community) presents too many obstacles to allow easy judgements about its admissibility as sound evidence for Anglo-papal connections.[54] The same goes for a brief claim in the twelfth-century *Liber benefactorum* of St Benedict's, Ramsey, stating that Oswald of York had acquired from John XIII a privilege guaranteeing the house's 'freedom and protection' (*libertas et munimen*) and its right for free abbatial elections. While unobjectionable, there is hardly enough in this claim by itself which allows us to pronounce confidently on its authenticity.[55] What then can we make of these scraps of uncertain material?

A good way to begin is by setting things in context and considering the wider evidence for appeals to papal privileges of this kind across the later tenth-century monastic movement. We may look both within and without the English kingdom. While thinly spread, slightly more evidence exists for interest in papal privileges within later tenth-century English monasticism than is usually appreciated. It has tended to go overlooked that King Æthelred's famous penitential diploma for Abingdon (993)—a lavish charter for the late Æthelwold's flagship abbey, restoring its exploited properties and confirming its free abbatial elections—names King Coenwulf and Pope Leo III as Æthelred's 'predecessors' through their patronage of the house. Presumably, this reflects some institutional memory of the privileges acquired from Leo for Coenwulf's network of familial minsters (798?), discussed in detail in Chapter 5.[56] Notably, the citation is so brief and generic that it bypasses the strictly proprietorial nature of those 200-year-old arrangements, which had little to do with the situation at millennial

---

[53] Tinti, 'England', pp. 173–80.

[54] ?†44. Accounts of the expulsion: *ASC, s.a.* 964 AEF; Wulfstan, *Life of St Æthelwold*, 17–18, pp. 30–3.

[55] ?†*45.   [56] *Abingdon*, 124 (S 876); 32, *33.

Abingdon or the aims of the Benedictines. Instead, Pope Leo's name (written in majuscule) assumes here a purely talismanic quality, lending ancient, Roman prestige to Æthelred's act. That same citation reappears elsewhere, in two forged royal diplomas produced at Abingdon within the same decade, attributed back to Kings Edgar and Eadwig (955–9).[57] Some 40 miles west, the Malmesbury community's translation into Old English of their seventh-century privilege of Sergius (689), placing them under papal 'jurisdiction' and guaranteeing free elections, possibly also dates to around these same years.[58] The circumstances of Malmesbury's revived interest in its papal past are obscure, but it may roughly coincide with its refoundation as a Benedictine institution in the last decades of the century.[59] Nor perhaps did Malmesbury's vernacularisation project stand alone: the now-lost translation of Glastonbury's privilege of Leo III (also 798?) might have also been a product of this time.[60] Yet the most vivid evocation of the importance of papal privileges to the Benedictine milieu comes from Byrhtferth of Ramsey's *Life of Ecgwine* (c. 1000, perhaps after 1016). As discussed in Part I, Byrhtferth's account of a probably legendary acquisition of a privilege from Pope Constantine for Evesham, and of its presentation before an imagined seventh- or eighth-century royal assembly, may draw upon memories of real ceremonial events publicising the delivery of papal privileges into the English kingdom in the author's own lifetime (perhaps even at Oswald's Ramsey).[61] More certainly, however, his narrative underscores a pattern seen in the evidence above: that we can find scattered indications of interest among the English Benedictines for papal privileges for monasteries; but, in all securely authentic contemporary evidence, this manifests itself as an enthusiasm for centuries-old acquisitions, not grants from contemporary popes.

In contrast to these snippets of backward-looking English material, the reliable continental evidence for papal privileges at later tenth-century monasteries is abundant and contemporary-facing. Zimmermann's edition of 'long tenth century' papal documents provides authentic texts of a full 272 privileges issued for continental monasteries between 896 and 1046, of which 62 belong to our sample period of 955–96. Even if we turn only to the pontificate of John XIII (965–72), the purported benefactor of

---

[57] *Abingdon*, 83–4 (S 658, 673); date and authenticity: Roach, *Forgery*, pp. 123, 138–46.
[58] 20; Rauer, 'Pope Sergius I's Privilege'.   [59] *Malmesbury*, pp. 24–5.   [60] 31.
[61] Byrhtferth, *Vita s. Ecgwini*, iii. 3–8, pp. 256–69 (probably the inspiration for the later †24–5); see above, p. 49.

Winchester and Ramsey, we find full texts of seven privileges granting the same combination of papal 'protection' (*patrocinium, tuitio*, etc.) and rights of free abbatial election which Ramsey later attributed to the pope, lending more credibility to those claims.[62] Individual cases can also be instructive. The near-contemporary *Chronicle* of Mouzon, on the West Frankish-Lotharingian border, gives an account of the papal-backed, epis-copal refoundation of the house which bears some notable resemblances to the situation later portrayed at Winchester. According to the *Chronicle*, in May 972 Archbishop Adalbero of Rheims had assembled a synod to publicise his refounding of the monastery, driving out its canons (as with Æthelwold, summoning the help of a small army), and installing Benedictine monks. The refoundation was sealed when Adalbero recited aloud before the assembly a papal privilege freshly acquired from John XIII, guaranteeing the refoundation's endowment: as the date of the surviving text indicates, John had granted it at the same Easter 972 imperial wedding at which Oswald may have received his pallium.[63] At face value, then, the continental evidence would appear to provide just enough contextual backing to Winchester and Ramsey's later claims to allow us to take them reasonably seriously: Rome issued a multitude of monastic privileges throughout these decades, and John XIII himself turns up in reliable, independent sources receiving and indulging the same kinds of petitions that the post-Conquest English records later attributed to him. From this view, successful requests for papal documentary support among the key institutions of the English Benedictine movement look plausible.

Such evidence can, however, only be stretched so far. Bar some superficial echoes, the sources either side of the Channel do not easily align. As much as the hundreds of monastic privileges from long-tenth-century continental Europe can help us imagine what a lost group of papal documents for English abbeys might have looked like, they also serve as a stark reminder of just how feeble the Anglo-Saxon record appears in comparison. (To reiterate a point already made in Chapter 1: the documentation of tenth-century Anglo-Saxon monastic archives otherwise survives relatively well, so we cannot simply attribute this disparity to problems of transmission.)[64]

---

[62] *PUU* 184, 186, 188, 213, 215–16, 219 (JL 3721, 3723, 3725, 3754, 3760–1, 3764).

[63] *PUU* 217 (JL 3762); *Chron. Mos.*, ii. 7, pp. 167–70. Adalbero also used the event to convene a special 'reform' commission, and present a further privilege acquired from John XIII for his diocese's flagship monastery of Saint-Rémi de Rheims: *PUU* 218 (JL 3763); Richer, *Historiae*, iii. 30–42, pp. 185–91. See further on this synod above, Chapter 2, p. 49.

[64] Above, pp. 11–12.

Even if the Winchester and Ramsey claims have some grounding in reality, we must take this severe imbalance in the overall quality and quantity of this source material seriously, and not argue around it. Moreover, we need to reflect on the different nature of the little which does exist. As just seen, the fragments of securely authentic evidence from England do after all indicate what looks like a revived interest in the use of papal privileges among at least three or four monastic communities, but in each instance the monks' gaze appears fixed several hundred years into the past, not—as with their continental counterparts—on the popes of the present.

The remainder of this section therefore aims to change tack, seeing what we might do to utilise the comparative paucity of evidence for tenth-century English monastic engagement with the contemporary papacy as a means for constructive enquiry. That is, it dwells not on 'what have we lost' or 'how reliable are our surviving remnants' (we simply do not know enough to go down this route), but rather asks: what might the extreme disparity between the Anglo-Saxon and mainland European material of this kind tell us about wider differences between these political zones in this period? We can start by assessing a more traditional interpretation, testing it against the current state of the evidence, before then moving on to an alternative hypothesis.

*   *   *

Let's start with an older model. One explanation lies ready at hand in the convergence of three classic themes in tenth- and eleventh-century European history: the descent of West Francia/France into 'feudal anarchy'; the first signs of the papacy's future as an independent source of authority, looking ahead to the notional emancipation of the church under the eleventh-century 'Gregorian Reform'; and the unusual strength of centralised government in the contemporary 'Anglo-Saxon State'. According to this approach (here much simplified), the retreat of royal power across much of France by the later tenth century compelled many vulnerable monasteries to turn to the popes as their new, alternative patrons. The papacy gladly took up this opportunity, and granted monasteries various privileges of immunity, thereby liberating them from local entanglements and tying them directly to Rome, building-up in the process the power base on which the later high-medieval papacy could depend. By contrast, the centralised strength of the Cerdicing Kingdom of the English at this time—unifying, and undergoing progressive state formation while the West Frankish realm splintered and collapsed—meant that such calls for help to popes were unnecessary (kings already did the job) and indeed probably unwelcome (papal grants of immunity to English monasteries would have undermined centralised institutions). Essentially, then, this is a 'weak state' vs 'strong state' approach, one in which later Anglo-Saxon monasticism stayed pope-free (for better or for worse, depending on the confessional perspective) thanks to the firm grip of the Cerdicing kings.[65]

Elements of the above sketch retain some validity, but much of it rests on outdated scholarship and a selective approach to the papal sources. While no one doubts that the exercise of royal power had become compromised across large parts of West Francia by the turn of the millennium, the causes and implications of this are now hotly debated, and the process of a 'feudal' break-up can no longer be taken as a straightforward fact.[66] West Francia anyway made up only one part of the picture. The usefulness of this traditional, Franco-centric explanation for the huge number of papal privileges for monasteries in these years, and of the validity of France as a comparandum for developments in England, is compromised by the evidence that the majority of papal documents went elsewhere: for the entire 896–1046 period, West Francia/France only accounts for 107 of the surviving 459 continental papal documents, behind 178 for Italy and 128 for East Francia/Germany;[67] in the period under review of 955–96, it ranks second in privileges for monasteries (15), behind the East Frankish realm (26) and just ahead of Italy (14), with a relatively substantial number also surviving from Catalonia (7), in these years emerging as a distinct polity.[68] These are of course imperfect figures, but they underline the point that Anglo-French comparisons alone cannot explain the reluctance of English monasteries to engage with the contemporary papacy.[69] Moreover, the tendency to

[65] The classic example of the proto-Gregorian, French 'feudal' explanation is Lemarignier, 'L'exemption', and Lemarignier, 'Structures'; Rennie, *Freedom*, provides a useful synthesis of the older bibliography and an updated approach; for critique of the Lemarignier thesis and its enduring popularity see Jones, 'Power', pp. 120 ff.; cf. also above, Chapter 4, pp. 115–17. The key, if only brief England–France, 'royalist' vs 'papalist' comparison is Wormald, 'Æthelwold', pp. 183–2, although his reading is subtle and looks momentarily beyond France. Centralised strength of Cerdicing government: Campbell, 'Late Anglo-Saxon State'.

[66] The literature is huge: West, *Reframing*, pp. 1–4, provides a helpful summary.

[67] Johrendt, *Papsttum*, p. 19.

[68] Geographical divisions follow Kortüm and Johrendt, but this and what follows are based on my own survey of the material. For simplification I have included Montmajour under 'France', although at the time it lay just within the border of the Provençal-Burgundian kingdom.

[69] For the Franco-normative orientation of much Anglophone (and of course French) medievalist scholarship until very recently, cf. Reuter, 'Debate'. Molyneaux, *Formation*, pp. 231–7, questions the usefulness of traditional England–France comparisons for the tenth and eleventh centuries.

prioritise attention on Franco-papal developments has had an especially distorting effect in the prominence it has given to the monastic privileges acquired by Abbo of Fleury (996) and Odilo of Cluny (998). These documents claimed extraordinary freedoms for these respective houses, guaranteeing direct relationships with Rome that almost cut out altogether regional power structures. They would in the longer term prove of great importance to the concept of papal 'exemption' (even papal primacy) as it later developed in the high-medieval period: scholarly interest in these texts is well justified.[70] From a tenth-century perspective, however, it is important to note that these probably beneficiary-penned texts were late, highly isolated cases, which did not necessarily find an immediate audience (Fleury's was condemned by Fulbert of Chartres, a prominent 'reform' figure; publicly threatened with torching; and its implementation obstructed for decades).[71] Their significance lay far ahead, in the unforeseeable future. In the tenth century, either privilege would have looked strange anywhere, and so the absence of their like from late Anglo-Saxon monasticism does not mean much.

That leads to the second, related problem with the above model: that its focus on the resurgence of papal immunities in this period both overestimates the preponderance of such documents, and, even in the cases where they did abound, arguably misreads their contemporary significance. Let's get things straight on the first point: whatever the interest of modern scholarship on the growth of papal liberties and immunities through these years, the bulk of extant privileges revolve around confirmations of pre-existing property rights.[72] Of course, this preoccupation with property is typical of church archivists, and will not shock anyone who has spent even the shortest amount of time leafing through a medieval cartulary. It nevertheless indicates a continuation of the development observed in the previous chapter, where we saw a marked shift in the content of privileges away from

---

[70] *PUU* †335 (JL *3872), authenticity defended in Mostert, *Political Theology*, pp. 58–9; *PUU* 351 (JL 3896). On both see Cowdrey, *Cluniacs*, pp. 22–36.

[71] André, *Vie de Gauzlin*, 18, pp. 52–3; Fulbert, *Letters*, 7–8, pp. 16–21; the case is summarised in Head, *Hagiography*, pp. 235–7. Abbo's acquisition appears so unusual that it was long deemed a forgery; in fact, Abbo may have been compelled to resort to creating a pseudo-ninth-century forgery of his own, attributed to Gregory IV (*Receuil des chartes*, ed. Prou and Vidier, i. 18: JE †2570), in order to support his petition: Mostert, 'Urkundenfälschungen'. A new study now argues that this forgery may be later, dating to *c.* 1067/72: if this is so, it nevertheless underlines the difficulty Fleury had in implementing their authentic privilege well into the latter half of the following century: Roach, *Forgery*, pp. 113–52 (cautiously suggesting the same date for Fleury's supporting forgery of Benedict VII: *PUU* †258; JL 3803).

[72] So frequently do they occur that it would be superfluous to list every example: see generally on privileges of this kind Johrendt, *Papsttum*, pp. 75–115.

concerns about 'jurisdiction' to more explicit guarantees over property rights from *c.* 750/80. This is not to understate these privileges' importance or historical interest. Securing property rights, and more clearly articulating and formalising them in documentary form, was central to the purposes of the monastic restoration programme, and the huge number of privileges suggests that, by the end of the tenth century, the popes had come to be seen across much of mainland European monasticism as trans-regional property guarantors of the highest order.[73] Acts 5, 1–10 had long associated Saint Peter with the safeguarding of church property and swift dispatch of its defrauders, a scene recalled in the 'Ananias and Saphira' charter sanctions characteristic of this period.[74] By *c.* 1000, it had become increasingly customary outside England to petition his incumbent successor to follow in his tradition. Any explanatory model for monastic enthusiasm for papal support in these years therefore needs to take into account that jurisdictional immunities and liberties were far from synonymous with 'papal privileges' in total, and were probably not the sort of documents with which contemporaries primarily associated the papacy. To overlook this or assume otherwise is teleological.

This is not to say that papal immunities did not matter at all in these years. Having disappeared from the record *c.* 750, by the tenth century they could be found in diverse forms at select elite monasteries across mainland Europe. They might involve three broad types of prerogative: the benefit of papal *iurisdicio* or 'jurisdiction', theoretically excluding the claims of certain regional ecclesiastical powers (a murky category, typically expressed in terms no way near as comprehensive as the exceptional Fleury and Cluny privileges mentioned above); the special right to papal 'protection' (*protectio, tuitio*); and the guarantee of free abbatial elections. These could overlap. Confirmations of the right to free elections—in the post-Carolingian world, often seen as a defining criterion of a 'royal monastery'[75]—might typically be combined with notions of 'protection': this emerging diplomatic category was almost certainly an *imitatio imperii* replica of the royal/imperial diplomas bestowing 'protection' or 'immunity-defence' upon high-status religious houses which proliferated in and after the Carolingian age.[76]

---

[73] Note that the texts of Adalbero's abovementioned privileges only concerned property, although they appear to have been advertised as thereby signifying 'reform' in a wider sense when publicly presented. On the increasing formalisation and articulation of ideas of property, see *inter alia* Innes, *State*, pp. 246–50, 262–3, and West, *Reframing*, pp. 171 ff.

[74] Rosé, 'Judas', esp. pp. 65–6.   [75] Bernhardt, *Itinerant Kingship*, pp. 70–5.

[76] See above, Chapter 5, pp. 158–9.

Whereas, however, royal/imperial 'protection' implied some kind of hard-power, military support for monasteries, the contemporary meaning of their papal doppelgängers remains harder to grasp, although a special right to lay claim to Roman spiritual sanctions was probably implied (see further below, for examples of when privileged monasteries may have appealed for formal interventions of papal excommunication). In turn, privileges bestowing 'protection' might combine with or become blurred into those outlining access to papal 'jurisdiction'. The line between these aspirations was fuzzy in this period, and a proper distinction between the two would not be invented until the later twelfth century: only then can we speak of papal 'jurisdiction'/'exemption' and 'protection' as defined legal categories.[77] If papal 'protection' was a product of the later Carolingian age by way of imperial influence, then 'jurisdiction' meant the resurrection around that same time of a category of papal privilege with fifth- and sixth-century roots and a seventh-century heyday, which nevertheless stopped being issued altogether in the mid-eighth (see in detail Chapter 4). It would appear that the resurgence of 'jurisdiction' privileges in the later Carolingian empire had its origins in a revived interest in the more ancient papal past, which then inspired the drafting and petitioning of new privileges from contemporary popes, following these antiquarian models. This looks like part of a bigger trend: the same culture that showed so much enthusiasm for Gregory the Great's *Register*, the *Liber pontificalis*, and the alternative late-antique papal history of Pseudo-Isidore seems to have had its interest piqued by the unusual 'jurisdiction' privileges found in the more ancient monastic archives.[78] The later Carolingian period provides the first manuscript witnesses to some of the earliest continental papal privileges reviewed in Chapter 4, when they may have been resurrected for contemporary disputes, and/or the petitioning of new confirmations.[79] Mid-to-late

---

[77] Falkenstein, *La papauté*, pp. 22–6.

[78] On the eighth-century disappearance of *iurisdicio* privileges: above, Chapter 5, p. 159, n. 25; for their late Carolingian resurgence: Rennie, *Freedom*, pp. 88–118. Late and post-Carolingian dissemination and influence of *Reg.* (mostly via the selective compilation 'R', first compiled under Hadrian I and disseminated via the Frankish royal court): Leyser, 'Memory'; transmission of *LP*: McKitterick, *Rome*, pp. 171 ff.; earlier letters and decretals: Jasper, 'Beginning'.

[79] e.g. JK 864 in a monastic compilation at Trier (s. ix): above, Chapter 4, p. 119, n. 21; JE 2017 in a Bobbio copy (s. ix/x), possibly first attested in a series of royal/imperial diplomas beginning 888: *Bobbio*, i. 69; and JE †2044, 2105, 2331 in the *Formulae Sancti Dionysii*, BnF, Lat. 2777, ff. 44–6, 53v–54: Große, 'La collection', now argues for its compilation for the arrival of John VIII at Troyes, 878; the manuscript is also a key early witness to the 'Donation of Constantine' (ff. 50–53v). Note also that our three known copies of *LD* were written in

ninth-century continental interest in the late antique papacy thus brought the idea of placing one's monastery under the exclusionary 'jurisdiction' of Rome back into circulation, and an intermittent flow of petitions for papal privileges of this kind outlived the Carolingian order into the tenth century and beyond.

So: newly acquired documents laying claim to papal-sponsored immunities did exist in some form in monastic archives across the tenth-century continent. The idea, however, that their acquisition was symptomatic of 'weak states' and collapsing authority (thereby explaining their absence from 'strong-state' Cerdicing England) does not stand up to closer scrutiny, especially when we look beyond France. To summarise this body of evidence as briefly as possible: claims to papal 'freedom and protection' could be found across much of the map of post-Carolingian Europe, most notably at sites associated with 'strong' centres of authority (cf. Map 6.1). In Ottonian East Francia during our 955–96 sample period, we find privileges of papal 'jurisdiction' or 'protection', usually matched with free abbatial elections at such major foundations as Fulda (961, 969, 994), Hersfeld (968), and Lorsch (982) in Franconia; St Gallen (967) and Ellwangen (979) in Swabia; and Quedlinburg (967), Bibra (963), Gandersheim (968), Thankmarsfelde/Nienburg (971, 983), and Corvey (989) in the Ottonian heartland of Saxony.[80] In many instances, these privileges went to monasteries which had already received imperial diplomas of 'immunity-defence' as a reward for the central role they played in *maintaining* public authority: they might double as royal mausolea, ecclesiastical palaces, itinerary stations, and nodes connecting imperial and aristocratic networks.[81] In some cases the papal privileges clearly served as prestigious, second-party Roman guarantees to their already existing imperial diplomas of 'immunity-defence', confirming and citing these as precedents, even reproducing their wording.[82] Nor was it

---

Caroline hands, *c.* 800–*c.* 900, although their purpose is obscure: above, Chapter 2, p. 28, n. 57. The popularity of *Reg.* also meant the widespread copying and distribution of its monastic privileges for Gaul (JK *926, JE 1457, 1745, 1875–7).

[80] *PUU* 150, 157, 178, 183–4, 186, <199, 213, 251, 274, <278, <289, <321 (JL 3688, 3694, 3716, 3721, *3733, 3723, 3739, 3754, 3799, 3811, 3818, 3832, 3853); see also the contemporary privileges for free elections and/or *iurisdicio* in the western duchy of Lotharingia, where property confirmations otherwise tended to be more prevalent, at Cologne (St Pantaleon), Trier (St Maximin), Gembloux and Seltz: *PUU* <244, 275, 291, 324 (JL 3788, 3817, 3827, 3857).

[81] Bernhardt, *Itinerant Kingship*; Wangerin, *Kingship*, pp. 60–6.

[82] e.g. *PUU* 185 (JL 2722) cites Otto I, *Diplomata*, 280, and its Carolingian *Vorurkunden*; *PUU* 230 (JL 2337) corresponds to privileges of Louis IV and Count Gauzfred of Empúries; *PUU* <289 confirms imperial and royal as well as papal privileges; *PUU* 305 (JL 3837) claims that the

unusual for these papal privileges to name the emperors or empresses as their sponsors and intercessors.[83] Here then, we see papal 'freedom and protection' invoked where central authority was strongest, not weakest (by contrast: we see no such monastic privileges in regions the emperors tended *not* to visit, notably Bavaria).[84] In Ottonian Italy we can observe a similar picture: the most generous papal immunities went to sites closest to imperial interests, whether at the royal city of Pavia and nearby Breme (all 972), or at the great abbeys of Montecassino (962, 977, 985, 989, 992/4) and San Vincenzo al Volturno (982) on the southern frontier, two houses which also functioned as important hubs for the maintenance of imperial authority.[85] In the West Frankish polity things looked different. A real divide emerges between our lack of evidence for any such privileges around the north/northeast,[86] and the good number we find in the south (968, 973, 975/ 83, 985, 992, 993) where royal power was generally much more attenuated.[87] Yet even here the 'strong' vs 'weak' authority model may not always suffice. The retreat of the south is perspectival. It requires historians to assume a royal view, looking outwards from the Seine. In some cases, rule may have come to be felt ever more firmly in the south, as local aristocrats intensified their own, more direct hold on power.[88] Monasteries were therefore not necessarily left stranded amidst the choppy waters of the 'feudal' sea, but potentially brought closer to the workings of power than ever before; those same local lords might act as their key patrons and protectors, and indeed some appear in the record as their intercessors at Rome.[89] A development of

monastery is under imperial as well as royal protection; *PUU* <278 (JL 3818) spells out the principle that the papal privileges for the monastery correspond to those granted by the emperor, according to the precedent of other dual papal-imperial arrangements granted elsewhere.

[83] e.g. Otto I appears as a named intercessor in *PUU* <159 (JL 3702) (with Empress Adelheid), 178, 184 (with Otto II), 186 (with Otto II), <199; Otto II in *PUU* 274-5, <278; Otto III in *PUU* 300 (JL 3834) (with Empresses Theophanu and Adelheid), <321; Theophanu in *PUU* 305 (with Bishop Hugo of Würzburg); Adelheid in *PUU* 324 (in memory of Ottos I and II); see further Johrendt, *Papsttum*, pp. 36-48. *PUU* 215, 219 (JL 3760, 3764) are addressed to Theophanu and Adelheid respectively.

[84] Cf. Davies and Fouracre, eds., *Property*, p. 15: 'exemption means closeness to the centre, not distance from it.'

[85] *PUU* <151, 215-16, 219, 244, <272, 287, 302, 310 (J³ 7794, JL 3760-1, 3764, 3791, 3810, J³ 8153, JL 3836, J³ 8231); imperial strategy at southern frontier monasteries: Loud, *Latin Church*, pp. 21-3, 31-2, 36.

[86] Only Ghent, in the Flemish principality, acquired a privilege of free election: *PUU* <313 (JL 3847).

[87] *PUU* 188 (Déols), 227 (Vézelay), 255 (Saint-Hilaire de Carcassonne), <238 (Charroux), 288 (Vézelay), 308 (Aniane), 318 (Lézat) (JL 3725, 3770, 3812, 3815, J³ 8156, 8213, JL 3850).

[88] Dunbabin, 'West Francia', pp. 375-6; West, *Reframing*.

[89] e.g. *PUU* 193 (JL 3735), 255; Böhmer-Zimmermann 244 (J³ *7738).

this kind may be observable above all in Catalonia. Just as this region began around this time to crystallise as a stand-alone polity, it was also becoming Europe's most 'privileged' single region, with full grants of combined papal 'jurisdiction' and 'protection' acquired at Gerri (966), Arles de Tec (968), Cuixà (968), Roda (974, 979, 990), and Besalù (979).[90] These privileges bear closest resemblance to those acquired in the Ottonian heartland. They look like confident assertions of establishment status, not desperate cries for help in the 'feudal' wilderness.

The purpose of this survey is to emphasise that the peculiar absence of good evidence for contemporary papal privileges for Anglo-Saxon monasteries in this period cannot be explained just by appealing to the strength of the 'Late Anglo-Saxon State'. We need not let the glare of Fleury's and Cluny's later, exceptional, super-immunities blind us to the variety of practice elsewhere. Most monastic privileges of this period concerned above all the confirmation of property. Where papal jurisdictional immunities and protections did exist, they came in diverse forms, stretching far beyond southern France, and were probably most prominent of all at some of the monasteries closest to the heart of Ottonian power. And even in the southwest of the former Carolingian world, where royal debility and papal 'freedom and protection' did indeed coincide, monastic appeals for Roman support did not necessarily always have to indicate structural weakness, but could instead reflect effective claims to international standing—by acquiring comparable privileges, some Catalan houses may have sought to assert themselves as distant equals to the likes of Fulda or Montecassino, with their regional patrons as players on that grander, extra-imperial stage. The tight grasp of the English kings over the monastic institutions of the 'Benedictine Reform' did not, therefore, rule out the possibility of their allowing or encouraging the monks to seek further pledges of apostolic 'freedom and protection'. It could well have enhanced, not undermined, their authority and prestige, as it appeared to do for their counterparts elsewhere. We therefore need to search for other explanations for their indifference or reluctance.

*　*　*

---

[90] *PUU* 171, 193–4, 230, 252, 254, 306 (JL 3710, 3734–5, 3777, 3798, 3800, 3838). For the region in this period and its local intensification of Carolingian forms of rule, see now Chandler, *Carolingian Catalonia*, pp. 229–74, superseding the older view (Kehr, *Papsttum*, pp. 12–22; Lewis, 'Papacy') that the turn towards the papacy at this time reflected the crumbling of the old older.

Turning once more to Map 6.1, one obvious point to make about its constellation of privileges is the degree to which it charts reasonably neatly over the shape of the former Carolingian empire, and hardly extends beyond it. This pattern of acquisitions seems to say much more about the long-term legacy of the Carolingian achievement—and its geographical limits—than it does anything about hot-spots of royal 'strength' or 'weakness' around the turn of the millennium. My argument here is that this ongoing Carolingian legacy is crucial to understanding the enthusiasm for contemporary papal support at monastic institutions in the long tenth century, and, therefore, its unusual absence from England. We can observe this aspect of the Carolingian legacy operating in continental Europe (and, I argue, not in the emerging English kingdom) on two, interrelated levels: the post-888 continuation of practices and attitudes which had begun to gather in momentum in the mid-to-late Carolingian period; and their intensification in the late and post-Carolingian world, as monastic politics and property holding became in some circumstances more complex. This is a huge topic. Only the briefest remarks are possible here, for the purposes of throwing the contrasting situation in the new Kingdom of the English into sharper relief.

First, later Carolingian roots and their continuity. The partnership of the Frankish sovereigns with the bishops of Rome had played a prominent role in the institutionalisation of Carolingian kingship since its inception. The increasing evidence for sustained ecclesiastical and aristocratic interest in papal documentary support by the mid-ninth century (as noted already at the beginning of this chapter) indicates a dissemination of this ideology far beyond the royal court. Importantly, these interests were not merely antiquarian. Fourth- and fifth-century papal decretals and the letters of Gregory the Great were copied en masse, and pseudo-ancient papal documents newly forged. But these efforts were increasingly undertaken alongside (and perhaps in order to provide models and precedents for) communications with contemporary popes, with new rulings, interventions, and privileges solicited from the Roman see's current incumbents, whose documents began by the mid-ninth century to be collected, perhaps for the first time since late antiquity, into substantial new collections of what might be categorised as updated papal canon law.[91] This interest in the intervention of immediately

---

[91] Jasper, 'Beginning', pp. 102–33.

contemporary popes even extended to forgeries in their name.[92] From Leo
IV (847–55) the number of recorded papal privilege acquisitions starts to
climb perceptibly.[93] By at least the later ninth century, the Carolingian
practice of 'confirmation politics' (*Bestätigungspolitik*)—the custom of seeking updated reissues of older diplomas from new rulers—had begun to
influence the interactions of Carolingian monasteries and their patrons
with the popes, with the effect that the momentum of new privilege acquisitions continued even at houses already boasting a rich tradition of papal
documentary support.[94] At an uneven pace, this pre-existing momentum
was then sustained beyond the threshold of 888 and into the long tenth
century.[95] The later tenth-century pattern of monastic privilege acquisitions
is a far call from that of the seventh and eighth centuries, but does not
seriously differ from that of the late ninth, bar some further extension into
regions such as Catalonia and Saxony. Practices on the ground also looked
alike: late antique (and now also late Carolingian) papal letters continued to
be copied in monastic scriptoria, and pseudo-ancient papal privileges duly
forged—but monks still looked upon the Rome of the present, using these
historical templates and/or falsifications in order to acquire *new* privileges
from *new* popes (thus Abbo of Fleury in 996).[96] Historians are no longer
inclined to think of the Carolingian age as an evanescent 'blip', all of
whose innovations, traditions, and practices suddenly died out in 888.[97]
The general picture of tenth-century monastic interest in contemporary
papal support looks undeniably post-Carolingian, in the sense of 'post-'
signifying that age's continuation and development, rather than negation.

Moreover, there is good reason to believe that the complexities proper to
the late and post-Carolingian age might have lent all the more appeal to the
seeking of papal guarantees for the properties, rights, and status of major

---

[92] e.g., notably the letter to 'all the bishops of Francia' attributed to Gregory IV (*c.* 830?):
MGH Epp. V, pp. 228–32 (JE 2578: on its dubious authenticity and use of 'Gregory' as a
mouthpiece for later Carolingian *admonitio* rhetoric, see now Renswoude, *Rhetoric*,
pp. 230–42).

[93] Above, n. 9.   [94] Above, Chapter 2, p. 23.

[95] Santifaller, 'Verwendung', pp. 98 ff.

[96] For the importance of *Reg.* (incl. its monastic privileges) for Abbo's thought and canonical
writings see Mostert, *Political Theology*, pp. 58, 65–76; the defensive statement of Aimo, *Vita
Abbonis*, 12, pp. 92–9 that the privilege Abbo had petitioned from Gregory V had drawn from
(quoted) *exempla* found in *Reg.*, thereby proving the former's legitimacy, is instructive in many
ways. Two volumes of *Reg.* (BnF, Lat. 2278, 11674) were apparently used at Fleury in the tenth
century and include annotations of documents cited elsewhere by Abbo, and of relevance to his
Roman petition: Mostert indicates that these may be his own manuscripts.

[97] 'Blip': Innes, *State*, p. 6.

monastic institutions. While few still consider the Treaty of Verdun's partition of the Carolingian empire (843) as a carving-up of the map into stand-alone sovereign states, it nevertheless signalled a 'real division', reifying political boundaries and presenting the imperial aristocracy (including the higher clergy) with access to multiple kings, courts, and political opportunities. In Matthew Innes' words, later ninth-century politics became 'a game of bewildering complexity played simultaneously on multiple boards', from the imperial to local level.[98] At least some of the great monasteries of the empire must have also had to play that multiple-board game, as properties, patrons, and familial and royal allegiances crossed political frontiers. Not everyone might have seen this as a bad thing, or a symptom of decline. As with their brothers, cousins, and donors in the lay aristocracy, some abbots probably welcomed the new opportunities and room for manoeuvre that the polycentricism of the late Carolingian world opened up. Nevertheless, the development of a situation whereby one's patrons, allies, and properties might lie across frontiers, within the territories of plural, horizontally aligned kings, must have greatly enhanced the attraction of seeking additional documentary support from contemporary popes. It does not appear to be a coincidence that it is around the mid-ninth century that the record of privilege acquisitions (as with other appeals to contemporary Roman authority) picks up. The post-888 world looks unlikely to have seen this complexity cancelled out, but rather all the more intensified: the post-Carolingian political ecosystem was one of porous, moving boundaries and trans-regnal connectivity; of interdependencies, intersecting dynasties, and overlapping hierarchies. On close inspection (to give one, already cited example), the decision of Adalbero to invoke John XIII's support for his later tenth-century monastic foundations and properties in his Rheims archdiocese and along the Lotharingian frontier—a zone of multiple loyalties and opportunities, if there ever was one—fits well into this picture.[99] That much was practical. Yet it is also possible that papal privileges played an increased symbolic role in the post-Carolingian landscape. In the long tenth century, new issues and reissues of these documents endured as the single format of diploma still shared across the monastic foundations of the

---

[98]   Ibid., pp. 195–222 (quotation at p. 218); 'real division': Airlie, *Making*, pp. 173 ff.

[99]   For Adalbero's multiple pulls of allegiance and interest, between his Ardennes clan, the Carolingians, the Capetians and the Ottonians, and his properties (both familial and ecclesiastical) between West Francia and East Frankish Lotharingia (including a papal-privileged monastery directly on their frontier), see Huysmans, 'Pious Foundation', with Parisse, 'Généalogie', pp. 24–5.

vast former empire. From 962, they were typically authenticated according to an imperial dating formula, even for beneficiaries in polities beyond the boundaries of Ottonian hard power.[100] Papal privileges thus contributed to the maintenance of a notion of unity across the post-Carolingian *ecclesia*. They harkened back to and renewed the memory of a shared past, while at the same time offering a way by which beneficiaries might negotiate their way around some of the multifaceted complexities of their present.

If the implication of the above is that the boom in monastic papal privilege acquisitions across the long tenth century was strongly rooted in traditions and circumstances characteristic of the post-Carolingian world, then it is significant that those same traditions and circumstances are more difficult to find in Cerdicing England. Although there has been a tendency over the past few decades to conceive of later Anglo-Saxon England as honorarily 'Carolingian', or even 'post-Carolingian',[101] we should remember that no known English sources from that age actually imagined the polity as sharing in a post-Carolingian identity. Of course, this was grounded in the fact that England had not formed part of the former empire. But it also reflected the distinct political and structural conditions of the new kingdom. The polycentric developments characteristic of the later and post-Carolingian age (and the rich literature of political thought they produced) did not apply to England, whose tenth-century state development followed its own quite separate path and chronology. English state formation enjoyed strong continental connections and influences, but it had neither Merovingian nor Carolingian foundations, and was built anew from the ground up, from just around the same time as the later Carolingian empire began to enter a period of transformation of its own.[102] Innes' 'game of bewildering complexity played simultaneously on multiple boards' does not ring especially true of current scholarly understandings of the late Anglo-Saxon experience. The English kingdom undoubtedly had its own regionalised political communities, allegiances, and rivalries, and much must remain hidden from us by the sparser source material. Nevertheless, after the short-lived, fraternal Eadwig–Edgar political division of 957–9, this comparatively small

---

[100] Above, Chapter 2, p. 45.

[101] e.g. Wickham, *Inheritance*, pp. 435–72 ('"Carolingian" England'), and the inclusion of Keynes, 'England, 900–1016' under 'Post-Carolingian Europe' rather than 'Non-Carolingian Europe' in the *New Cambridge Medieval History III*.

[102] Molyneaux, *Formation*, *passim*; and pp. 237–45, for the argument that 'outer European' polities such as León-Castile and Hungary may have closer resemblances to English state formation than the traditional Carolingian models.

realm only knew one king and one royal court.[103] It lacked internal royal boundaries, and lacked the magnetic pull and multi-directional entanglements of plural courts. We do not currently have evidence from this period for Anglo-Saxon abbeys having either properties or patrons overseas;[104] even within the kingdom, many of the great Benedictine monasteries lay securely in its West Saxon heartland. In England, things were probably just simpler. This is not to reassert the old 'strong state' vs 'weak state' paradigm under a different guise, but rather to sketch the emerging Cerdicing kingdom as a polity and ecclesiastical landscape of *relative* simplicity, against the *relative* complexity of much of the late and post-Carolingian world. Many of the factors contributing to the appeal of seeking papal support as a way of getting ahead in the post-Carolingian board-game may have therefore been absent from contemporary England.

Simplicity also features in the key monastic narratives of the English Benedictine movement, especially those associated with Æthelwold at Winchester. Again, this is emphatically not to say that other stories did not lie below the surface of some of the more controlled, formalised 'reform' narratives: Oswald's Ramsey, with its blend of regional, ealdormanic patronage and continental influences makes a good case in point.[105] However, Æthelwoldian texts such as the preface to the *Regularis Concordia* (*c.* 966/73), the New Minster refoundation charter (966), or the vernacular *King Edgar's Establishment of the Monasteries* (*c.* 966/84) can still tell us much about the movement's self-perception and self-presentation.[106] Most significant for our current discussion are these narratives' assertive insularity, noting continental currents only in passing, if at all;[107] and, relatedly, their chronological linearity with respect to the role of the papacy in the history of the Anglo-Saxon church and its monastic heritage. Echoing the epic Creation-to-Fall-to-Redemption monastic history of the New Minster charter, the *Concordia* and *Establishment* craft a straightforward, linear story whereby Gregory the Great converts the English in the distant past,

---

[103] The seriousness of the division is contestable: Keynes, 'England, 900–1016', argues for 'a political settlement amicably agreed by all the parties concerned'.

[104] The purported 'Anglo-Saxon' charters later claimed by Ghent (S 728, 997a, 1205b) and Saint-Denis (S 133, 868, 960; with †37) are widely deemed spurious, *pace* Atsma and Vezin, 'Le dossier'.

[105] See, from the perspective of the Loire, Aimo, *Vita Abbonis*, 4–5, pp. 50–5.

[106] *Regularis concordia*, pp. 1–9; *Winchester NM*, 23 (S 745); CS I, i. 32.

[107] *Regularis concordia*, p. 3, and Wulfstan, *Life of St Æthelwold*, 13, pp. 26–7 (a nod to Fleury and Ghent); B., *Vita s. Dunstani*, 23, pp. 72–3 mentions Dunstan's *incerta Galliarum exilia* but says nothing of Ghent. Byrhtferth, *Vita s. Oswaldi*, paints a more complex picture (involving Ramsey and Fleury), but this work may not have had a wide readership.

before the nation falls to ruin, and is then restored to its former monastic splendour in the present day by Edgar, scion of the ruling dynasty (no others are even mentioned).[108] The historical role of the papacy is therefore revered, but the role that might or might not be played by the latter-day bishops of Rome within the new Kingdom of the English and its restored monastic landscape is entirely passed over: Saint Gregory lives safely in the idyll of the distant past.

One can draw analogies here to the above evidence for late Anglo-Saxon Benedictine interest in chiefly (perhaps exclusively) ancient, pre-Viking papal privileges for monasteries. But this treatment of the papacy as having an institutional significance primarily in the past, not present, also reflects the degree to which some of the intellectual and legal traditions of the late Anglo-Saxon churches stood quite apart from those which had developed under the different conditions of their late- and post-Carolingian counterparts. We have just seen how, from the mid-ninth century onwards, papal letters and laws began to be collected and forged anew across the Carolingian world, with the late antique canon of substantially patristic popes opened up to include rulings of more contemporary bishops of Rome. By contrast, the groundbreaking research of Michael Elliot has now demonstrated the extraordinary conservatism of later Anglo-Saxon canon law against this 'new wave' of late- and post-Carolingian legal thinking. English monastic scriptoria continued to copy and cite from the rich corpus of late antique, patristic canon law that had circulated throughout the continent up to the ninth century. Yet they opted out of engaging with the new (and, arguably, increasingly Rome-orientated) legal thinking characteristic of continental Europe from c. 840/50 onwards.[109] Similarly, Archbishop Wulfstan's legal writings, while often characterised as 'Carolingian' in tone, hardly made use of *later* Carolingian material.[110] Quite remarkably, even Gregory the Great's *Register*—which circulated widely in the empire, and is now thought to have been one of the most influential texts for developments in ideas about canon law and the role of the papacy in the late- and post-Carolingian world—has left little trace of any later

---

[108] *Regularis concordia*, pp. 1–4; *CS* I, i. 32; see also B., *Vita s. Dunstani*, 2–3, pp. 8–11.

[109] Elliot, 'Canon Law', esp. pp. 278–80.

[110] Wormald, *Making*, pp. 213–18, 344: the apparent exception would be Wulfstan's excerpts from Radulf of Bourges (853/66) (*Capitula*, ed. Brommer, pp. 227 ff.), but in fact the passages concerned are almost entirely *ad uerbatim* copies from the *Capitula* of Theodulf (798/818), the Council of Chalon (813), Halitgar's penitential (820), and Ansegis' *Collectio* (827).

Anglo-Saxon readership.[111] If, in long-tenth-century Europe, Gregory provided a precedent and textual model for new acquisitions from contemporary popes, then in the English monastic imaginary he existed firmly in the past: a saint, church father, and 'Apostle of the English', but not a template for the role of Roman documentary culture in the refashioning of Anglo-Saxon monasticism. The fervent interest shown by the later Carolingian world in the possibilities of papal canon law and the role of contemporary popes in supporting ecclesiastical institutions may be one of the most influential developments of that age—a significant legacy to continental developments of the tenth and eleventh century. The argument here is that the later Anglo-Saxon ignorance of, or at best indifference to, these *later* Carolingian textual traditions can go some way towards making sense of the peculiar absence of evidence for papal documentary support for the English Benedictine monastic refoundations.

To sum up. Treated by itself, the scattered, partly dubious evidence for the use of papal privileges within the English Benedictine movement gives away little. However, by zooming out and viewing it alongside the comparatively substantial corpus of acquisitions at contemporary mainland European monasteries, we can turn this paucity of evidence on its head, and use it to ask instead a positive research question: what might such a disparity between the English and continental evidence do to illuminate what was different about monastic attitudes to the papacy within the Cerdicing kingdom? We cannot fall back on the easy answer, that the late Anglo-Saxon kings maintained such a tight grip over its monasteries that they simply did not need papal institutional support. Evidence from elsewhere demonstrates that some of the great continental abbeys closest to imperial, royal, or comital power could also be those enjoying the most sumptuous papal privileges: the prestige of one such authority might be invoked to enhance, not counteract, the other. Instead, the real value of our meagre English evidence is that it is suggestive of the degree to which the Wessex-led Benedictine movement was relatively uninfluenced by certain later Carolingian trends. From the mid-ninth century, Carolingian monasteries had turned more frequently to confirmations and reconfirmations of papal institutional guarantees as a way of negotiating the increasing complexities of the political landscape, using ancient papal texts as precedents and models for ever more acquisitions and forgeries in the names of contemporary

---

[111] Late- and post-Carolingian significance: Leyser, 'Memory', pp. 193–201. Absence in England: Gretsch, Ælfric, pp. 46–9; Savill, 'Consul'.

popes. By contrast, the refounded monasteries of the new Kingdom of the English, only coming of age well into the tenth century, had not inherited these post-Carolingian practices. When Æthelwold invoked the authority of Rome in the story of Anglo-Saxon monasticism, he meant the primordial, ground-zero age of Gregory I, not the potential contribution of the living popes and Lateran functionaries of his own day. When the monks of Abingdon, Malmesbury, Glastonbury, and Evesham made appeals to their status as institutions living under the guarantees of papal 'freedom' or 'jurisdiction', they referred back to texts (real or imagined) from the pre-Viking age of the seventh and eighth centuries. And when the English Benedictines turned to forgery to safeguard their rights and properties, they did so in the names of Insular monarchs, not recent popes.[112] It is not impossible that a later claim such as Ramsey's, that Oswald had once acquired a papal guarantee for the house's 'freedom and protection', had some grounding in the truth. It is appealing to think of him petitioning it during his pallium expedition of 972: conceivably, amid the full splendour of the Otto-Theophanu wedding, rubbing shoulders with Adalbero amongst many others. However, as with the archiepiscopal privileges discussed above, we have little evidence that such a document, once brought back to England, had much of an impact in directing the shape and self-understanding of the late Anglo-Saxon monastic movement. Such privileges were characteristic of continental monasticism's shared post-Carolingian legacy, to which the fledgling Kingdom of the English was not a direct heir.

III. Papal Excommunication: Ælfric of Hampshire and the Monks of Glastonbury

One final piece of evidence needs addressing, which may at first sight undermine this sketch. Part I noted the rough date (985/96) and authenticity of a letter from John (XV) to Ealdorman Ælfric (of Hampshire) concerning the property of the major Benedictine house of Glastonbury. Reworked by the mid-twelfth century into a privilege listing and confirming the properties concerned, in its earliest state it took the form of a short letter of admonition directed at the ealdorman, threatening above all his excommunication:

---

[112] Charter forgeries: Roach, *Forgery*, pp. 113–52; cf. also the so-called 'Laws of Edward and Guthrum', long recognised as the work of Wulfstan: Whitelock, 'Wulfstan'; the same now goes for the 'Tithe Ordinance' attributed to Æthelstan: Ivarsen, 'Æthelstan'.

... and since, though unworthy, we do not doubt that we, through blessed Peter the apostle, have taken up the care of all the churches and the solicitude of all the faithful, so do we warn your beloved that, for the love of the apostles Peter and Paul, and out of reverence for us, you cease from plundering the properties of that place and invading its *villae* and possessions. For if you do not, let it be known to you that by our authority, on behalf of the prince of the apostles, you will be excommunicated, separated from the company of the faithful, placed under perpetual anathema, and perennially bound with the traitor Judas in the eternal fire.[113]

The letter probably belongs to the phase of royal and aristocratic attacks upon ecclesiastical landholdings characteristic of Æthelred's early reign, before his penitential resumption of the programme of monastic endowment in 993.[114] Ælfric of Hampshire, 'whom the king trusted most', would later go down in a *c.* 1020-penned, anti-Æthelredian section of the *Anglo-Saxon Chronicle* as a figure of unusual notoriety, whose 'old tricks' included deserting two crucial battles in 992 and 1003.[115] John's letter at least indicates that the ealdorman had earned his infamy among monastic circles as early as *c.* 985/93, to a sufficient degree that the authority of the pope had been invoked against him. Of particular interest to us here is the question of whether John's letter indicates that Glastonbury laid claim to a now-lost privilege of papal 'protection' akin to those found at numerous continental monasteries in the later tenth century. Is this letter a rare witness to such 'protection' being called into action: that is, with the pope actually making good his or his predecessors' claims, stepping in with the threat of excommunication when word had reached Rome that the house was in danger? Could late tenth-century Glastonbury—perhaps the wealthiest house in the kingdom[116]—have seen itself as an institutionally 'papal' monastery of the Benedictine movement after all?

Patrick Wormald drew comparisons between this text and a slightly later diploma-letter in the name of Benedict VIII (1012–24) to 'all the archbishops and bishops in Burgundy, Aquitaine and Provence' concerning attacks on Cluny's property by eleven named 'persecutors'. Those offenders were to make restitution by Michaelmas (29 September) 1021/3, or else find themselves 'cursed and anathematised', according to the long formula of

---

[113] 47.   [114] Roach, *Æthelred*, pp. 100–11.
[115] *ASC, s.a.* 992, 1003 CDE.   [116] *Glastonbury*, pp. 1–74.

maledictions with which the letter ends.[117] However, while its case-specific threat of papal anathematisation has parallels to the Glastonbury letter, the exceptional importance of Cluny by the 1020s, together with the sheer bombastic scope of this document—effectively addressed to the entire southern French clergy, and as lavish in its length and formulation as any public act of the early middle ages—makes it a difficult comparator. Far closer to the Glastonbury text is the same Benedict's letter to Count Hug of Empúries (Catalonia), concerning Sant Pere de Roda (1021).[118] Cutting the rhetoric and getting straight to the point, Benedict accuses Hug of invading the 'inheritance' of Roda, namely the castle of Verdere and its properties. He promises Hug 'innumerable agonies and tears' if he does not make amends, and outlines the excommunication and anathematisation of him and his tenants if this does not happen by Easter Sunday. In both letters these case-specific interventions relate to earlier papal privileges. We have already seen that Roda acquired a number of privileges granting papal 'protection' (and confirming named properties, including Verdere) in the late tenth century,[119] while Benedict's letter for Cluny cites the 'written privileges' and 'freedom' granted by 'all our predecessors'. Such interventions doubt-lessly relied on the initiative of the monastery concerned, and on the cooperation of the regional clergy and aristocracy if their threats were ever going to mean much. Nevertheless they indicate that by the early eleventh century the bishops of Rome were expected in some regions to follow through the pledges of their privileges. This may have implications for the background of the Glastonbury letter, but there are also two important differences. One is specificity. The naming in the Benedict VIII letters of the properties concerned; of the date on which restitution was to be made; and, in the case of Cluny, the guarantors of the pope's threat in the person of the regional episcopate—all these suggest a real, urgent intention to see through the ultimatum, absent from the brief, more generalised admonition of John XV. The second concerns preservation. The survival of these documents at Cluny and Roda suggests that they were directed primarily towards the monasteries themselves, and kept there long after these one-off cases had been settled as part of their wider series of privileges: they continued to function as confirmations of the property concerned, warnings against future malefactors, and markers of their identity as 'papal'

---

[117] *PUU* 530 (JL 4013); Wormald, 'Æthelwold', p. 183. It was probably composed at Cluny: Kortüm, *Zur päpstlichen Urkundensprache*, pp. 254–7.
[118] *PUU* 531 (JL *4034).   [119] Above, p. 209.

institutions. While it is unfair to compare any Anglo-Saxon archive with the stupendous survivals of either Cluny or the Catalan region, the manuscript tradition of the John XV letter nonetheless suggests that it did not the hold the status of a documentary record at Glastonbury until much later.

The early version of the text survives as one of the last items in British Library, Cotton Tiberius A. xv. Donald Bullough demonstrated that this badly damaged manuscript, probably put together at Christ Church, Canterbury, c. 1000 or shortly thereafter, drew upon the same (now lost) exemplar as the contemporary Cotton Vespasian A. xiv, ff. 114–79, a letter collection associated with Archbishop Wulfstan of York.[120] From what now survives, we can gather that it consisted substantially of the correspondence of Alcuin (d. 804) and certain other items from within or just after his lifetime, together with some earlier Northumbrian materials going back to the seventh century, and a miscellany of later letters dating up to the time of compilation, mostly from the tenth century and relating to the church province of Canterbury. Most of these later items survive only through the last section of the 'Canterbury Letter Book' (ff. 144v–173r). It is known from his other works that William of Malmesbury consulted this Tiberius manuscript or its exemplar.[121] Since William included an interpolated copy of the John XV letter into the later ('C') version of his *Gesta regum Anglorum* (1125/35), but oddly not in his *On the Antiquity of Glastonbury* (c. 1130, the research for which took him to that monastery's archive), it would appear that he probably knew of the letter only from Canterbury. The earliest secure evidence for interest in the letter at Glastonbury is from the turn of the fourteenth century, in a marginal addition to *On the Antiquity* which copies the *Gesta regum* text.[122] We should therefore think of the immediate, millennial setting of John XV's letter primarily from the perspective of archiepiscopal Canterbury, and at best put only a question mark over the possibility of any great weight being placed on the document at Glastonbury itself before the high middle ages.

What, then, was it doing at Canterbury? The latest identifiable items in the Letter Book date from the archbishopric of Sigeric (990–4). Susan Kelly has proposed that the letter could derive from his pallium expedition of 990.[123] This fits well with the context outlined above, especially since Sigeric has been identified as an instrumental figure in steering royal policy

[120] Bullough, *Alcuin*, pp. 81–102.
[121] Thomson, *William*, pp. 154–67; Thacker, 'Pope Sergius I's Letter', pp. 115–16.
[122] Cambridge, Trinity College, R. 5. 33, f. 13.   [123] *Glastonbury*, pp. 568–9.

back towards the Benedictine programme and its restoration of monastic property by 993.[124] We can easily imagine Abbot Ælfweard of Glastonbury (975/88–1009), whom the same manuscript shows to have corresponded with Sigeric,[125] asking the archbishop to present a petition during his embassy. Even if the letter was acquired by other means, there may have been a convention for missives of this kind to pass through the archbishop's circle before their formal delivery—conceivably, via the public forum of the royal assembly.[126] Perhaps an assertion of that role of the archbishops of Canterbury as mediators between the politics of the English kingdom and the 'international' church lay behind this letter collection. In view of its date and location, it was probably compiled under Sigeric's successor, Archbishop Ælfric, whom we met earlier visiting Gregory V in 997 at Pavia (perhaps for the synod concerning Rheims, Robert II's marriage, Aachen and Fulda) and joining on his return journey Abbo of Fleury.[127] Bullough could find no discernible rationale behind Tiberius A. xv's choice of letters.[128] But as a specialist in Anglo-continental connections in an earlier century, he may in this case have failed to see the wood for the trees: Tiberius A. xv has an unmistakably cosmopolitan, even international-relations flavour. Alcuin's letters make up the greater part of the codex (ff. 1–144v). His unique career as Charlemagne's Anglo-Saxon courtier, and correspondent of some of the great churchmen across his empire, already therefore gives this collection a particular character. The non-Alcuinian material included within this section only reinforces this tone—for example, a letter of Sergius I to Abbot Ceolfrith of Wearmouth-Jarrow (*c.* 700), asking him to send an English scholar to Rome (ff. 50v–52).[129] Of the twenty-six letters which make up the remaining section, the Letter Book proper, at least twelve (several others remain unidentified) are cross-Channel missives, usually involving either archbishops Dunstan, Æthelgar (988–90), and Sigeric, or tenth-century kings of the English. At least two more concern solely continental affairs. These 'international' items hail from Saint-Bertin, Rheims, Ghent, Brittany, Saint-Ouen, Flanders, Saint-Vaast, Paris, and Fleury, and end with two papal documents: our John XV letter concerning Glastonbury and—the closing piece—a legatine document in his name, announcing the peace agreed between King Æthelred and Duke Richard of Normandy at

[124] Roach, *Æthelred*, pp. 137, 145, 153–4, 158.
[125] BL, Cotton Tiberius A. xv, ff. 172v–173; *Memorials*, ed. Stubbs, pp. 400–3.
[126] Cf. Roach, *Kingship*, pp. 147–60, on 'further business' at the *witangemot*.
[127] Above, p. 197.   [128] Bullough, *Alcuin*, p. 96.
[129] HS, iii, pp. 248–9 (JE 2138); Thacker, 'Pope Sergius I's Letter'.

Rouen (991).[130] One message seems clear. The Cerdicings and their arch-bishops of Canterbury followed in the tradition of international renown and connectivity that Alcuin had enjoyed in Age of Charlemagne, and which even Sergius I had recognised when he sought scholarly assistance from Wearmouth-Jarrow in the Age of Bede. And all this just in time for the Channel-crossing marriage of Æthelred to Emma of Normandy in 1002.[131]

So, to recalibrate. We might do better by approaching John XV's letter primarily from the perspective of (archiepiscopal) Canterbury's boasts to overseas connectivity, rather than (monastic) Glastonbury's own, perhaps doubtful, self-identification as a house under any kind of post-Carolingian-style 'papal protection'. With Canterbury's cross-Channel influences in mind, however, one central aspect of John's letter deserves special attention: its emphasis on papal excommunication as a game-changing coercive meas-ure. This may betray something of the contemporary Gallic *Zeitgeist*. Short sanctions including threats of excommunication and/or anathema had closed papal privileges—as with diplomas across the post-Roman world—since early times, and we already explored in Chapter 5 the possibility that one such sanction may have helped bring about the suspension of an early-ninth-century archbishop.[132] There is, however, a wave of evidence from *c.* 1000 that hints at a novel interest in and around the millennial West Frankish realm in the idea of the bishops of Rome as supreme agents of excommunication, for whom the exercise of this spiritual weapon was not merely one feature of their office, but one of its defining characteristics. We have from the early decades of the eleventh century a fascinating series of diplomatically innovative charters from the western regions of the post-Carolingian world, which after being issued within their prospective local-ities were then purportedly confirmed with an added papal pledge of excommunication or anathema. New privileges were not sought. Rather, these declarations of excommunication were inscribed directly onto the single-sheet document via a papal subscription, with (in at least one case) the further attachment of the pope's *bulla*.[133] Our earliest surviving record of this type dates to 1005, but Abbo of Fleury's writings indicate that this idea of the pope as the supreme excommunicator had begun to gain some traction a decade or two before. In the chapter of his canon law collection

---

[130] Keynes, 'Canterbury Letter-Book'.
[131] *ASC* CDE, *s.a.* 1002; Bullough, *Alcuin,* p. 97, briefly ponders a link.
[132] Above, Chapter 2, p. 45 and Chapter 5, pp. 181–2.
[133] *PUU* 417 (Marseille), 459 (Urgell), 467 (Peillonex), 514 (Thiers) (J³ 8533, 8603, 8733, 8721).

'On Privileges', Abbo defines the 'singular excellence' of the popes as their capacity to protect the rights (*lex*) of churches through 'the anathema of excommunication'.[134] Two chapters later, he distinguishes royal-imperial diplomas (*praecepta*) from papal privileges, defining the former as documents 'confirmed by the authority of their command (*iussio*)', the latter those 'decreed under the anathema of excommunication'.[135] This is hardly advanced legal theory, but the close relationship between the papacy and excommunication in Abbo's thinking here is evident. Moreover, his abject failure to dig up any canonical authorities or precedents to support these statements only highlights that this was quite new. In his letters, Abbo likewise emphasises the importance of papal authority to the protection of property via the 'rod' (*virga*) or 'penalty' (*epitimium*) of papal excommunication. Albert of Micy quoted Abbo's words on this principle in his own petition to John XVIII (1004–9) for a privilege.[136]

Yet for perhaps the most impressive example of this millennial Gallic trend we need, paradoxically, to look to the heart of the *Reich*. There, the so-called 'Pope Leo Formula' makes its first datable appearance at just this time. This liturgical text, a dramatic, lengthy ritual excommunication formula aimed at transgressors of church property, took the peculiar hybrid form of a rite-cum-letter attributed to a 'Pope Leo'. Over the next two centuries it enjoyed a wide circulation thanks to its inclusion in the tradition of liturgical handbooks now known as the Romano-German Pontifical.[137] Scholars have usually understood this letter as a production of the early-to-mid-tenth century, even narrowing down its forger's original attribution to Leo VII (936–9). But there are no good reasons for confidently dating it much earlier than its first manuscript appearance in the Emperor Henry II's Bamberg Pontifical (1007/12); it is potentially attributable to any Pseudo-Leo (Leo the Great or Leo III may have made more attractive candidates).[138] Despite the pontifical's imperial setting, the letter's origins probably lay further west, in *Gallia* rather than *Germania*. 'Leo' addresses himself to the episcopate, abbots and monks *in Francia*, and the letter's style is reminiscent of the kind of monastic maledictions known from contemporary France. As Henry Parkes has now shown, the Pontifical's compilers were pointedly eclectic when it came to the origins of their texts, gathering diverse liturgical materials as 'spolia' from all across the Latin church, including the rites

---

[134] *PL* 139. 479.   [135] *PL* 139. 480.   [136] *PL* 139. 419–22, 439–40.
[137] *Le pontificale*, ed. Vogel and Elze, i, pp. 315–17; see now with Parkes, 'Questioning'.
[138] Bamberg, Staatsbibliothek, Msc. Lit. 53, ff. 191r–v.

'according the Gauls'.[139] We are probably, therefore, looking here as well at a western text, originating in the same papal excommunication milieu as above. Versions of this 'Pope Leo Formula' were also adapted as monastery-specific privileges threatening papal excommunication at Fleury, Santa Maria de Ripoll, and St Maximin and St Martin in Trier, although their late manuscript traditions do not permit accurate dating.[140] Altogether, the diverse evidence points towards a seemingly new intensification of a discourse that tightly linked together the idea of the papacy with the exercise of excommunication (especially in defence of church property) west of the Rhine from around the 990s onwards. Why is unclear. We know at least that excommunication had become increasingly institutionalised as an episcopal prerogative since the late Carolingian period, and by the tenth century may have felt especially tied to episcopal identity.[141] This later, Rome-facing aspect presumably emerged in dialogue with those developments, perhaps as a reaction against them. In any case, the papal excommunication threats brandished by Cluny and Roda in these years must be seen as one part of this wider cultural moment. So too should that for Glastonbury, as mediated and preserved by the Channel-hopping archbishops of Canterbury.

John XV's short letter of reprimand to Ealdorman Ælfric fascinates in many ways. It offers a glimpse of the sort of ideas and connections passing between at least Canterbury and continental Europe in the later tenth century, despite the sometimes inward-looking rhetoric of the English Benedictine movement; about the kinds of 'other business' that may have arisen at the Lateran during the archbishops' pallium embassies; and— reminiscent of the Dunstan Pontifical—the enthusiasm of the archbishops to promote this image of their cross-Channel connectivity, at least among their inner Christ Church circle. Perhaps the most important consequence of the letter's rare preservation is that it provides a context for the penitential resumption of the monastic programme in the 990s. It suggests that a key instrument in pushing those close to the king back onto this 'reform' path were public threats of excommunication and malediction, perhaps reminiscent of the sort of showdowns we are used to seeing in the literature of the 'Peace of God' movement in parts of contemporary West Francia. These did not have to evoke the idea of Rome: we have scraps of contemporary English

---

[139] Parkes, 'Henry II', pp. 128–32.

[140] *PUU* †88–9 (J³ †7617, 7620), †90–1 (JL 3610–11); there are several problems with Zimmermann's attempts to date and locate these documents, which deserve renewed study.

[141] Edwards, *Ritual Excommunication*; Hamilton, 'Remedies'; Hamilton, 'Interpreting'; Hamilton, 'Law'; Hamilton, 'Medieval Curses'; Jaser, *Ecclesia*, pp. 54–268.

evidence elsewhere that show excommunication exercised in these years through the usual episcopal channels, and this was probably the norm.[142] John's letter nevertheless has a special value in showing that, on at least one occasion, contemporary West Frankish interests in the idea of the pope as an especially effective agent of excommunication may have had some influence on English practices. What it does *not* provide is any good evidence that Glastonbury, one of the foremost centres of the later Anglo-Saxon monastic movement, laid claim to special privileges of papal 'protection' or 'jurisdiction' remotely comparable to anywhere like Fulda, Montecassino, Cluny, or Roda—or indeed, dozens of other monasteries across the map of post-Carolingian Europe. Whoever penned Pope John's letter, they 'only' went as far as claiming that he bore responsibility for 'the care of *all* the churches and the solicitude of *all* the faithful', a statement so all-encompassing as to render it almost innocuous. It indicated no hint of special treatment for Glastonbury, nor any other English monastery.

IV. Conclusions

In some ways this chapter has had a negative flavour, deconstructing and downgrading the already slight evidence for papal privileges in tenth-century England, rather than attempting the usual path of rehabilitation. Instead, it has emphasised important peculiarities and contradictions. It has sought to demonstrate just how odd it looks that these remarkable Roman documents, proliferating at this time all across the Latin church, and even becoming characteristic markers of its most important archbishoprics and monasteries, raised such little interest in tenth-century England—that is, despite this emerging polity's considerable continental connections and influences; its historic interest in apostolic authority; and its high-profile maintenance of relations with the Roman see through gifts, embassies, and pilgrimages. The best way of understanding this difference lies in the observation that Anglo-Saxon England never became strictly speaking 'post-Carolingian', and was in fact relatively uninfluenced by some of the developments of late Carolingian politics. The perception of Rome and the papacy that developed through much of France and Germany, Catalonia and northern-central Italy in the long tenth century, and the political

---

[142] Hamilton, 'Law', pp. 288–90.

practices that grew out of this, owed much to the shared (late) Carolingian inheritance of these regions, at a structural as well an ideological level. This disinclination of Edgar, Æthelred, and their religious leaders to play the same tune reflects their profound distance from that shared legacy— something that historians, in talking up the honorarily Carolingian aspects of West Saxon rule, have not always been quick to concede. Perhaps more importantly, it may hint at the underlying causes of wider English divergences from continental political thought and practice in this period, stemming from this same *peculiarity* of foundations onto which the new English kingdom was being built.

How might a revised sketch of 'England and the Papacy in the Tenth Century' look? One major distinction lay between what we might call 'foreign' versus 'domestic policy'. The West Saxon court and its prelates had a sharp sense of papal Rome as a political symbol, and even as an attractive third-party arbitrator in overseas politics, as the use of a papal intermediary (*apocrisarius*) at the Rouen peace negotiations shows. Sending relatively regular embassies to Rome, now sometimes headed by archbishops and their entourages, maintained their stake in this world. Not least, it made the new Cerdicing kingdom visible on the international stage. This may be the best way to understand the uniquely English phenomenon of Peter's Pence. Doubtlessly, it was taken extremely earnestly as a spiritual gift to Saint Peter. But it also meant flooding Rome every year with huge sums of coins minted in the name of the king of the English and bearing his image. The Ottos sought to ensure that every papal document leaving the Eternal City was authenticated in their name and regnal year; Edgar and Æthelred arranged matters so that the flocks of pilgrims and petitioners already there might hold an image of their own crowned heads in their hands. Thietmar, bishop of Merseburg (1009–18) noted in his *Chronicle* the sad irony that the English of his day, known as the *tributarii* of Saint Peter, had now come to pay tribute to the Danes.[143] What is most interesting here is that 'Peter's Pence' had proven such a successful PR exercise for the English kingdom that this prelate on the outer Saxon frontier thought in these terms at all. And yet: for all that the Cerdicings invested into Rome, we see relatively little interest in bringing contemporary apostolic authority back to play in the workings of their own church. Archiepiscopal privileges may have been unexceptional, and of little interest to archivists. Monastic privileges were

---

[143] Thietmar, *Chronicon*, vii. 36, pp. 442–3.

rare-to-non-existent. When papal letters did make their way into the Insular world, they concerned not the *in perpetuum* privileges of ecclesiastical institutions, but one-off cases addressing the sins of named individuals. Thus John XV's reprimand of Ealdorman Ælfric, or the curious series of short, personalised papal certificates brought back by penitential pilgrims from the city.[144] This domestic reluctance to engage with the contemporary papacy on an institutional level feeds into the second key distinction of this period: what we have identified as a sense of ancient papal history *qua* ancient papal history. Gregory was venerated; late antique decretals copied; old privileges translated, or imagined anew in hagiography. But the past stayed the past. More recent decretal collections were not sought; papal forgeries apparently unattempted; old privileges left unrenewed; new monastic privileges not petitioned. Viewed from the post-Carolingian world, this would have all looked by the turn of the millennium rather strange. As we will see in the next chapter, some of that strangeness would endure well into the transformative age of the eleventh-century 'papal revolution'.

---

[144] Above, n. 5.

7

Papal Privileges in England and the Coming of the 'Papal Revolution' (1049–73)

When Ealdred got mugged, he must have hardly believed his luck. Returning to England after the Roman Easter Synod of 1061, the would-be archbishop of York had left the Eternal City scorned and empty-handed. In a humiliating and unprecedented step, Pope Nicholas II and his cardinals, before an assembly of bishops hailing from Troyes, Nevers, Meaux, Metz, Le Mans, Wells, and Hereford, had rejected his petition for the privilege of the archiepiscopal pallium. In the ruling of the synod, the fact that Ealdred had already held since 1046 the see of Worcester—hitherto something of an informal tradition for late Anglo-Saxon prelates graduating to York—had utterly disqualified him from the archiepiscopate. Here was a flagrant breach of the ancient canonical prohibition against episcopal translation. The crowning moment of Ealdred's career had suddenly, unexpectedly, become one of unimagined dishonour: his public degradation before a gathering of prelates from across the Latin west, at the very threshold of the apostles. He can have hardly set off for home in high spirits—but then, just outside the city gates, his fortune in a strange way changed. A force led by Count Gerardo of Galeria, an advocate of the Roman 'old aristocracy' and opponent to its new reformist leadership, ambushed the sizeable English embassy. Spoils were taken, men were killed. The party hurried back inside the city walls and sought the pope's aid. Considering Gerardo's ties, Nicholas must have recognised the symbolism of this attack. What good were the reform papacy's claims to the universal protection of the world's churches when its guests were being assaulted outside its own front door? The cardinals reconsidered their severity against Ealdred; their previous humiliation of the bishop must have now looked rather different in light of the count's bloody postscript. Taking counsel, they softened their position, and granted Ealdred the archiepiscopal pallium after all. Nicholas' privilege did not hesitate to stress, however, that they had made an unrepeatable exception:

England and the Papacy in the Early Middle Ages: Papal Privileges in European Perspective, c. 680–1073.
Benjamin Savill, Oxford University Press. © Benjamin Savill 2023. DOI: 10.1093/oso/9780198887058.003.0007

the battered petitioner had to resign Worcester, and never again could he or any other bishop expect such leniency. Ealdred rode home, an archbishop once more.[1]

This exceptionally well-documented case is fascinating in its own right, but it comprises just one part of a sudden flurry of evidence for Anglo-papal documentary interactions beginning in the late 1040s. At its forefront stands a series of twelve plausibly authentic privileges or credible *deperdita* issued between the pontificates of Leo IX (1049–54) and Alexander II (1061–73). Together, these form the single densest cluster of evidence for acquisitions of papal privileges in England before the twelfth century.[2] The correlation between this sudden, late upswing and the first decades of the papal 'reform movement' or 'revolution' that began to play out through the wider Latin church at just this time does not look like much of a coincidence, and is arguably not wholly surprising. It nevertheless serves as a reminder that the interconnections between this heavily documented mid-eleventh-century religious and political phenomenon and the late Anglo-Saxon church have still not received the full attention they deserve. The issue may above all be historiographical, relating to where specialists within different national traditions draw their dividing lines. For historians of Rome, the papacy, and the German and Italian *Reich*, the formal inauguration of the reform programme at the Council of Sutri of 1046—when the Emperor Henry III enforced his *coup d'état* at Rome by imposing Pope Clement II upon the local clergy and aristocracy—and then its rapid acceleration following the inauguration of Leo IX in 1049, has long held a central place in the master-narrative. In French historiography, this meanwhile tends to be the point at which the controversies about 'the feudal mutation' come to an end. In work on Iberia, it has correlated with the traditional paradigms of *reconquista* and Europeanisation. Yet 1046/9 hardly features in English models, where 1066 remains the sacred threshold between the distinct research agendas of Anglo-Saxon and Anglo-Norman historiography.[3] Consequently, the evidence for the interactions between the newly energised reform regime and the last generation of pre-Norman government has often gone overlooked,

---

[1] 59; *ASC, s.a.* 1061 D; *Life of King Edward*, i. 5, pp. 52–7; Peter Damian, *Briefe*, iv. 2. 89, pp. 566–7; Tinti, 'Pallium'; Gresser, *Synoden*, pp. 53–6. Gerardo and the 'old aristocracy': Wickham, *Medieval Rome*, pp. 217–20. On the pallium in England and Worcester-York translations: above, Chapter 6, pp. 190–96; for the use of the (not unproblematic) term 'reform', p. 187, n. 1.

[2] *49, ?†50, *51, 53–4, 57–9, *62, *63, 64–5.

[3] Savill, 'England and the Papacy', pp. 307–8, paraphrased here.

with the story of English church renewal depicted as beginning instead in the age of Archbishops Lanfranc (1070–89) and Anselm (1093–1109). This has had two effects. It has privileged from the perspective of English history the more rigorous, confrontational period of reform ushered in by the pontificates of Gregory VII (1073–85), Urban II (1088–99), and Paschal II (1099–1118) as effectively *the* reform. Worse still, it has sometimes meant judging, as a result, the state of late Anglo-Saxon Christianity according to those same post-*c.* 1073 standards, perceiving the pre-Conquest clergy as living in a state of naïve obliviousness to the transformations underway through the rest of Latin Europe—thereby replicating, in effect, the prejudices and propaganda of the Anglo-Norman regime.[4]

The question of how far, and in what ways, pre-Conquest England had already become involved in the wider European reform movement of the eleventh century awaits a dedicated study of its own. This chapter takes only the first steps towards that task by investigating the evidence of this undervalued cluster of papal privileges acquired by English institutions during the final two Anglo-Saxon decades and the opening phase of the Norman Conquest. We saw in Chapter 6 that Anglo-Saxon interactions with Rome probably intensified from the later ninth century onwards as part of the consciously 'international' image cultivated by the ascendant Cerdicing regime, but that this contrasted in style and scope to the relationships with the papacy we see across much of the rest of the Latin church: this development did not appear to involve any substantial engagement with contemporary papal legal and documentary culture, something which grew with ever increasing momentum in much of Francia, northern and central Italy, and Catalonia. It was argued that at the root of this lay the peculiar quality of the Anglo-Saxon polity as a decidedly *non*-post-Carolingian state, which had not inherited the same shared legal or documentary landscape, ecclesiastical memories and tensions, cross-border complexities, or understandings of the role of Rome, as found elsewhere in the post-Carolingian world. The main question posed in this chapter is simply—what changed from the late 1040s onwards? Does this cluster of privileges indicate that England suddenly become pulled into a post-Carolingian mainstream, and if so, were the forces driving this generated within the polity itself, or did they come from the outside, under papal

---

[4] Ibid., pp. 308–10; the commonplace that the reform papacy took a dim view of the Anglo-Saxon church and sanctioned the events of 1066 is not supported by contemporary evidence: Morton, 'Pope Alexander'.

direction? Does this shift of gear reveal a late Anglo-Saxon enthusiasm for the continental reform project, or is the picture more complex?

I. Understanding the Early Papal Reform Movement

Before looking closer at the evidence, we need some clarity as to what we mean by the early papal reform. The history of the papacy from the mid-eleventh century onwards is characterised by a massive increase in its documented activity, revealing the growing influence of the popes and their cardinal clergy as important players in their own right in European and Mediterranean politics. German historians, attempting to defuse the confessional problem of whether or not this was a 'good thing', have adopted in recent years the more neutral terminology of a *papstgeschichtliche Wende* for this shift (blandly anglicised, the 'turning-point in papal history', but for its intended audience evocative of the German *Wende* of 1989–90). This sees the transformations of 1046/9 onwards as a real revolution, but one less of papal ideology than sheer productivity, distinguished above all by its proactive, self-driven character: the popes themselves now took their own initiatives more often, in contrast to their predominantly responsive, petitioner-driven early medieval predecessors.[5] This is useful for getting us beyond the old dogmas that understood the papal reform as either the liberation of the church from the Dark Ages, where it had languished in the grasp of the state, or its hostile takeover by a scheming, power-hungry Roman centre. Nevertheless it is not by itself sufficient for thinking around the enormous complexities of the eleventh century, in particular this critical phase of the later 1040s to early 1070s.

Two points need emphasis. Firstly, the more famous aspect of this 'turning-point'—wherein the popes and cardinals exercised their power in an aggressively self-driven fashion, bringing about a true 'Church vs. State' conflict in the form of the Investiture Crisis—had to wait for the more radical stage of the reform inaugurated under Gregory VII, not beginning until 1076 at the earliest.[6] Instead, the key papal reformers in its initial phase came from within the *Reich*, and were intimate with (and dependent upon) the imperial court, which had imposed their party upon the less-than-enthusiastic city of Rome. Even once this relationship became more strained

---

[5] Schieffer, '*Motu*'.   [6] Miller, 'Crisis', pp. 1570–3.

from the later 1050s under the minority of Henry IV, the predominant discourse remained one of cooperation and unity.[7] Secondly, the teleological significance traditionally imposed upon the early papal reform must not blind us to the fact that it initially constituted only one part of a wider European eleventh-century reform movement, already well advanced by 1046/9. The best recent work on reform has prioritised the diverse on-the-ground, regional developments beginning c. 1000, involving increased agitation around the issues of church property, clerical sexuality, and the demarcation between the sacred and profane. From these, the papal reform later took its cues. Real changing attitudes to the meaning and future direction of the Christian church stirring up well beyond Rome now look more important than the political and institutional manoeuvres later taking place within it. In the words of John Howe, 'before there was a centre, there was reform.'[8]

From this perspective, the ideology-free and centralising, institution-focused approach to papal reform that proponents of the 'turning-point' might advocate feels outmoded. In current research, the political centre is out, ideas are back in. That centre, however, proves on closer inspection difficult to pin down. My argument here is that the dynamics of the papacy peculiar to this transitional period of 1046/9–73 betray this centre/periphery distinction as essentially misleading. We must recognise how unusual the Henrician coup of 1046 was in its radical decentring of Rome from the idea of the papacy. There are rare, isolated earlier cases of emperors imposing external bishops on Rome, but such instances were unpopular, short-lived, and had no serious impact upon the workings or identity of the Roman church. By contrast, from the mid-1040s many among the Lateran clergy and bureaucracy, together with their Roman aristocratic supporters who had so much at stake in the institution, found themselves displaced for at least a generation.[9]

This came about through a number of transformations. At the top, it meant importing distant bishops as popes: Bishops Suidiger of Bamberg (Pope Clement II, 1046–7), Poppo of Brixen (Damasus II, 1048), Bruno of Toul (Leo IX, 1049–54), Gebhard of Eichstätt (Victor II, 1055–7), Gerhard of Florence (Nicholas II, 1058–61), and Anselm of Lucca (Alexander II,

---

[7] Robinson, *Papal Reform*, pp. 5–12.

[8] Howe, *Church Reform*, p. 160; Cushing, *Reform*; Savill, 'England and the Papacy', pp. 310–12.

[9] Wickham, *Medieval Rome*, pp. 29, 247.

1061–73). Abbot Frederick of Montecassino (Stephen IX, 1057–8) stands out as a non-episcopal appointment, but as a former imperial chancellor and member of the Lotharingian ducal house, he too was an outsider.[10] These bishops did not just break canonical prohibitions on translation by moving to Rome, but also continued to hold their former sees, assuming dual identities as both (local) bishop and (universal) pope.[11] Although their decisions to adopt new names would in time become one of the more famous papal traditions, in the eleventh century this was still quite innovative. It signposted their dual insider-outsider identities, and harkened back to the antique papacy via names familiar outside Rome through the pages of Pseudo-Isidore: Clement (c. 100), Alexander (c. 110), Victor (189–98), Damasus (366–84), and Leo the Great (440–61).[12] Even Gerhard's seemingly anomalous nod to Nicholas I (858–67) invoked the most impressive pope of the later Carolingian period, under whom Pseudo-Isidore had first flourished, and whose own writings became absorbed into the post-Carolingian canon law tradition.[13] Such naming practices therefore looked closer to notions about the papacy prevalent within the post-Carolingian churches from which these bishops originated, rather than in Rome itself, purposefully eschewing the names characteristic of the city's own clergy (e.g., John, Benedict, Sergius).[14] Equally unusually, these popes spent a great deal of time outside Rome. While aspects of their travels doubtlessly had pastoral overtones,[15] one should refrain from thinking of these journeys as principally efforts to revive 'the international responsibility of the Roman Church',[16] still less an exercise in 'Europolitik avant la lettre'.[17] Often, these outsider-popes left Rome because its clergy and aristocracy had driven them out; what is more, they tended to head back to their own regional power-bases of Lotharingia, Germany, and later Tuscany, organising much of their activity from there. That our best narrative source for the pontificate of Leo IX comes from Lotharingia, and admits little knowledge of Roman affairs, is telling.[18]

---

[10] Gresser, Clemens; Bischoff and Tock, eds., Léon, Hägermann, Papsttum; Schmidt, Alexander.

[11] Goez, 'Papa'.

[12] Decretales, ed. Hinschius, pp. 3–66, 94–105, 127–30, 180–9, 498–520, 565–630.

[13] Above, Chapter 6, pp. 188–9; see e.g. Burchard's Decretum: PL 140. 616, 776, 801, 819, 823, 922; 170 of his letters survive, for which the tradition stems almost entirely from recipient-end collections within the Carolingian world: Jasper, 'Beginning', pp. 110–25.

[14] Cf. Santifaller, Saggio, pp. 70–145.   [15] Johrendt, 'Reisen'.

[16] Morris, Papal Monarchy, p. 86.   [17] Schmieder, 'Peripherie', p. 359.

[18] Die Touler Vita Leos IX, esp. ii. 27, pp. 242–3.

This same decentring of Rome from the papal idea manifested itself also on an administrative and aesthetic level, as we saw in Chapter 2, with the transformation of the output of the papal writing-office. From 1049 the popes resolved to abandon permanently the iconic, centuries-old papyral scrolls characteristic of Rome, replacing them for good with parchment diplomas modelled on the transalpine imperial chancery. That transformation resulted in part from a supplanting of personnel, as Roman scribes became phased-out in favour of northerners, who travelled with the frequently itinerant papal household.[19] This in turn reflected the most effective institutional shake-up instigated by these outsider-popes, especially Leo IX: filling vacancies in the Roman clergy and administration with new, external candidates—typically, again, from within the German *Reich*.[20] Refashioning the cardinal clergy in this way presumably magnified the extra-Roman ideas, texts, and political and proprietorial connections surrounding the pope, and ensured institutional continuity of this culture change beyond the reigns of individual pontiffs. Only in 1073, with the elevation of Archdeacon Hildebrand to the see as Gregory VII, did the papal leadership fall back into the hands of a Roman cleric.[21] That story, however, lies beyond the scope of this book.

We can therefore speak of a revolutionary de-Romanising of the papacy in the mid-eleventh century. From this perspective, the scholarly opposition between writing histories of the early papal reform that focus on institutional transformations at the 'centre', and those that prioritise the earlier, regionalised reforms of the 'periphery', begins to collapse in on itself. To study the papacy in the mid-1040s to early 1070s is to bring centre and periphery together. The first phase of the 'turning-point in papal history' really did involve a seizing of the initiative by the pope and those around him. But this did not come from within the bishopric of Rome as it had been hitherto understood. Rather, its personnel, expertise, networks, frameworks of reference, aesthetics, aristocratic and military support—not to mention, for many years, its very theatre of operations—were all extra-Roman: a development of the Carolingian and post-Carolingian world we explored in Chapter 6. We have seen over and over again in this book that if we want

---

[19] Above, Chapter 2, pp. 28, 39–43.

[20] Morris, *Papal Monarchy*, p. 86; Parisse, 'L'entourage', pp. 436–41; Wickham, *Medieval Rome*, p. 247.

[21] Wickham, *Medieval Rome*, p. 30; Cowdrey, *Pope Gregory*, pp. 27–74. Even Hildebrand (a Tuscan, but a member of the Roman clergy) had spent 1046–8/9 in Germany, perhaps attached to Henry III's court: Cowdrey, *Pope Gregory*, pp. 29–30.

to understand the papacy in the earlier middle ages, we need to set our sights on how those outside the orbit of the Lateran and Vatican conceived of it and used it as a resource, rather than focus on Rome, since it was with the former that the real initiative and creativity lay. The argument here is that 1046/9 did not see the reversal of this early medieval model, but rather its radical intensification. Rather than simply influencing and steering the direction of individual papal acts through appeals and petitions, peripheral forces within the post-Carolingian Latin church now seized control of the papal apparatus, reshaping it in their own image.

Once again, therefore, if we wish to make sense of the privileges acquired in these years, we need to continue looking at impulses within the wider world of their beneficiaries, rather than Roman politics, from which even the popes made themselves scarce for much of this period. Looking at the distribution of the 276 surviving privileges acquired between 1049 and 1073 (Map 7.1), several trends stand out.[22] Firstly, the core zone of acquisitions remains that of the post-Carolingian regions of northern and central Italy (133), the East Frankish *Reich* (67), and the West Frankish kingdom (49), joined by Catalonia (4). Together this suggests a continuation and, broadly speaking—if not necessarily on a region-by-region level— intensification of the developments observed in the previous chapter, with a particular density around a Lotharingian–Burgundian–Italian 'central zone'. To these we can add three further, smaller groupings of privileges just beyond the borders of the Carolingian world, in southern Italy (12), Aragon (3), and England (8, with 4 *deperdita*). The first two at least reflect short bursts of contacts made between members of the reform party and the emerging polities of Norman Italy and Aragon: these nevertheless look marginal to the wider pattern. Next, by following the chronology of these acquisitions, we can observe that they tend to follow the itineraries of these outsider-popes far beyond Rome, much in the same way that the issuing of diplomas by contemporary sovereigns might reflect their own itinerant regimes, moving between beneficiaries, particularly in the regions central to their rule. Of these 276 privileges, less than half of those whose dating clauses survive state that they were granted in Rome, a truly exceptional figure compared to any earlier period.[23] Through the trail left by Leo's

---

[22] There is no equivalent to either *PUU* or Johrendt, *Papsttum*, for this period, and there is no space for a full survey of the material here: the data is drawn from J³, and the reader is directed there for further information.

[23] Eighty-two of 173 privileges.

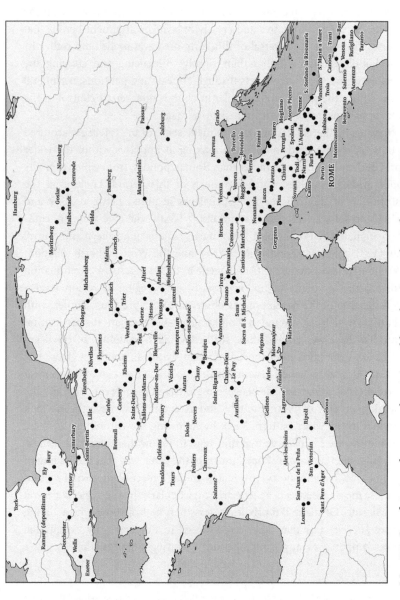

Map 7.1 Beneficiaries of extant authentic/possibly authentic papal privileges, 1049–73

privileges, one can trace his departure from Rome early in his pontificate in 1049, his tour of his own power-base in and around the Lotharingian region, and then his visit to the court of his cousin Henry III in Mainz (in terms of documentation, one of the single most productive phases of the early reform).[24] Hints of something comparable emerge from the more poorly documented pontificate of Victor, who spent much of 1055–7 back in his German heartland.[25] Later, in the pontificates of Nicholas and Alexander, we can observe a swing in the distribution of beneficiaries away from the *Reich*, Burgundy, and (to a lesser degree) France, towards a more Italian field of play under these Tuscan popes, who spent a good proportion of their pontificates back in their own bishoprics of Florence[26] and Lucca.[27] Overall, then, the evidence points foremost in this period to an intensification of the regional trends seen in the long tenth century, with the added dynamic of the opportunities for acquisitions of privileges becoming markedly affected by the itinerancy (and, presumably, pre-existing networks and connections) of the outsider-popes, typically within those same regions where they had operated before their papal election. We now need to consider how our English material fits into this wider context.

II. England's Early Reform Privileges: Four Categories of Evidence

(a) New Bishoprics: The Exceptional Case of Leofric of Exeter?

In 1050, perhaps on the feast of Saints Peter and Paul (29 June), King Edward the Confessor (1042–66) took Queen Edith in his left hand, and Bishop Leofric in his right, and entered the monastery of Sts Peter and Mary, Exeter. Inside, he presented over its altar his diploma uniting the *dioceses* of Cornwall and Crediton (Devon), establishing the house as their new episcopal see, with Leofric its incumbent.[28] This magnificent charter, surviving

---

[24] Böhmer-Frech 555–729, J³ *9277–*9431.

[25] Böhmer-Frech 1249–80, J³ *10017–*10049.

[26] Nicholas spent the better part of his pontificate banished from Rome, including a spell at his see of Florence from November 1059 till about March 1060 (J³ *10342–*10377).

[27] Alexander appears to have taken up residence at his Lucca bishopric for substantial portions of at least 1062 (J³ *10535–*10570), 1066 (J³ 10833–*10847), 1068 (J³ *10961–11000), 1070 (J³ *11071–11081) and 1072 (J³ *11160–11164).

[28] CS I, i. 71 (S 1021); Roach, 'Public Rites', pp. 189–90.

as an apparent original,[29] sets out the stage-directions for this ritual, and puts into Edward's mouth the statement that his actions confirmed a ruling of Pope Leo. We have seen that something approximating just such a mandate survives. In a letter-privilege addressed to Edward, Leo IX 'marvels' at the news that Leofric held a see without a city (*civitas*), and 'commands and beseeches' the king to move it from the 'little villa' (*uillula*) of Crediton to the *civitas* of Exeter.[30] If this looks at face value like an early example of a reform pope dispatching orders to a sovereign and intervening in the restructuring of a distant church, we must appreciate that no other example of a privilege of this kind survives from this period. This is a unique document, and if anything looks like a bespoke response (whether real or contemporaneously forged) to a peculiarly Insular problem. Indeed, what we see here may correspond to the *longue durée* effect of the developments observed in Chapter 4, where the severely de-urbanised landscape of post-Roman Britain compelled the Anglo-Saxon church's earliest bishoprics to take shape first around peoples rather than cities, with rural minsters then taking the role of their sees.[31] In the later Anglo-Saxon period, the location and even permanency of such non-urban sees continued to be unusually fluid, perhaps more so than ever before.[32] Outsiders may have found something disconcerting about it. Perhaps it should not seem surprising, then, that this early attempt to bring the shape of the English episcopal church more firmly into line with city-based European norms should have been instigated under a king who had spent the better part of his life on the continent, and his bishop, Leofric, who (despite his Anglo-Saxon name) had a Lotharingian background.[33] These actions of 1050 thus provide a foretaste of the better-known and more comprehensive efforts to move sees from *uillulae* to *ciuitates* under the Norman regime in 1074/5,[34] and hint at the anxieties the foreign-trained ecclesiastics newly resident in Edward's England had about the strangely rural condition of its church. Nevertheless, this papal support for the urban resettlement of a newly imported, Lotharingian clergy may have also had an earlier Insular precedent: the foundation of the see of Dublin, Ireland's first urban bishopric, by a group of Lotharingian canons in or shortly after 1028, following a journey by King

---

[29] Exeter, D&C, 2072.   [30] ?†50.   [31] See above, pp. 135–9.

[32] See the evidence collected in *WBEASE*, pp. 539–66. Even Reuter, in an essay otherwise keen to stress tenth-century Anglo-continental commonalities, conceded that England was peculiar in this respect: 'Europe', pp. 23–6.

[33] Licence, *Edward*, pp. 39–79; *GP*, I, ii. 94, pp. 314–15; Bihrer, *Begegnungen*, pp. 186–90.

[34] *CS* I, ii. 92.

Sihtric to Rome that year, where he may have received the blessing of John XIX.[35] The further evidence of links between the developing western port towns of Exeter and Dublin—and perhaps even Sihtric's connections between the two[36]—make these parallels intriguing. Some sort of Dublin influence over the Exeter foundation in the time of Bishop Donatus (1028–74) must remain hypothetical, but we cannot rule it out entirely. What we can say with more certainty is that both instances point to foreign clerics implanted into the under-urbanised Insular world making their own adjustments to their local environment, and not to any centralised papal policy.

Still: given the weight of this regional initiative, Edward's support, and even the likelihood that Leofric composed the king's diploma himself,[37] we might ask why such pains were taken to call in the additional backing of Leo IX. One clue may lie in the context of the privilege's reproduction in the 'Leofric Missal', a pontifical belonging to the bishop and part of his foundation-bequest to the new see of Exeter (Figure 7.1). The manuscript opens with a narrative account written in two contemporary hands.[38] The first recounts a dubious legend, which enjoyed wider circulation around this time, that in the days of King Edward the Elder (899–924), Pope Formosus (891–6: *sic*) had sanctioned the reorganisation of the West Saxon bishoprics, thereby following up the work of Gregory I.[39] Later, the new King Edward took the throne, and in 1046 appointed his chaplain Leofric to the bishopric of Crediton and Cornwall. Faced with the 'devastations of barbaric pirates', the latter sought to move his see to the 'city' of Exeter, but reflected that he could not do so 'without Roman authority', and so dispatched his priest Lambert to seek approval from Leo. The scribe then reproduces Leo's letter.[40] The narrative strategy here is obvious. It justifies the actions of Leofric and his Lotharingian canons—who presumably faced opposition from the monks and clerics of Cornwall and Devon—by depicting the world of Edward and Leo as a renewal of an imagined West Saxon golden age overseen by the Elder Edward and Formosus, itself a renaissance of the era of Gregory. Controversial eleventh-century innovations thus drew their

---

[35] Ó Riain-Raedel, 'New Light'.

[36] Hudson, 'Knútr', pp. 330–2; but cf. Downham, 'England', pp. 62–3.

[37] Cf. Licence, *Edward*, pp. 263–81.

[38] Oxford, Bodleian Library, Bodley 579, ff. 2–3v; Drage, 'Bishop Leofric', pp. 161–7.

[39] *CS* I, ii. 35. 1–2 (S 1296, 1451a); later picked up by William of Malmesbury's *Liber pontificalis* (Cambridge, University Library, Kk 4. 6, f. 277; BL, Harley 633, f. 56), and thereafter *HN*, 5, pp. 271–2; *GP*, I, ii. 80, pp. 276–9; *GR* I, ii. 128–9, pp. 204–5. Cf. also *†46.

[40] Oxford, Bodleian Library, Bodley 579, ff. 3r–v.

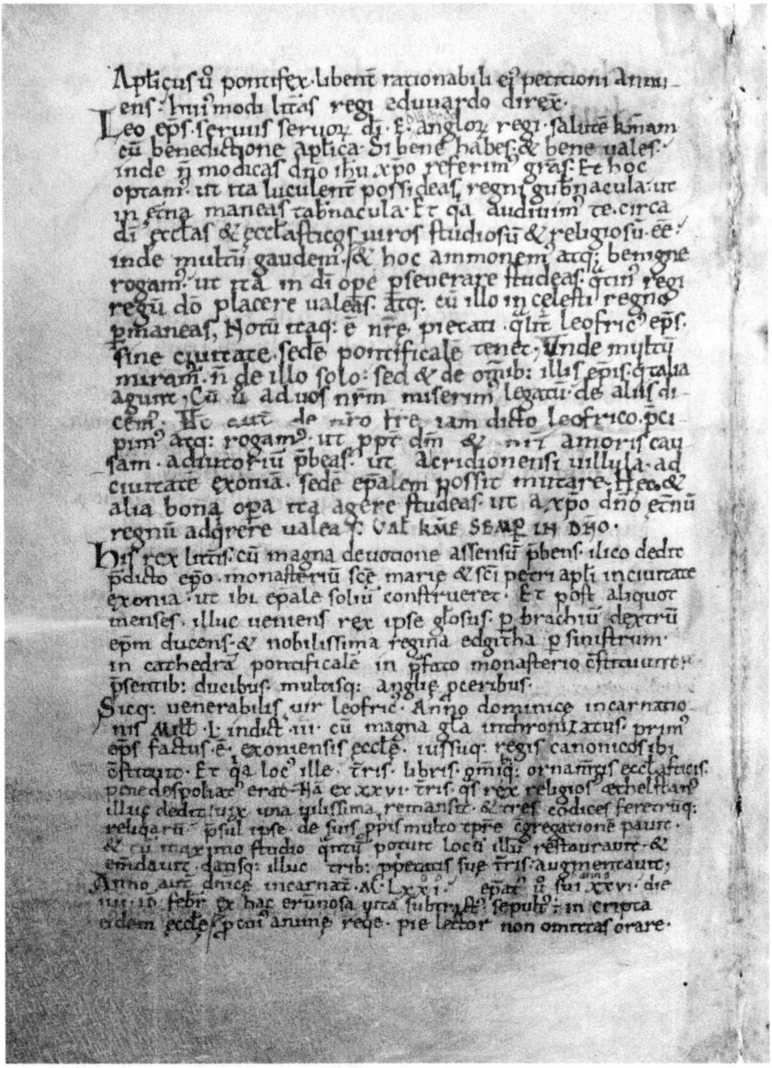

Figure 7.1 Leo IX for Crediton-Exeter (1049/50) (JL 4208), copy in the Leofric Missal: Oxford, Bodleian Library, Bodley 579, f. 3v (Digital Bodleian, CC-BY-NC 4.0 licence).

authority from their supposed connection to an idealised past. Indeed, one could argue that the entire codex of the Leofric Missal embodied a comparable attitude. The manuscript's core comprises a splendid, late ninth-century Carolingian or Canterbury sacramentary; to this are added tenth-century, Canterbury elements; then come the final Lotharingian additions, courtesy of Leofric and his canons once the codex arrived in Exeter.[41] Within that most recent section, a relic list reveals the ancient artefacts kept at the new see upon its foundation: fragments of the Holy Land and the martyrs, virgins, and confessors of antiquity, supposedly granted to the older Exeter minster by King Æthelstan (927–39).[42] Whether these treasures really went back to that king's heroic age is doubtful. What really mattered for the probably not-so-popular incomers to this new see in 1050, however, is that, bundled together with the bequest of more ancient liturgical manuscripts, and the gift of a papal privilege which supposedly harkened back to the traditions of Æthelstan's father and even Gregory I, these claims helped to form a legitimising package which could overcome the jarring novelties of the present by building a bridge to antiquity's dazzling authority.

Leofric nevertheless used his unique privilege cautiously, even strategically. That Edward's diploma remarks upon its precedent so briefly and imprecisely may not have come as an accident. What remains of the papal document suggests that Leo had merely acknowledged that Leofric's see should transfer to an urban centre. The decision made by the time of the 1050 ceremony to merge the Devon and Cornwall *parrochiae* together in this process, thereby subduing the latter's autonomy, had received no mention in the privilege. This was a clever fudge. Moreover, with the birthing pains of the new see out of the way, Exeter does not seem to have gone on to maintain much sense of a papal identity. In 1069 William I issued an uncharacteristically sumptuous diploma for the cathedral, emulating the aesthetics of Edward's foundation charter, and so linking his authority to that of the dead king.[43] It did not mention Leo, whose role thereupon fades from the bishopric's institutional memory.

(b) Seats, Sandals, and Mitres: Canterbury's Short-Lived Prerogatives

The emissary Lambert had probably met Leo during the latter's tour of Lotharingia and its environs in 1049–50. One possible occasion came at the Council of Rheims in October 1049, attended by at least three English dignitaries: Bishop Duduc of Wells, Abbot Wulfric of Sts Peter and Paul, Canterbury, and Abbot Ælfwine of Ramsey, all sent on Edward's orders.[44] This three-day event marked one of the most dramatic showdowns of the

---

[41] *Leofric Missal*, i, pp. 5, 207–9.   [42] Oxford, Bodleian Library, Bodley 579, ff. 6r–v.
[43] Exeter, D&C, 2528 (*AAWI*, 138).   [44] *ASC, s.a.* 1046 E, 1050 D.

early reform.[45] Held to observe the consecration of the new basilica at Saint-Rémi, some 60 miles west of the *Reich*'s Lotharingian frontier, the assembly probably enjoyed the sponsorship of Leo's cousin, Emperor Henry III.[46] King Henry of France, in whose realm it notionally took place, declined to attend.[47] The Cerdicing delegation found itself dwarfed by a gathering of some of the major prelates of Francia's western and central regions. Besides abbots from houses including Saint-Rémi, Cluny, Gorze, and Corbie, the consecration saw the arrival of such heavyweights as Archbishops Wido of Rheims, Eberhard of Trier, Halinard of Lyon and Hugh of Besançon, together with the bishops of Soissons, Thérouanne, Senlis, Metz, Langres, Coutances, Séez, Lisieux, Bayeux, Avranches, Verdun, Nevers, Angers, Nantes, and (as part of the papal entourage) Porto.[48]

A gathering on this scale was exceptional. It is the first such 'international'-level event for which we have definite records of English delegates in attendance.[49] It is a shame, then, that we find no trace of their taking part in the reform fireworks that blew up once these mid-eleventh-century prelates got together in one room. Accusations and excommunications flew forth against simonists, adulterers, murderers, the incestuous, sodomites, and arms-bearing clerics. Tearful confessions were extracted; croziers snapped; advocates of the accused struck dumb in the presence of Saint Remigius' holy corpse. One prelate was deposed on the spot. Another fled in the night.[50] Duduc, Wulfric, and Ælfwine do not, however, appear to have made themselves conspicuous amid these proceedings. In his detailed *History* of the council, Anselm of Saint-Rémi fails to ascribe any actions to the three, forgets Duduc's name, and lists the two abbots only at the very end of his roll-call of attendees.[51] This is no small point, for the problem of presence, visibility, and spatial precedence was the first of the controversies to erupt at this council: who among the archbishops of Rheims, Trier, Lyon, and Besançon should sit closest to the pope? Anselm describes the negotiated solution, with an eye to detail suggestive of the scale of the argument. Ultimately, the bishops resolved to form a circle in the church, with the altar as its easternmost point. The abbots sat behind them, then Leo, ingeniously,

---

[45] *Konzilien*, ed. Jasper, 27, pp. 224–50; Gresser, *Synoden*, pp. 17–21.

[46] At least one English writer was under the (in this case, mistaken) impression that the emperor had presided: *ASC s.a.* 1050 D.

[47] *Konzilien*, ed. Jasper, 27, pp. 230–1.   [48] Ibid., pp. 232–3.

[49] Possibility of (unrecorded) English attendance at some major Ottonian councils: above, Chapter 6, pp. 196–8.

[50] Hefele, *Histoire*, iv, pp. 1011–28; Cushing, *Reform*, pp. 125–8.

[51] *Konzilien*, ed. Jasper, 27, p. 233.

sat at the circle's centre, thus equidistant from all the bishops, with Lyon to his immediate right, Besançon at his left, and Trier and Rheims either side of Saint-Rémi's altar, which he faced directly.[52] As for Abbot Wulfric—sitting half-ignored, somewhere at the back as this explosive council then began to play out—we at least get the impression that he had paid attention to this opening dispute. The following spring, at the less fraught Roman Synod of 1050, Bishop Hermann of Ramsbury interceded with Leo on his behalf, acquiring for the abbots of Sts Peter and Paul the privilege of sitting beside no less an authority than the abbot of Montecassino at future synods. He purportedly extracted from the pope the further guarantee that the archbishop of Canterbury might sit next to the cardinal bishop of Silva Candida. Over a decade later, Wulfric's successor Æthelsige made another acquisition, receiving from Alexander II the further privilege of donning the prestigious vestments of the mitre and Roman sandals.[53]

These privileges of conciliar seating and precedence, and of ornate embellishments to priestly garb, together helped shape a newly emerging sub-category of papal diploma concerned with visual self-representation. We must recognise that they originated within a peculiar, post-Carolingian context. If we look back from the high and later middle ages, so-called *pontificalia* such as the mitre seem utterly commonplace—part of anyone's idea today of what a bishop looks like. However, in the mid-eleventh century they represented unusual, even provocative innovations, claimed by only a handful of prelates. Our first proper evidence anywhere for the mitre comes from a privilege of Leo IX from Easter 1049 for its use by Archbishop Eberhard of Trier.[54] Over the following years, papal permission to wear this conspicuous prestige-item was also sought by the archbishops of Mainz (1052) and Hamburg (1053), the cathedral canons of Bamberg (1052), the bishop of Halberstadt (1063), and the abbots of Echternach (1069).[55] Understood as a peculiarly 'Roman insignia',[56] it joined a growing range of privileges of material self-representation sought by high-status churches around this time, including the supposedly Roman-style dalmatic and

[52] Ibid., pp. 232–3; Hefele, *Histoire*, iv, p. 1018. [53] *49, *62.

[54] *Konzilien*, ed. Jasper, 25A (JL 4158). The origins of the mitre remain uncertain, including its relationship to the papal tiara (first reliably depicted together in the Montecassino Exultet Roll of 1087: Ladner, *Papstbildnisse*, iii. 109): see Braun, *Die liturgische Gewandung*, pp. 431–47, and Miller, *Clothing*, pp. 191–4, 201; I am not convinced that the coinage of Sergius III (904–11) already depicts an early form of such a garment: Serafini, *Le monete*, i. 19.

[55] PL 143. 695, 697, 701 (JL 4281, 4283, 4290); *AA inedita*, i. 39 (JL 4498); *Geschichte der Grundherrschaft Echternach*, ed. Wampach, 195 (JL 4667).

[56] PL 143. 703.

sandals/*caligae* (first attested at late tenth-century Metz, Corvey, Lobbes, and Seltz; later at Reichenau, Fulda, Corbie, Besançon, Cologne, Nienburg, Trier, Montecassino, and sometimes granted alongside the right to call one's clergy 'cardinals'); the processional cross (Cologne, Mainz, Hamburg, Trier, Embrun, 1050s); and the *naccus*, a sort of stately horse-cloth—thus extending the splendour of one's garments to one's steed (Cologne, Mainz, Hamburg, Trier, 1050s).[57] In the case of at least the dalmatic, the *Liber pontificalis* indicates that sixth-century Roman clerics had understood this as having papal associations, while both the *Life* of Caesarius of Arles and Gregory I's *Register* reveal that the popes of that century might approve of their use by the deacons of other select churches.[58] We lack, however, comparable evidence suggesting that these other vestimentary privileges also had a late antique or papal background. Moreover, we should not assume any simple continuity between even this attested sixth-century practice and the new enthusiasm we see from the 970s among German prelates wishing to dress their clergy in a 'Roman' fashion.[59] It is surely significant that the petitions for privileges of this kind came from within the Ottonian and Salian *Reich*, and picked up in frequency as clerics from that region took control of the papal machine. Maureen Miller has now shown that the broader 'ornate style' of ecclesiastical dress, characteristic of the high middle ages, originated and flourished within this same northern, post-Carolingian imperial church culture. It was neither a late antique nor Mediterranean legacy.[60] It therefore seems quite possible that these petitions for elaborate, nominally Roman vestments in the later tenth and eleventh centuries in fact reflected regionalised, Franco-German aesthetic innovations, attributed from-the-outside-in to the authority of Rome. Copies of the *Liber pontificalis* and Gregory's *Register*, stalwarts of the post-Carolingian library,[61] could have served as the main source of inspiration, rather than any lived experience of contemporary Roman practice.

---

[57] *PUU* <204, 264, 305, 324, 592, 622 (JL 3741, 3806, 3837, 3857, 4093, J³ 9063); *PL* 143. 609, 641, 668, 687, 695, 701, 824, 826, 831, 834, 1305 (JL 4170, 4212, 4249, 4273, 4281, 4290, 4364, 4396, 4368, 4369, 4397); *PL* 146. 1301, 1325 (JL 4557, 4630); *Codex diplomaticus Anhaltinus*, ed. Heinemann, i. 131 (JL 4335). See further Braun, *Die liturgische Gewandung*, pp. 247–58, 396–9.

[58] *LP*, i. 34, p. 171; Caesarius, *Opera*, ii, p. 313; *Reg.*, ix. 220, pp. 790–1 (JE 1748).

[59] The exceptional instance between these two periods is Stephen II's purported privilege for the use of dalmatics by Saint-Denis' deacons (752/7): *PUU Saint-Denis*, 5a (JE 2332). If genuine, it is worth noting that Fulrad, then-abbot, could have been a key figure in the transmission of *LP* in Carolingian Francia: McKitterick, *Rome*, pp. 212–13, 216–18; if a forgery, it can be no later than its earliest manuscript appearance in the *Formulae Sancti Dionysii* (c. 878?): above, Chapter 6, p. 207, n. 79.

[60] Miller, *Clothing*, pp. 96–140.   [61] See above, Chapter 6, p. 206, 215–16.

Miller suggests that the wider emergence of the 'ornate style' reflected a concern among the uppermost clergy to articulate their position as a distinct caste within the religious and political hierarchy: it was 'a shared language of power'.[62] However, these additional privileges of high-prestige 'accessories' for select, individual churches also encourage us to think about competition *within* that highest ecclesiastical rank. We saw in the previous chapter how the archbishops of the Ottonian polity and its wider orbit devised additions to their pallium privileges, increasing the possible occasions on which they might wear this special garment, probably as a means of differentiating themselves within the complex, overlapping hierarchies of the post-Carolingian church.[63] These later privileges for yet further *pontificalia* indicate an intensification of this tendency within that same political community as the decades progressed. It is no coincidence that petitions for prerogatives of this kind arose around the same time as those for special, custom-overriding seating privileges at church councils,[64] and, moreover, within this same early reform period in which the number and scale of councils dramatically increased.[65] Miller notes that, with time, papal councils became important legislating bodies on regulations to clerical clothing.[66] Councils were not, however, just legislative occasions, but highly ritualised events,[67] during which super-high-profile ecclesiastics had the relatively rare opportunity to come face-to-face, indeed while wearing their vestments. At imperial and papal synods, certain archbishops, bishops, and abbots who felt themselves the centre of the universe within their own regions suddenly had to deal with prelates considered their equals or even betters. Egos were at stake. Already at the first ever synod convened by the reform faction in 1047, a 'seating fight' (*iurgium sedendi*) broke out between the patriarch of Aquileia and archbishops of Ravenna and Milan, in the course of which supposed proofs of precedence were rustled up by all sides, in the form of dubious synodal *acta* of Pope Symmachus (498–514) and presumably forged

---

[62] Miller, *Clothing*, pp. 120, 178–83; cf. Patzold, *Episcopus*.

[63] Above, Chapter 6, pp. 194–6.

[64] e.g. *PUU* 592 (JL 4093); *PL* 143. 687, 831, 1305 (JL 4273, 4368, 4397); *Konzilien*, ed. Jasper, 24B (JL 4141). Traditionally, bishops took seating precedence according to their date of consecration: see e.g. 'Ordo 2' (s. vii), widely circulated in pre-Gratianic canonical collections: *Konzilordines*, ed. Schneider, pp. 176–7. 'Ordo 7' (*c.* 800), transmitted through the later and post-Carolingian liturgical tradition, does not address seating: *Konzilordines*, ed. Schneider, p. 305. On seating disputes as an especially post-Carolingian phenomenon: Fichtenau, *Living*, pp. 8–20.

[65] Gresser, *Synoden*. The frequency of councils wearied even Peter Damian: *Briefe*, iv. 4. 164, p. 165.

[66] Miller, *Clothing*, pp. 35–6.   [67] Laudage, 'Ritual'.

privileges of Popes John I (523–6) and XIX (1024–32).[68] We ought to think of the emerging genre of petitions for additional *pontificalia* as resulting from these same struggles over precedence and differentiation at super-provincial councils. These privileges helped contribute to a spectrum of 'strategies of distinction'[69] whereby the high-priests of the most prestigious churches of the post-Carolingian world sought to negotiate their way through—and better articulate their position within—its hierarchical complexity.

These privileges of seating and 'Roman' dress were therefore both situational and relational: the products of a particular political community—chiefly, operating in that same 'central' zone of the *Reich* and its environs—and parts of a conversation about power and prerogatives taking place within it. The abbot of Echternach presumably sought and used his privileges for the dalmatic, sandals, and mitre in dialogue with the abbots of Fulda and Nienburg, who already claimed the two former items, and with the nearby archbishops of Trier, who pioneered the use of the latter. Likewise, the archbishops of Cologne, Mainz, and Trier acquired privileges for more and more elaborate liturgical ornaments in competition with one another. To some degree this may, in this early phase, have been culturally specific. Montecassino joined this visual arms race from 1057, but only under its Lotharingian abbot, Frederick of Liège. With this in mind, we might recall that Wulfric did not petition Bruno-Leo himself, but used as his intercessor Hermann of Ramsbury, yet another Lotharingian. Goscelin, our only source for these English petitions, hailed from Saint-Bertin and may have travelled as part of Hermann's entourage.[70] Indeed, one may wonder what these privileges for mitres, sandals, and elevated seating at continental synods actually meant back in contemporary England. It is fun to imagine Abbot Æthelsige attending the *witangemot*, uniquely dressed in the tall hat and special footwear currently fashionable among the *Reich*'s highest clergy. But if such visual items drew their meaning from their relationships to one another within a particular culture, and functioned chiefly within the competitive hierarchies of the imperial church, we cannot really say that they would have been read the same way, or borne anything like the same kind of meaning and function, once taken out of that particular context and used as a one-off within the later Anglo-Saxon church. What the image of Abbot Æthelsige in a mitre means to us may have had little bearing among many English contemporaries, who probably lacked our (and the post-Carolingian

---

[68] *Konzilien*, ed. Jasper, 24B (JL 4141).   [69] Above, Chapter 6, p. 198.
[70] Goscelin, *De translatione*, p. 432; Bihrer, *Begegnungen*, p. 186–7; Barlow, 'Goscelin'.

church's) points of reference. It does not, in any case, seem to have caught on. Whereas elsewhere in the post-Carolingian world privileges of this kind flourished from the 1070s onwards, Goscelin remarks that Æthelsige's successors gave up these rights, and we see no evidence of comparable petitions made from England until well beyond the period covered here.[71]

(c) Ecclesiastical Properties, Rights, and 'Protections'

The above prerogatives were rarely conveyed through their own dedicated documents. Typically, they featured among an increasing number of supplementary clauses within more broadly ranging privileges confirming the properties and/or rights of the clerical or monastic institutions concerned. Once again, formulaic confirmations of this kind—approximately mirroring the diplomatic norms of post-Carolingian sovereign diplomas—make up the majority of papal documents petitioned in this period. Generally speaking, the surviving corpus of 1049–73 looks like an intensified development of the later ninth- and tenth-century trends we explored in the last chapter (that is, overwhelmingly involving confirmations of pre-existing property claims, with further grants made in some circumstances for the 'freedoms' of papal 'jurisdiction' and 'protection', and the rights of electing heads of houses), and as such does not need much further discussion here.[72] A few aspects nevertheless merit brief remark.

Firstly, we see some minor changes to the range and extent of beneficiaries' geographical distribution. This involved a slight (but only slight) expansion beyond the old Carolingian frontiers, and a correlation between petitions and papal itineraries. It also meant a move away from the privileging of major Saxon institutions such as Magdeburg, Quedlinburg, or Gandersheim, doubtlessly an outcome of the passing of imperial rule from the Ottonian family. It is worth noting here—in light of the disproportionate focus in older scholarship on the papacy's supposedly French-centred 'privilege-policy' at this time—that West Frankish institutions, including monasteries, again only make up a portion of a much wider pool of beneficiaries.[73]

---

[71] Goscelin, *De translatione*, p. 433; Braun, *Die liturgische Gewandung*, pp. 399, 453.

[72] Above, pp. 203–10.

[73] Of the 161 extant privileges for monasteries, 42 were in the West Frankish realm, compared to 75 in Italy, 32 in the German-Burgundian *Reich*, and 7 in Iberia.

Next, the range of types of beneficiaries has widened, going beyond the typical addressees of monasteries and archbishops, to include multiple non-monastic churches (often only vaguely defined, but including canonries, *pieve*, and hospitals), suffragan bishops, and cathedral chapters as well as a number of 'wildcards', including individual clerics,[74] the 'clergy and people' of Lucca,[75] an association of lords wishing to construct an oratory in their castle,[76] and two freshly canonised saints (in whose case the precise beneficiary is not entirely clear).[77] These types of recipient are themselves subject to geographical particularity. Thus, cathedral clergies appear as papal beneficiaries frequently in Italy; only occasionally in the Burgundian kingdom and Lotharingia; and never in West Francia, Iberia, or Germany proper. Almost all the 'wildcards' are Italian.

Lastly, when we talk about the intensification of tenth-century trends, this applies on two fronts: on the one hand, the sheer number of privileges (again, especially in Italy); on the other—and perhaps this is the most significant shift of all—the increasing detail into which many of these texts go, and the numerous small varieties they show from one another. This is an especially important point to make, since work on papal documents in this period has often focused on how certain, selectively chosen, monastic privileges (typically in France) outlined arrangements which in retrospect approximate the fully-fledged 'exemptions' of the high middle ages.[78] This is true, and it is important. But it is not the whole story, and reflects just one aspect of a far wider and more interesting development—the growing desire among petitioners of all kinds across the post-Carolingian world to seek privileges delineating in more and more specific detail precisely what their rights and entitlements supposedly were. These appear, moreover, bespoke to different institutions on a case-by-case basis. What we seem to find here, then, is less a core change in papal diplomatic or 'privilege-policy' (let alone a centralised reform strategy or a new, *Zeitgeist*-defining drive for 'exemption'),[79] but rather a reflection in these texts of an increasing tendency on-the-ground, already well observed in non-papal scholarship, towards a formalisation of rights, regulations, and conceptions of property, and a sharper sense of boundaries (both territorial and

---

[74] *AA inedita*, ii. 130, 134 (JL 4490–1).   [75] *PL* 146. 1393 (JL 4724).

[76] *PL* 143. 1350 (JL 4455).

[77] *Konzilien*, ed. Jasper, 30B (JL 4219); *PL* 146. 1413 (JL 4756).

[78] Most recently Falkenstein, *La papauté*, and Rennie, *Freedom*.

[79] For a subtle revision of the received orthodoxy, and a call for further research, see Kéry, 'Klosterexemtion'.

conceptual) requiring recognition and confirmation.[80] The real upside of this for historians is that papal privileges simply get much more interesting in eleventh-century Europe, offering a fascinating insight into local conflicts and assertions over such matters as poll taxes paid in wine;[81] ducal courts;[82] coin minting;[83] the benefices of married clerics and their redistribution;[84] the construction of castles;[85] episcopal control over markets;[86] women-excluding spaces;[87] monks' liabilities to port tolls in light of their poverty rule;[88] the burial of pilgrims;[89] the non-burial of the excommunicated;[90] lake-fishing and watermill privileges;[91] episcopal gate-dues and destraint within a five-mile radius;[92] monastic rights to preaching and baptism;[93] the relationship between clerics and secular judges;[94] private jurisdiction;[95] episcopal shares of canons' tithes;[96] permission to avoid known simonists;[97] linen production;[98] or, among other matters, the expectation that twelve citizens furnish their city's canons with a ship.[99]

All we need to observe here is that our brief flurry of papal privileges confirming monastic and episcopal rights and properties in England does not—sadly, but perhaps also tellingly—contain anything so particular. They are for the most part generic, all-encompassing texts. Nicholas II's privilege for Bishop Giso of Wells of 1061 may briefly pique our interest in its promise to confirm the 'castles' or 'fortifications' (*castri*) claimed by this Somerset church, but it becomes clear upon reading the wider corpus that this has simply been pilfered from a formulation drawn up two years earlier, in response to a request from Bishop Giovanni of Penne in the Abruzzo.[100] Moreover, whereas the sanction of the earlier text spells out an arrangement whereby Penne and the Lateran will share between them a fine of £10 gold paid by any transgressors, the absence of this clause from the Wells version suggests rather weaker expectations about Nicholas' pledges actually being followed through. The same pope's privilege for Bishop Wulfwig of Dorchester, granted eight days later, appears for the most part similarly

---

[80] Above, Chapter 6, p. 205, n. 73.   [81] *PL* 143. 628 (JL 4192).
[82] *PL* 143. 697 (JL 4283).   [83] *PL* 143. 879 (JL 4385).   [84] *PL* 143. 671 (JL 4254).
[85] *PL* 143. 1341 (JL 4435).   [86] *Konzilien*, ed. Jasper, 27, pp. 249–50 (JL 4177).
[87] *PL* 143. 829 (JL 4367).   [88] *PL* 143. 731 (JL 4298).
[89] *PL* 143. 704–23 (JL 4292-3).   [90] *PUU Frankreich*, v. 2 (J³ 9447).
[91] *PL* 143. 678 (fragment, reconstructed in Böhmer-Frech 931) (JL 4263).
[92] *PL* 146. 1314 (JL 4596).
[93] *Geschichte der Grundherrschaft Echternach*, ed. Wampach, 195 (JL 4667).
[94] *PL* 143. 734 (JL 4306).   [95] *PUU Ile-de-France*, 9 (JL 4183).
[96] *PL* 146. 1309 (JL 4569).   [97] *AA inedita*, ii. 131 (JL 4493).
[98] *PL* 143. 633 (JL 4195).   [99] *PL* 143. 808 (JL 4338).
[100] 57; *PL* 143. 1311 (JL 4402).

generic, although it contains an important bespoke clause on Dorchester's rights in the *parrochia* of Lindsey, to which we will return shortly.[101] Victor II's privileges for Chertsey and Ely (1055/7), are unique in their (largely shared) formulation, but they make only very general, all-encompassing guarantees of properties and rights—that is, assuming that the Ely privilege's extra clause on banning the entry of clerics and officials reflects a later interpolation, which seems almost certainly the case.[102] For the most part, all that these documents confirm are broad rights which do not clearly indicate the exceptional status of any one church, let alone matters of reform. Ramsey's *Liber benefactorum* hazily claims that Abbot Ælfwine had availed himself of a Leonine privilege for his house's *iura* at Rheims in 1049, but one suspects this concerned general rights and properties rather than anything approximating 'exemption' (or else we might expect the chronicler to be less coy).[103]

Our single significant exception is the privilege acquired by Abbot Baldwin of Bury St Edmunds from Alexander II in October 1071. This recognised the unique importance of his monastery and placed it under the 'particular authority' (*propria ius*) of the Roman see, where it would enjoy its 'protection and defence' (*tutela et defensio*), and, most urgently, the guarantee that it should never become an episcopal centre.[104] Here at last we see a definite privilege of monastic 'freedom' on a classic continental, post-Carolingian model, one acquired in the peculiar circumstances of a conflict between Baldwin and the incoming Norman bishop Herfast, who wished to move his see to Baldwin's prosperous monastery. Nevertheless, this looks on closer inspection like a singular case, one without grounding in contemporary English 'horizons of expectation', nor achieving it seems any real success. Baldwin—himself another figure with a background in the Lotharingian world, who until the 1060s had spent his career between Alsace and Saint-Denis—had acquired his privilege only a few days after two grants with similar formulations had been drawn up for the Aragonese houses of Loarre and Sobarbre (part of an exceptional burst of communications between King Sancho Ramirez and the cardinal legate Hugo Candidus).[105] These somehow came to the attention of an opportunistic Baldwin, who may have initially arrived in Rome on other business, and served as his

---

[101] 58.   [102] 53–4.   [103] *49.

[104] 64; for this and the rest of this paragraph see Savill, 'Prelude'.

[105] *PUU Spanien*, ii. 3–4 (J³ 11113–14); cf. *Chartes et documents*, ed. Monsabert, pp. 75–8 (JL 4714).

model. Archbishop Lanfranc anyway confiscated the privilege once Baldwin had returned to England, compelling the abbot to resort to forging Anglo-Saxon royal diplomas to pursue the same ends. When the papacy began granting a new series of papal privileges for Bury from the 1120s onwards, these made no mention of Alexander's grant. This formed part of a bigger pattern. None of these privileges for English monasteries and bishoprics were reissued in the fashion typical of the 'confirmation politics' familiar to continental Europe, and after autumn 1071 no comparable documents entered England until the much changed conditions of the early-to-mid-twelfth century. Once again, we see from the late 1040s a tantalising burst of activity, across a single generation—which then abruptly grinds to a halt.

(d) Archbishop Ealdred and the End of Anglo-Saxon Episcopal Translation

Baldwin had probably visited Rome at least once before. A privilege of Nicholas II from the Easter Synod of 1061, confirming the rights and possessions of Saint-Denis' Alsatian 'little abbey' of Lièpvre, dates to Baldwin's stint as prior of that house, and he may have attended the council to acquire the document in person.[106] If so, he would have witnessed there the humiliation and subsequent reconciliation of Archbishop Ealdred of York, with which this chapter began. Long neglected by historians, this English embassy of 1061, apparently led by Earl Tostig and Ealdred, and accompanied by Bishops Giso and Walter of Hereford (who, like Giso, was consecrated in Rome by Nicholas) and other dignitaries (including one Burgheard, possibly son of Earl Ælfgar, who died on the return journey), has recently enjoyed the attention of several studies. Thanks to this work, we can now be confident of the authenticity of the surviving, undated text of Ealdred's privilege, and recognise its importance in showing the commitment of the new, post-1046 regime to upholding reform principles by withholding customary privileges to those who did not comply. We can also appreciate the role played by the embassy in pressing the claims of the Mercian Leofwineson family (perhaps represented in part by Burgheard) against the ecclesiastical province of York (in the person of Ealdred) over

---

[106] *PUU Saint-Denis*, 17 (JL 4456); Savill, 'Prelude', pp. 813–14.

control over the *parrochia* of Lindsey, via the church of St Mary's at Stow.[107] Only two further remarks are therefore needed here. Both, however, are critical to understanding the circumstances under which Ealdred finally acquired his pallium.

Firstly: its date, and the deal done. The humiliating Easter Synod ran from 15–23 April, and Giso of Wells' privilege was subsequently granted on 25 April, that is, the pre-eminent Roman procession day of the Greater Litany.[108] Wulfwig of Dorchester's representatives, perhaps led by Burgheard,[109] had to wait another eight days for his privilege, granted on 3 May. This included the clause recognising Dorchester's claim to the Lindsey *parrochia* via Stow, thus depriving it from the archbishopric of York, and tightening the Leofwinesons' hold over their network of proprietary churches.[110] This eight-day delay between the two dated privileges is revealing. It suggests that the episode of the English party's initial departure and ambush took place within this interim, and that Ealdred's pallium privilege was wrestled out of Pope Nicholas not only because of his change of heart following the attack, but also through some deal-brokering, with Ealdred agreeing to give up Lindsey in exchange for support for his pallium claims. It is unclear whether that deal was made with the pope and his cardinals, or with in fact the Leofwineson party—who then pledged to add their decisive support to the claim Ealdred was pushing with the papacy— but the latter may be more likely.[111] If so, it is a reminder that the raising of the York-Leofwineson dispute at Rome may not have necessarily resulted from a premediated high-court appeal, being 'an ecclesiastical matter which required a judgment from the pope',[112] but perhaps came about as the result of something more opportunistic, wangled on the spot by the Dorchester-Leofwineson party, who suddenly saw their chance. If this was the case, it probably gives us a date for Ealdred's truncated pallium privilege—on or close to 3 May, when the deal was agreed—and may even explain its imperfect state. It is not impossible that compromising details about relinquishing Stow (a claim York later resumed) conveniently disappeared from later copies.

[107] 59. Tinti, 'Pallium'; Baxter, 'Death'; Schoenig, 'Withholding'; Schoenig, *Bonds*, pp. 321–2, 348, 374, 379–80; Licence, 'New Source'; Licence, *Edward*, pp. 197–200.

[108] Litany: Wickham, *Medieval Rome*, pp. 324–6.

[109] Burgheard: Baxter, 'Death' (but cf. Licence, *Harold*).

[110] Baxter, *Earls*, pp. 152–203, esp. p. 188.

[111] The privilege remarks that witnesses had now come forward to support Ealdred's claims that he had been translated unwillingly.

[112] Licence, *Edward*, p. 197.

Secondly, that Ealdred wound up in this situation at all says a lot about the distance of the late Anglo-Saxon church from post-Carolingian legal norms. We saw in Chapter 6 how the new canonical collections of papal letters and decretals, popular in the Carolingian world from the mid-ninth-century onwards, had failed to make a mark in contemporary England. Similarly, the emerging English predilection for a career ladder of 'stepping-stone sees', whereby bishops would work their way up towards the great archbishoprics via lesser *sedes*, not only ran counter to the continental anxieties about these practices, but constituted a flagrant breach of the strict taboos against episcopal translation that featured in legal collections such as Pseudo-Isidore, which had contributed to its characterisation as a kind of 'fornication' or 'adultery' (while also outlining the possibility for its allowance under only exceptional circumstances).[113] By the mid-eleventh century, these post-Carolingian taboos remained, while Anglo-Saxon practices continued. Easter 1061 marks the point at which the former—embodied in the Pseudo-Isidore-influenced personnel of the new outsider-regime at Rome[114]—finally clashed with the latter. The reformers, themselves products of the world of these post-Carolingian legal norms, did not take kindly to spontaneous episcopal translation. While it is true that they themselves had translated to Rome, and, once there, claimed the prerogative of issuing special privileges for episcopal translation, it is important to recognise that these exceptional practices only reinforced the general rule. As Werner Goez demonstrated, translation to Rome became justified on the emerging principle that the *papatus* was not, after all, another *episcopatus*, and thus not subject to the same laws. Meanwhile, the very idea that other bishops now required an exceptional papal privilege in order to translate legally from see-to-see simply served to *underline* the idea that this was otherwise prohibited.[115] Nicholas' privilege for Ealdred, which emphasises its allowance of his translation to York as an unrepeatable exception, echoes Pseudo-Isidore,[116] and is the single privilege for England within this group

---

[113] Above, p. 196; see above all Leyser, 'Episcopal Office', especially its comments on the pollution discourse as a Carolingian development; see also Scholz, *Transmigration*; Sommar, 'Episcopal Translation'. Pseudo-Isidore is sometimes seen as encouraging a relaxation of translation laws; I would rather argue that, by outlining their exemption under exceptional conditions, it further reinforced their general inadmissibility: cf. my remarks on formal and substantive rationality above, p. 146, n. 108.

[114] Fuhrmann, *Einfluß*, ii, pp. 339–45.

[115] Goez, 'Papa'. For an early reform-era translation privilege: *Konzilien*, ed. Jasper, 25B (JL 4163).

[116] 'non ambitione set iussione filii nostri regis coactum', cf. *Decretales*, ed. Hinschius, p. 152 (JK †90).

that we can certainly identify as reflecting contemporary reform concerns. This was, however, 'reform' by way of chastisement, working *against* the existing traditions of the Anglo-Saxon church, and not driven by any 'reforming' interests within it. What is most remarkable from our perspective is that English attitudes towards episcopal translation endured for so long against the grain of contemporary post-Carolingian practices and taboos, seemingly without raising any cause for concern. That as late as 1061 a prelate as well-connected as Ealdred seems to have assumed that he could get away with his multiple translations suggests a great deal about the late Anglo-Saxon church's distinct position within the wider post-Carolingian world, and its divergence from some of its norms and discourses.

Nicholas' privilege for Ealdred marked the end of the emerging practice of late Anglo-Saxon bishops (foremost of Worcester) translating upwards to the archiepiscopal see of York. It was in that sense a papal ruling with a far-reaching long-term effect, and a real instance of 'reform in action'. The pallium grant made in 1071 to his successor, Thomas of Bayeux, looks completely conventional and bypasses the problem altogether.[117] Things had moved on. Nevertheless, it is difficult to grasp just how much close attention was paid over the next few decades to the texts of either the York or Dorchester privileges that came out of this stand-off in May 1061. As (papal-approved) episcopal translation underwent a gradual process of normalisation in the twelfth century, Ealdred's conflict with Nicholas became misremembered as having concerned the former's plurality, an issue on which the contemporary sources stay silent.[118] The closest we come to seeing this privilege mentioned again, meanwhile, is in a bizarre, forged diploma of Edward the Confessor for York, possibly datable to the early twelfth century. Its *narratio* imagines Pope Formosus (d. 896) granting the bishopric of Worcester to Archbishop Oswald of York (d. 991!), before going on to claim that the relevant privilege was lost in a fire, prompting Ealdred to request that Nicholas renew its terms.[119] As for the transfer of Lindsey to Dorchester, the post-Conquest relocation of the latter see to Lincoln effectively confirmed this territorial grab (with the unusually huge medieval diocese of Lincoln its enduring legacy).[120] Nevertheless, the dispute

---

[117] 65.

[118] William of Malmesbury, *Vita Wulfstani*, i. 10, pp. 42–3; *GP*, I, iii. 115, pp. 382–3. Scholz, *Transmigration*, p. 252, sees Ealdred's case as mainly about plurality, but is dependent upon these later sources.

[119] *Northern Houses*, 11 (S 1037a), citing *†46.

[120] Cf. *AAWI*, 177: see Appendix, p. 286.

with York over Stow continued to drag on, long after the fall of the Leofwinesons in 1071. Attempts to resolve the matter came through diplomas of King William Rufus and Paschal II. Notably, neither mentioned Nicholas II's earlier ruling.[121] Here again, we struggle to find continuity between the Anglo-papal relations of the early reform-era and those of the high middle ages.

III. Making Sense of the Evidence

How, then, can we account for this late upswing in papal acquisitions, together with its sudden cessation? What might it reveal about the wider workings of mid-eleventh-century politics? On the strength of the above evidence, we can begin by dismissing some of the more tempting explanations. Firstly, a pope-centred hypothesis cannot suffice. The idea that the papacy of these years earnestly pursued its own, self-driven strategy, aimed at extending its authority into England does not hold much weight. Of course, papal activity increased in general in this time, and this probably had a knock-on effect upon the rise in Anglo-papal interactions. This is especially true of councils, which provided the occasions for many of the acquisitions discussed above. We should also take seriously the prospect that the emergence of the reform party as a political force in its own right—often visibly intertwined in imperial foreign politics, including its military operations[122]—encouraged the English court to reach out to it more often with embassies as part of its wider concerns with maintaining good 'international relations'. To this, our corpus of privileges may have arisen only as a secondary afterthought. Nevertheless, these factors cannot account for everything. As seen in Chapter 6, politically savvy English embassies to emperor-friendly popes had already taken place throughout the tenth century. Moreover, it was just as papal activity became yet more intense elsewhere from the 1070s that English petitions for privileges once again halted, leaving even the most recent acquisitions unconfirmed and half-forgotten. Besides, as now made abundantly clear, privileges were across Europe petitioner-driven, and those petitioners tended to come from

---

[121] *Historians of the Church of York*, ed. Raine, iii. 7, 12; Hugh, *History*, pp. 14–17; *Registrum Antiquissimum*, ed. Foster and Major, i. 4.
[122] English chroniclers did not fail to note Leo IX's association with Henry III's Flanders campaign *ASC, s.a.* 1049 C, 1050 D.

regions already *au fait* with papal documentary culture. Responding to pre-existing demand, and working within the regions where they had pre-existing power bases, the activity of the early reform popes was not equally spread, with little practical attempt at exerting universal episcopacy. Acquisitions largely followed patterns already familiar from the later ninth century onwards. Looking through the vast corpus of papal documentary material generated continent-wide in these decades, one would have to adopt a very Insular perspective indeed to think that the ascendant reform party had expended much of its energy or anxiety over the English.

We can also dismiss the possibility that these acquisitions reflected any urgent interest within the mid-eleventh-century English church in the wider European project of religious reform. This is not to write off the existence of English reform tendencies altogether in the 1040s–70s, only to say that we do not find much evidence for it within this corpus of texts. Many of these English acquisitions look formulaic, and could well have belonged to an earlier century. The closest we come to evidence of a reforming tendency from the petitioner's side is arguably in the most unique item of the group, Leofric's privilege to move his see to Exeter. Considering its stated concern for a return to the ancient convention of situating episcopal sees in cities, and its adherence to the most practical contemporary conception of *refor-mare* as a project of building churches anew,[123] one could read it as drawing from eleventh-century discourses of religious renewal. Nevertheless, even here, Leofric and his clergy's personal experiences in more urbanised Lotharingia may have contributed most to their discomfort about the rural state of much of the Anglo-Saxon church, rather than any lofty canonical ideals. The only privilege that looks like an explicit assertion of an aspect of the reform programme is that for Ealdred, banning all future translations. But as we have seen, this was not reform by demand but as punishment, and if anything it betrays the degree to which senior prelates and aristocrats in England were hitherto unaffected by this controversy. Some of these privileges also include (courtesy of their papal draftsmen, not petitioners) the formulaic notice in their *protocol* that they are addressed only to the recipient and their 'canonically elected' successors.[124] For us, knowing the bigger picture, that short phrase instantly recalls the place of simony

---

[123] Barrow, 'Developing', p. 503. Fuhrmann, *Einfluß*, ii, p. 341, saw Leofric's privilege as having Pseudo-Isidorian influences, but the principle of bishoprics being in *ciuitates* not *uillulae* was an ancient one which was already well known through the older canonical tradition.

[124] 57–9, but the formula is general.

in contemporary reform debates; but whether it had the same effect on readers in mid-eleventh-century England, we cannot know. Elsewhere in privileges for English beneficiaries, we do not find the slightest evidence that simony, celibacy, and the boundaries between the sacred and profane had enveloped European discourse in these years. If these documents for English recipients were the only texts that had survived at all from the papacy of this period, one would hardly guess that the apostolic see had become embroiled in the movement for reform at all.

As for the sudden end to these acquisitions in the 1070s and their subsequent drift into oblivion, we should avoid the temptation of simply explaining this away with the arrival of the Great Men William the Conqueror (1066–87) and Gregory VII (1073–85). Neither is properly a subject of study in this book, but they need addressing briefly, if only to underline the point that we cannot treat them as inevitabilities towards whom all earlier developments must have led, nor *dei ex machina* that solve all our questions about the early-to-high-medieval transition. Their effect in their respective jurisdictions was of course transformative, and naturally played a role in the problem posed here. It is, anyway, generally accepted that Anglo-papal relations often came under strain in the Norman-Hildebrandine age, with papal communications hotly monitored by William and his sons, and this provides some of the context for the lack of interest in these documents after 1071.[125] William's grimly loyal collaborator Lanfranc was a powerful figure in his own right when it came to enforcing the new dispensation, as his abovementioned confiscation of Bury's privilege shows.[126] Nevertheless, invoking these personalities cannot make sense of the whole picture. Whatever the success of Lanfranc in stamping down on papal documents not to his liking, his ability to do this so quickly and effectively in England surely depended on the state of what came before him. Gregory and his successors meanwhile made their influence felt everywhere (and caused more than just 'strain'), yet it was only England that ceased to engage with papal privileges from the 1070s. Besides: the Kingdom of the English was far from the only polity transformed by conquest, colonisation, and crisis in the later eleventh and early twelfth century; it may not have even seen the greatest upheavals of the 1070s.[127] Later eleventh-century ruptures of course mattered enormously. But in a study such as this we need to look beyond two or three individuals or decisive

---

[125] Barlow, *English Church*, pp. 105–8.   [126] Cowdrey, *Lanfranc*, esp. pp. 197–205.
[127] Leyser, 'Crisis'; Bisson, *Crisis*; Bartlett, *Making*; Moore, *First European Revolution*.

battles, and towards the deeper peculiarities within later Anglo-Saxon political and ecclesiastical culture that might help explain why this sudden wave of interest in papal documentary support arose, and why it could not then be sustained once those famous ruptures came.

The most obvious approach comes through addressing the issue of our ecclesiastical personnel and their origins. It will have already become evident over the course of this chapter that some significance must lie in the fact that many of these English recipients were, strictly speaking, not 'Anglo-Saxons' per se, but clerics with backgrounds in the Lotharingian region. The preponderance of Lotharingians among the higher English clergy in the 1040s–60s—what Simon Keynes has called the 'Lotharingian Connection' or even 'Conspiracy' of the late Anglo-Saxon church—has long been recognised.[128] Far less attention has been paid to the fact that this neatly coincided with a comparable takeover of Lotharingians into papal positions of power from 1046 onwards, and, as explored above, a period in which papal activity often found itself focused around this Middle Kingdom region of the former Carolingian empire.[129] Through these privileges, we can thus see Keynes' Lotharingian Connection extending outwards across the continent. Leofric and the canons he brought with him in his takeover of the Devon and Cornwall churches had origins in the region, and left a markedly Lotharingian stamp on its library through its calendars, obits, liturgies, and Rule of communal living; an argument has even been made for Leofric receiving his early education at Toul, perhaps under Bishop Bruno (1026–52), the future Leo IX.[130] Lambert, the priest he sent to acquire his privilege, had a characteristically Lotharingian name, traditionally associated with Liège.[131] If he did petition Leo at Rheims, he may well have travelled there with the sole English episcopal attendee, Duduc of Wells (1033–61), whom John of Worcester also later identified as a Lotharingian.[132] Duduc's successor Giso hailed from Sint-Truiden, near Liège.[133] The contemporary copy of his privilege from Nicholas II is in a characteristically *liègeois* hand: plausibly that of Giso himself, or a member of his household.[134] Evidence from the wider corpus of single-sheet survivals suggests that the original was

---

[128] Keynes, 'Giso', pp. 205–13.

[129] For what follows: Savill, 'Prelude', pp. 814–15; Savill, 'England and the Papacy', pp. 317–18. Lotharingian ecclesiastics in Rome: Frech, 'Lothringer'.

[130] Above, n. 33; Barlow, 'Leofric'.   [131] Bihrer, *Begegnungen*, p. 188.

[132] John of Worcester, *Chronicle*, s.a. (1060); Bihrer, *Begegnungen*, pp. 182–3, prefers an 'Old Saxon' identification.

[133] Keynes, 'Giso'.   [134] Wells, Dean and Chapter, CF/3/2.

in the similar hand of the scribe 'Nicholas II A', possibly a Florentine of Lotharingian background or training.[135] It would have received its authenticating clause from no less a figure than the papal librarian Humbert of Moyenmoutier, the Lotharingian bishop of Silva Candida.[136] Nicholas, as we have seen, had personally consecrated Giso in Rome, the same day as he had Walter of Hereford, another Lotharingian.[137] The pope himself, alias Gerhard, may have had a Lotharingian (or Burgundian) background,[138] as did his patron Gottfried, Duke of Lotharingia and Tuscany, the brother of Frederick of Liège, abbot of Montecassino and ultimately Pope Stephen IX— himself once a member of the chapter at Liège, alongside the same Gerhard-Nicholas.[139] Present also at this 1061 meeting were (probably) Baldwin, future recipient of Alexander's privilege for Bury of 1071, and at that point based at Lièpvre (Upper Lotharingia), and of course Ealdred. Although not a Lotharingian himself, the latter had spent time at Cologne, and had joined Hermann of Ramsbury at the Roman Synod of 1050. Its two main items of business appear to have been the canonisation of Gerhard of Toul, a giant of tenth-century Lotharingian politics, and the condemnation of Berengar of Tours, *bête noire* of the Liège school and its alumni, a number of whom were by then members of the papal entourage.[140] We have come across this council already, for it was probably there that Hermann, another Lotharingian, petitioned Canterbury's arguably Lotharingian-style vestments from Bruno-Leo.[141]

Evidently, something was going on here. To say that Anglo-papal interactions in the 1040s–70s must have arisen in part from Lotharingian networks is surely on the right track, although what this meant in practice is harder to grasp. Centres such as Liège would have played a role in nurturing and maintaining the interpersonal relationships, lines of communication, and feelings of trust which both the incoming reform papacy and significant elements of the late Anglo-Saxon clergy could tap into for mutual benefit from the later 1040s. Nevertheless, this can only have facilitated arrangements,

---

[135] Kehr, 'Scrinium', p. 91, n. 4.

[136] Humbert died 5 May: this is one of the last four documents in his name (JL 4457–60).

[137] John of Worcester, *Chronicle*, s.a. (1060–1).   [138] Hägermann, 'Nikolaus'.

[139] De Jong, 'Adelman'; Parisse, 'Généalogie', pp. 35–6.

[140] Cologne: *ASC, s.a.* 1054 CD; 1050 synod: *Konzilien*, ed. Jasper, 30B, with Gresser, *Synoden*, pp. 23–5, although this wrongly claims no English bishops attended, misreading Leo IX's letter to absentees in *Britannia* as meaning 'England', rather than Brittany: *PL* 143. 648 (JL 4225); Berengar, Liège, and the reformers: De Jong, 'Adelman', with Cowdrey, 'Lanfranc, the Papacy'.

[141] John of Worcester, *Chronicle*, s.a. (1045); Bihrer, *Begegnungen*, p. 186; above, p. 243.

rather than created them out of nothing, and as George Molyneaux has pointed out, just because people know each other, does not necessarily mean they like each other—often, quite the opposite applies.[142] Might the religious and political culture of Lotharingia itself explain the pro-papal sentiments of its émigrés in this period? The idea that this region may have been exceptionally predisposed to the movement for church reform has a vintage in modern scholarship, but that may rest to some degree on early twentieth-century confessional and national prejudices;[143] in any case, one finds little especially 'reforming' about the privileges granted to the Anglo-Lotharingian party. A more important factor, one suspects, was simply that this former Middle Kingdom of the Frankish empire—a multi-direction-facing frontier-zone if any existed[144]—had long stood firmly enmeshed in the political, ecclesiastical, legal, and documentary culture of the post-Carolingian world which we explored in Chapter 6, within which legal and documentary invocations of the contemporary papacy ('reform' or otherwise) played an integral part. England, as we saw, had taken a different path, and did not share in many of the conventions and expectations of that Carolingian inheritance. It cannot be a coincidence, therefore, that just as a generation of senior ecclesiastics arrived into the English kingdom who had spent their formative years in that environment, so then do we begin to see a sudden upswing in what look like characteristically post-Carolingian activities in relation to the papacy, with bishops and abbots seeking contemporary papal confirmations for royal privileges; involving themselves in conciliar meetings with French, German, and Italian colleagues; even adopting elements of the 'Roman'-style dress then popular among the imperial clergy. Leofric, Lambert, Duduc, Hermann, Giso, Walter, and Baldwin had come of age in the world of Pseudo-Isidore, Gregory's *Register*, and of churches whose sense of identity and security depended in part on frequent re-confirmations of written papal authority. These figures arrived into the peculiar world of the Anglo-Saxon church, bringing with them a shared playbook of characteristically post-Carolingian practices, expectations, and solutions. Papal privileges would have been among them.

---

[142] Molyneaux, *Formation*, p. 49.

[143] Fliche, *La réforme*, iii, pp. 113–28 is the classic statement; but note that this work, published in inter-war Louvain, betrays contemporary nationalist anxieties in its depiction of *la réforme lorraine* as following a distinct, superior path to that of the rest of Germany, independent of imperial spiritual authority.

[144] Margue, 'Lotharingien', p. 37.

The prominence of this Lotharingian vanguard among the English higher clergy can therefore account for a greater receptivity to contemporary papal legal instruments. Their connections, leading from Liège to Tuscany to Rome, presumably facilitated their acquisition. Why, however, did they and, following their lead, several of their Anglo-Saxon counterparts, seek this external support in the first place? Here again much of the answer may lie in interpersonal connections—but in this case, their *weakness* within England. Scholars have long noted the prominence of foreign-born or -trained ecclesiastics in Edward's kingdom, the most famous besides the Lotharingian party being the Norman Robert of Jumièges (archbishop of Canterbury 1051–2, who also sought support from the reform papacy during his short tenure, although did not, as far as we can tell, acquire any privileges).[145] What has hardly received remark is the fact that this was the first time such a number of overseas clerics had ever held power in England since the seventh-century conversions. Again, this contrasts with much of the Carolingian and post-Carolingian world, where the *ambitio* of far-travelling ecclesiastics through Latin Europe partly explains the intensification of the translation taboo.[146] From that perspective, the much-fêted explosion of vernacular religious texts in late ninth- to early eleventh-century England had a parochial side to it as well, reflecting a hierarchy somewhat closed to wider foreign-language personnel.[147] Edward's outsider-appointees had belonged to the royal chapel, and some traced their connections back to Edward's youth-in-exile in Normandy; Duduc looks like a comparable import of the Danish conqueror Cnut (1016–35).[148] Beyond the king, however, it seems unlikely that these ecclesiastics had any wider structural support within England: no kin, perhaps few friends, no family lands, and no cultural capital from demonstrable links to ancient 'native' traditions. In the early medieval world this was a dangerous situation to be in, not least when even King Edward, having grown up in exile in Normandy, during a quarter-century Cerdicing fall from power, lacked his forebears' deep entrenchment in the kingdom's power structures.

---

[145] Licence, 'Robert'; idem, *Edward*, pp. 131–4, 155–8.   [146] Leyser, 'Episcopal Office'.
[147] Grimbald of Saint-Bertin (d. 901), John the Old Saxon (fl. 890), and Abbo of Fleury (at Ramsey 985–7), scholarly invitees who never held episcopal office, were rare birds: for further examples see Wood, 'Carolingian Scholar'. It is possible that the obscure Theodred, bishop of London and the East Angles (s. x$^{2/4}$) had a German background, although this is uncertain: ibid., p. 137.
[148] Bihrer, *Begegnungen*, pp. 182–6.

The career of Archbishop Robert, violently exiled in 1052 when Edward's authority hit a low ebb, serves as case in point.[149]

Without kith or kin at home, distant papal backing for one's rights and possessions, however imprecise, must have taken on a special appeal. That other, non-foreign-born ecclesiastics soon followed their lead also makes sense, moreover, when we observe how fragile even their position may have been within the structures of mid-eleventh-century England. Recent work has uncovered another long-overlooked peculiarity of the later Anglo-Saxon church: the complete lack of evidence that there was any serious overlap between the major families of the lay aristocracy and the episcopate. Ealdormen and earls virtually never had bishops (nor even abbots) for brothers or sons.[150] Perhaps in the long tenth century, the English clerical elite had found stability via their kin within lower strata of the landholding aristocracy, and their own connections to an all-powerful Cerdicing court. By the 1040s, however, much of that safety-net had disappeared. Cnut's arrival in 1016 had wiped out the better part of the old English aristocracy (including churchmen: Ramsey's abbot and Wulfwig's predecessor were among those killed by the new conqueror at Assandun).[151] A 'rootless elite' of 'new men' with 'new wealth' had risen in their place, and in the Godwinesons and Leofwinesons, the kingdom became dominated by two small, hitherto comparatively obscure lay families.[152] Six unpredictable, often violent royal successions from 1014–42, culminating in yet another king-from-across-the-sea whose own succession looked increasingly in jeopardy, must have shaken faith in the security of court patronage. Eyes turned to alternative patrons and guarantors. The promise of papal authority took on a new shine.

The uncertainty, instability, and recurrent crises of the inter-conquest period of 1016–66 may have also engendered a greater openness to novel political ideas, even creative experimentation. The disintegration of the old order could create space for something new. There are signs of wider, quite sudden transformations in elite culture, consumption, identity, and political memory as this 'new rich' took power—transformations which Edward could not magically reset after the Cerdicing restoration of 1042.[153]

---

[149] *ASC*, s.a. 1052 CDE; *Life of King Edward*, i. 3–4, pp. 28–45.

[150] Cubitt, 'Bishops', p. 123; Barrow, *Clergy*, pp. 139–41; Blanchard, 'New Perspective'. No sons or brothers as prelates does not rule out links with more distant kinsmen, although even these appear with 'striking scarcity' (Barrow).

[151] *ASC*, s.a. 1016 CDE.   [152] Fleming, *Kings*, pp. 21–104; Fleming, 'New Wealth'.

[153] Insley, 'Why'; Fleming, 'New Wealth'; Williams, 'Thegnly Piety'.

We can see one aspect of that transformation in the kingdom's documentary culture: to return to a concept set out in Chapter 2, England by the 1040s was suddenly becoming quite a different 'documentary landscape'.[154] Already within Cnut's reign, the centuries-old, diplomatically and aesthetically conservative instrument of the Anglo-Saxon royal diploma fell into decline, in what looks less like a case of poor survival than a marked shift in political and legal culture.[155] We find open complaint that the old Latin diplomas did not 'avail anything', with the royal offer of new issues declined;[156] clues that the royal chancery, a core governmental enterprise of the tenth-century Cerdicings, had folded its operations, outsourcing to beneficiaries and regional bishops;[157] and, in the middle of Edward's reign, a near-decade-long hiatus in known diploma production.[158] The question of whether or not this decline came about through the emergence of a new kind of written instrument in this same period, the royal writ-charter—a short, vernacular document bearing the king's seal, and sent to shire courts to announce grants of properties and rights[159]—feels less important here than the fact that such an innovation could have arisen at all in England's conservative documentary culture. In the 1060s we also begin to see royal diplomas issued in the form of *pancartes*: charters confirming an institution all its rights and possessions, a genre originating in the Carolingian world, and popular in contemporary France.[160] One gets the sense of a political culture in creative turmoil, with new men, in positions of structural insecurity, compelled to toy with unfamiliar forms of legal expression as old certainties fell by the wayside. Appeals to the written authority of the energetic new reform popes touring Europe, themselves transforming their own chancery in just these same decades, came as part of a bigger trend of searching for something new. The multi-genre dossier of texts Giso put together during his time at Wells (in grand sum: six writ-charters of Edward (1061/66), two of Queen Edith (1061/6–1066/75), and one each of Kings Harold (1066), William (1068/83), and Queen Mathilda (1072/83); a self-penned *pancarte* in Edward's name

---

[154] Above, pp. 51–2.   [155] Insley, 'Where'; Insley, 'Why', pp. 7–15.

[156] *Christ Church*, 150A (S 986).

[157] The point is controversial: see now Licence, *Edward*, pp. 263–81; for the case against, Keynes, 'Regenbald'.

[158] Licence, *Edward*, pp. 263–4.

[159] Sharpe, 'Use'; Licence, *Edward*, pp. 262, 277–81. The argument that writ-charters were not evidentiary deeds, but ephemeral written orders, misses the point that—however their issuing authority thought they 'ought' to have been used—they might have been interpreted in different ways by different audiences. Clearly some recipients considered the texts evidentiary, or else none would survive today.

[160] Licence, *Edward*, pp. 272–7; Guyotjeannin, Pycke, and Tock, *Diplomatique*, p. 106.

(1065); a diploma in William's, restoring Harold's confiscations (1068); a narrative account of his acts;[161] and of course Nicholas' privilege, reproduced in facsimile) points to an individual acutely conscious of how tenuously his position hung, and wise enough to set up multiple layers of safety-net. His background in the heart of the post-Carolingian world gave him the contacts, ideas, and openness to foreign innovations to put him among the avant-garde of this experimental age.

It would, however, only prove to be a phase. The importance and influence of the Lotharingian Connection in the 1040s–70s generation of the English church really had, I have argued here, a fundamental role in opening up receptivity to papal documentary culture, especially in this inter-conquest age of uncertainty and experimentation. However, it's also necessary to emphasise that mapping out prosopographical connections cannot be enough to explain major transformations in documentary, legal, religious, and political culture. As Conrad Leyser has demonstrated, efforts to explain away the eleventh-century reform simply by drawing dots between elite individuals and assuming cynical influence, faction, and collusion can take us dangerously close to the world of Lewis Naimier- or Ronald Syme-style 'Tory history', unhelpfully downplaying the real significance of new ideas or structural change.[162] That is true here, but it does not contradict the argument about the Lotharingian Connection having a crucial role to play in this *temporary* phase of English enthusiasm for petitioning papal support. Rather, taking a prosopographical approach, but with a healthy scepticism about its limits, can do much to explain not merely why this influx of papal privileges arrived when it did, but also why much of what was acquired looks formulaic and superficial, and why the project withered away after a generation. The Lotharingian vanguard and their associates opened up new possibilities in negotiating English property and politics, bringing in the know-how and right contacts for appealing to papal authority at a time when it was in the ascendant on the continent, and when the English political scene was particularly vulnerable and open to new ideas. They found themselves building, however, from scratch. Importing papal documentary culture into a world where virtually no privileges appear to have been acquired for over two hundred years, and whose libraries suggested little-to-no interest nor familiarity with post-late-antique papal politics,

---

[161] *Anglo-Saxon Writs*, ed. Harmer, 64–9, 70–2 (S 1111–16, 1163, 1240–1); *Bath and Wells*, 40 (S 1042); *AAWI*, 286–9; Keynes, 'Giso', pp. 254–60.
[162] Leyser, 'Church Reform', pp. 483–4.

writings, or laws, could not be expected to have an instant effect, nor an enduring one. What we see through 1049–71 look like tentative trials on unfamiliar terrain, failing to lay down any of the structural foundations that would allow this new interest in papal support to be replicated in the same way into the next generation—foundations that would have needed to be strong indeed to weather the shock of the new Conquest of 1066. By the time Baldwin acquired his privilege for Bury in 1071, the older Lotharingian party with which he might have identified had already begun to die out and fade in prominence at the top of both the English and papal hierarchies. Meanwhile, almost the entire Anglo-Saxon aristocracy found itself—once again—well advanced along its 'terrible slide towards annihilation' in the wake of the second Conquest.[163] Baldwin's privilege was confiscated upon his return, and no known comparable petitions made for another half-century. A lively, late Anglo-Saxon experiment had fizzled out without serious consequence. A different order would be built anew under the Anglo-Normans.

IV. Conclusions

Mid-eleventh-century England requires treatment on its own terms. A cosmopolitan period of upheaval, inventiveness, and continental connectivity of its own peculiar distinction, its course was not inevitably set for, nor even a precursor of, the transformative new regime of William I and his descendants. The evidence of papal privileges makes that clear. After two centuries of only limited engagement with papal law and letters, 1049–71 saw a new cadre of foreign clerics trained in old Carolingian customs burst onto the scene, introducing Trier-style vestments into the Canterbury cloister; guarantees for 'castles' first formulated in the Abruzzo into the Somerset levels; the papal-mandated urbanisation of the Cornish-Devonian church; and Roman protections for an East Anglian monastery which mirrored those of *reconquista* Spain. All this proved not a foreshadowing of the coming Norman age, but rather a soon-abandoned, alternative path. Its traces were disappearing already (together with many of its protagonists) by the 1070s, and not picked up again until the early-to-mid-twelfth century, when things had to begin once over from square one. To understand how quickly it fell apart, looking backwards is more helpful than projecting into

---

[163] Fleming, *Kings*, p. 144.

the future. It is difficult not to see the obstruction and disappearance of these privileges as rooted in the conditions sketched in Chapter 6, with the nascent, long-tenth-century Cerdicing state developing along lines quite different to those of later Carolingian, and certainly post-Carolingian Europe. Active engagement with papal petitions and privileges remained by the middle of the eleventh century a decidedly post-Carolingian political language. The Kingdom of the English still endured, despite its turbulence and the arrival of new influences, as a distinct political, cultural, and legal unit.

Viewing the evidence from this angle also helps us put the early decades of the papal reform movement into perspective. Observing the amazing energy of its early leaders, and coupling this with what we now know would emerge over the next century and a half—nothing less than the emergence of the papacy as one of *the* major institutions in world history—it is tempting to see Leo and his protégés as already papal monarchs, precocious harbingers of the high-medieval order. Instead, their ultimately only limited, temporary impact in England, which was perhaps only mediated in the first place through the influence of their pre-existing networks in the Lotharingian Connection, reminds us of the vast constraints within which they operated. Pre-existing, regional demand for the papal idea remained absolutely key; bar some very minor forays into southernmost Italy and Aragon, the reformers' field of play was still that of their long-tenth-century predecessors. As for reform itself, the virtual absence of its core ideas from the privileges sent to England shows how much its direction relied not on papal leadership but local initiatives (among the English clergy, it seems, pretty thin on the ground). The picture is one familiar throughout this book, and thoroughly early medieval. Just like their counterparts in earlier centuries, the early papal reform faction depended on those petitioning from familiar or at least flexible 'documentary landscapes', who would present their acquisitions to audiences which already had a place for papal documentary culture within their 'horizons of expectation'. In mid-eleventh-century England, an elite cadre of personnel hailing from the core of the old Frankish world may have done more to encourage the reception of these documents than anyone since the days of Cynethryth and Cwoenthryth. But it was hardly enough to be more than a phase. Ultimately, the early reform papacy was a post-Carolingian institution, built out of—and operating within—the conventions, ambitions, and political geography of the post-Carolingian order.

8

Coda

Remembering, Inventing, and Forgetting

Before concluding, a brief word is needed on the afterlife of our privileges, and their reinvention in the historical record in the twelfth century. A sketch must suffice for now.

At the beginning of the 1120s, Eadmer recounted how he had lately rifled through the half-millennium-old archives of Canterbury cathedral, searching for evidence to support the archbishopric's claims to primacy over the English church. As he did so, the history of England and the papacy in the early middle ages began to crumble apart between his fingers:

> [Certain privileges], as we said before, were found in the archives of the church of the Lord Saviour, and we have thought it absurd not to commend them to the memory of future times. And indeed many others were found, but some were unreadable on account of their great age, while others were composed on sheets of papyrus, and written in a strange script. These too had for the most part disintegrated, so they could not, in any case, aid our understanding. And so, fearing to make note of things unknown, we have by necessity excluded them from this work...[1]

Eadmer's story neatly coincides with the first decades in which the manuscript evidence for papal privileges for early medieval England begins in real earnest. This was, of course, part of something bigger. One can observe a comparable pattern across the corpus of pre-Conquest documentary culture as a whole, with the cartulary boom of the twelfth and thirteenth centuries having a profound effect over the shape of the record now extant.[2] Nonetheless, with papal privileges this looks far more pronounced. Of the

---

[1] *HN*, 5, p. 276. Eadmer dates this to spring 1120; he worked on *HN* until 1122: Southern, *Saint Anselm*, pp. 307–9.

[2] Davis, pp. xiv–xx; Clanchy, *From Memory*, pp. 103–5. See generally Guyotjeannin, Morelle, and Parisse, eds., *Cartulaires*; Geary, *Phantoms*, pp. 81–114; Bouchard, *Rewriting*, pp. 9–37.

England and the Papacy in the Early Middle Ages: Papal Privileges in European Perspective, c. 680–1073.
Benjamin Savill, Oxford University Press. © Benjamin Savill 2023. DOI: 10.1093/oso/9780198887058.003.0008

1,937 known Anglo-Saxon charters (authentic and forged), almost a third are attested by pre-1100 manuscripts.[3] The same can only be said of eight of the papal documents listed in Chapter 3 from English archives, two of which are early items from Bede's *Historia*, and none original single-sheets.[4] By contrast, a full thirty privileges—some authentic or interpolated, but most outright forged—first appear in manuscripts dating to the early-to-mid-twelfth century.[5] This sudden surge of reinterest in the Anglo-papal trad-ition is all the more noteworthy given, as we saw in the last chapter, the cessation of new acquisitions in the 1070s and the lack of interest shown in older privileges in the decades that followed. Eadmer's ransacking of the archive highlights a number of issues important for understanding this new campaign.

Foremost was an urgent need to delve into the Anglo-papal past, driven by a new-found interest in what was up for grabs in the present. From the time of Calixtus II (1119–24), English institutions at last began fervently participating in the post-Carolingian tradition of routinely seeking papal privileges and their reconfirmations—a practice that had been gaining in momentum in mainland Europe since the later ninth century, and rocketing since the late eleventh.[6] Of chief interest were guarantees of monastic 'freedoms'; meanwhile at the archbishoprics of Canterbury and York, papal confirmations of claims to respective pre-eminence or independence became the main objects of desire. Turning up so late to the party, however, created difficulties. Successful petitions to an increasingly legalistic papal Curia required documentary proof, preferably older privileges that could then be reconfirmed. Missing out on much of the past three centuries of papal documentary culture meant that whatever their expectations, English monks and clerics would have found their archives sorely lacking in papal privileges of any kind. Even petitioners from houses rich in royal diplomas going back centuries must have ransacked their strongboxes in vain, finding nothing of the continuous history of papal documentation otherwise taken for granted in many of the institutions of post-Carolingian Europe. We get a glimpse of this strange chasm in Anglo-papal historical memory at the turn

---

[3] Data retrieved from S.

[4] 1, 5, 20 (Old English), 41, 47, ?†50, 57, 64. Not included is 29, in an Italian MS.

[5] †2, †3 (but see below, n. 11), †6, †8, †10, †11, 14, †15, †18, 20 (Latin), †22, †24, †25, 27, †28, 32, 35, 36, †37, †39, †40, 47 (interpolated), †43, 47 (interpolated), †52, 53, 58, †60, †66.

[6] Barlow, *English Church*, pp. 108 ff.; Robinson, *Papacy*; Santifaller, 'Verwendung', pp. 121 ff.; Johrendt, 'Italien', pp. 186–7. Besides the written evidence, the archaeological record for papal documents in post-Conquest England is comparably silent until Calixtus II: *PAS*, DUR-A82CF6.

of the twelfth century in William of Malmesbury's *Liber pontificalis* (1119, or shortly after). His earliest known work, it provides an enhanced edition of the Roman *Liber pontificalis* as far as the late eighth century, embellished along the way with William's own-sourced material. It continues thereafter solely with items found by the author.[7] William has added documents from English archives, where he can find them. But it is remarkable how little he has at hand, even in comparison to his own later works. After Leo III (795–816), he has almost nothing to say for the two and a half centuries that follow, providing blank entries for one pope after another until Nicholas II (1059–61).[8] Scanning back from the 1110s, a sort of abyss had become visible in the Anglo-papal documentary record after the early ninth century; even the documentation of the two centuries before looked comparatively slight. This was the void Anglo-Norman ecclesiastics now had to stare into and pull *something* out of if they were to have much hope of acquiring fresh privileges from the papacy in its new, alluringly powerful twelfth-century incarnation. Thus the hurried retreat of William's contemporaries, including Eadmer, back into their archives at just this same time.

Their researches were not always in vain. There remained scraps of a past to put to use. A handful of Bedan-era acquisitions for Canterbury, Malmesbury, Chertsey, and Bermondsey-Woking; some mauled privileges of the Mercian age; a few tenth-century documents; a late flourish of odds and ends from the time of Edward the Confessor: if things looked pretty meagre by continental standards, it still might have sufficed to reassure some institutions that they were dealing with more than self-delusion or local legend. Eadmer preceded the passage quoted above with his copies of what *had* been found, or so he claimed, during that same archival search. We know that two of those items, Leo III's privilege for Æthelheard (802) and John XII's for Dunstan (960), were authentic documents.[9] Neither of these privileges as Eadmer reproduces them are, however, without textual problems, and comparison with the tenth-century 'Dunstan Pontifical' shows that the second was tampered with to make it a far more impressive grant

---

[7] Thomson, *William*, pp. 119–36; Cambridge, University Library, Kk. 4. 6, ff. 224–80 (s. xii^in: 'C'); BL, Harley 633, ff. 4–71 (s. xii^ex: 'L').

[8] William inserts **20** (C only); Sergius to Ceolfrith (*c.* 700: C only): above, p. 221, n. 129 (JE 2138); †**24** (C only); Paul I to Eadberht and Ecgberht (757/8): see Appendix, p. 283 (JE 2337); memorandum on Formosus (891–6): above, p. 239 (S 1451a); John XV on Æthelred and Normandy (991): above, pp. 188, 222 (JL 3840); †**66**, †**67**. The Formosus and John XV items constitute William's only material between 816 and 1059: the first is a dubious local legend, the second misattributed to Gerbert of Rheims.

[9] *HN*, 5, pp. 270–1 (**35**), 274–6 (**41**).

of rights to Canterbury. As for the other items he supplies—far more effective in their support for Canterbury's primacy claims—these are, as a venerable literature now attests, almost entirely spurious.[10] They did not exist alone. Forged privileges first appeared around this same time at Evesham, Peterborough, Glastonbury, St Paul's, Westminster, (probably) Winchester Old Minster, Canterbury St Augustine's, and (less certainly) the monastic community of Canterbury Christ Church.[11] It is true that forgeries do not always need an immediate practical purpose. But the fact these particular items first emerged in the manuscript record at about the same time that English institutions revived, after a long hiatus, their interest in *new* papal privileges suggests that these phenomena were linked, and that the composition of these *spuria* did not therefore long predate their first manuscript witnesses.[12] In some cases we can observe their use as supporting evidence for petitions at the Curia.[13] This too followed continental precedent. In the 1060s and 1070s, comparable dossiers of papal forgeries had been put together at institutions such as Saint-Denis, Corbie, and Fleury to support

---

[10] *HN*, 5, pp. 261–2 (†3), 262–3 (†6), 263–5 (†8), 265–6 (†10), 266–7 (JE 2132: below, Appendix, p. 283), 267–8 (†22), 268–70 (†28), 271–2 (S 1451a), 273–4 (†38). I follow Southern, 'Canterbury', over Boehmer, *Fälschungen*.

[11] †3 is transmitted with Canterbury's archiepiscopal forgeries but concerns the Christ Church monks. It could predate the primacy dossier, since its appearance in BL, Cotton Claudius, A. iii, f. 7, in a 'Style IV' hand, may be s. xi[2]: *Christ Church*, pp. 90–3. Prof. Crick (pers. comm.) notes, however, that there are irregularities with this frail hand which 'could well be later than the 1070s' and 'could easily be after 1100'; we know of other Canterbury scribes writing in 'Style IV' into the first two decades of the twelfth century.

[12] Savill, 'Prelude', pp. 816–17.

[13] Succesfully: Calixtus II for St Augustine's, 1120: *PUU England*, iii. 10 (JL 6878), citing †2, †11, **14**, †39, †40; Eugenius III for Chertsey, 1150: ibid., iii. 46 (J not listed), citing **16**, †48, 54. Humiliating defeat: Canterbury's primacy dossier before Calixtus II, 1123: Hugh, *History*, pp. 192–5. A special case is Durham's Gregory VII forgery (*PUU England*, ii. 2: JL 5265): an unusually late pope to attribute a *spurium* of this kind, but the earliest possible given the date of Durham's monastic refoundation. Symeon (*Libellus*, iv. 2, pp. 226–9) alleged Gregory's involvement as early as 1103/15, but it is doubtful that any text then existed: see above, Chapter 3, p. 107, n. 146. In 1126 Calixtus II was notified by petitioners of this supposed Gregorian *preceptum* when they sought to obtain an authentic privilege, but the resulting document (*PUU England*, ii. 5: J not listed) indicates this claim was made only orally: the extant text dates to Durham's s. xii[2] forgery campaign (Bates, 'Forged Charters'). Presumably, claiming a false privilege from so recent a pope raised more difficulties than would an ancient pontiff: the 1126 petitioners did not dare bring a forgery of '1083' to the Curia. Another distinct example is Westminster's †52, †60, inserted into Osbert, *Vie de S. Édouard*, for presentation to the papal legate in 1138. This was in order to obtain a privilege of canonisation from Innocent II, who refused the petition on account of insufficient information, and Westminster ultimately had to wait until 1161: *PL* 179. 568 (JL 8182), *PL* 200. 106 (JL 10653). The incorporation of these documents within this text—as with their insertion elsewhere into *spuria* attributed to Edward (K 824–5; S 1041, 1043)—had a 'Trojan Horse' quality which helped alleviate the risks of submitting forgeries by recent popes to Curial scrutiny.

upcoming petitions to Rome;[14] behind this lay precedents of forging or falsifying papal documents in the Carolingian regions going back at least two centuries. It is another sign of their postponed arrival into continental traditions of papal documentary culture that the English churches—otherwise no strangers to forgery[15]—only followed suit at a somewhat later date. Lying about the relationship between one's institution and the popes of old presumably only had a limited appeal, until one felt there was enough to gain from those of the present day.

We must therefore take Eadmer's remarks about his discovery of other, unreadable privileges which he could not reproduce in his *Historia* with a pinch of salt. Yet we should not proceed too cynically. Christ Church Canterbury's surviving archive really did go back to at least the seventh century,[16] and besides, Eadmer's story needed to sound plausible if he were to bother with it at all. By the early twelfth century his account would have struck a chord with many contemporary archivists: the material record of the early medieval papacy had already begun to fall to pieces. Papyrus did not keep well, while Roman *curialis*, the 'strange script' of which Eadmer complained, had by his time become obsolete. As early as the 790s, the compilers of the *Codex Carolinus* had declared that one of their main incentives in collecting papal letters from the past five decades was to rescue these fragile texts, 'already partly ruined and destroyed', for posterity.[17] Less than a century later, a Roman cleric boasting of the late antique papyrus records of the papal *scrinium* nevertheless had to use a recent Carolingian redaction when it actually came to reproducing them.[18] Once we get to the beginning of the twelfth century, the remark in Italian sources that papyri urgently needed transcribing before they became 'consumed by age' appears repeatedly;[19] in contemporary Rome, at least one notary made a living transcribing tenth-century papyri for monastic clients.[20] Early medieval Roman documents were thus already well on their way to becoming the reserve of professional palaeographers. As stylised as his account may be, Eadmer probably did find his hopes frustrated by certain ancient, illegible

---

[14] *PUU Saint-Denis*, p. 26; Geary, *Phantoms*, p. 109; Morelle, 'Moines'; Roach, *Forgery*, pp. 185–8 (listing further examples).

[15] Brooks, *Early History*, pp. 191–7; Cubitt, 'Finding'; Crick, 'Insular History'; Roach, *Forgery*, pp. 113–52; Clanchy, *From Memory*, pp. 318 ff.

[16] Even today it begins with an original diploma of 679 (for Reculver, but at Canterbury by c. 800): BL, Cotton Augustus ii. 2 (*Christ Church*, 2; S 8); but cf. *Christ Church*, p. 44, for the possibility that much of the earliest archive was lost in the eighth century.

[17] *MGH Epp.* III, p. 476.   [18] Above, Chapter 2, p. 27, n. 53.

[19] Carbonetti Vendittelli, 'Sicut'.   [20] Wickham, *Medieval Rome*, p. 285.

fragments, and once *his* generation had dismissed them as unusable, some may have never been read again. Indeed, by the close of the twelfth century, much of the materiality of that past may have vanished altogether. In his *Historia* of Evesham abbey, Thomas of Marlborough recounted a visit to the Curia in 1205, where he was compelled to defend his house's claims to episcopal exemption by handing over to Innocent III its papal dossier, including two 'original' privileges of Pope Constantine (709, 713):

> The pope instructed me to produce them, and I did so. He took them in his own hands and pulled between the *bulla* and the document to see if he could separate the *bulla* from the cord. Scrutinizing them very carefully, he handed them to the cardinals for them to scrutinize, and when they had gone the rounds of them all they came back to the pope. Holding up a privilege of Constantine, he said, 'Privileges of this kind...are very well known to us, and could not be forged...These are genuine', and he returned everything to me. I am not going to tell you how fearful I was...[21]

In fact, these privileges *weren't* genuine: Thomas probably understated his 'fearful' moment.[22] Extraordinarily, contemporary single-sheets of both survive today, probably the same two that Innocent and his cardinals manhandled. What is most remarkable is that they are, from a modern scholarly perspective, so utterly unconvincing. Compared to the great papyrus rolls of the early middle ages, they are sad, scrawny little things: produced on parchment, only 36 × 25 cm and 38 × 22 cm in size, and written *c.* 1200 in an imitative, archaising script, reminiscent of a later Anglo-Saxon hand—in other words, quite unlike anything that came out of the early papal chancery (Figure 8.1).[23] These are forgeries produced by a scribe who had never seen an early medieval papal document. But apparently they worked: by implication, their intended audience had never seen one either, nor even may have certain members of the Curia—including Innocent III, for all his purported bluster. As the thirteenth century began, much of whatever remained of early medieval papal documentary culture which had not been transcribed and reworked may have already been lost forever.[24]

---

[21] Thomas, *History*, iii. 300, pp. 298–9.   [22] Clanchy, *From Memory*, p. 325.

[23] Evesham, Almonry Museum, 127 (36 × 25 cm) (†24); BL, Cotton Cleopatra E. i, ff. 64–5 (38 × 22 cm) (†25).

[24] Even reports of exceptional pockets of surviving papyri in the thirteenth century confirm this impression: of the stash of 10 decaying papal papyri from Silva Candida and Porto, transcribed into the register of Gregory IX in 1236 for their emergency preservation, the oldest was dated only as early as 905; the rest ranged from 992–1057: Gregory IX, *Les registres*, ii, cols. 585–98. See further Savill, 'Donation.'

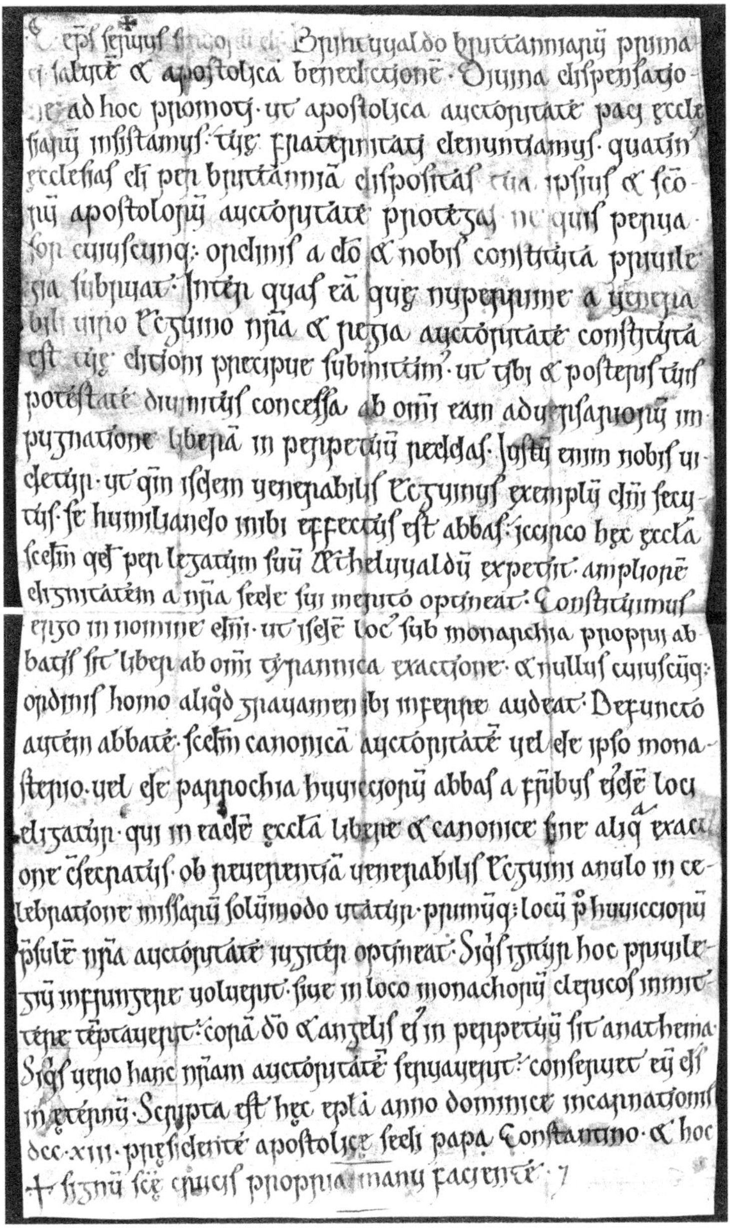

Figure 8.1 Forgery, c. 1200: 'Constantine I' for Evesham, '713' (JE †2149): BL, Cotton Cleopatra E. i, ff. 64–5 (British Library, with permission).

The age of Eadmer therefore constituted a decisive moment in the history of the material covered—and coverable—in this book. The explosion of papal government in the twelfth century, and England's new engagement with it, prompted a hurried search through the archive. Some church store chests yielded disintegrating, barely legible fragments; others nothing at all. With what they had at hand, a new generation set about transcribing, mistranscribing, interpolating, or simply inventing a more useful Anglo-papal past, while probably consigning the unreadable or undesirable to the waste-papyrus bin. By 1200, the noise of the ceaseless chancery output of the new, high-medieval papacy had drowned out what little evidence there was of the early Anglo-papal past, and contorted its remnants into something more suitable to contemporary tastes. A paradox familiar already to students of Anglo-Saxon history rings especially true here: with the turn of the twelfth century, our story of papal privileges in early medieval England not only ends—in some ways, it also begins.

9

Conclusions

We have covered more than four hundred years over the course of this investigation. Does a single, tidy narrative of the role and development of papal privileges in early medieval England stand out, one easily summarisable here? The answer is no—but then that is the point. Whatever the efforts of later archivists or writers in tracing a neat line of development between the use of papal documents in conversion-era England up to the world of the high middle ages, the picture that emerges on close analysis is one of fits and starts. No evolutionary papal grand narrative yet existed in the first millennium, and contemporaries did not need to play into one. For the *Angli*, consciously living at the world's distant, barely urbanised 'corner' (*angulus*),[1] the city of Rome in all its complexity, connectivity, and sheer enormity was a fascinating resource: of relics, texts, stories and ideas, and of more abstract notions of legitimacy and authority. If we are to characterise the middle ages as a time of fervent experimentation,[2] then Rome was a source of laboratory materials par excellence. Papal privileges played one part in this. At opportune moments, English pilgrim-petitioners sought to tap into the incomparably rich resources of Rome's documentary and hagiological culture, acquiring huge, sumptuous decrees drawn-up in the pope's name and bearing the charisma of the apostles, which they might then bring back into their own community as aids to negotiating their way through more immediate, local concerns. These were bright flashes, big moments; sometimes game-changing, sometimes obstructed or forgotten (when most controversial, as in early ninth-century Mercia, they could be both). What they did *not* do was form part of a continuous *habitus*, tradition, or routine, let alone one that played a role in a coherent scheme of evolving papal government. These were experiments—occasionally false starts or dead ends, and more interesting for it. As for their success, failure, meaning, even existence: these depended foremost on contingent circumstances and horizons of expectation in England, rather than grand strategy

---

[1] O'Reilly, 'Multitude'.   [2] Holmes and Standen, 'Introduction', pp. 37–9.

England and the Papacy in the Early Middle Ages: Papal Privileges in European Perspective, c. 680–1073.
Benjamin Savill, Oxford University Press. © Benjamin Savill 2023. DOI: 10.1093/oso/9780198887058.003.0009

at the Lateran palace. One historian has imagined the miracle-working saints' cults of the early middle ages not as ceaselessly operative, institutional constants, but more akin to volcanic sites: usually lying dormant, yet characterised by blasts of activity, sometimes decades or centuries apart.[3] We might picture the on-off bursts of engagement with papal documentary culture within early medieval English society (itself, after all, one aspect of its cult of Saint Peter) as working in a similar way.

How did this compare to elsewhere? Above all, one must still think throughout this period in terms of diversity, regional differences, local impulses, and micro-narratives which did not consciously engage with any masterplan of centralising, papal unity. Nevertheless, we can tentatively observe a movement from the mid-to-late ninth century onwards of an increasingly similar pattern of engagement with the contemporary papacy in many of the regions of the Carolingian and post-Carolingian world. This involved more frequent petitions by a widening range of individuals and institutions for papal privileges (or reconfirmations of existing privileges) broadly analogous to the kinds of imperial and royal diplomas which were also sought and issued within those polities, to which they often played a supporting role. They were frequently drafted with the input of these petitioner-beneficiaries. They were acquired against the backdrop of a range of other Rome-facing activities in those same regions. These included new compilations (and especially forgeries) of papal law; occasional summons for papal representatives to intervene in local disputes; and an interest in the works of a more recent generation of popes, whose more contemporary letters were compiled and circulated, or integrated into collections of law previously the domain of late antique (essentially, patristic) pontiffs. That a more uniform pattern developed under the Carolingians will surprise few. What needs emphasising, however, is that this outlived their empire: both despite its break-up, and because of it. As argued in Chapter 6, the practice of turning to the contemporary papacy as a live source of legal and documentary authority of continuing importance had built up enough momentum by the end of the ninth century to continue into the tenth and eleventh. Investing into this papal culture after the 880s appears to have constituted one important way by which a pan-Carolingian, imperial identity might still be expressed, and the intensifying complexities of a more fragmented, polycentric political landscape could be negotiated. Within this world,

[3] Smith, 'Saints', p. 591.

papal privileges could moreover have had a relational quality which meant that the more were successfully acquired, the more effective they became: that is, the odds of having one's own acquisition respected and implemented by the wider political and ecclesiastical community increased significantly when others had their own skin (or rather, Egyptian bulrush) in the game. This interdependent stakeholding in the idea of papal authority could then snowball, reaching a critical mass towards the end of the eleventh century. Significantly, we do not see anything like this in contemporary England, which followed its own, quite different path. A key lesson is that we must avoid the trap of thinking of the nascent Kingdom of the English as either a bite-size, later spin-off from the Carolingian project, or as a simple constituent of the wider post-Carolingian community. Its foundations and setting were distinct, and the way it engaged with the papacy symptomatic of this.

This disinclination in England to build up a more systematic engagement with contemporary papal documentary culture did not mean, however, that its communities had necessarily any less interest in Rome. Rather, their engagement was different in nature. Rome attracted English pilgrims throughout the early medieval period. They brought and received gifts, sought penance, and stayed (sometimes died) there, besides the *scholae* of Franks and Frisians outside San Pietro; kings, prelates, and other ambassadors used the city as platform for political communication. English churches thought of Gregory the Great as their apostle, and collected in their libraries decretals, inscriptions, itineraries, and other writings associated with the late antique bishops and martyrs of Rome. Where they seem to have differed most from many of their contemporaries in the Frankish kingdoms or northern-central Italy from the later ninth century onwards was in their lack of sustained interest in the papal laws, privileges, legates, and letters of subsequent generations, either authentic or forged, and their apparent reluctance to bring papal documentary culture more systematically into play in religious or political life. This participation in only elements of the papal tradition is instructive. It serves as a reminder that the 'papacy' and 'papal authority'—besides being far from synonymous with 'Rome'—were not fixed concepts which early medieval societies chose or chose not to engage with or recognise: they represented constellations of practices and ideas, the most salient aspects of which varied according to time and place. In the Cerdicing kingdom, the role of Rome and the papacy as a living reference-point for written decrees, interventions, or legal confirmations does not appear to have had anything like the same kind of resonance as it did in much of mainland Europe. This does not mean, however, that the

Kingdom of the English was 'behind', 'out-of-step', or isolated from the mainstream, and to imply as much is teleological, privileging the master-narrative that sees the papacy's high-medieval incarnation as its definitive manifestation. In the early middle ages, there existed plural, coexisting versions of what Rome and its bishops could or should mean, and myriad possible futures. The shifting polities of the English engaged on-and-off with ideas of papal authority for half a millennium before the transformations of the twelfth century, and they left enough of a record to allow us to reconstruct a great part of it. This was a remarkable phenomenon in and of itself, and does not need to be forced into the same developmental models used to explain events in the Frankish culture zone, or the later emergence of a 'papal monarchy' in the central middle ages.

If this meant a different sort of relationship to the popes and Rome, it does not necessarily follow that it was therefore a 'special' one. Chapter 1 briefly addressed the older historiographical opinion that the early English had enjoyed a unique, 'special relationship' with papal Rome, something apparently characteristic of the pre-Conquest centuries, and arguably contrasting in its degree of intimacy to what was experienced or perceived elsewhere. Having now looked comparatively at the full corpus of early medieval papal privileges, we can say that nothing supports this idea within this particular body of source material. Such a reading is, at best, only possible if one studies the papal documents for England in isolation. This is not to say that Anglo-Saxon engagement with Rome did not have its unusual aspects. Above all, the tenth- and eleventh-century traditions of Peter's Pence or in-person archiepiscopal petitions for the pallium were genuinely odd, and as such deserve the attention they have received. Moreover, one finds nothing to suggest that the English saw their relationship with Rome as banal or deficient either. Perhaps we would do best to approach the 'special relationship' paradigm in a way analogous to recent scholarship's deconstruction of another held-truth, the idea that the Anglo-Saxons also thought of themselves as God's chosen people.[4] That is, we can now reject—on the basis of a simple absence of evidence—the idea that the English believed themselves in a peculiarist sense as *the* elect or, in this case, *the* closest to Rome, while still entertaining the prospect that they might have understood themselves as part of a wider community of chosen *peoples* or papal *favourites*. Besides: a lack of frequency in Anglo-papal interactions,

---

[4] Molyneaux, 'Did'; O'Brien, 'Chosen Peoples'.

especially of the documentary kind, did not have to mean a lack of intensity. As suggested in Chapter 2, Rome's geographical and cultural distance from Britain; the expense, time, and danger involved in getting there; or the probably more exotic quality of its written materials within the Anglo-Saxon 'documentary landscape'—all could have at times added to the 'wow-effect' of papal privileges in early medieval England, in contrast to regions where acquisitions took place more easily and regularly. In the spirit of the cliché that distance makes the heart grow fonder, one could perhaps still argue along such lines for the 'special' quality of the Anglo-papal relationship within the early medieval period: one in which the remoteness of Rome and its documentary culture from England might have on certain occasions heightened its aura to a degree unusual elsewhere.

Uncovering what those occasional intersections between the papal *scrinium* and the Anglo-Saxon *witan* can do to further our understanding of early medieval England has been the main aim of Part II. By turning the focus away from the popes and towards their petitioners and beneficiaries, we have seen something of the tensions between monastic and episcopal space and authority in the early Christian kingdoms; familial inheritance strategies in eighth- and ninth-century Mercia; changed attitudes to Rome and its political instrumentalisation under the Cerdicing regime; and the openness to novel documentary strategies and overseas connections under the new men and new politics of the mid-eleventh century, as well as their failure to last beyond a generation. Nonetheless, we may end by asking a question largely outside the book's remit so far: what can the acquisitions of these privileges across the early middle ages tell us about the contemporary papacy?

The most important recurring motif throughout this study has been the sheer degree of dependency of the early medieval papacy upon the perceptions, expectations, traditions, and contingent political practices within any of the given regions with which it communicated. This is not merely about the papacy's ability to extend its authority or 'enforce' its decisions (any such enforcement of course taking place on-the-ground, within and by those societies themselves). Rather, the popes depended markedly upon external forces to determine the very shape of where and with whom they communicated; what those communications might look like and mean; and how they would later be remembered. This is not to suggest that the papacy was impotent or meaningless, only that, when dealing with the outside world, its potency and meaning was generated from within that same 'periphery'. Popes held real power in their immediate environs. In the early middle ages, the main job of most bishops of Rome, above all in the eyes of the Romans who had put them in office, was to govern their own megacity and its patrimonies. Next to this, whatever happened elsewhere, not to mention in England, probably remained until the 1040s of secondary concern at best.[5] The papacy's ability to communicate its power within Rome through its artistic and architectural projects, and in the spectacular output of its unique chancery, meanwhile helped generate the magnetic field which drew petitioners to the city. However, reliance on beneficiary initiative, input, interpretation, implementation, and preservation/registration in the worlds beyond its own power base meant that in some sense—to adopt a currently popular turn of phrase—the papacy did not control its own narrative. More precisely: given the diverse manifestations of engagement with papal Rome that took place across different times and places, it did not control its own *narratives*. We have looked at some of those shaped in England here, but they formed part of a wider mosaic. One of the most significant upsets brought about by the coming of the reform party in the mid-eleventh century was their imposition of one particular post-Carolingian idea of the papacy over the city of Rome; in time, theirs would become the dominant narrative. Yet as we saw in Chapter 7, this 'papal revolution' attracted only bursts of interest in England in its earliest decades, when it remained overwhelmingly reliant on the continued input of many of those same communities which had already engaged most with papal documentary culture in the generations prior. If the central apparatus of the papacy had changed, its ability to impose its version of events where it liked had not. How that came about, however, is a story for another book, set in a very different world.

As for approaches to the early papacy, hopefully this book has done its part to help extricate the subject from at least some of the teleological 'morbidity' with which its traditional scholarship was once characterised.[6] Papal historiography can and should break beyond the artificial boundaries cordoning it off as a stand-alone field. The papacy was shaped by the diverse societies of contemporary Europe, and so it is to the study of those societies that papal historians must turn, engaging more rigorously with wider research into late antiquity and the early middle ages. And as for Anglo-Saxon England: I hope the foregoing has contributed to our sense that we can only really begin to understand its ideas about a supra-regional

---

[5] Cf. Wickham, *Medieval Rome*, p. 15.   [6] Noble, 'Morbidity'; see above, p. 10.

phenomenon such as the papacy (or even, the church in general) when we look beyond its shores and think comparatively. That means more than just boiling down the English experience to an extension of the bigger European picture, or treating its developments as smaller scale variations on what we find elsewhere. Subtle arguments for difference and peculiarity, even exceptionality, *are* possible. But they will not be convincing, nor very interesting, if made only in isolation.

A Note on Some Items Excluded from the Handlist

The following twelve items have not been listed as privileges. They do not appear in Chapter 3's Handlist, and receive at best limited discussion elsewhere. Nevertheless, readers may query certain omissions, or at least wish to know which texts did not make the cut (and why).

?†(i) *Sergius I to Æthelred, Aldfrith and Aldwulf, 'kings of the English', recommending Berhtwald, archbishop of Canterbury*
(693?)
Incipit: Donum gratiae spiritualis
Edited: *HN*, v, pp. 266–7; Boehmer, *Fälschungen*, p. 151; *GP*, I, i. 34, pp. 70–2.
Registered: JE 2132; Conte, *Chiesa*, †280; J³ ?3568.
Comment: Sergius praises the kings and their *gens sancta*, *genus electum* and recommends to them Berhtwald. Although transmitted as part of Canterbury's 'primacy forgeries' and complementary to an almost certainly falsified/heavily interpolated letter in Sergius' name to the bishops of England (†22), this short letter makes no unreasonable claims and may be authentic. Note that, unlike †22, the letter does not state that Berhtwald visited Rome, although a reference in *LP* (i. 86, p. 376) to Sergius having 'ordained' Berhtwald as 'archbishop of Britain' nevertheless makes some sort of meeting possible. Compare, however, Bede, who tells us that Berhtwald travelled to Gaul to be ordained by Gudinus of Lyon, but says nothing of further travels: *HE*, v. 8, 11, pp. 474–5, 484–5.

(ii) *Paul I to Eadberht, king (of the Northumbrians), and Ecgbert archbishop (of York), urging the return of monasteries at Stonegrave, Coxwold, and 'Donaemuthe'*
(757/8)
Incipit: Arbiter rerum et
Edited: HS, iii, pp. 394–6.
Registered: JE 2337; J³ 4145.
Comment: Admonitory letter to the king. Abbot Forthred has complained in Rome that Eadberht has seized three of his monasteries and given them to the *patricius* Moll. Paul urges Eadberht to return the houses to Forthred, stressing eternal rewards, although he threatens no sanctions should he fail to comply. He adds as a general rule that lay persons should not invade 'religious places'. While its extant *inscriptio* also names Ecgbert, the letter appears only to address the king. It is transmitted with the letters of Alcuin (above, Chapter 6, p. 220), a sometime subject of Eadberht and oblate to Ecgbert.

†*(iii) *Hadrian I pledges to Offa, king of the Mercians, that, when he has held a council in England conferring liberties and properties to the monastery of St Albans, the apostolic see will confirm these with its own privileges, and adopt St Albans as its 'special daughter'*
(793)
Incipit: n/a (report from St Albans, s. xiii)
Edited: Roger of Wendover, *Chronica*, i, pp. 255–9; Matthew Paris, *Chronica*, i, pp. 359–61; *Lives of the Two Offas*, pp. 113–14.
Registered: No.
Comment: This tale, first related by Roger of Wendover (*c.* 1220/36), is certainly fictitious (*pace* Sayers, 'Papal Privileges', p. 58), and part of a wider web of late forgeries and legends inventing a post-Bedan history for St Albans (*St Albans*, pp. 8–45, 56–74). The story imagines Offa travelling to Rome, seeking from Hadrian the canonisation of Alban, and then resolving to send a monetary tribute, thus linking St Albans and its post-Conquest privileges to an origin myth for Peter's Pence. One notable feature of the story (and the reason for its relegation to this appendix) is that Hadrian does not actually grant a privilege. Rather, he pledges to do so in the future tense, having told Offa to return to England and promulgate privileges of his own in council. Presumably the author's strategy was to get around the fact that no such document existed in the St Albans archive. Perhaps he also envisioned a situation wherein contemporary popes might feel obliged to fulfil at last Hadrian's promises (St Albans' series of papal privileges only began with Calixtus II in 1122: *PUU England*, iii. 5). However fantastical, such legends about Offa might nevertheless have had some distant relation to the authentic Hadrianic privilege now known to have been acquired by the king for his monasteries dedicated to Peter (**29**).

(iv) *Gregory V to Ælfric, 'bishop of the Anglo-Saxons' (archbishop of Canterbury), concerning a penitential pilgrim to Rome*
(996/9)
Incipit: Notum fieri uolumus
Edited: Aronstam, 'Penitential Pilgrimages', p. 80; *PUU* 234.
Registered: Böhmer-Zimmermann 799a; J³ 8371.
Comment: Gregory informs Ælfric that he has ordered the bearer of the letter, who accidentally killed his son, to undertake penance for seven years. Part of a series of penitential letters issued in the names of popes and addressed to English prelates, probably brought back by the penitents as proof of pilgrimage. See further Aronstam, 'Penitential Pilgrimages', and Tinti, 'England', p. 82.

(v) *John (XVIII) to (Wulfstan), archbishop (of York), concerning a penitential pilgrim to Rome*
(1003/9)
Incipit: Huius igitur ostensorem
Edited: Aronstam, 'Penitential Pilgrimages', p. 80; *PUU* 408.
Registered: Böhmer-Zimmermann 983a; J³ 8569.
Comment: John informs the archbishop that the bearer of the letter has taken up a regime of penance from him. This letter seems to have been preserved within

England for formulaic purposes: the archbishop is not named and the penitent referred to as 'N'. See above, (iv).

(vi) *John (XVIII) to an (English) bishop, concerning a penitential pilgrim to Rome* (1003/9)
Incipit: Dignum duximus dilectioni
Edited: Aronstam, 'Penitential Pilgrimages', p. 81; *PUU* 409.
Registered: Böhmer-Zimmermann 983b; J³ 8570.
Comment: John informs the bishop that 'this man' has taken up a regime of penance from him. This letter seems to have been preserved within England for formulaic purposes, with the bishop named as 'N'. See above, (iv).

(vii) *John (XVIII) to Wulfstan, archbishop (of York), concerning a penitential pilgrim to Rome* (1003/9)
Incipit: Iste uir pro
Edited: Aronstam, 'Penitential Pilgrimages', p. 81; *PUU* 410.
Registered: Böhmer-Zimmermann 983c; J³ 8571.
Comment: John informs Wulfstan that 'this man', a fratricide, has come to 'the thresholds of the holy apostles' and sought penance from him; he then describes the regime. See above, (iv).

(viii) *John (XIX) to an (English) archbishop, concerning a penitential pilgrim to Rome* (1024/32)
Incipit: Visis apostolorum liminibus
Edited: Aronstam, 'Penitential Pilgrimages', p. 81; *PUU* 410.
Registered: Böhmer-Frech 24; J³ 8953.
Comment: John informs the archbishop that the bearer of the letter, who has accidentally killed his child, has come to the 'thresholds of the apostles' and 'tearfully' sought penance; he then describes the regime, to last fourteen years. This letter seems to have been preserved within England for formulaic purposes, with the archbishop named as 'N'. See above, (iv).

(ix) *Leo IX to E(adsige), archbishop 'of the English' (Canterbury), concerning the priest Andrew, a penitent(ial pilgrim to Rome?)* (1049/50)
Incipit: Hunc Andream presbiterum
Edited: Aronstam, 'Pope Leo', p. 541; Aronstam, 'Penitential Pilgrimages', p. 82.
Registered: Böhmer-Frech 510; J³ 9541.
Comment: John informs Eadsige that he has absolved Andrew, 'your priest', who has committed homicide, 'if it is so' (*si ita est*) that he has undertaken seven years' penance. He cites as a precedent a (forged) decretal of Calixtus (from Pseudo-Isidore: *Decretales*, ed. Hinschius, pp. 137–43: JK †86). This is the last of a series of penitential letters issued in the names of popes and addressed to English prelates. In this case it is not clear if it was acquired by the penitent as part of a pilgrimage to Rome. See further Aronstam, 'Penitential Pilgrimages'.

(x) *Alexander II informs Ordric, abbot of Abingdon, that has been unable to retain 'our son' Ælfgeat by any justification, even though he has the right to choose whom he wishes from monasteries and canonries if they prove 'useful and necessary' for the apostolic see*
(1061/6)
Incipit: Licet nostre auctoritatis
Edited: *Epistolae*, ed. Loewenfeld, 69.
Registered: JL 4478; J³ 10585.
Comment: Fragment or paraphrase from an otherwise unknown letter of Alexander, found in the unique manuscript of the *Collectio Britannica* canon law compilation, probably compiled in Italy, *c.* 1090/95 (BL, Add. 8873, f. 40: Ewald, 'Papstbriefe', p. 330; Kéry, 'Kanonessammlungen', pp. 286–92). It is very difficult to reconstruct the context of this 32-word excerpt, or the form and purpose of the original document. The identity of Ælfgeat (*Aliuetus*) is unknown, although presumably he was attached to Abingdon. Domesday records an Ælfgeat *presbiter* holding land in Somerset in 1086 (*Domesday*, ed. Morris et al., viii, 16. 5) and an Ælfgeat *presbiter* holding land from the abbot of Ely either side of the Conquest (ibid., xviii, 5. 40), but it is impossible to draw any connection.

?*(xi) *Alexander II and his legates lend their 'authority and counsel' to the relocation of the see of Dorchester-on-Thames to Lincoln*
(1067/73) (1071?)
Incipit: n/a (*deperditum*: cited in a charter of William I)
Edited: *AAWI*, 177.
Registered: No.
Comment: Mentioned by William I in an original writ-charter of 1072/87 for Bishop Remigius of Dorchester/Lincoln. It is difficult to tell whether this 'authority and counsel', if genuinely given, ever took documentary form (if it had, it may have resembled ?†50), or whether proceedings were primarily verbal. If there had been a document, there is no trace of Lincoln ever retaining a copy (compare 58, apparently brought from Dorchester following the relocation of see). One possible occasion for seeking Alexander's 'counsel' was during Remigius' journey to Rome alongside Lanfranc, Thomas, and Baldwin in 1071 (*HN*, i, pp. 10–11, when 64–5 were acquired), but the reference to Alexander's 'legates' indicates otherwise.

†(xii) *Alexander II to Lanfranc, archbishop of Canterbury, concerning the monastic community at (Old Minster) Winchester*
(1071/3)
Incipit: Peruenit ad aures
Edited: *PL* 146. 1416.
Registered: JL 4762; J³ ?11171.
Comment: Complementary letter to the probably forged privilege in Alexander's name addressed to Winchester (†67). See Cowdrey, 'Lanfranc, the Papacy', pp. 493–5, which suggests that although parts may be genuine, in its extant form it appears to have been rewritten to support the claims of the twelfth-century Winchester monks.

Bibliography

Manuscripts

Amiens, Bibliothèque municipale, 526 n. 1
Bamberg, Staatsbibliothek, Msc. Lit. 53
Barcelona, Arxiu de la Corona d'Aragó, Butlla de Joan XVIII
Barcelona, Arxiu de la Corona d'Aragó, Butlla de Silvestre II
Bergamo, Biblioteca civica, Papiro di Giovanni XVIII
Bologna, Archivio capitolare, Caps. 14 n. 1
Cambridge, Corpus Christi College, 146
Cambridge, Corpus Christi College, 161
Cambridge, Gonville and Caius College, 249/277
Cambridge, Peterhouse, 74
Cambridge, Trinity College, O. 2. 41
Cambridge, Trinity College, R. 5. 16
Cambridge, Trinity College, R. 5. 33
Cambridge, University Archives, Luard 115
Cambridge, University Archives, Luard 115*a*
Cambridge, University Library, Ii. 2. 3
Cambridge, University Library, Kk. 4. 6
Cambridge, University Library, Mm. 4. 19
Cambridge, University Library, Peterborough Dean and Chapter I
Canterbury, Dean and Chapter, Register A
Dijon, Bibliothèque municipale, 909
Dublin, Trinity College, 641
Durham, Cathedral Library, B. iv. 18
Egmond-Binnen, Sint-Adelbertabdij, Biblioteek Ms. G. ii
Evesham, Almonry Museum, 127
Exeter, Dean and Chapter, 2072
Exeter, Dean and Chapter, 2528
Florence, Archivio capitolare, 1032
Girona, Arxiu Capitular, Butlla del papa Formós
Girona, Arxiu Capitular, Butlla del papa Romà
Gloucester, Gloucestershire Archives, D678/1 M4/1
Le Puy, Bibliothèque municipale, 117 n. 1
Lincoln, Dean and Chapter, A/1/5
London, British Library, Add. 8873
London, British Library, Add. 10,972
London, British Library, Add. 14,847

London, British Library, Cotton Augustus ii. 2
London, British Library, Cotton Augustus ii. 38
London, British Library, Cotton Augustus ii. 61
London, British Library, Cotton Augustus ii. 78
London, British Library, Cotton Ch. vi. 2
London, British Library, Cotton Claudius A. iii
London, British Library, Cotton Claudius B. vi
London, British Library, Cotton Claudius C. ix
London, British Library, Cotton Claudius D. x
London, British Library, Cotton Claudius E. v
London, British Library, Cotton Cleopatra E. i
London, British Library, Cotton Faustina A. iii
London, British Library, Cotton Faustina B. vi
London, British Library, Cotton Julius D. ii
London, British Library, Cotton Otho A. xviii
London, British Library, Cotton Otho C. i/1
London, British Library, Cotton Tiberius A. xiii
London, British Library, Cotton Tiberius A. xv
London, British Library, Cotton Tiberius E. iv
London, British Library, Cotton Vespasian A. ix
London, British Library, Cotton Vespasian A. xiv
London, British Library, Cotton Vespasian B. vi/1
London, British Library, Cotton Vespasian B. xv
London, British Library, Cotton Vespasian B. xx
London, British Library, Cotton Vespasian B. xxiv
London, British Library, Cotton Vespasian E. xvi
London, British Library, Cotton Vitellius A. ii
London, British Library, Cotton Vitellius A. xiii
London, British Library, Detached seal xxxviii. 5
London, British Library, Egerton 2733
London, British Library, Harley 76
London, British Library, Harley 633
London, British Library, Harley 1761
London, British Library, Harley 3763
London, British Library, Lansdowne 402
London, British Library, Royal 13 B. xix
London, British Library, Royal 13 D. ii
London, British Library, Royal 13 D. v
London, British Library, Stowe Ch. 15
London, British Library, Stowe 944
London, Metropolitan Archives, CLC/313/B/001/MS25504
London, Metropolitan Archives, CLC/313/B/012/MS25501
London, The National Archives, Public Record Office C 52/4
London, The National Archives, Public Record Office E 164/27
London, The National Archives, Public Record Office E 164/28

London, Society of Antiquaries, 60
London, Westminster Abbey, W.A.M. xx
Longleat, Marquess of Bath, 39
Marburg, Staatsarchiv, Stiftsarch. Fulda 1024
Marburg, Staatsarchiv, Stiftsarch. Fulda 1049 June 13
Marburg, Staatsarchiv, Stiftsarch. Fulda 1064
Milan, Bibliotheca Ambrosiana, i. 2 sup.
Munich, Bayerisches Hauptstaatsarchiv, Bamberg Urk. 68
Munich, Bayerisches Hauptstaatsarchiv, Bamberg Urk. 120
Munich, Bayerische Staatsbibliothek, Clm 8112
Munich, Bayerische Staatsbibliothek, Clm 28118
Münster, Landesarchiv Nordrhein-Westfalen Abteilung Westfalen, B 605u/Stift
　Heerse (Neuenheerse)/Urkunden Nr. 3
Oxford, Bodleian Library, Bodley 297
Oxford, Bodleian Library, Bodley 579
Oxford, Bodleian Library, Bodley 718
Oxford, Bodleian Library, Eng. Hist. a. 2, no. iv
Oxford, Bodleian Library, Laud Misc. 636
Oxford, Bodleian Library, Lyell 15
Oxford, Bodleian Library, Rawlinson A 287
Oxford, Bodleian Library, Rawlinson B 333
Oxford, Bodleian Library, Wood empt. I
Oxford, Bodleian Library, Wood empt. 5
Oxford, Christ Church, 138
Oxford, Christ Church, 341
Paris, Archives nationales, K 7 n. 9/2
Paris, Archives nationales, K 13 n. 10/4
Paris, Archives nationales, K 17 n. 6
Paris, Archives nationales, L 220 n. 3; K 15 n. 3/2
Paris, Archives nationales, L 221 n. 1
Paris, Archives nationales, L 844 n. 3
Paris, Archives nationales, LL 1156
Paris, Archives nationales, LL 1158
Paris, Bibliothèque nationale de France, Lat. 943
Paris, Bibliothèque nationale de France, Lat. 2278
Paris, Bibliothèque nationale de France, Lat. 2777
Paris, Bibliothèque nationale de France, Lat. 8840
Paris, Bibliothèque nationale de France, Lat. 10837
Paris, Bibliothèque nationale de France, Lat. 11674
Paris, Bibliothèque nationale de France, NAL 1609
Paris, Bibliothèque nationale de France, NAL 2507
Paris, Bibliothèque nationale de France, NAL 2580
Perpignan, Bibliothèque municipale, 72
Ravenna, Archivio arcivescovile, Papiro n. 4
Rome, Biblioteca Angelica, ms. or. 62 (C.3.6)

Urgell, Museu Diocesà, Butlla atorgada pel papa Silvestre II al bisbe Sala
Vatican City, Archivio Segreto Vaticano, Misc. arm. xi, 19
Vatican City, Biblioteca Apostolica Vaticana, Pap. vat. lat. 1
Vatican City, Biblioteca Apostolica Vaticana, Vat. lat. 4939
Vic, Arxiu Episcopal, 405
Vic, Arxiu Episcopal, 406
Vic, Arxiu Episcopal, 407
Vic, Arxiu Episcopal, 445
Vic, Arxiu Episcopal, 624
Wells, Dean and Chapter, CF/3/2
Winchester, Dean and Chapter, A/3/1
Winchester, Dean and Chapter, A/3/2
Winchester, Hampshire Record Office, 21 M65/A1/1
York, Minster Library and Archives, L 2/1

Printed Primary Sources

Abbo of Fleury, *Opera omnia*, in *Patrologiae*, ed. Migne, 139, cols. 417–578.

Abbots of Wearmouth and Jarrow, ed. and trans. C. Grocock and I.N. Wood (Oxford, 2013).

Acta pontificum Romanorum inedita, ed. J. von Pflugk-Harttung, 3 vols. (Tübingen, 1880–8).

Aelred of Rievaulx, *Vita sancti Ædwardi regis et confessoris*, in *Aelredi Rievallensis Opera omnia*, ed. F. Marzella (Turnhout, 2017), pp. 11–182.

Agobard of Lyon, *Epistolae*, ed. E. Dümmler, in *Epistolae Karolini aevi III. Monumenta Germaniae Historica. Epistolae V* (Berlin, 1895), pp. 150–239.

Aimo of Fleury, *Vita et passio sancti Abbonis*, ed. and trans. R.-H. Bautier and G. Labory, in *L'abbaye de Fleury en l'an mil* (Paris, 2004), pp. 3–137.

Alcuin, *Epistolae*, in *Epistolae Karolini aevi II*, ed. E. Dümmler, *Monumenta Germaniae Historica. Epistolae IV* (Berlin, 1895), pp. 1–493.

Aldhelm, *Opera*, ed. R. Ewald, *Monumenta Germaniae Historica. Auctorum Antiquissimorum XV* (Berlin, 1919).

Alexander II, *Epistolae et diplomata*, in *Patrologiae*, ed. Migne, 146, cols. 1279–1430.

Alexander III, *Epistolae et privilegia*, in *Patrologiae*, ed. Migne, 200.

André de Fleury, *Vie de Gauzlin, abbé de Fleury*, ed. and trans. R.-H. Bautier and G. Labory (Paris, 1969).

The Anglo-Saxon Chronicle: a Collaborative Edition, ed. D.N. Dumville and S. Keynes, 17 vols. (Cambridge, 1983–).

Anglo-Saxon Writs, ed. F.E. Harmer (Manchester, 1952).

Annales camaldulensis ordinis sancti Benedicti, ed. J.-B. Mittarelli and A. Costadoni, 9 vols. (Venice, 1755–73).

B., *Vita s. Dunstani*, in *The Early Lives of St Dunstan*, ed. and trans. M. Winterbottom and M. Lapidge (Oxford, 2012), pp. 1–110.

Bede, *Ecclesiastical History of the English People*, ed. and trans. B. Colgrave and R.A.B. Mynors (Oxford, 1969).

Bede, *Epistola ad Ecgbertum episcopum*, in *Abbots*, ed. and trans. Grocock and Wood, pp. 123–61.

Bede, *Historia abbatum*, in *Abbots*, ed. and trans. Grocock and Wood, pp. 21–75.

Bede, *Homelia in natale s. Benedicti*, in *Abbots*, ed. and trans. Grocock and Wood, pp. 1–19.

Benedicti regula. Editio altera emendata, ed. R. Hanslik (Vienna, 1977).

Boniface and Lul, *Epistolae*, ed. M. Tangl, *Monumenta Germaniae Historica. Epistolae selectae I* (Berlin, 1955).

Burchard of Worms, *Decretorum liber*, in *Patrologiae*, ed. Migne, 140, cols. 537–1084.

Byrhtferth of Ramsey, *The Lives of St Oswald and St Ecgwine*, ed. and trans. M. Lapidge (Oxford, 2009).

Byrhtferth of Ramsey, *Vita s. Ecgwini*, in Byrhtferth, *Lives*, ed. and trans. Lapidge, pp. 205–304.

Byrhtferth of Ramsey, *Vita s. Oswaldi*, in Byrhtferth, *Lives*, ed. and trans. Lapidge, pp. 1–204.

Caesarius of Arles, *Opera omnia nunc primum in unum collecta*, ed. G. Morin, 2 vols. (Maredsous, 1937–42).

Capitula episcoporum. Erster Teil, ed. P. Brommer, *Monumenta Germaniae Historica. Capitula Episcoporum I* (Hanover, 1984).

Capitularia regum Francorum, ed. A. Boretius and V. Krause, *Monumenta Germaniae Historica. Leges II*, 2 vols. (Hanover, 1883–97).

The Cartae antiquae Rolls 1–10, ed. L. Landon (London, 1939).

Cartularium Saxonicum: a Collection of Charters Relating to Anglo-Saxon History, ed. W. de Gray Birch, 3 vols. (London, 1885–93).

The Cartulary of Montier-en-Der, 666–1129, ed. C.B. Bouchard (Toronto, 2004).

Charters of Abingdon Abbey, ed. S.E. Kelly, 2 vols. (Oxford, 2000–1).

Charters of Barking Abbey and Waltham Holy Cross, ed. S.E. Kelly (Oxford, 2021).

Charters of Bath and Wells, ed. S.E. Kelly (Oxford, 2007).

Charters of Chertsey Abbey, ed. S.E. Kelly (Oxford, 2015).

Charters of Christ Church Canterbury, ed. N.P. Brooks and S.E. Kelly, 2 vols. (Oxford, 2013).

Charters of Glastonbury Abbey, ed. S.E. Kelly (Oxford, 2012).

Charters of Malmesbury Abbey, ed. S.E. Kelly (Oxford, 2005).

Charters of the New Minster, Winchester, ed. S. Miller (Oxford, 2001).

Charters of Northern Houses, ed. D.A. Woodman (Oxford, 2012).

Charters of Peterborough Abbey, ed. S.E. Kelly (Oxford, 2009).

Charters of Rochester, ed. A. Campbell (Oxford, 1973).

Charters of Shaftesbury Abbey, ed. S.E. Kelly (Oxford, 1996).

Charters of Sherborne, ed. M.A. Donovan (Oxford, 1988).

Charters of St Albans, ed. J. Crick (Oxford, 2007).

Charters of St Augustine's Abbey, Canterbury and Minster-in-Thanet, ed. S.E. Kelly (Oxford, 1995).

Charters of St Paul's, London, ed. S.E. Kelly (Oxford, 2004).

Chartes et documents pour servir a l'histoire de l'abbaye de Charroux, ed. D.P. de Monsabert (Poitiers, 1910).

Chronicon abbatiae Rameseiensis, ed. W.D. Macray (London, 1886).

Chronique ou livre du fondation du monastère de Mouzon, ed. and trans. M. Bur (Paris, 1989).

Codex Carolinus, ed. W. Gundlach, in *Epistolae Merowingici et Karolini aevi, Monumenta Germaniae Historica. Epistolae III* (Berlin, 1892), pp. 469–657.

Codex diplomaticus aevi Saxonici, ed. J.M. Kemble, 6 vols. (London, 1839–48).

Codex diplomaticus Anhaltinus, ed. O. von Heinemann, 4 vols. (Dessau, 1867–79).

Codex diplomaticus Langobardiae, ed. G. Porro Lambertenghi (Turin, 1873).

Codice diplomatico del Monastero di S. Colombano di Bobbio fino all'anno MCCVIII, ed. C. Cipolla, 3 vols. (Rome, 1918).

Codice diplomatico longobardo, ed. L. Schiaparelli, C. Brühl, and H. Zielinski, 5 vols. (1929–2003).

Concilia Galliae A. 314 – A. 506, ed. C. Munier (Turnhout, 1963).

Concilia Galliae A. 511 – A. 695, ed. C. de Clercq (Turnhout, 1963).

Concilium universale Chalcedonense, ed. E. Schwartz (Berlin, 1932–8).

Councils and Ecclesiastical Documents Relating to Great Britain and Ireland, ed. A.W. Haddan and W. Stubbs, 3 vols. (Oxford, 1869–78).

Councils and Synods, With Other Documents Relating to the English Church I, A.D. 871–1204, ed. D. Whitelock, M. Brett, and C.N.L. Brooke, 2 vols. (Oxford, 1981).

The Crawford Collection of Early Charters and Documents now in the Bodleian Library, ed. A.S. Napier and W.H. Stevenson (Oxford, 1895).

Decretales Pseudo-Isidorianae et capitula Angilramni, ed. P. Hinschius (Leipzig, 1863).

Diplomata, chartae, epistolae, leges aliaque instrumenta ad res Gallo-Francicas spectantia, ed. J.M. Pardessus, 2 vols. (Paris, 1843–9).

Domesday Book, ed. J. Morris et al., 35 vols. (Chichester, 1975–86).

Eadmer, *Historia novorum in Anglia*, ed. M. Rule (London, 1884).

Eadmer, *Vita s. Oswaldi*, in Eadmer, *Lives and Miracles of Saints Oda, Dunstan, and Oswald*, ed. and trans. A.J. Turner and B.J. Muir (Oxford, 2006), pp. 213–89.

The Early Charters of Eastern England, ed. C.R. Hart (Leicester, 1966).

Eddius Stephanus [Stephen of Ripon], *The Life of Bishop Wilfrid*, ed. and trans. B. Colgrave (Cambridge, 1927).

Eigil, *Vita Sturmi abbatis*, ed. P. Engelbert, in P. Engelbert, *Die Vita Sturmi des Eigil von Fulda. Literarkritisch-historische Untersuchung und Edition* (Marburg, 1968), pp. 129–63.

English Episcopal Acta XXXI: Ely 1109–1197, ed. N. Karn (Oxford, 2005).

Epistolae pontificum romanorum ineditae, ed. S. Loewenfeld (Leipzig, 1885).

Eynsham Cartulary, ed. H.E. Salter, 2 vols. (Oxford, 1907).

Felix, *Life of Saint Guthlac*, ed. and trans. B. Colgrave (Cambridge, 1956).

Flodoard of Reims, *Historia Remensis ecclesiae*, ed. M. Stratmann, *Monumenta Germaniae Historica. Scriptores XXXVI* (Hanover, 1998).

Formulae collectionis sancti Dionysii, in *Formulae Merowingici et Karolini aevi*, ed. K. Zeumer, *Monumenta Germaniae Historica. Leges V* (Hanover, 1886), pp. 493–511.

The Fourth Book of the Chronicle of Fredegar: with its Continuations, ed. and trans. J.M. Wallace-Hadrill (London, 1960).

Fulbert of Chartres, *Letters and Poems*, ed. and trans. F. Behrends (Oxford, 1976).

Geschichte der Grundherrschaft Echternach im Frühmittelalter. I. 2. *Quellenband*, ed. C. Wampach (Luxembourg, 1930).

Die Gesetze der Angelsachsen, ed. F. Liebermann, 3 vols. (Halle, 1903–16).

Goscelin, *De translatione sancti Augustini*, ed. D. Papebroch, *Acta Sanctorum, Maii* vi (Antwerp, 1688), pp. 373–433.

Gregory the Great, *Registrum epistolarum*, ed. P. Ewald and Ludwig M. Hartmann, *Monumenta Germaniae Historica. Epistolae I–II*, 2 vols. (Berlin, 1887–99).

Gregory the Great, *Registrum epistularum*, ed. D. Norberg, 2 vols. (Turnhout, 1982).

Gregory IX, *Les registres de Grégoire IX*, ed. L. Auvray, 3 vols. (Paris, 1896–1907).

Gregory of Tours, *Libri historiarum X*, ed. B. Krusch and W. Levison, *Monumenta Germaniae Historica. Scriptores rerum Merovingicarum I. 1, editio altera* (Hanover, 1951).

Historia ecclesie Abbendonensis: the History of the Church of Abingdon, ed. and trans. J. Hudson, 2 vols. (Oxford, 2002–7).

The Historians of the Church of York and its Archbishops, ed. J. Raine, 3 vols. (London, 1879–94).

Hugh the Chanter, *The History of the Church of York, 1066–1127*, ed. and trans. C. Johnson, rev. M. Brett, C.N.L. Brooke, and M. Winterbottom (Oxford, 1990).

Ibn Hawqal, *Configuration de la terre (Kitab Surat al-ard)*, trans. J.H. Kramers and G. Wiet (Beirut and Paris, 1964).

Innocent II, *Epistolae et privlegia*, in *Patrologiae*, ed. Migne, 179, cols. 53–658.

John the Deacon, *Vita s. Gregorii magni*, in *Patrologiae*, ed. Migne, 75, cols. 59–242.

John of Worcester, *The Chronicle of John of Worcester*, ed. P. McGurk and R.R. Darlington, trans. Jennifer Bray and P. McGurk, 3 vols. (Oxford, 1995–).

Jonas, *Vita Columbani abbatis discipulorumque eius libri II*, in Jonas, *Vitae sanctorum Columbani, Vedastis, Iohannis*, ed. B. Krusch, *Monumenta Germaniae Historica. Scriptores rerum Germanicarum XXXVII* (Hanover and Leipzig, 1905), pp. 1–294.

Die Konzilien Deutschlands und Reichsitaliens 1023–1059, ed. D. Jasper, *Monumenta Germaniae Historica. Concilia VIII* (Hanover, 2010).

Die Konzilordines des Früh- und Hochmittelalters, ed. H. Schneider, *Monumenta Germaniae Historica. Ordines de celebrando concilio* (Hanover, 1996).

Landboc, siue registrum monasterii beatae Mariae uirginis et sancti Cénhelmi de Winchelcumba, ed. D. Royce, 2 vols. (Exeter, 1892).

Lanfranc, *Letters*, ed. H. Clover and M. Gibson (Oxford, 1979).

Leo IX, *Epistolae et decreta pontificia*, in *Patrologiae*, ed. Migne, 143, cols. 591–794.

The Leofric Missal, ed. N. Orchard, 2 vols. (London, 2002).

Liber diurnus Romanorum pontificum, ed. H. Foerster (Bern, 1958).

Liber Eliensis, ed. E.O. Blake (London, 1962).

Le Liber pontificalis, ed. L. Duchesne, 3 vols. (Paris, 1884–1957).

The Life of King Edward Who Rests at Westminster, ed. and trans. F. Barlow, 2nd edition (Oxford, 1992).

The Lives of the Two Offas, ed. and trans. M. Swanton (Crediton, 2010).

Matthew Paris, *Chronica majora*, ed. H.R. Luard, 7 vols. (London, 1872–83).

Memorials of Saint Dunstan, Archbishop of Canterbury, ed. W. Stubbs (London, 1874).

Monasticon Anglicanum, ed. W. Dugdale, new edition, ed. J. Caley, H. Elis, and B. Bandinel, 6 vols. (London, 1846).

Nicholas II, *Epistolae et diplomata*, in *Patrologiae*, ed. Migne, 139, cols. 1301–62.

The Old English Martyrology, ed. and trans. C. Rauer (Cambridge, 2013).

The Old English Version of Bede's Ecclesiastical History of the English People, ed. and trans. T. Miller, 2 vols. (London, 1890–8).

Osbert de Clare, *La Vie de S. Édouard le Confesseur*, ed. M. Bloch, *Analecta Bollandiana*, 41 (1923), pp. 51–131, reprinted in M. Bloch, *Mélanges historiques* (Paris, 1963), pp. 948–1030.

Otto I, *Diplomata*, ed. T. Sickel, *Monumenta Germaniae Historica. Diplomatum regum et imperatorum Germaniae I* (Hanover, 1882), pp. 80–638.

Papsturkunden 896–1046, ed. H. Zimmermann, 3 vols. (Vienna, 1984–9).

Papsturkunden in England, ed. W. Holtzmann, 3 vols. (Berlin, 1930–52).

Papsturkunden in Frankreich, ed. W. Wiederhold, 7 vols. (Berlin, 1906–13).

Papsturkunden in Frankreich, Neue Folge 7. Nördliche Ile-de-France und Vermandois, ed. D. Lohrmann (Göttingen, 1976).

Papsturkunden in Frankreich, Neue Folge 9. Diözese Paris II. Abtei Saint-Denis, ed. R. Grosse (Göttingen, 1998).

Papsturkunden in Italien. Reiseberichte zur Italia Pontificia, ed. P. Kehr, 6 vols. (Vatican City, 1977).

Papsturkunden in Spanien. Vorarbeiten zur Hispania Pontificia, ed. P. Kehr, D. Berger, K. Herbers, and T. Schlauwitz, 3 vols. (Berlin, 1926–2020).

Patrologiae cursus completus, series Latina, ed. J.P. Migne, 221 vols. (Paris, 1841–64).

Peter Damian, *Die Briefe des Petrus Damiani*, ed. K. Reindel, *Monumenta Germaniae Historica. Die Briefe der Deutschen Kaiserzeit IV*, 4 vols. (Munich, 1983–93).

Le pontificale romano-germanique du dixième siècle, ed. C. Vogel and R. Elze, 3 vols. (Vatican City, 1963–72).

Pontificum Romanorum diplomata papyracea quae supersunt in tabulariis Hispaniae Italiae Germaniae, ed. C. de Silva Tarouca and C. Erdmann (Rome, 1929).

The Privileges of the University of Cambridge; Together with Additional Observations on its History, Antiquities, Literature, and Biography, ed. G. Dyer, 2 vols. (London, 1824).

Recueil des chartes de l'abbaye de Saint-Benoît-sur-Loire, ed. M. Prou and A. Vidier, 2 vols. (Paris and Orléans, 1900–32).

Regesta regum Anglo-Normannorum: the Acta of William I (1066–1087), ed. D. Bates (Oxford, 1998).

Il regesto di Farfa, ed. I. Giorgio and U. Balzani, 5 vols. (Rome, 1879–1914).

The Registrum Antiquissimum of the Cathedral Church of Lincoln, ed. C.W. Foster and K. Major, 10 vols. (Hereford, 1931–73).

Regularis concordia, ed. and trans. T. Symons (London, 1953).

Richer of Saint-Remi, *Historiae*, ed. H. Hoffmann, *Monumenta Germaniae Historica. Scriptores XXXVIII* (Hanover, 2000).

Roger of Wendover, *Chronica siue flores historiarum*, ed. H.O. Coxe, 4 vols. (London, 1841–4).

Symeon of Durham, *Libellus de exordio atque procursu istius, hoc est Dunhelmensis, ecclesie: Tract on the Origins and Progress of this the Church of Durham*, ed. and trans. D. Rollason (Oxford, 2000).

Thietmar of Merseburg, *Chronicon*, ed. R. Holtzmann, *Monumenta Germaniae Historica. Scriptores rerum Germanicarum in usum scholarum nova series IX* (Berlin, 1935).

Thomas of Marlborough, *History of the Abbey of Evesham*, ed. and trans. J. Sayers and L. Watkiss (Oxford, 2003).

Die Touler Vita Leos IX, ed. H.-G. Krause, *Monumenta Germaniae Historica. Scriptores rerum Germanicarum LXX* (Hanover, 2007).

Tudor Royal Proclamations, ed. P.L. Hughes and J.F. Larkin, 3 vols. (New Haven and London, 1964–9).

Die Urkunden Ludwigs des Frommen, ed. T. Kölzer, *Monumenta Germaniae Historica. Diplomata Karolinorum II*, 3 vols. (Wiesbaden, 2016).

Die Urkunden der Merowinger, ed. T. Kölzer, *Monumenta Germaniae Historica. Diplomata regum Francorum e stirpe Merovingica*, 2 vols. (Hanover, 2001).

Die Urkunden Pippins, Karlmanns und Karls des Grossen, ed. A. Dopsch, J. Lechner, M. Tangl, and E. Mühlbacher, *Monumenta Germaniae Historica. Diplomata Karolinorum I* (Hanover, 1906).

Victor II, *Epistolae et diplomatica*, in *Patrologiae*, ed. Migne, 139, cols. 803–38.

Vita Ceolfridi, in *Abbots*, ed. and trans. Grocock and Wood, pp. 77–121.

Vita et miraculi sancti Kenelmi, in *Three Eleventh-Century Anglo-Latin Saints' Lives*, ed. and trans. R.C. Love (Oxford, 1996), pp. 49–90.

William of Malmesbury, *De antiquitate Glastoniensis Ecclesie*, ed. J. Scott, in J. Scott, *The Early History of Glastonbury: an Edition, Translation and Study of William of Malemsbury's* De antiquitate Glastonie Ecclesie (Woodbridge, 1981), pp. 40–172.

William of Malmesbury, *Gesta pontificum Anglorum: the History of the English Bishops*, ed. and trans. M. Winterbottom with the assistance of R.M. Thomson, 2 vols. (Oxford, 2007).

William of Malmesbury, *Gesta regum Anglorum: the History of the English Kings*, ed. and trans. R.A.B. Mynors, completed by R.M. Thomson and M. Winterbottom, 2 vols. (Oxford, 1998).

William of Malmesbury, *Vita Wulfstani*, in William of Malmesbury, *Saints' Lives: Lives of SS. Wulfstan, Dunstan, Patrick, Benignus and Indract*, ed. and trans. M. Winterbottom and R.M. Thomson (Oxford, 2002), pp. 1–155.

Willibald, *Vita Bonifatii*, in *Vitae sancti Bonifatii*, ed. W. Levison, *Monumenta Germaniae Historica. Scriptorum rerum Germanicarum* [57] (Hanover and Leipzig, 1905), pp. 1–58.

The Winchcombe and Coventry Chronicles: Hitherto Unnoticed Witnesses to the Work of John of Worcester, ed. and trans. P.A. Hayward, 2 vols. (Tempe, 2010).

Wulfstan of Winchester, *The Life of St Æthelwold*, ed. and trans. M. Lapidge and M. Winterbottom (Oxford, 1991).

Secondary Works

Airlie, S., 'Semper fideles? Loyauté envers les Carolingiens comme constituant de l'identité aristocratique', in R. Le Jan, ed., *La royauté et les élites dans l'Europe carolingienne (début IXe siècle aux environs de 920)* (Lille, 1998), pp. 111–28.

Airlie, S., *Making and Unmaking the Carolingians, 751–888* (London, 2020).

Althoff, G., 'Colloquium familiare–colloquium secretum–colloquium publicum. Beratung im politischen Leben des früheren Mittelalters', *Frühmittelalterliche Studien*, 24 (1990), pp. 154–67.

Anton, H.H., *Studien zu den Klosterprivilegien der Päpste im frühen Mittelalter unter besonderer Berücksichtigung der Privilegierung von St. Maurice d'Agaune* (Berlin and New York, 1975).

Anton, H.H., 'Der Liber Diurnus in angeblichen und verfälschten Papstprivilegien der früheren Mittelalters', in *Fälschungen im Mittelalter*, 3, pp. 115–42.

Appadurai, A., 'Introduction: Commodities and the Politics of Value', in A. Appadurai, ed., *The Social Life of Things: Commodities in Cultural Perspective* (Cambridge, 1986), pp. 3–63.

Appelt, H., 'Die Anfänge des päpstliche Schutzes', *Mitteilungen des Instituts für österreichische Geschichtsforschung*, 62 (1954), pp. 101–11.

Aronstam, R.A., 'Pope Leo IX and England: an Unknown Letter', *Speculum*, 48 (1974), pp. 535–41.

Aronstam, R.A., 'Penitential Pilgrimages to Rome in the Early Middle Ages', *Archivum Historiae Pontificiae*, 13 (1975), pp. 65–83.

Ashe, L. and E.J. Ward, eds., *Conquests in Eleventh-Century England: 1016, 1066* (Woodbridge, 2020).

Atsma, H. and J. Vezin, 'Le dossier suspect des possessions de Saint-Denis en Angleterre revisité (VIIIe–IXe siècles)', in *Fälschungen im Mittelalter*, 4, pp. 211–36.

Austin, J.L., *How to Do Things with Words: The William James Lectures Delivered at Harvard University in 1955*, ed. J.O. Urmson and M. Sbisà, 2nd edition (Oxford, 1975).

Barlow, F., *The English Church, 1066–1154: a History of the Anglo-Norman Church* (London and New York, 1979).

Barlow, F., 'Goscelin (b. c. 1035, d. in or after 1107)', in Matthew and Harrison, eds., *Oxford Dictionary*, 22, pp. 1020–1.

Barlow, F., 'Leofric (d. 1072)', in Matthew and Harrison, eds., *Oxford Dictionary*, 33, p. 397.

Barrow, J., 'English Cathedral Communities and Reform in the Late Tenth and the Eleventh Centuries', in Rollason, Harvey, and Prestwich, eds., *Anglo-Norman Durham*, pp. 25–39.

Barrow, J., 'Ideas and Applications of Reform', in Noble and Smith, eds., *Cambridge History*, pp. 345–62.

Barrow, J., *The Clergy in the Medieval World: Secular Clerics, Their Families and Careers in North-Western Europe, c. 800–c. 1200* (Cambridge, 2015).

Barrow, J., 'Developing Definitions of Reform in the Church in the Ninth and Tenth Centuries', in R. Balzaretti, J. Barrow, and P. Skinner, eds., *Italy and Early Medieval Europe: Papers for Chris Wickham* (Oxford, 2018), pp. 501–11.

Barthes, R., 'The Death of the Author', in R. Barthes, *Image-Music-Text*, trans. S. Heath (London, 1977), pp. 142–8.

Bartlett, R., *The Making of Europe: Conquest, Colonisation and Cultural Change, 950–1350* (London, 1994).

Bassett, S.R., 'A Probable Mercian Royal Mausoleum at Winchcombe, Gloucestershire', *Antiquaries Journal*, 65 (1985), pp. 82–100.

Bates, D., 'The Forged Charters of William the Conqueror and Bishop William of St Calais', in Rollason, Harvey, and Prestwich, eds., *Anglo-Norman Durham*, pp. 111–24.

Baxter, S., *The Earls of Mercia: Lordship and Power in Late Anglo-Saxon England* (Oxford, 2007).

Baxter, S., 'The Death of Burgheard Son of Ælfgar and its Context', in P. Fouracre and D. Ganz, eds., *Frankland: the Franks and the World of the Early Middle Ages. Essays in Honour of Dame Jinty Nelson* (Manchester, 2008), pp. 266–84.

Beaumont, C., 'Monastic Autonomy, Episcopal Authority and the Norman Conquest: the Records of Barking Abbey', *Anglo-Norman Studies*, 38 (2016), pp. 35–50.

Bernhardt, J.W., *Itinerant Kingship and Royal Monasteries in Early Medieval Germany, c. 936–1075* (Cambridge, 1993).

Beumann, H., *Theutonum nova metropolis. Studien zur Geschichte des Erzbistums Magdeburg in ottonischer Zeit* (Cologne, Weimar, and Vienna, 2000).

Bihrer, A., *Begegnungen zwischen dem ostfränkisch-deutschen Reich und England (850–1100). Kontakte—Konstellationen—Funktionalisierungen—Wirkungen* (Ostfildern, 2012).

Bischoff, G. and B.-M. Tock, eds., *Léon IX et son temps* (Turnhout, 2006).

Bisson, T.N., *The Crisis of the Twelfth Century: Power, Lordship and the Origins of European Government* (Princeton, 2009).

Blair, J., 'Frithuwold's Kingdom and the Origins of Surrey', in S. Bassett, ed., *The Origins of Anglo-Saxon Kingdoms* (London and New York, 1989), pp. 97–107.

Blair, J., 'The Minsters of the Thames', in J. Blair and B. Golding, eds., *The Cloister and the World: Essays in Medieval History in Honour of Barbara Harvey* (Oxford, 1996), pp. 5–27.

Blair, J., 'A Saint for Every Minster? Local Cults in Anglo-Saxon England', in A. Thacker and R. Sharpe, eds., *Local Saints and Local Churches in the Early Medieval West* (Oxford, 2002), pp. 455–494.

Blair, J., *The Church in Anglo-Saxon Society* (Oxford, 2005).

Blair, J., *Building Anglo-Saxon England* (Princeton and Oxford, 2018).

Blanchard, M., 'A New Perspective on Family Strategy in Tenth- and Eleventh-Century England: Ealdorman Status and the Church', *Historical Research*, 92 (2019), pp. 244–66.

Boehmer, H., *Die Fälschungen Erzbischof Lanfranks von Canterbury* (Leipzig, 1902).

Boshof, E., 'Köln, Mainz, Trier. Die Auseinandersetzung um die Spitzenstellung im deutschen Episkopat in ottonisch-salischer Zeit', *Jahrbuch des kölnischen Geschichtsvereins*, 49 (1978), pp. 9–48.

Boshof, E., 'Trier, Oberlothringen und das Papsttum im 10./11. Jahrhundert', in Große, ed., *L'église*, pp. 365–91.

Bouchard, C.B., *Rewriting Saints and Ancestors: Memory and Forgetting in France, 500–1500* (Philadelphia, 2015).

Bourdieu, P., *Distinction: a Social Critique of the Judgement of Taste*, trans. R. Nice (London, 2010).

Bourdon, L., 'Les voyages de saint Mayeul en Italie. Itinéraires et chronologie', *Mélanges d'archéologie et d'historie*, 43 (1926), pp. 61–89.

Boureau, A., 'Privilege in Medieval Societies from the Twelfth to the Fourteenth Centuries, or: How the Exception Proves the Rule', in Linehan and Nelson, eds., *Medieval World*, pp. 621–34.

Brandi, K., 'Der byzantinische Kaiserbrief aus St. Denis und die Schrift der frühmittelalterlichen Kanzleien', *Archiv für Urkundenforschung*, 1 (1908), pp. 5–86.

Braun, J., *Die liturgische Gewandung im Occident und Orient nach Ursprung und Entwicklung, Verwendung und Symbolik* (Freiburg, 1907).

Bresslau, H., *Handbuch der Urkundenlehre für Deutschland und Italien*, 2nd edition, 2 vols. (Berlin and Leipzig, 1912–31).

Brooks, N., *The Early History of the Church of Canterbury: Christ Church from 597 to 1066* (London and New York, 1984).

Brooks, N., 'Canterbury, Rome and the Construction of English Identity', in J.M.H. Smith, ed., *Early Medieval Rome and the Christian West: Essays in Honour of Donald A. Bullough* (Leiden, 2000), pp. 221–46.

Brown, W.C., M. Costambeys, M. Innes, and A.J. Kosto, eds., *Documentary Culture and the Laity in the Early Middle Ages* (Cambridge, 2013).

Bullough, D., 'St Oswald: Monk, Bishop and Archbishop', in N. Brooks and C. Cubitt, eds., *St Oswald of Worcester: Life and Influence* (London and New York, 1996), pp. 1–22.

Bullough, D., *Alcuin: Achievement and Reputation* (Leiden, 2004).

Burton, J.E., 'The Monastic World', in I.W. Rowlands and B.K.U. Weiler, eds., *England and Europe in the Reign of Henry III (1216–1272)* (Aldershot, 2002), pp. 121–36.

Campbell, J., 'The Late Anglo-Saxon State: a Maximum View', *Proceedings of the British Academy*, 87 (1994), pp. 39–65.

Carbonetti Vendittelli, C., '"Sicut inveni in thomo carticineo iam ex magna parte vetustate consumpto exemplavi et scripsi atque a tenebris ad lucem perduxi." Condizionamenti materiali e trasmissione documentaria a Roma nell'alto medioevo', in C. Braidotti, E. Dettori, and E. Lanzillotta, eds., Ου παν εφημερον: scritti in memoria di Roberto Pretagostini, 2 vols. (Rome, 2009), 1, pp. 47–69.

Chandler, C.J., *Carolingian Catalonia: Politics, Culture and Identity in an Imperial Province, 779–987* (Cambridge, 2019).

Chaplais, P., 'The Original Charters of Herbert and Gervase, Abbots of Westminster (1121–1157)', in P.M. Barnes and C.F. Slade, eds., *A Medieval Miscellany for Doris Mary Stenton* (London, 1962), pp. 89–112.

Chaplais, P., 'Some Anglo-Saxon Diplomas on Single Sheets: Originals or Copies?', *Journal of the Society of Archivists*, 3 (1965–9), pp. 313–36.

Chaplais, P., 'Who Introduced Charters into England? The Case for Augustine', *Journal of the Society of Archivists*, 3 (1965–9), pp. 526–42.

Charles-Edwards, T.M., 'Anglo-Saxon Kinship Revisited', in J. Hines, ed., *The Anglo-Saxons from the Migration Period to the Eighth Century: an Ethnographic Perspective* (Woodbridge, 1997), pp. 171–210.

Charles-Edwards, T.M., *Wales and the Britons 350–1064* (Oxford, 2013).

Cheney, C.R., 'Some Features of Surviving Original Papal Letters in England', *Annali della Scuola Speciale per Archivisti e Bibliotecari dell' Università di Roma*, 12 (1972), pp. 1–25.

Clanchy, M.T., *From Memory to Written Record: England 1066–1307*, 3rd edition (Oxford, 2013).

Clark, C. and W. Kaiser, eds., *Culture Wars: Secular–Catholic Conflict in Nineteenth-Century Europe* (Cambridge, 2003).

Clayton, M., *The Cult of the Virgin Mary in Anglo-Saxon England* (Cambridge, 1990).

Clayton, M., *The Apocryphal Gospels of Mary in Anglo-Saxon England* (Cambridge, 1998).

Clover, H., 'Alexander II's Letter "Accepimus a quibusdam" and its Relationship with the Canterbury Forgeries', in *La Normandie bénédictine au temps de Guillaume le conquérant (XIᵉ siecle)* (Lille, 1967), pp. 417–42.

Constable, G., 'Opposition to Pilgrimage in the Middle Ages', in S. Kuttner and A.M. Stickler, eds., *Melanges G. Fransen*, 2 vols. (Rome, 1976), 2, pp. 123–46.

Conte, P., *Chiesa e primato nelle lettere dei papi del secolo VII* (Milan, 1971).

Conte, P., *Regesto delle lettere dei papi del secolo VIII* (Milan, 1984).

Costambeys, M., *Power and Patronage in Early Medieval Italy: Local Society, Italian Politics and the Abbey of Farfa* (Cambridge, 2007).

Cowdrey, H.E.J., *The Cluniacs and the Gregorian Reform* (Oxford, 1970).

Cowdrey, H.E.J., 'Lanfranc, the Papacy, and the See of Canterbury', in G. D'Onofrio, ed., *Lanfranco di Pavia e l'Europa del secolo XI nel IX centenario della morte (1089–1989)* (Rome, 1993), pp. 439–500.

Cowdrey, H.E.J., *Pope Gregory VII, 1073–1085* (Oxford, 1998).

Cowdrey, H.E.J., 'Archbishop Thomas I of York and the *pallium*', *Haskins Society Journal*, 11 (2003), pp. 31–41.

Cowdrey, H.E.J., *Lanfranc: Scholar, Monk, and Archbishop* (Oxford, 2003).

Crick, J., '"Pristina Libertas": Liberty and the Anglo-Saxons Revisited', *Transactions of the Royal Historical Society*, 6th series, 14 (2004), pp. 47–71.

Crick, J., 'Insular History: Forgery and the English Past in the Tenth Century', in Rollason, Leyser, and Williams, eds., *England*, pp. 515–44.

Crick, J., 'Historical Literacy in the Archive: Post-Conquest Imitative Copies of Pre-Conquest Charters and Some French Comparanda', in M. Brett and D.A. Woodman, eds., *The Long Twelfth-Century View of the Anglo-Saxon Past* (Farnham, 2015), pp. 169–90.

Cubitt, C., *Anglo-Saxon Church Councils c. 650–c. 850* (London and New York, 1995).

Cubitt, C., 'Finding the Forger: an Alleged Decree of the 679 Council of Hatfield', *English Historical Review*, 114 (1999), pp. 1217–48.

Cubitt, C., 'Bishops and Succession Crises in Tenth- and Eleventh-Century England', in Körntgen and Waßenhoven, eds., *Patterns*, pp. 111–26.

Cubitt, C., 'St Wilfrid: a Man for his Times', in Higham, ed., *Wilfrid*, pp. 311–47.

Cushing, K.G., *Reform and the Papacy in the Eleventh Century: Spirituality and Social Change* (Manchester, 2005).

Dahlhaus, J., 'Aufkommen und Bedeutung der Rota in der Papsturkunde', in Rück, ed., *Graphische Symbole*, pp. 407–23.

Dahlhaus, J., 'Rota oder Unterschrift. Zur Unterfertigung päpstlicher Urkunden durch ihre Aussteller in der zweiten Hälfte des 11. Jahrhunderts', in Fees, Hedwig, and Roberg, eds., *Papsturkunden*, pp. 249–304.

Davies, W. and P. Fouracre, eds., *The Settlement of Disputes in Early Medieval Europe* (Cambridge, 1986).

Davies, W. and P. Fouracre, eds., *Property and Power in the Early Middle Ages* (Cambridge, 1995).

Davies, W. and P. Fouracre, eds., *The Languages of Gift in the Early Middle Ages* (Cambridge, 2010).

Davis, G.R.C., *Medieval Cartularies of Great Britain and Ireland*, rev. C. Breay, J. Harrison, and D.M. Smith (London, 2010).

d'Avray, D.L., *Medieval Religious Rationalities: a Weberian Analysis* (Cambridge, 2010).

d'Avray, D.L., *Dissolving Royal Marriages: a Documentary History, 860–1600* (Cambridge, 2014).

Diem, A., 'Who is Allowed to Pray for the King? Saint-Maurice d'Agaune and the Creation of a Burgundian Identity', in W. Pohl and G. Heydemann, eds., *Post-Roman Transitions: Christian and Barbarian Identities in the Early Medieval West* (Turnhout, 2013), pp. 47–88.

Downham, C., 'England and the Irish-Sea Zone in the Eleventh Century', *Anglo-Norman Studies*, 26 (2004), pp. 55–74.

Dumas, A., 'Protection apostolique', in Naz, ed., *Dictionnaire*, 7, cols. 381–8.

Dumville, D.N., 'The Anglian Collection of Royal Genealogies and Regnal Lists', *Anglo-Saxon England*, 5 (1976), pp. 23–50.

Dunbabin, J., 'West Francia: the Kingdom', in Reuter, ed., *New Cambridge Medieval History*, pp. 372–97.

Edwards, G.S., *Ritual Excommunication in Medieval France and England, 900–1200* (Ann Arbor, 1997).

Edwards, H., 'Two Documents from Aldhelm's Malmesbury', *Bulletin of the Institute for Historical Research*, 139 (1986), pp. 1–19.

Elze, R., 'Das Deutsche Historische Institut in Rom 1888–1988', in R. Elze and A. Esch, eds., *Das Deutsche Historische Institut in Rom 1888–1988* (Tübingen, 1990), pp. 1–32.

Ewald, P., 'Studien zur Ausgabe des Registers Gregors I', *Neues Archiv der Gesellschaft für ältere deutsche Geschichtskunde*, 3 (1878), pp. 429–625.

Ewald, P., 'Die Papstbriefe der Britischen Sammlung', *Neues Archiv der Gesellschaft für ältere deutsche Geschichtskunde*, 5 (1880), pp. 274–414, 505–96.

Ewig, E., 'Beobachtungen zu den Klosterprivilegien des 7. und frühen 8. Jahrhunderts', in J. Fleckenstein and K. Schmidt, eds., *Adel und Kirche. Gerd*

Tellenbach zum 65. Geburtstag dargebracht von Freunden und Schülern (Freiberg, Basel, and Vienna, 1968), pp. 66–77.

Ewig, E., 'Das Privileg des Bischofs Berthefrid von Amiens für Corbie von 664 und die Klosterpolitik der Königin Balthild', *Francia*, 1 (1973), pp. 66–77.

Ewig, E., 'Bermerkungen zu zwei merowingichen Bischofsprivilegien und einem Papstprivileg des 7. Jahrhunderts für merowingischen Klöster', in A. Borst, ed., *Mönchtum, Episkopat und Adel zur Gründungszeit des Klosters Reichenau* (Sigmaringen, 1975), pp. 215–49.

Falkenstein, L., *La papauté et les abbayes françaises aux XIe et XIIe siècles. Exemption et protection apostolique* (Paris, 1997).

Fälschungen im Mittlelalter. Internationaler Kongreß der Monumenta Germaniae Historica, München, 16.–19. September 1986, 5 vols. (Hanover, 1988).

Fees, I., 'Zur Bedeutung des Siegels an den Papsturkunden des frühen Mittelalters', in W. Maleczek, ed., *Urkunden und ihre Erforschung. Zum Gedenken an Heinrich Appelt* (Vienna, 2014), pp. 53–70.

Fees, I., 'Rota und Siegel der Päpste in der zweiten Hälfte des 11. Jahrhunderts', in C. Alraum, A. Holndonner, H.-C. Lehner, C. Scherer, T. Schlauwitz, and V. Unger, eds., *Zwischen Rom und Santiago. Festschrift für Klaus Herbers zu seinem 65. Geburtstag* (Bochum, 2016), pp. 285–98.

Fees, I., A. Hedwig, and F. Roberg, eds., *Papsturkunden des frühen und hohen Mittelalters. Äußere Merkmale—Konservierung—Restuarierung* (Leipzig, 2011).

Feissel, D. and J. Gascou, eds., *La pétition à Byzance* (Paris, 2004).

Fentress, J. and C. Wickham, *Social Memory* (Oxford, 1992).

Fichtenau, H., *Arenga. Spätantike und Mittelalter im Spiegel von Urkundenformeln* (Graz and Cologne, 1957).

Fichtenau, H., *Das Urkundenwesen in Österreich vom 8. bis frühen 13. Jahrhundert* (Vienna, Cologne, and Graz, 1971).

Fichtenau, H., '"Politische" Datierungen des frühen Mittelalters', in H. Wolfram, ed., *Intitulatio II. Lateinische Herrscher- und Fürstentitel im neunten und zehnten Jahrhundert* (Vienna, Cologne, and Graz, 1973), pp. 453–548.

Fichtenau, H., *Living in the Tenth Century: Mentalities and Social Orders*, trans. P.J. Geary (Chicago and London, 1991).

Fleming, R., *Kings and Lords in Conquest England* (Cambridge, 1991).

Fleming, R., 'The New Wealth, the New Rich and the New Political Style in Late Anglo-Saxon England', *Anglo-Norman Studies*, 23 (2000), pp. 1–22.

Fliche, A., *La réforme gregorienne*, 3 vols. (Paris and Leuven, 1924–37).

Fogliasso, E., 'Exemption des religieux', in Naz, ed., *Dictionnaire*, 5, cols. 646–65.

Foot, S., 'By Water in the Spirit: the Administration of Baptism in Early Anglo-Saxon England', in J. Blair and R. Sharpe, eds., *Pastoral Care Before the Parish* (Leicester, London, and New York, 1992), pp. 171–92.

Foot, S., *Veiled Women*, 2 vols. (Aldershot, 2000).

Foot, S., *Monastic Life in Anglo-Saxon England, c. 600–900* (Cambridge, 2006).

Foot, S., 'Reading Anglo-Saxon Charters: Memory, Record or Story?', in E.M. Tyler and R. Balzaretti, eds., *Narrative and History in the Early Medieval West* (Turnhout, 2006), pp. 39–66.

Foot, S., *Æthelstan: the First King of England* (New Haven and London, 2011).

Foster, M., 'Custodians of St Cuthbert: the Durham Monks' Views of their Predecessors, 1083–c. 1200', in Rollason, Harvey, and Prestwich, eds., *Anglo-Norman Durham*, pp. 53–65.

Fouracre, P., 'Eternal Light and Earthly Needs: Practical Aspects of the Development of Frankish Immunities', in Davies and Fouracre, eds., *Property*, pp. 53–81.

Fox, Y., *Power and Religion in Merovingian Gaul: Columbanian Monasticism and the Frankish Elites* (Cambridge, 2014).

Frech, K.A., *Regesta Imperii III. 5. Papstregesten 1024–1058*, 2 vols. (Cologne, Weimar, and Vienna, 2006–11).

Frech, K.A., 'Lothringer in Rom in der Zeit der "deutschen" Päpste', in Herbers and Müller, eds., *Lotharingien*, pp. 68–88.

Frenz, T., 'Graphische Symbole im päpstlichen Urkunden (mit Ausnahme der Rota)', in Rück, ed., *Graphische Symbole*, pp. 399–405.

Frenz, T., *Papsturkunden des Mittelalters und der Neuzeit*, 2nd edition (Stuttgart, 2000).

Fuhrmann, H., *Einfluß und Verbreitung der pseudoisidorichen Fälschungen. Von ihrem Auftauchen bis in die neuere Zeit*, 3 vols. (Stuttgart, 1972–4).

Fuhrmann, H., 'Papstgeschichtsschreibung. Grundlinien und Etappung', in A. Esch and J. Petersen, eds., *Geschichte und Geschichtswissenschaft in der Kultur Italiens und Deutschlands* (Tübingen, 1989).

Fuhrmann, H., 'The Pseudo-Isidorian Forgeries', trans. T. Reuter, in Jasper and Fuhrmann, *Papal Letters*, pp. 135–95.

Garipzanov, I.H., *Graphic Signs of Authority in Late Antiquity and the Early Middle Ages* (Oxford, 2018).

Geary, P.J., *Phantoms of Remembrance: Memory and Oblivion at the End of the First Millennium* (Princeton, 1994).

Giele, E., J. Peltzer, and M. Trede, 'Rollen, Blättern und (Ent)Falten', in T. Meier, M.R. Ott, and R. Sauer, eds., *Materiale Textkulturen. Konzepte–Materialen–Praktiken* (Berlin, Munich, and Boston, 2015), pp. 677–94.

Gilsdorf, S., *The Favor of Friends: Intercession and Aristocratic Politics in Carolingian and Ottonian Europe* (Leiden, 2014).

Ginzburg, C., 'Spie. Radici di un paradigma indiziario', in A. Gargani, ed., *Crisi della ragione. Nuovi modelli nel rapporto tra sapere e attività* (Turin, 1979), pp. 95–136.

Gittos, H., *Liturgy, Architecture, and Sacred Places in Anglo-Saxon England* (Oxford, 2013).

Goetting, H., 'Zur Kritik der älteren Gründungsurkunde des Reichsstifts Gandersheim', *Mitteilungen des österreichischen Staatsarchivs*, 3 (1950), pp. 362–403.

Goez, W., 'Papa qui et episcopus. Zum Selbstverständnis des Reformpapsttums im 11. Jahrhundert', *Archivum Historiae Pontificiae*, 8 (1970), pp. 27–59.

Goffart, W., *The Narrators of Barbarian History (A.D. 550–800): Jordanes, Gregory of Tours, Bede, and Paul the Deacon* (Princeton, 1988).

Goodson, C.J., *The Rome of Pope Paschal I: Papal Power, Urban Renovation, Church Rebuilding and Relic Translation, 817–824* (Cambridge, 2010).

Gresser, G., *Die Synoden und Konzilien in der Zeit des Reformpapsttums in Deutschland und Italien von Leo IX. bis Calixt II. 1049–1123* (Paderborn, 2006).

Gresser, G., *Clemens II. Der erste deutsche Reformpapst* (Paderborn, Munich, Vienna, and Zürich, 2007).

Gretsch, M., *Ælfric and the Cult of Saints in Late Anglo-Saxon England* (Cambridge, 2005).

Grimm, Brüder, *Kinder- und Hausmärchen. Ausgabe letzter Hand mit einem Anhang sämtlicher, nicht in allen Auflagen veröffentlicher Märchen*, ed. H. Rölleke (Stuttgart, 2012).

Grob, E.M., *Documentary Arabic Private and Business Letters on Papyrus* (Berlin and New York, 2010).

Große, R., ed., *L'église de France et la papauté (X^e–XIIIe siècle): actes du Colloque Historique Franco-Allemand* (Bonn, 1993).

Große, R., 'Frühe Papsturkunden und Exemtion des Klosters Saint-Denis? (7.–12. Jh.)', in Hiestand, ed., *Hundert Jahre*, pp. 167–88.

Große, R., ed., *L'acte pontifical et sa critique* (Bonn, 2007).

Große, R., 'Die beiden ältesten Papsturkunden für das Domkapitel von Paris (JL 3949 und 3951)', in Große, ed., *L'acte*, pp. 15–29.

Große, R., 'La collection de formules de Saint-Denis (Bibl. nat. Fr., lat. 2777): un dossier controversé', *Bibliothèque de l'École des chartes*, 172 (2014), pp. 185–97.

Gullick, M., 'The Hand of Symeon of Durham: Further Observations on the Durham Martyrology Scribe', in D. Rollason, ed., *Symeon of Durham: Historian of Durham and the North* (Stamford, 1998), pp. 14–31.

Guyotjeannin, O., L. Morelle, and M. Parisse, eds., *Les cartulaires. Actes de la Table ronde organisée par l'Ecole nationale des chartes et le GDR 121 du CNRS* (Paris, 1993).

Guyotjeannin, O., J. Pycke, and B.-M. Tock, *Diplomatique Médiévale*, 3rd edition (Turnhout, 2006).

Hack, A.T., *Codex Carolinus. Päpstliche Epistolographie im 8. Jahrhundert*, 2 vols. (Stuttgart, 2006).

Hägermann, D., 'Nikolaus II', in G. Kruase and G. Müller et al., eds., *Theologische Realenzyklopeädie*, 38 vols. (Berlin and New York, 1976–2007), 24, pp. 540–3.

Hägermann, D., *Das Papsttum am Vorabend des Investiturstreits. Stephan IX. (1057–1058), Benedikt X. (1058) und Nikolaus II. (1058–1061)* (Stuttgart, 2008).

Halfond, G.I., *The Archaeology of Frankish Church Councils, AD 511–768* (Leiden and Boston, 2010).

Halfond, G.I., 'Caring for Churches, Orphans and Widows in Late Merovingian Francia: Contemporary and Carolingian Perspectives', *Revue d'histoire ecclésiastique*, 113 (2018), pp. 544–75.

Hamilton, S., 'Remedies for "Great Transgressions": Penance and Excommunication in Late Anglo-Saxon England', in F. Tinti, ed., *Pastoral Care in Late Anglo-Saxon England* (Woodbridge, 2005), pp. 83–105.

Hamilton, S., 'The Early Pontificals: the Anglo-Saxon Evidence Reconsidered from a Continental Perspective', in Rollason, Leyser, and Williams, eds., *England*, pp. 411–28.

Hamilton, S., 'Interpreting Diversity: Excommunication Rites in the Tenth and Eleventh Centuries', in H. Gittos and S. Hamilton, eds., *Understanding Medieval Liturgy: Essays in Interpretation* (Farnham, 2016), pp. 125–58.

Hamilton, S., 'Law and Liturgy: Excommunication Records, 900–1050', in S. Greer, A. Hicklin, and S. Esders, eds., *Using and Not Using the Past after the Carolingian Empire, c. 900–c. 1050* (New York, 2020), pp. 282–302.

Hamilton, S., 'Medieval Curses and their Users', *Haskins Society Journal*, 30 (2020), pp. 21–52.

Härtel, R., *Notarielle und kirchliche Urkunden im frühen und hohen Mittelalter* (Vienna, Cologne, and Weimar, 2011).

Hartmann, F., *Hadrian I. (772–795). Frühmittelalterliches Adelspapsttum und die Lösung Roms vom byzantinischen Kaiser* (Stuttgart, 2006).

Hayward, P., 'Gregory the Great as "Apostle of the English" in Post-Conquest Canterbury', *Journal of Ecclesiastical History*, 55 (2004), pp. 19–57.

Head, T., *Hagiography and the Cult of Saints: the Diocese of Orléans, 800–1200* (Cambridge, 1990).

Hefele, C.J., *Histoire des conciles d'apres les documents originaux*, trans. and rev. H. Leclerq, 11 vols. (Paris, 1907–52).

Heidecker, K., ed., *Charters and the Use of the Written Word in Medieval Society* (Turnhout, 2000).

Helmholz, R.H., *The Spirit of Classical Canon Law* (Athens and London, 1996).

Helms, M.W., *Craft and the Kingly Ideal: Art, Trade, and Power* (Austin, 1993).

Herbers, K., *Regesta Imperii I. 4. Papstregesten 800–911, 2. 844–872*, 2 vols. (Cologne, Weimar, and Vienna, 1999–2012).

Herbers, K., 'Im Dienste der Universalität oder der Zentralisierung? Das Papsttum und die „Peripherien" im hohen Mittelalter – Schlussbemerkungen und Perspektiven', in Johrendt and Müller, eds., *Römisches Zentrum*, pp. 323–44.

Herbers, K., *Geschichte des Papsttums im Mittelalter* (Darmstadt, 2012).

Herbers, K., F. Engel, and F. López Alsina, eds., *Das begrenzte Papsttum. Spielräume päpstlichen Handelns: Legaten, delegierte Richter, Grenzen* (Berlin, 2013).

Herbers, K. and I. Fleisch, eds., *Erinnerung–Niederschrift–Nutzung. Das Papsttum und die Schriftlichkeit im mittelalterlichen Westeuropa* (Berlin, 2011).

Herbers, K. and J. Johrendt, eds., *Das Papsttum und das vielgestaltigte Italien. Hundert Jahre Italia Pontificia* (Berlin, 2009).

Herbers, K. and W. Könighaus, eds., *Von Outremer bis Flandern. Miscellanea zur Gallia Pontificia und zur Diplomatik* (Berlin, 2013).

Herbers, K. and H. Müller, eds., *Lotharingien und das Papsttum im Früh- und Hochmittelalter. Wechselwirkungen im Grenzen zwischen Germania und Gallia* (Göttingen, 2017).

Hiatt, A., *The Making of Medieval Forgeries: False Documents in Fifteenth-Century England* (London, 2004).

Hiestand, R., ed., *Hundert Jahre Papsturkundenforschung: Bilanz–Methoden–Perspektiven* (Göttingen, 2003).

Higham, N.J., ed., *Wilfrid: Abbot, Bishop, Saint* (Donnington, 2013).

Holmes, C. and N. Standen, eds., *The Global Middle Ages* (Oxford, 2018).

Holmes, C. and N. Standen, 'Introduction: Towards a Global Middle Ages', in Holmes and Standen, eds., *Global Middle Ages*, pp. 1–44.

Howe, J., *Church Reform and Social Change in Eleventh-Century Italy: Dominic of Sora and His Patrons* (Philadelphia, 1997).

Howe, N., 'Rome: Capital of Anglo-Saxon England', *The Journal of Medieval and Early Modern Studies*, 34 (2004), pp. 147–72.

Hudson, B., 'Knútr and Viking Dublin', *Scandinavian Studies*, 3 (1994), pp. 319–35.

Huschner, W., *Transalpine Kommunikation im Mittelalter. Diplomatische, kulterelle und politische Wechselwirkungen zwischen Italien und dem nordalpinen Reich (9.–11. Jahrhundert)*, 3 vols. (Hanover, 2003).

Huschner, W., 'Benevent, Magdeburg, Salerno. Das Papsttum und die neuen Erzbistümer in ottonischer Zeit', in Herbers and Johrendt, eds., *Papsttum*, pp. 87–108.

Huysmans, O., 'Pious Foundation or Political Masterstroke? The *Chronicon Mosamense* and the Reform of Mouzon by Archbishop Adalbero of Rheims (969–989)', *Revue d'histoire ecclesiastique*, 110 (2015), pp. 263–81.

Innes, M., *State and Society in the Early Middle Ages: the Middle Rhine Valley 400–1000* (Cambridge, 2000).

Insley, C., 'Where Did All the Charters Go? Anglo-Saxon Charters and the New Politics of the Eleventh Century', *Anglo-Norman Studies*, 24 (2001), pp. 109–28.

Insley, C., 'Looking for Charters that Aren't There: Lost Anglo-Saxon Charters and Archival Footprints', in J. Jarrett and A.S. McKinley, eds., *Problems and Possibilities of Early Medieval Charters* (Turnhout, 2013), pp. 171–87.

Insley, C., 'Why 1016 Matters; or, The Politics of Memory and Identity in Cnut's Kingdom', in Ashe and Ward, eds., *Conquests*, pp. 3–22.

Internullo, D., 'Du papyrus au parchemin. Les origines médiévales de la mémoire archivistique en Europe occidentale', *Annales*, 74 (2019), pp. 523–57.

Ivarsen, I., 'Æthelstan, Wulfstan and a Revised History of Tithes in England', *Early Medieval Europe*, 28 (2021), pp. 225–52.

Jaffé, P., *Regesta pontificum Romanorum ab condita ecclesia ad annum post Christum natum MCXCVIII*, 2nd edition, rev. W. Wattenbach, S. Loewenfeld, F. Kaltenbrunner, and P. Ewald, 2 vols. (Leipzig, 1885–8).

Jaffé, P., *Regesta pontificum Romanorum ab condita ecclesia ad annum post Christum natum MCXCVIII*, 3rd edition, rev. K. Herbers, M. Schütz, J. Werner et al., 4 vols. to date (Göttingen, 2016–).

Jarrett, J., 'Archbishop Ató of Osona: False Metropolitans on the Marca Hispanica', *Archiv für Diplomatik*, 56 (2010), pp. 1–42.

Jaser, C., *Ecclesia maledicens. Rituelle und zeremonielle Exkommunikationsformen im Mittelalter* (Tübingen, 2013).

Jasper, D., 'The Beginning of the Decretal Tradition: the Origin of the Genre through the Pontificate of Stephen V', trans. S. Rowan, rev. M. Sommar, in Jasper and Fuhrmann, *Papal Letters*, pp. 1–134.

Jasper, D. and H. Fuhrmann, *Papal Letters in the Early Middle Ages* (Washington, DC, 2001).

Jauss, H.R., *Toward an Aesthetic of Reception*, trans. T. Bahti (Minneapolis, 1982).

John, E., '"Secularium Prioratus" and the Rule of St. Benedict', *Revue Bénédictine*, 75 (1965), pp. 212–39.

Johrendt, J., 'Die Reisen der frühen Reformpäpste – Ihre Ursachen und Funktionen', *Römische Quartalschrift*, 96 (2001), pp. 57–94.

Johrendt, J., 'Der Empfängereinfluß auf die Gestaltung der Arenga und Sanctio in den päpstlichen Privilegien (896–1046)', *Archiv für Diplomatik*, 50 (2004), pp. 1–11.

Johrendt, J., *Papsttum und Landeskirchen im Spiegel der päpstlichen Urkunden (896–1046)* (Hanover, 2004).

Johrendt, J., 'Italien als Empfängerlandschaft (1046–1198): ein Vergleich aus der Perspektive des Urkundenalltags in Ligurien, Umbrien and Kalabrien', in Herbers and Johrendt, eds., *Papsttum*, pp. 183–214.

Johrendt, J., 'Papsturkunden und Papstbriefe bis zu Bonifaz VIII', *Archiv für Diplomatik*, 66 (2020), pp. 331–56.

Johrendt, J. and H. Müller, eds., *Römisches Zentrum und kirchliche Peripherie. Das universale Papsttum als Bezugspunkt der Kirchen von den Reformpäpsten bis zu Innocent III* (Berlin and New York, 2008).

Johrendt, J. and H. Müller, eds., *Rom und die Regionen. Studien zur Homogenisierung der lateinischen Kirche im Hochmittelalter* (Berlin, 2012).

Jones, A.T., 'The Power of an Absent Pope: Privileges, Forgery, and Papal Authority in Aquitaine, 877–1050', in U.-R. Blumenthal, A. Winroth, and P. Landau, eds., *Canon Law, Religion, and Politics: Liber Amicorum Robert Somerville* (Washington, DC, 2012), pp. 118–35.

Kehr, P.F., 'Scrinium und Palatium. Zur Geschichte des päpstlichen Kanzleiwesens im 11. Jahrhundert', *Mitteilungen des Instituts für Österreichische Geschichtsforschung. Ergänzungs-Band*, 6 (1901), pp. 70–112.

Kehr, P.F., *Das Papsttum und der katalanische Prinzipat bis zur Vereinigung mit Aragon* (Berlin, 1926).

Keller, H., 'The Privilege in the Public Interaction of the Exercise of Power: Forms of Symbolic Communication Beyond the Text', in Mostert and Barnwell, eds., *Medieval Legal Process*, pp. 75–108.

Kelly, S., 'Some Forgeries in the Archive of St Augustine's Abbey, Canterbury', in *Fälschungen im Mittlelalter*, 4, pp. 347–69.

Kelly, S., 'Anglo-Saxon Lay Society and the Written Word', in R. McKitterick, ed., *The Uses of Literacy in Early Medieval Europe* (Cambridge, 1990), pp. 36–62.

Kelly, S., 'Cynethryth (fl. c. 770–798)', in Matthew and Harrison, eds., *Oxford Dictionary*, 14, pp. 861–2.

Kéry, L., *Canonical Collections of the Early Middle Ages (ca. 400–1140): a Bibliographical Guide to the Manuscripts and Literature* (Washington, DC, 1999).

Kéry, L., 'Klosterexemtion in der Einöde? Bonifatius und das Privileg des Papstes Zacharias für Fulda (751)', *Archiv für mittelrheinische Kirchengeschichte*, 60 (2008), pp. 75–110.

Kéry, L., 'Kanonessammlungen als Fundorte für päpstliche Schreiben', in Herbers and Johrendt, eds., *Papsttum*, pp. 261–74.

Kéry, L., 'Klosterfreiheit und päpstliche Organisationsgewalt. Exemtion als Herrschaftsintrument des Papsttums?', in Johrendt and Müller, eds., *Rom*, pp. 83–144.

Keynes, S.D., *The Diplomas of King Æthelred 'the Unready' 978–1016: a Study in their Use as Historical Evidence* (Cambridge, 1980).

Keynes, S.D., 'Regenbald the Chancellor (*sic*)', *Anglo-Norman Studies*, 10 (1987), pp. 185–222.

Keynes, S.D., 'The Control of Kent in the Ninth Century', *Early Medieval Europe*, 2 (1993), pp. 111–31.

Keynes, S.D., *The Councils of Clofesho* (Leicester, 1994).

Keynes, S.D., 'England, 700–900', in R. McKitterick, ed., *The New Cambridge Medieval History, II c. 700–c. 900* (Cambridge, 1995), pp. 18–42.

Keynes, S.D., 'Giso, Bishop of Wells (1061–88)', *Anglo-Norman Studies*, 19 (1997), pp. 203–71.

Keynes, S.D., 'England, 900–1016', in Reuter, ed., *New Cambridge Medieval History*, pp. 456–84.

Keynes, S.D., 'Ely Abbey 672–1109', in P. Meadows and N. Ramsay, eds., *A History of Ely Cathedral* (Woodbridge, 2003), pp. 3–59.

Keynes, S.D., 'King Æthelred's Charter for Sherborne Abbey', in K. Barker, D.A. Hinton, and A. Hunt, eds., *St Wulfsige and Sherborne: Essays to Celebrate the Millennium of the Benedictine Abbey, 998–1998* (Oxford, 2005).

Keynes, S.D., 'Foreword', in *Codex diplomaticus aevi Saxonici*, ed. J.M. Kemble, Cambridge Library Collection reprint, 6 vols (Cambridge, 2011), 1, pp. v–xxiv.

Keynes, S.D., 'The "Canterbury Letter-Book": Alcuin and After', in C. Breay and J. Story, eds., *Manuscripts in the Anglo-Saxon Kingdoms: Cultures and Connections* (Dublin, 2021), pp. 119–40.

Klingshirn, W.E., *Caesarius of Arles: The Making of a Christian Community in Late Antique Gaul* (Cambridge, 1994).

Knibbs, E., 'Ebo of Rheims, Pseudo-Isidore, and the Date of the False Decretals', *Speculum*, 92 (2017), pp. 144–83.

Koch, P., 'Urkunde, Brief und Öffentliche Rede. Eine diskurstraditionalle Filiation im "Medienwechsel"', *Das Mittelalter. Perspektiven mediävistischer Forschung*, 3 (1998), pp. 13–44.

Körntgen, L. and D. Waßenhoven, eds., *Patterns of Episcopal Power: Bishops in Tenth and Eleventh Century Western Europe* (Berlin, 2011).

Kortüm, H.-H., *Zur päpstlichen Urkundensprache im frühen Mittelalter. Die päpstlichen Privilegien 896–1046* (Sigmaringen, 1995).

Koziol, G., *Begging Pardon and Favor: Ritual and Political Order in Early Medieval France* (Ithaca, 1992).

Koziol, G., *The Politics of Memory and Identity in Carolingian Royal Diplomas: the West Frankish Kingdom (840–987)* (Turnhout, 2012).

Koziol, G., 'The Conquest of Burgundy, the Peace of God, and the Diplomas of Robert the Pious', *French Historical Studies*, 37 (2014), pp. 173–214.

Ladner, G.B., *Die Papstbildnisse des Altertums und des Mitelalters*, 3 vols. (Vatican City, 1941–84).

Lapidge, M., 'The Career of Aldhelm', *Anglo-Saxon England*, 36 (2007), pp. 15–69.

Lapidge, M., J. Blair, S.D. Keynes, and D. Scragg, eds., *The Wiley Blackwell Encyclopedia of Anglo-Saxon England*, 2nd edition (Oxford, 2014).

Laudage, J., 'Ritual und Recht auf päpstlichen Reformkonzilien (1049–1123)', *Annuarium historiae conciliorum*, 29 (1997), pp. 287–334.

Lemarignier, J.-F., *Étude sur les privilèges d'exemption et de juridiction ecclésiastique des abbayes normandes depuis les origines jusqu'en 1140* (Paris, 1937).

Lemarignier, J.-F., 'L'exemption monastique et les origines de la réforme grégorienne', in *A Cluny. Congrès scientifique, fêtes et cérémonies liturgiques en l'honneur des saints Abbés Odon et Odilon, 9–11 juillet 1949* (Dijon, 1950), pp. 288–340.

Lemarignier, J.-F., 'Structures monastiques et structures politiques dans la France de la fin du Xe et des débuts du XIe siècle', *Settimane di Studio*, 4 (1957), pp. 357–400.

Levison, W., *England and the Continent in the Eighth Century: the Ford Lectures Delivered in the University of Oxford in the Hilary Term, 1943* (Oxford, 1946).

Lewis, A.R., 'The Papacy and Southern France and Catalonia, 840–1417', in A.R. Lewis, *Medieval Society in Southern France and Catalonia* (London, 1984), pp. 1–10.

Leyser, C., 'Episcopal Office in the Italy of Liutprand of Cremona, c. 890–c. 970', *English Historical Review*, 125 (2010), pp. 795–817.

Leyser, C., 'From Maternal Kin to Jesus as Mother: Royal Genealogy and Marian Devotion in the Ninth-Century West', in C. Leyser and L. Smith, eds., *Motherhood, Religion and Society in Medieval Europe, 400–1400: Essays Presented to Henrietta Leyser* (Farnham, 2011), pp. 21–40.

Leyser, C., 'Church Reform – Full of Sound and Fury, Signifying Nothing?', *Early Medieval Europe*, 24 (2016), pp. 478–99.

Leyser, C., 'The Memory of Gregory the Great and the Making of Latin Europe, 600–1000', in K. Cooper and C. Leyser, eds., *Making Early Medieval Societies: Conflict and Belonging in the Latin West, 300–1200* (Cambridge, 2016), pp. 181–201.

Leyser, K., 'The Crisis of Medieval Germany', in K. Leyser, *Communications and Power in Medieval Europe: The Gregorian Revolution and Beyond*, ed. T. Reuter (London and Rio Grande, 1994), pp. 21–50.

Leyser, K., 'The Ottonians and Wessex', in K. Leyser, *Communications and Power in Medieval Europe: The Carolingian and Ottonian Centuries*, ed. T. Reuter (London and Rio Grande, 1994), pp. 73–104.

Licence, T., 'Robert of Jumièges, Archbishop in Exile (1052–5)', *Anglo-Saxon England*, 42 (2013), pp. 311–29.

Licence, T., 'A New Source for the *Vita Ædwardi regis*', *Journal of Medieval Latin*, 29 (2019), pp. 1–20.

Licence, T., *Edward the Confessor: Last of the Royal Blood* (New Haven, 2020).

Licence, T., *Harold* (forthcoming).

Liebermann, F., 'Aethelwolds Anhang zur Benediktineregel', *Archiv für das Studium der neueren Sprachen und Litteraturen*, 108 (1902), pp. 375–7.

Lin, S., 'The Merovingian Kingdoms and the Monothelete Controversy', *Journal of Ecclesiastical History*, 71 (2020), pp. 235–52.

Linehan, P. and J.L. Nelson, eds., *The Medieval World* (London, 2001).

Loud, G.A., *The Latin Church in Norman Italy* (Cambridge, 2007).

Mabillon, J. and M. Germain, *Museum Italicum seu collectio veterum scriptorum ex bibliothecis italicis*, 2 vols. (Paris, 1687).

McDougall, S., *Royal Bastards: the Birth of Illegitimacy, 800–1230* (Oxford, 2017).

McKitterick, R., *Rome and the Invention of the Papacy: the Liber pontificalis* (Cambridge, 2020).

Margue, M., 'Lotharingien als Reformraum (10. bis Anfang des 12. Jahrhunderts)', in Herbers and Müller, eds., *Lotharingien*, pp. 12–38.

Markus, R.A., *Gregory the Great and His World* (Cambridge, 1997).

Matthew, H.C.G. and B. Harrison, eds., *Oxford Dictionary of National Biography*, 60 vols. (Oxford, 2004); rev. online at https://www.odnb.com (accessed 11/02/2022).

Matthews, S., *The Road to Rome: Travel and Travellers between England and Italy in the Anglo-Saxon Centuries* (Oxford, 2007).

Mazel, F., ed., *L'espace du diocèse. Genèse d'un territoire dans l'Occident médiéval (V^e–XIIIe siècle)* (Rennes, 2008).

Mazel, F., *L'évêque et le territoire. L'invention médiévale de l'espace (V^e–XIIIe siècle)* (Paris, 2016).

Mersiowsky, M., 'Towards a Reappraisal of Carolingian Sovereign Charters', in Heidecker, ed., *Charters*, pp. 15–26.

Mersiowsky, M., *Die Urkunde in der Karolingerzeit. Originale, Urkundenpraxis und politische Kommunikation*, 2 vols. (Wiesbaden, 2015).

Miller, M.C., 'The Crisis in the Investiture Crisis Narrative', *History Compass*, 7 (2009), pp. 1570–80.

Miller, M.C., *Clothing the Clergy: Virtue and Power in Medieval Europe, c. 800–1200* (Ithaca, 2014).

Molyneaux, G., 'Did the English Really Think They Were God's Elect in the Anglo-Saxon Period?', *Journal of Ecclesiastical History*, 65 (2014), pp. 721–37.

Molyneaux, G., *The Formation of the English Kingdom in the Tenth Century* (Oxford, 2015).

Moore, R.I., *The First European Revolution, c. 970–1215* (Oxford, 2000).

Morelle, L., 'Moines de Corbie sous influence sandionysienne? Les préparatifs du synode romaine du 1065', in Große, ed., *L'église*, pp. 197–218.

Morelle, L., 'La liberté de Luxeuil et son expression diplomatique. À propos d'une charte épiscopale absente et d'un privilège pontifical encombrant (Jean IV, 640–642)', in S. Bully, A. Dubreucq, and A. Bully, eds., *Colomban et son influence. Moines et monastères du haut Moyen Âge en Europe* (Rennes, 2018), pp. 239–60.

Morris, C., *The Papal Monarchy: the Western Church from 1050 to 1250* (Oxford, 1989).

Morton, C., 'Pope Alexander II and the Norman Conquest', *Latomus*, 34 (1975), pp. 362–82.

Mostert, M., *The Political Theology of Abbo of Fleury: a Study of Ideas about Society and Law of the Tenth-Century Monastic Reform Movement* (Hilversum, 1987).

Mostert, M., 'Die Urkundenfälschungen Abbos von Fleury', in *Fälschungen im Mittlelalter*, 4, pp. 287–318.

Mostert, M. and P.S. Barnwell, eds., *Medieval Legal Process: Physical, Spoken and Written Performance in the Middle Ages* (Turnhout, 2011).

Müller-Mertens, E., 'The Ottonians as Kings and Emperors', in Reuter, ed., *New Cambridge Medieval History*, pp. 233–66.

Naismith, R., 'Peter's Pence and Before: Numismatic Links between Anglo-Saxon England and Rome', in Tinti, ed., *England*, pp. 217–53.

Naismith, R., *Medieval European Coinage: with a Catalogue of Coins in the Fitzwilliam Museum, Cambridge. 8. Britain and Ireland, c. 400–1066* (Cambridge, 2017).

Naismith, R. and F. Tinti, 'The Origins of Peter's Pence', *English Historical Review*, 134 (2019), pp. 521–52.

Naz, R., ed., *Dictionnaire de droit canonique*, 7 vols. (Paris, 1935–65).

Nelson, J.L., 'The Second English *Ordo*', in J.L. Nelson, *Politics and Ritual in Early Medieval Europe* (London, 1986), pp. 361–74.

Nelson, J.L., 'Church Properties and the Propertied Church: Donors, the Clergy and the Church in Medieval Western Europe from the Fourth Century to the Twelfth', *English Historical Review*, 124 (2009), pp. 355–74.

Niermeyer, J.F, *Mediae latinitatis lexicon minus*, 2 vols (Leiden, 2002).

Noble, T.F.X., 'Morbidity and Vitality in the History of the Early Medieval Papacy', *Catholic Historical Review*, 81 (1995), pp. 505–40.

Noble, T.F.X., 'The Rise and Fall of the Archbishopric of Lichfield in English, Papal, and European Perspective', in Tinti, ed., *England*, pp. 291–305.

Noble, T.F.X. and J.M.H. Smith, eds., *The Cambridge History of Christianity: Early Medieval Christianities, c. 600–c. 1100* (Cambridge, 2008).

O'Brien, C., 'Hwaetberht, Sicgfrith and the Reforming of Wearmouth and Jarrow', *Early Medieval Europe*, 25 (2017), pp. 301–19.

O'Brien, C., 'Chosen Peoples and New Israels in the Early Medieval West', *Speculum*, 95 (2020), pp. 987–1009.

O'Hara, A., *Jonas of Bobbio and the Legacy of Columbanus: Sanctity and Community in the Seventh Century* (Oxford, 2018).

O'Hara, A. and I. Wood, 'Introduction', in Jonas of Bobbio, *Life of Columbanus, Life of John of Réomé, and Life of Vedast*, trans. A. O'Hara and I. Wood (Liverpool, 2017), pp. 1–84.

O'Reilly, J., 'The Multitude of Isles and the Corner-stone: Topography, Exegesis, and the Identity of the *Angli* in the *Historia Ecclesiastica*', in J. Roberts and L. Webster, eds., *Anglo-Saxon Traces* (Tempe, 2011), pp. 201–28.

Ó Riain-Raedel, D., 'New Light on the Beginnings of Christ Church Cathedral, Dublin', *Medieval Dublin*, 17 (2019), pp. 63–80.

Ortenberg, V., 'The Anglo-Saxon Church and the Papacy', in C.H. Lawrence, ed., *The English Church and the Papacy in the Middle Ages*, 2nd edition (Stroud, 1999), pp. 29–62.

Orton, F. and I. Wood, with C.A. Lees, *Fragments of History: Rethinking the Ruthwell and Bewcastle Monuments* (Manchester and New York, 2007).

Parisse, M., 'Généalogie de la Maison d'Ardenne', in *La maison d'Ardenne X^e–XIe siècles* (Luxembourg, 1981), pp. 9–41.

Parisse, M., 'L'entourage de Léon IX', in Bischoff and Tock, eds., *Léon IX*, pp. 435–56.

Parker, M., *De antiquitate Britannicae ecclesiae et priuilegiis ecclesiae Cantuariensis cum archiepiscopis eiusdem 70* (London, 1572).

Parkes, H., *The Making of Liturgy in the Ottonian Church: Books, Music and Ritual in Mainz, 950–1050* (Cambridge, 2015).

Parkes, H., 'Questioning the Authority of Vogel and Elze's *Pontifical romano-germanique*', in H. Gittos and S. Hamilton, eds., *Understanding Medieval Liturgy: Essays in Interpretation* (Farnham, 2016), pp. 75–102.

Parkes, H., 'Henry II, Liturgical Patronage and the Birth of the "Romano-German Pontifical"', *Early Medieval Europe*, 28 (2020), pp. 104–41.

Patzold, S., *Episcopus. Wissen über Bischofe im Frankreich des späten 8. bis 10. frühen Jahrhunderts* (Ostfildern, 2008).

Pfaff, V., 'Die päpstlichen Klosterexemtionen in Italien bis zum Ende des zwölften Jahrhunderts. Versuch einer Bestandsaufnahme', *Zeitschrift der Savingy-Stiftung für Rechtsgeschichte. Kanonistische Abteilung*, 72 (1986), pp. 76–114.

Pflugk-Harttung, J. von, *Specimina Selecta Chartarum Pontificum Romanorum* (Stuttgart, 1885).

Pitz, E., *Papstreskript und Kaiserreskript im Mittelalter* (Tübingen, 1971).

Pitz, E., 'Erschleichung und Anfechtung von Herrscher- und Papsturkunden vom 4. bis 10. Jahrhundert', in *Fälschungen im Mittlelalter*, 3, pp. 69–113.

Pohl, B., 'The (Un)Making of a History Book: Revisiting the Earliest Manuscripts of Eadmer of Canterbury's *Historia novorum in Anglia*', *The Library*, 7th series, 20 (2019), pp. 340–70.

Pollard, R.M., 'The Decline of the Cursus in the Papal Chancery', *Studi Medievali*, 50 (2009), pp. 1–40.

Prinz, F., *Frühes Mönchtum im Frankenreich. Kultur und Gesellschaft in Gallien, den Rheinland und Bayern am Beispiel der monastischen Entwicklung (4. bis 8. Jahrhundert)* (Munich and Vienna, 1965).

Purcell, N., 'Postal Service', in S. Hornblower and A. Spawforth, eds., *The Oxford Classical Dictionary*, 4th edition (Oxford, 2012), pp. 1197–8.

Rauer, C., 'Pope Sergius I's Privilege for Malmesbury', *Leeds Studies in English*, new series, 37 (2006), pp. 261–81.

Rabikauskas, P., *Die römische Kuriale in der päpstlichen Kanzlei* (Rome, 1958).

Rabikauskas, P., 'Zur fehlenden und unvollständingen Skriptumzeile in den Papstprivilegien des 10. und 11. Jahrhunderts', *Miscellanea historiae pontificiae*, 21 (1959), pp. 91–116.

Rabikauskas, P., *Diplomatica generalis (praelectionum lineamenta)*, 5th edition (Rome, 1998).

Radiciotti, P., 'Una bolla papale ritrovata: il papiro Tjäder †56 nell'Ang. Or. 62', *Studi di Egittologia e Papirologia*, 1 (2004), pp. 139–45.

Rasmussen, N.K., *Les pontificaux du haut moyen âge. Genèse du livre de l'évêque* (Louvain, 1998).

Rathsack, M., *Die Fuldaer Fälschungen. Eine rechtshistorische Analyse der päpstlichen Privilegien des Klosters Fulda von 751 bis ca. 1158*, trans. P.K. Mogensen, 2 vols. (Stuttgart, 1989).

Rennie, K.R., *The Foundations of Medieval Papal Legation* (Basingstoke, 2013).

Rennie, K.R., *Freedom and Protection: Monastic Exemption in France, c. 590–c. 1100* (Manchester, 2018).

Renswoude, I. van, *The Rhetoric of Free Speech in Late Antiquity and the Early Middle Ages* (Cambridge, 2019).

Reuter, T., 'Debate: the "Feudal Revolution" III', *Past and Present*, 155 (1997), pp. 177–95.

Reuter, T., ed., *The New Cambridge Medieval History, III c. 900–c. 1024* (Cambridge, 1999).

Reuter, T., 'A Europe of Bishops: the Age of Wulfstan of York and Burchard of Worms', in Körntgen and Waßenhoven, eds., *Patterns*, pp. 17–38.

Riches, T., 'The Peace of God, the "Weakness" of Robert the Pious and the Struggle for the German Throne, 1023–5', *Early Medieval Europe*, 18 (2010), pp. 202–20.

Rio, A., *Legal Practice and the Written Word in the Early Middle Ages: Frankish Formulae, c. 500–1000* (Cambridge, 2009).

Roach, L., 'Public Rites and Public Wrongs: Ritual Aspects of Diplomas in Tenth- and Eleventh-Century England', *Early Medieval Europe*, 19 (2011), pp. 182–203.

Roach, L., *Kingship and Consent in Anglo-Saxon England, 871–978: Assemblies and the State in the Early Middle Ages* (Cambridge, 2013).

Roach, L., *Æthelred the Unready* (New Haven, 2016).

Roach, L., *Forgery and Memory at the End of the First Millennium* (Princeton, 2021).

Roberts, E., 'Bishops on the Move: Rather of Verona, Pseudo-Isidore and Episcopal Translation', *Medieval Low Countries*, 6 (2019), pp. 117–38.

Roberts, E., *Flodoard of Rheims and the Writing of History in the Tenth Century* (Cambridge, 2019).

Robertson, N., 'Dunstan and Monastic Reform: Tenth-Century Fact or Twelfth-Century Fiction?', *Anglo Norman Studies*, 28 (2006), pp. 153–67.

Robinson, I.S., *The Papacy 1073–1198: Continuity and Innovation* (Cambridge, 1990).

Robinson, I.S., *The Papal Reform of the Eleventh Century: Lives of Pope Leo IX and Pope Gregory VII* (Manchester, 2004).

Rollason, D., M. Harvey, and M. Prestwich, eds., *Anglo-Norman Durham 1093–1193* (Woodbridge, 1994).

Rollason, D., C. Leyser, and H. Williams, eds., *England and the Continent in the Tenth Century: Studies in Honour of Wilhelm Levison (1876–1947)* (Turnhout, 2010).

Roper, M., 'Wilfrid's Landholdings in Northumbria', in D.P. Kirby, ed., *Saint Wilfrid at Hexham* (Newcastle upon Tyne, 1974), pp. 61–80.

Rosé, I., 'Judas, Dathan, Abiron, Simon et les autres. Les figures bibliques-repoussoirs dans les clauses comminatoires des actes originaux français', *Archiv für Diplomatik*, 62 (2016), pp. 59–106.

Rosenthal, J., 'The Pontifical of St Dunstan', in N. Ramsay, M. Sparks, and T. Tatton-Brown, eds., *St Dunstan: His Life, Times and Cult* (Woodbridge, 1992), pp. 143–63.

Rosenwein, B.H., *Negotiating Space: Power, Restraint, and Privileges of Immunity in Early Medieval Europe* (Ithaca, 1999).

Rosenwein, B.H., 'One Site, Many Meanings: Saint-Maurice d'Agaune as a Place of Power in the Early Middle Ages', in M. de Jong and F. Theuws, eds., *Topographies of Power in the Early Middle Ages* (Leiden, Boston, and Cologne, 2001), pp. 271–90.

Rosenwein, B.H., 'Inaccessible Cloisters: Gregory of Tours and Episcopal Exemption', in K. Mitchell and I. Wood, eds., *The World of Gregory of Tours* (Leiden, Boston, and Cologne, 2002), pp. 181–198.

Rück, P., 'Die Urkunde als Kunstwerk', in A. von Euw and P. Schreiner, eds., *Kaiserin Theophanu. Begegnung des Ostens und Westens um die Wende des ersten Jahrtausends*, 2 vols. (Cologne, 1991), 2, pp. 311–34.

Rück, P., ed., *Graphische Symbole in mittelalterlichen Urkunden. Beiträge zur diplomatischen Semiotik* (Sigmaringen, 1996).

Rück, P., 'Beiträge zur diplomatischen Semiotik', in Rück, ed., *Graphische Symbole*, pp. 13–47.

Rück, P., 'Die hochmittelalterliche Papsturkunden als Medium zeitgenössicher Ästhetik', in E. Eisenlohr and P. Worm, eds., *Arbeiten aus dem Marburger hilfswissenschaftlichen Institut* (Marburg an der Lahn, 2000), pp. 3–30.

Rustow, M., *The Lost Archive: Traces of a Caliphate in a Cairo Synagogue* (Princeton and Oxford, 2020).

Sansterre, J.-M., 'La date des formules 60–63 du "Liber Diurnus"', *Byzantion*, 48 (1978), pp. 226–43.

Santifaller, L., 'Die Verwendung des Liber Diurnus in den Privilegien der Päpste von den Anfangen bis zum Ende des 11. Jahrhunderts', *Mitteilungen des Instituts für österreichische Geschichtsforschung*, 49 (1935), pp. 225–366, reprinted in Santifaller, *Liber Diurnus: Studien und Forschungen*, ed. H. Zimmermann (Stuttgart, 1976).

Santifaller, L., *Saggio di un Elenco dei funzionari, impiegati e scrittori della Cancellaria Pontificia dall'inizio all'anno 1099*, 2 vols. (Rome, 1940).

Santifaller, L., *Beiträge zur Geschichte der Beschreibstoffe im Mittelalter mit besonderer Berücksichtigung der päpstlichen Kanzlei. Erster Teil: Untersuchungen* (Graz and Cologne, 1953).

Santifaller, L., G. Rill, and W. Szaivert, 'Chronologisches Verzeichnis der Urkunden Papst Johanns XIX (1014–1032)', *Römische Historische Mitteilungen*, 1 (1956-7), pp. 35–76.

Savill, B., 'Prelude to Forgery: Baldwin of Bury Meets Pope Alexander II', *English Historical Review*, 132 (2017), pp. 795–822.

Savill, B., 'England and the Papacy between Two Conquests: the Shadow of "Reform"', in Ashe and Ward, eds., *Conquests*, pp. 307–30.

Savill, B., 'The Consul Vanishes: On Using and Not Using Gregory the Great's *Register* in Early Medieval England', *Early Medieval Europe* (forthcoming).

Savill, B., 'The Donation of Pope Constantine', *Anglo-Norman Studies* (forthcoming).

Sawyer, P.H., *Anglo-Saxon Charters: an Annotated List and Bibliography* (London, 1968); rev. S.E. Kelly and R. Rushforth et al. online at https://esawyer.lib.cam.ac.uk (accessed 11/02/2022).

Sayers, J.E., 'Papal Privileges for St. Albans Abbey and its Dependencies', in D.A. Bullough and R.L. Storey, eds., *The Study of Medieval Records: Essays in Honour of Kathleen Major* (Oxford, 1971), pp. 57–84.

Sayers, J.E., '"Original," Cartulary and Chronicle: the Case of the Abbey of Evesham', in *Fälschungen im Mittlelalter*, 4, pp. 371–95.

Schieffer, R., '*Motu Proprio*. Über die papstgeschichtliche Wende im 11. Jahrhundert', *Historisches Jahrbuch*, 122 (2002), pp. 27–41.

Schieffer, R., 'Die päpstlichen Register vor 1198', in Herbers and Johrendt, eds., *Papsttum*, pp. 261–74.

Schmidt, T., *Alexander II. (1061–1073) und die römische Reformgruppe seiner Zeit* (Stuttgart, 1977).

Schmieder, F., 'Peripherie und Zentrum Europas. Der nordalpine Raum in der Politik Leos IX. (1049–1054)', in B. Flug, M. Matheus, and A. Rehberg, eds., *Kurie und Region. Festschrift für Brigide Schwarz zum 65. Geburtstag* (Stuttgart, 2005), pp. 341–58.

Schoenig, S.A., 'Withholding the Pallium as a Tool of the Reform', in P. Erdö and A Szuromi, eds., *Proceedings of the Thirteenth International Congress of Medieval Canon Law* (Vatican City, 2010), pp. 577–88.

Schoenig, S.A., *Bonds of Wool: the Pallium and Papal Power in the Middle Ages* (Washington, DC, 2016).

Scholz, S., *Transmigration und Translation. Studien zum Bistumswechsel der Bischöfe von der Spätantike bis zum Hohen Mittelalter* (Cologne, Weimar, and Vienna, 1992).

Scholz, S., *Politik–Selbstverständnis–Selbstdarstellung. Die Päpste in karolingischer und ottonischer Zeit* (Stuttgart, 2006).

Schwarz, W., 'Jurisdicio und Condicio. Eine Untersuchung zu den Privilegia libertatis der Klöster', *Zeitschrift der Savigny-Stiftung für Rechtsgeschichte. Kanonistische Abteilung*, 45 (1959), pp. 34–98.

Scott, J.C., *The Art of Not Being Governed: an Anarchist History of Upland Southeast Asia* (New Haven and London, 2009).

Serafini, C., *Le monete e le bolle plumbee pontificie del madagliere vaticano*, 4 vols. (Milan, 1910–28).

Sharpe, R., 'Charters, Deeds, and Diplomatics', in F.A.C. Mantello and A.G. Rigg, eds., *Medieval Latin: an Introduction and Bibliographical Guide* (Washington, DC, 1996), pp. 230–40.

Sharpe, R., *A Handlist of the Latin Writers of Great Britain and Ireland before 1540* (Turnhout, 1997).

Sharpe, R., 'The Use of Writs in the Eleventh Century', *Anglo-Saxon England*, 32 (2003), pp. 247–91.

Sharpe, R., 'King Caedwalla's Roman Epitaph', in K. O'Brien O'Keeffe and A. Orchard, eds., *Latin Learning and English Lore: Studies in Anglo-Saxon Literature for Michael Lapidge*, 2 vols. (Toronto, 2005), 1, pp. 171–93.

Sharpe, R., 'King Ceadwalla and Bishop Wilfrid', in S. DeGregorio and P. Kershaw, eds., *Cities, Saints and Communities in Early Medieval Europe: Essays in Honour of Alan Thacker* (Turnhout, 2020), pp. 195–222.

Short, I., 'Archives de la cathédrale d'Ely en langue vernaculaire', *Romania*, 138 (2020), pp. 261–75.

Sickel, T.E. von, 'Prolegomena zum Liber Diurnus I', *Sitzungsberichte der Philosophisch-historischen Klasse der kaiserlichen Akademie der Wissenschaften*

Wien, 117.7 (1889), pp. 1–76; 'Prolegomena zum Liber Diurnus II', ibid., 117.13 (1889), pp. 1–94.

Sijpesteijn, P.M., 'Arabic Papyri and Islamic Egypt', in R.S. Bagnall, ed., *The Oxford Handbook of Papyrology* (Oxford, 2009), pp. 452–72.

Sims-Williams, P., *Religion and Literature in Western England, 600–800* (Cambridge, 1990).

Smith, J.M.H., 'Saints and their Cults', in Noble and Smith, eds., *Cambridge History of Christianity*, pp. 581–605.

Snook, B., 'Who Introduced Charters into England? The Case for Theodore and Hadrian', in B. O'Brien and B. Bombi, eds., *Textus Roffensis: Law, Language and Libraries in Early Medieval England* (Turnhout, 2015), pp. 257–89.

Southern, R.W., 'The Canterbury Forgeries', *English Historical Review*, 287 (1958), pp. 193–226.

Southern, R.W., *Saint Anselm and his Biographer: a Study of Monastic Life and Thought, 1059–c. 1130* (Cambridge, 1963).

Sowerby, R., 'The Heirs of Bishop Wilfrid: Succession and Presumption in Early Anglo-Saxon England', *English Historical Review*, 134 (2019), pp. 1377–1404.

Squatriti, P., 'Pornocracy', in C. Kleinhenz, ed., *Medieval Italy: an Encyclopedia*, 2 vols. (New York, 2004), 2, pp. 926–7.

Stafford, P., 'Political Women in Mercia, Eighth to Early Tenth Centuries', in M.P. Brown and C.A. Farr, eds., *Mercia: an Anglo-Saxon Kingdom in Europe* (London and New York, 2001), pp. 35–49.

Stancliffe, C., 'Columbanus's Monasticism and the Sources of His Inspiration: From Basil to the Master?', in F. Edmonds and P. Russell, eds., *Tome: Studies in Medieval Celtic History and Law in Honour of Thomas Charles-Edwards* (Woodbridge, 2011), pp. 17–28.

Stancliffe, C., 'Dating Wilfrid's Death and Stephen's Life', in Higham, ed., *Wilfrid*, pp. 17–26.

Stenton, F.M., *Preparatory to Anglo-Saxon England*, ed. D.M. Stenton (Oxford, 1970).

Stenton, F.M., *Anglo-Saxon England*, 3rd edition (Oxford, 1971).

Story, J., *Carolingian Connections: Anglo-Saxon England and Carolingian Francia, c. 750–870* (Aldershot, 2003).

Story, J., 'Aldhelm and Old St Peter's, Rome', *Anglo-Saxon England*, 39 (2010), pp. 7–20.

Story, J., 'Bede, Willibrord and the Letters of Pope Honorius I on the Genesis of the Archbishopric of York', *English Historical Review*, 527 (2012), pp. 783–818.

Thacker, A., 'Kings, Saints and Monasteries in Pre-Viking Mercia', *Midland History*, 10 (1985), pp. 1–25.

Thacker, A., 'Rome: the Pilgrims' City in the Seventh Century', in Tinti, ed., *England*, pp. 89–140.

Thacker, A., 'Pope Sergius' Letter to Abbot Ceolfrith: Wearmouth-Jarrow, Rome and the Papacy in the Early Eighth Century', in J. Hawkes and M. Boulton, eds., *All Roads Lead to Rome: the Creation, Context and Transmission of the Codex Amiatinus* (Turnhout, 2019), pp. 115–28.

Thomson, R.M., *William of Malmesbury*, rev. edition (Woodbridge, 2003).

Thomson, R.M., *Descriptive Catalogue of the Medieval Manuscripts in the Library of Peterhouse, Cambridge* (Cambridge, 2016).

Tinti, F., 'England and the Papacy in the Tenth Century', in Rollason, Leyser, and Williams, eds., *England*, pp. 163–84.

Tinti, F., 'The Archiepiscopal Pallium in Late Anglo-Saxon England', in Tinti, ed., *England*, pp. 307–42.

Tinti, F., ed., *England and Rome in the Early Middle Ages: Pilgrimage, Art and Politics* (Turnhout, 2014).

Tinti, F., 'The Pallium Privilege of Pope Nicholas II for Archbishop Ealdred of York', *Journal of Ecclesiastical History*, 70 (2019), pp. 1–23.

Tinti, F., *Europe and the Anglo-Saxons* (Cambridge, 2021).

Tosi, M., 'I monachi colombaniani del sec. VII portano un rinnovamento agricolo-religioso nella fascia littorale Ligure', *Archivum Bobiense*, 14–15 (1992–3), pp. 5–246.

Unger, V., *Regesta Imperii I. 4. Papstregesten 800–911, 3. 872–882* (Vienna, Cologne, and Weimar, 2013).

Unger, V., *Päpstliche Schriftlichkeit im 9. Jahrhundert. Archive, Register, Kanzlei* (Vienna, Cologne, and Weimar, 2018).

Vollrath, H., *Die Synoden Englands bis 1066* (Paderborn, Munich, Vienna, and Zürich, 1985).

Wangerin, L.E., *Kingship and Justice in the Ottonian Empire* (Ann Arbor, 2019).

Werner, J., *Papsturkunden vom 9. bis ins 11. Jahrhundert. Untersuchungen zum Empfängereinfluß auf die äußere Urkundengestalt* (Berlin, 2017).

West, C., *Reframing the Feudal Revolution: Political and Social Transformation between Marne and Moselle, c. 800–c. 1100* (Cambridge, 2013).

Whitelock, D., 'Wulfstan and the So-Called Laws of Edward and Guthrum', *English Historical Review*, 56 (1941), pp. 1–21.

Whittow, M., 'Sources of Knowledge; Cultures of Recording', in Holmes and Standen, eds., *Global Middle Ages*, pp. 45–87.

Wickham, C., 'Problems in Doing Comparative History', in P. Skinner, ed., *Challenging the Boundaries of Medieval History: the Legacy of Timothy Reuter* (Turnhout, 2009), pp. 5–28.

Wickham, C., *The Inheritance of Rome: a History of Europe from 400 to 1000* (London, 2010).

Wickham, C., *Medieval Rome: Stability and Crisis of a City, 900–1150* (Oxford, 2015).

Wickham, C., 'Consensus and Assemblies in the Romano-Germanic Kingdoms', in V. Epp and C.H.F. Meyer, eds., *Recht und Konsens im frühen Mittelalter* (Ostfildern, 2017), pp. 389–426.

Wiedemann, B., *Papal Overlordship and European Princes, 1000–1270* (Oxford, 2022).

Williams, A., 'Thegnly Piety and Ecclesiastical Patronage in the Late Old English Kingdom', *Anglo-Norman Studies*, 24 (2001), pp. 1–24.

Wollasch, J., 'Monasticism: the First Wave of Reform', in Reuter, ed., *New Cambridge Medieval History*, pp. 163–85.

Wood, I., 'A Prelude to Columbanus: the Monastic Achievement in the Burgundian Territories', in H.B. Clarke and M. Brennan, eds., *Columbanus and Merovingian Monasticism* (Oxford, 1981), pp. 2-32.

Wood, I., 'Jonas, the Merovingians, and Pope Honorius: *Diplomata* and the *Vita Columbani*', in A.C. Murray, ed., *After Rome's Fall: Narrators and Sources of Early Medieval History. Essays Presented to Walter Goffart* (Toronto, 1998), pp. 99-120.

Wood, I., 'Notes', in T. Head, ed., *Medieval Hagiography: an Anthology* (New York and London, 2001), pp. 131-5.

Wood, I., 'Genealogy Defined by Women: the Case of the Pippinids', in L. Brubaker and J.M.H. Smith, eds., *Gender in the Early Medieval World: East and West, 300-900* (Cambridge, 2004), pp. 234-56.

Wood, I., 'The Foundation of Bede's Wearmouth-Jarrow', in S. DeGregorio, ed., *The Cambridge Companion to Bede* (Cambridge, 2010), pp. 84-96.

Wood, I., 'The Gifts of Wearmouth and Jarrow', in W. Davies and P. Fouracre, eds., *The Languages of Gift in the Early Middle Ages* (Cambridge, 2010), pp. 89-115.

Wood, I., 'The Continental Connections of Anglo-Saxon Courts from Æthelbert to Offa', *Settimane di Studio*, 58 (2011), pp. 443-80.

Wood, I., 'The Continental Journeys of Wilfrid and Biscop', in Higham, ed., *Wilfrid*, pp. 200-11.

Wood, I., *The Modern Origins of the Early Middle Ages* (Oxford, 2013).

Wood, I., 'Between Rome and Jarrow: Papal Relations with Francia and England, from 597 to 716', *Settimane di Studio*, 61 (2014), pp. 297-320.

Wood, I., 'The Irish in England and on the Continent in the Seventh Century: Part I', *Peritia*, 26 (2015), pp. 171-98.

Wood, I., 'Columbanus, the Columbanian Tradition, and Caesarius', in D.G. Tor, ed., *The 'Abbasid and Carolingian Empires: Comparative Studies in Civilizational Formation* (Leiden, 2017), pp. 153-68.

Wood, M., 'A Carolingian Scholar in the Court of King Æthelstan', in Rollason, Leyser, and Williams, eds., *England*, pp. 135-62.

Wood, S., *The Proprietary Church in the Medieval West* (Oxford, 2006).

Wormald, P., 'Bede and Benedict Biscop', in G. Bonner, ed., *Famulus Christi: Essays in Commemoration of the Thirteenth Centenary of the Birth of the Venerable Bede* (London, 1976), pp. 141-69, reprinted with additions in Wormald, *Times*, pp. 3-29.

Wormald, P., *Bede and the Conversion of England: the Charter Evidence* (Jarrow, 1984), reprinted with additions in Wormald, *Times*, pp. 135-66.

Wormald, P., 'Æthelwold and his Continental Counterparts: Contact, Comparison, Contrast', in B. Yorke, ed., *Bishop Æthelwold: His Career and Influence* (Woodbridge, 1988), pp. 13-42, reprinted with additions in Wormald, *Times*, pp. 207-28.

Wormald, P., 'Lordship and Justice in the Early English Kingdom: Oswaldslow Revisited', in Davies and Fouracre, eds., *Property*, pp. 114-36.

Wormald, P., *The Making of English Law: King Alfred to the Twelfth Century. Volume I: Legislation and Its Limits* (Oxford, 1999).

Wormald, P., 'Earconwald (d. 693)', in Matthew and Harrison, eds., *Oxford Dictionary*, 17, pp. 559-60.

Wormald, P., *The Times of Bede: Studies in Early English Christian Society and Its Historian*, ed. S. Baxter (Oxford, 2006).

Wright, C.D., 'Vercelli Homily XV and the *Apocalypse of Thomas*', in S. Zacher and A. Orchard, eds., *New Readings in the Vercelli Book* (Toronto, 2009), pp. 151–84.

Wright, R., *A Sociophilological Study of Late Latin* (Turnhout, 2002).

Yorke, B., *Wessex in the Early Middle Ages* (London and New York, 1995).

Yorke, B., 'Æthelwold [St Æthelwold, Ethelwold] (904x9–984)', in Matthew and Harrison, eds., *Oxford Dictionary*, 1, pp. 434–8.

Zimmermann, H., 'Ottonische Studien', *Mitteilungen des Instituts für österreichische Geschichtsforschung. Ergänzungsband* 20 (1962), pp. 122–90, reprinted in H. Zimmermann, *Im Bann des Mittelalters. Ausgewählte Beiträge zur Kirchen- und Rechtsgeschichte*, ed. I. Eberl and H.-H. Kortüm (Sigmaringen, 1986), pp. 1–69.

Zimmermann, H., *Regesta Imperii II. 5. Papstregesten 911–1024*, 2nd edition (Vienna, Cologne, and Weimar, 1998).

Zotz, T., '*Pallium et alia quaedam archiepiscopatus insignia*: Zum Beziehungsgefüge und zu Rangfragen der Reichskirchen im Spiegel der päpstlichen Privilegierung des 10. und 11. Jahrhunderts', in H. Maurer and H. Patze, eds., *Festschrift für Berent Schwineköper zu seinem siebzigsten Gerburtstag* (Sigmaringen, 1982), pp. 155–75.

Unpublished Secondary Works

De Jong, S., 'The Involvement of Adelman of Liège (d. 1061) in the Berengarian Controversy and its Resonance in Liège', paper given to the Medieval History Seminar, German Historical Institute, Washington, DC, 17 October 2015.

Drage, E.M., 'Bishop Leofric and Exeter Cathedral Chapter (1050–1072): a Reassessment of the Manuscript Evidence', DPhil thesis, University of Oxford, 1978.

Elliot, M.D., 'Canon Law Collections in England *ca* 600–1066: the Manuscript Evidence', PhD thesis, University of Toronto, 2013.

Goldberg, E.J., 'King Ecgfrith of Northumbria, Wearmouth-Jarrow and the Battle of Dún Nechtain (685)', paper given to the International Medieval Congress, University of Leeds, 9 May 2008.

Sommar, M.E., 'The Changing Role of the Bishop in Society: Episcopal Translation in the Middle Ages', PhD thesis, Syracuse University, 1998.

Online-Only Resources

Chartes originales antérieures à 1121 conservées en France, http://telma.irht.cnrs.fr/outils/originaux/index/ (accessed 11/02/2022).

Keynes, S.D., 'A Provisional Checklist of Papal Letters and Privileges for Recipients in Anglo-Saxon England [June 2013]', *Kemble: the Anglo-Saxon Charters*

Website,   http://dk.robinson.cam.ac.uk/sites/default/files/files/Checklist%20Papal %20Letters(1).pdf (accessed 11/02/2022).

Portable Antiquities Scheme, https://finds.org.uk/database (accessed 11/02/2022).

'Ravenna: S. Apollinare in Classe: Apse Mosaic: Constantine IV Pogonatus', *ARTSTOR*, https://library.artstor.org/asset/ARTSTOR_103_41822001125762 (accessed 11/02/2022).

Index

For the benefit of digital users, indexed terms that span two pages (e.g., 52–53) may, on occasion, appear on only one of those pages.